19/20

SLC

The Art of Chinese Management

THE ART OF
Chinese
Management

THEORY, EVIDENCE, AND APPLICATIONS

Kai-Alexander Schlevogt

OXFORD
UNIVERSITY PRESS

2002

OXFORD
UNIVERSITY PRESS

Oxford New York
Auckland Bangkok Buenos Aires Cape Town Chennai
Dar es Salaam Delhi Hong Kong Istanbul Karachi Kolkata
Kuala Lumpur Madrid Melbourne Mexico City Mumbai Nairobi
São Paulo Shanghai Singapore Taipei Tokyo Toronto

and an associated company in Berlin

Published by Oxford University Press, Inc.
198 Madison Avenue, New York, New York 10016

www.oup.com

Oxford is a registered trademark of Oxford University Press.

Library of Congress Cataloging-in-Publication Data

Schlevogt, Kai-Alexander.
    The art of Chinese management : theory, evidence, and applications /
    by Kai-Alexander Schlevogt.
      p. cm.
    Includes bibliographical references and index.
    ISBN 0-19-513644-6
    1. Industrial management—China. 2. Business enterprises—China
    3. Corporate culture—China. 4. Industrial management—China—Case studies.
    I. Title
    HD70.C5 S35 2001
    658'.00951—dc21   2001024731

9 8 7 6 5 4 3 2 1

Printed in the United States of America
on acid-free paper

TO THE PEOPLE OF CHINA

Can the strength of a hundred people be greater than that of one thousand people? It can and is, when the one hundred are organized.

V. I. LENIN

Science is systematized knowledge. . . . Art is knowledge made efficient by skill.

J. F. GENUNG

Preface

Ye Emperors, Kings, Dukes, Marquises, Earls, and Knights, and all other
people desirous of knowing the diversities of the races of mankind, as well
as the diversities of kingdoms, provinces, and regions of all parts of the
East, read through this book, and ye will find in it the greatest and most
marvelous characteristics of the people.

—*The Travels of Marco Polo*

The superior man understands righteousness, the inferior man understands
profit.

—Confucius

子曰："君子喻于义，小人喻于利."

This book tells the story of a journey to the East, in search of new ideas
about organizing and managing human activity, which are shaped by an
ancient Oriental culture. It is the outcome of my preoccupation and interaction with the Chinese people for almost a decade. The story that
emerges is both similar to and different from the *Journey to the West*, the
famous Chinese classical novel. Whereas the latter is a biting satire of
society and Chinese bureaucracy, this journey's gist is the discovery of the
art of management as practiced by Chinese companies, particularly the
newly founded private enterprises. What is similar is that both journeys
reveal human striving and perseverance—the novel, in the form of an al-
legorical tale; the present work, by reporting empirical results from the
first large-scale and quantitative survey of Chinese organizations. It is
unique in its detailed coverage of private and state enterprises in the north
and south of China, based on standardized face-to-face interviews with
124 CEOs and several in-depth case studies. These findings allow for

groundbreaking statistical generalizations previously unknown in the field.

Art is a combination of heart, thought, and action. The web-based model of private Chinese management justifies this description. The newly founded private Chinese enterprises on the mainland revive traditional Chinese family-based cultural values (which transcend the simple quest for profit) and readopt the clever business practices of their overseas Chinese compatriots. This powerful model explains much of the dynamism inherent in the private enterprise revolution we are witnessing in China.

This book combines facts with design. It is thus relevant for two groups of readers. First, scholars will be interested in my explanation of the distinctive organizational choices made in Chinese companies, their driving forces, and performance outcomes. Second, business leaders and policy makers dealing with China and other emerging markets will want to understand the key success factors in the Chinese market, and learn how to design new, effective organizations living up to the challenges of the new millennium. Both groups will benefit from the strong fact base of the study, which differentiates it from the usual anecdotes.

The management of mainland Chinese private enterprises is a new, exciting research topic with important implications for organizational theory and practice. I hope that by undertaking this pioneering study, I will stimulate further research in this new area, which translates into performance-enhancing managerial advice.

Kai-Alexander Schlevogt,
Spring/Summer 1999

Acknowledgments

This royal throne of kings, this scepter'd isle,
This earth of majesty, this seat of Mars,
This other Eden, demi-paradise;
This fortress built by nature for herself,
Against infection, and the hand of war;
This happy breed of men, this little world;
This precious stone set in the silver sea . . .
This blessed plot, this earth, this realm, this England
　　　　　　—Shakespeare, *Richard II*, II.i.40

"Dominus illuminatio mea" (God is my light) is an appropriate prayer for men of erudition and faith. It also suits a university like Oxford that wants to promote truth in knowledge and blessed learning. This grand institution is the cradle of enlightened scholarship and its everlasting beacon. Too well-known to be pointed out, it matches elegance of thought with gracious style and refinement of manners. Like the venerable colleges in the bustling city, the university as a whole is an oasis of deep and orderly reflection in a superficial and chaotic world. Its collective brightness of motifs, feelings, and thoughts has lit the way of the leaders of the world. Whoever gained the privilege of admission to this unique community, soon felt and embraced its ideals and spirit, and was transformed forever. He acquired the intellectual and social skills to excel in the world, whether as statesman, scientist, or in other vocations. I am greatly indebted to this academic kingdom and scholar paradise—"et in arcadia ego" aptly describes my special attachment. I would like to express my sincere gratitude to Dr David Barron of Jesus College, who was an important source of suggestions and encouragement throughout my research time at Oxford. I also thank Dr Richard Whittington of New College for his valuable advice.

　　I extend my special appreciation to Christ Church (Aedes Christi), Oxford's most famous college—the only one to be founded by a reigning king

(Henry VIII) and to educate as many as 14 Prime Ministers and 11 Rulers of India. I am grateful for its support of my field research in China through generous grants. I am particularly indebted to the erudite Dean, the Very Reverend John Drury, for accepting me in its community of great men and guiding me through his example of devotion, faith, scholarship and understatement, blending the best of ages gone-by, the present, and the promise of the future. When I went down, he presented me with works of John Ruskin, a fellow member of "the House" (1836). Even though not intended that way, it happened to shape the way I conceptualized art, both in the original sense and, as in this book, applied to human skills.

Let me now leave the dreaming spires of Oxford and its "splendid isolation" and other-worldliness, in a move from inspiring thought to determined action, from the spiritual to the political center of a former empire and sovereign of the seas. I would like to express my sincere gratitude to Professor Peter Abell, the Director of the Interdisciplinary Institute of Management at the London School of Economics and Political Science (LSE). He inspired me ever since I first met him with his intelligence, seemingly effortless power of reasoning, sharp wit, candor, and his nonchalant, unassuming, and affable demeanors, which are fitting garments particularly for a man of such high distinction in such a magnificent place. Because of its invaluable human, intellectual and social capital, the LSE is the unrivalled international leader in the esemplastic social sciences. It taught me rigorous economics with a human face.

To complete my appreciation of the trustworthy Albion (when not at war with Germany), its people and institutions, I would like to express my gratitude to the British Economic and Social Research Council for the generous award that I won in their national research competition.

Home is where one begins his journey and achievement is where one ends. From the old world I ventured to the new world in the West, which strives hard to surpass its master, and to the even newer old world in the East, which is on the way to revive its ancient excellence. At Harvard University, I thank the two successive Directors of the Fairbank Center of East Asian Research, Asia Center, where this book was written, for inviting me to their exclusive community of world-class scholars. The breadth and depth of the various scholarly activities at the center is impressive. The praise of the Chinese President during his visit to Harvard was therefore clearly deserved. I also extend my thanks to Prof. Yasheng Huang for inviting me to join the Harvard Business School, which is one of the most outstanding centers of business administration on the planet.

I first met Professor Lex Donaldson of the Australian Graduate School of Management in Oxford. We had independently pursued rigorous macro-structural analysis, but soon discovered our shared interest in striving for truth and true knowledge, embracing the positivist beliefs and aspirations despite the difficulties of realizing them. I was very impressed by his outstanding scholarship, and his unrelenting pursuit of the highest standards of integrity in research and social interaction. I thank him very much for his inspiration and valuable advice.

I am greatly indebted to the dedication and commitment of the Oxford University Press (OUP) teams responsible for editing, production, and marketing. Even a German cannot help but be impressed by the meticulous work and outstanding quality of the OUP staff. One advantage of having one's work chosen for publication with OUP is that the submitted manuscript underwent a double blind peer review that decided its acceptance. All publications bear the special Oxford University Press quality imprint, which differentiates it from most other book publishers, which do not mandate such a rigorous selection process. Like top academic journals, OUP invites in-depth reviews from two anonymous world experts in the respective subject area. Apart from its staff, this exacting selection is one of the major factors explaining the prestige and reputation associated with the Oxford name. The review process helps to identify the best books, full of powerful ideas and rigorous scientific methods, avoids faddishness, and ensures long book lives. Its rigor places onerous demands on the reviewers. I would like to thank the two anonymous experts for reviewing my work and providing me with helpful comments, which further improved my work.

Finally, I would like to extend my gratitude to all the Chinese leaders who spent a considerable amount of their precious time with me for the interviews. Because I promised them confidentiality, I cannot list their names, but I thank them all.

Contents

PART I
Introduction and Development of Theory: Laying the Groundwork

1

Setting the Stage:
The Miraculous Rebirth of
Private Enterprise in China

Napoleon's warning has become reality. The sleeping giant, one of the oldest civilizations on the surface of the planet, dating back more than five thousand years and having written records for nearly three thousand years, has reawakened.[1] The titan, comparable in size to the whole of Europe, has finished the long period of hibernation, stretches his legs, and is ready to walk tall again. Due to the success of its economic reforms, the People's Republic of China (P.R.C.) has become strategically important in both political and economic terms. Politically, it has developed into a powerhouse in the Pacific Rim with ever increasing military might. Economically, China boasted double-digit growth rates for most of the 1990s, making it the third largest economy in the world. In addition, given that over one-fifth of the human race lives in China, the increase in purchasing power makes it the largest, and potentially also one of the most profitable, national markets in the world. As a consequence of its growing importance, China, as the "last true business frontier" (Johnson 1996, p. 39), attracts increasing interest from both businessmen and academics in diverse disciplines, including political science, economics, management, and anthropology.

One particularly spectacular but little researched aspect and driving force of this rapid development is what I like to call the "entrepreneurial revolution" taking place in China, that is, the dramatic growth in private economic activity, fueled mainly by the success of domestic private enterprises, with foreign direct investment producing less uplifting results from the investors' point of view. The scale and speed of this revolution are unrivaled by any other enterprise boom in the world—nothing comparable has happened at any time in human history. Domestic private firms already represent the largest share of the enterprise population in terms of numbers. The core belief expressed in this book is that much of this boom and many of these dramatic changes are associated with new forms of organizational structures and management, particularly in the private sector. Complementing the usual macroeconomic reasons explaining development, it shifts and broadens the perspective on potential sources of economic growth by emphasizing the importance of structure and management, i.e., microeconomic forces, for economic development.

The key theme of this book is to argue that the distinctive management of Chinese private enterprises has contributed to the rapid development of the private sector and constitutes a form of art, in the sense of the "skill of doing something well." Their sophisticated techniques are also pieces of art or cultural artifacts, influenced by long-standing Chinese cultural traditions. What is more, in their unique combination, they potentially can serve as a new management paradigm for the twenty-first century. I will show that Chinese private enterprises have readopted a particular "Web-based Chinese Management" (WCM) model, parts of which so far have been assumed to be practiced only in overseas Chinese communities. The term "management model" describes the structural and managerial choices of an organization.[2] Much as the advent of traditional Chinese medicine has helped patients in the West, so the new "managerial drug" will help businessmen to meet the key challenges of the new millennium in a systemic and holistic way. WCM might become the Eastern acupuncture needle of management to heal organizational diseases and strengthen corporate power in the West. As mentioned above, this management model is closely intertwined with and causally related to the reemphasis on traditional Chinese cultural values in private enterprises and, due to its emphasis on social capital, informal structures, and adaptable leadership style, is a highly effective instrument for dealing with the increasing uncertainty and complexity of economic transactions (compared to a few decades ago), as well as with motivational problems of employees in large companies. The classical models of organizational strategy, structure, and process, tailored to predictable and stable environments, have proven to be inadequate for these tough new (or reemerging) issues (Schlevogt, 2000, p. 9).

It should be noted that despite frequent comments referring to the essential stability and stagnation of Chinese society, there is no nation on Earth that has undergone more violent times of turbulence and change than the Central Kingdom. Examples range from the Warring States period to the Great Cultural Revolution. The alleged "unprecedented" change taking place everywhere in the world in the wake of globalization is therefore only a caricature in comparison to these dramatic upheavals in China. How can anybody seriously compare the recently somewhat more intensive advertising battles and jockeying for position in international markets with the fundamental life-and-death struggle of a people? This assessment can come only from people who lack historical perspective and are greedy to come up with new ideas, although they have no original insights for the present times.

Due to their familiarity with uncertainty, complexity, and change we can be confident that the Chinese developed distinctive leadership, management and other organizational design skills that alone were powerful enough to cope with this turbulence, making it possible to adapt to new circumstances and ensure the survival of a great civilization. These skills may lie dormant now in some quarters, but they did not die. Having experienced so much turmoil, the Chinese might have concluded that it is necessary to actively foster continuity instead of mindlessly calling for ever more change (but not improvement). The ancient Chinese thus put great emphasis on social relations and social capital, mutual obligations and cooperation, as well as on harmony and cohesion in society. Above all, they understood that all things move in cycles and do not extend linearly. Their time horizon surely was longer than fifty years. But we do not have to go back to long-gone ages to show that the present global turbulence is not unique. Look what happened in the twentieth century: trade and factor mobility (especially labor mobility through immigration) on a global scale before World War I, recovery in the 1920s, Trotsky's speculation about an integrated world economy, then nationalism, followed by World War II and "global integration" again. Everything that integrates will fall apart later. The next wave of breakup—be it along ethnic or other lines—will soon come. It is good to be prepared with time-proven management tools.

The bare branches that survived for centuries and centuries will bear blossoms again.

Given all these facts, it is my vision that China's long historical connection with the development of strategy and organization and the transfer of managerial ideas to the West would, after a long interruption, find a continuation in the twenty-first century, which might once again be a period of great Chinese influence in Asia and the rest of world. The bare branches that survived for centuries and centuries will bear blossoms again. The inflow of advanced management ideas from the West will be greeted by an outflow of new strategic and organizational ideas from China.

My mission is to set this process in motion. To narrow the huge research gap related to Chinese management, this book has the main objective of laying down a theoretical and empirical basis for the study of enterprises in mainland China, particularly private enterprises. In the process, I will analyze key factors for success in China. The work will also illuminate ways of improving the lackluster performance of many multinational companies in China. To achieve the research objective, based on the first large-scale and quantitative survey of 124 Chinese companies and several case studies, I will analyze the nature, causes, and effectiveness of organizational structures and management practices of private and state enterprises located in the north and the south of China; I also will translate the empirical findings into best practice recommendations for executives. The term "state enterprise" covers both state-owned and collective enterprises and is used to mark the contrast of this group of enterprises with private enterprises. Although anecdotal evidence has suggested that significant differences exist between private and state enterprises, as well as between companies in the north and the south of China, systematic research on these issues has been rare. The quantitative nature of this pioneering study makes it possible, for the first time, to draw statistical generalizations, and the case studies help to embed the findings in real-world contextual richness. Unlike many other books, this work includes all research instruments in an appendix, to enable other scholars to replicate and extend its findings.

This chapter is organized in eight sections. First, I will provide some context for the study by painting a broad historical canvas of the long-standing Chinese preoccupation with organizing. I will not elaborate on traditional warfare strategies, which warrant a separate study. The aim of this section is to show that, with this study, organizational theory arrives back at the place where the first concepts of organizational structure and management were developed (Lui 1996, p. 390) and from which they were most probably transferred to the West. This historical sketch is followed by a quick look at the most recent organizational experiment, that is, the present economic reforms and emergence of private enterprise. The dramatic impact of domestic and foreign private investment makes the organization of Chinese companies a compelling research object. Next, I will briefly outline the general research question and benefits for academic and practitioner readers in terms of study contributions. This section is followed by an outline of the basic research model and theory, and methods employed to test it. The final part provides an overview of the chapters.

Historical background of organization in China: Back to the origins

A journey of 1,000 li starts with the first step
—Ancient Chinese Proverb

千里之行，始于足下

Visitors to China in 1978 and even later were surely startled by its relative poverty, and thought that they were visiting a desert. They were like people seeing a gaunt and bare mountain whose vegetation had been cut by farmers and trampled by cattle. Although the mountain was once covered with lovely trees and flowers, the visitors most probably imagined that it was bare from the start. Like the mountain, the natural state of China was very different in the past from what now appears, but there is no reason to doubt that it can return to the golden state of old or reach an even higher level of civilization.

Whether teaching in Lanzhou, Shenzhen, Shanghai, or Beijing, I usually start the inaugural lecture by showing my students a simple picture. It shows a huge, ancient Chinese ritual vessel, the *Si Mu Wu* tetrapod. The first question I ask is when the vessel was made. The students usually dramatically underestimate its age—oldest dates guessed being about twenty-five hundred years. In fact, it was made more than three thousand years ago, during the first historical dynasty (the earliest dynasty to leave written records), the (late) Shang (1766–1122 B.C.). Upon hearing this, the students are usually astonished, some of them amazed by the high level of craftsmanship, but they then expect me to start lecturing about a *more important topic*—that is, management—because that was why they came to listen to me. The reader of this book might feel the same.

But the vessel *does* tell us a great story—a tale about management and about China. It is evidence for the sophisticated organizational skills of the Chinese at a time when the Western peoples were still living in primitive conditions. It is also a powerful testimony to China's past glory. Think about it for a moment. The vessel weighs 875 kilograms and is beautifully decorated. It clearly proves the high level of indigenously developed technological competence in China at this early period of human history. Could anybody have produced it alone? No. Large-scale, labor-intensive metal production was needed for a bronze casting of this size and character. A huge group of people with very different skill sets and levels, and different characters and temperaments, ranging from creative artists to manual laborers (ore miners, fuel gatherers, foundry workers, ceramists, etc.), had to divide their work and be managed by a project leader. This prescriptive control by the model designer and labor manager required coordinative mechanisms such as centralized direction, hierarchy, rules, and procedures. Incidentally, the prestige of owning such a metal object came partly from having political control over other people. To sustain this incredible effort it was also necessary to motivate the human resources by devising incentive schemes and methods of punishment that would lead to high levels of social discipline. Much of the control was possibly implicit, through socialized values—a forerunner of the implicit contracts of corporate culture. We can conclude that the ancient Chinese were masters of coordination and control, the two essential prerequisites of successful management.

The descendants of these early illustrious masterminds maintained the momentum of innovation and progress. It is well recognized that until about A.D. 1400 China outperformed the West in terms of living standards, and probably also with respect to social order and cohesiveness. The trade deficits of Rome with China are famous, as are the four great technological inventions: paper, printing, fire powder, and compass. They were later adopted or, if we trust ethnocentric Western account, "(re-)discovered" by the Occident. In the spiritual area, Confucianism was the most ambitious design and grandest project ever undertaken to realize the dream of the perfect human society. These lessons in social engineering, unfortunately, were never learned by the West, which went in almost exactly the opposite direction—rampant and aggressive individualism—eventually destroying the fabric of its society.

As regards the art of government, the first emperor, Qin Shi Huang (259 B.C.–210/209 B.C.), was one of the earliest known organizer-managers on earth and one of the greatest leaders of all time. The ancient city of Xi'An, the capital he established in 221 B.C., was the starting point of the world-famous Silk Road, along which, in ancient times, together with people and goods, the extremely advanced knowledge and ideas of China traveled to the West (Fukuda 1989). Among those ideas there presumably were concepts of organization. After unifying the nation into an empire, Qin envisioned and implemented networks of roads, canals, and fortresses that he eventually linked to form the Great Wall. Early on, he also understood the importance of universal standardization. He is celebrated for establishing not only the basic measures and weights, but also standardizing things like the axle lengths of carts, the written language, and laws. Standardization is still highly relevant—just think about arguments over standards for such technologies as high-definition television and "smart" cards.

Voltaire pointed out that the Chinese administrative system was the most perfect structural arrangement the world has ever known.

Another of Qin's organizational innovations was a fully centralized administration and strong military organization, which helped to avoid the rise of independent satrapies. This made China the first bureaucratic nation-state in the world. The term "mandarin" is still epithet for a bureaucrat, though with negative connotations in our times.[3] Voltaire pointed out that the Chinese administrative system was the most perfect structural arrangement the world has ever known—the fact that China is the only ancient civilization that still survives is a powerful testimony to its historical effectiveness, inner strength, and adaptability. The bureaucratic and administrative structure created by the first emperor remained the enduring basis of all subsequent dynasties in China, even though he was officially criticized by later dynasties. The attacks were particularly strong in the Han dynasty, which wanted to propagate its new state ideology of Confucianism, whose aim was to achieve control through cultural values, which were to glue society together and facilitate cooperative economic efforts. Its rules of social behavior promoted morality and moderation. The use of learning for self-cultivation and rituals and music for socialization purposes was originally espoused by Confucius and Mencius, and later systematized by Xun Zi—the molder of ancient Confucianism and, given his impact in such a large and populous country, one of the greatest philosopher the world has ever known. It contradicted Qin's totalitarian legalism, which followed in the theoretical footsteps of Han Fei Zi, the leading legalist philosopher of the classical period. The Confucian ideology helped the Han dynasty (206 B.C.–220 A.D.) to become the longest lasting empire in Chinese history.

The administrative system, which unlike in the later state of Prussia, for example, was not replicated for the management of private enterprises, was rooted in a meritocracy based on selection through rigorous testing in the imperial exams and promotion according to capability. Its flexibility and capacity for survival were demonstrated by the fact that it allowed for transitions from incompetent leaders to new dynasties. Both meritocracy and flexibility were impressively evidenced by the ascent of a former beggar, Zhu Yuan Zhang, who became emperor by founding the Ming dynasty (1368–1644).

China was the most advanced country in the world—it regarded the rest of the world as inferior and barbarian.

Thirteenth-century China was remarkable for its modernism (Gernet 1962, p. 17) and innovation. An analysis of its government, economy, technology, infrastructure, transport, trade and arts, provides startling evidence for this assertion. Through bureaucratic excellence, the government efficiently managed pivotal institutions and thus could control the economy. An important corollary of the well-functioning administrative system was the efficient collection of taxes. This provided a solid revenue stream for investments in government-sponsored projects. The economy was strictly monetary, without any trace of barter. Regional division of labor was marked; enterprises producing tea and salt were sophisticated. The city of Hangzhou became the richest and most populous metropolis in the world. Besides, the technological achievements impress us even today. The transportation infrastructure was highly developed and used intensively. Trade flourished both nationally and internationally. An armada of vessels sailed natural waterways and an extensive web of intercity canals. Large seagoing junks reached India, Arabia, and East Africa to trade in silk and porcelain. In the arts, China reached ever new peaks. In almost any field of social organization and creation, it thus was the most advanced country in the world. From its ethnocentric perspective as the Middle Kingdom, it regarded the rest of humankind as "barbarian" (yeman). Who could really criticize this snobbish attitude?

> The Japanese sages were right that the reputation of a thousand years may
> be determined by the conduct of one hour.

After this glorious period full of original thoughts on leadership and
organization, the Chinese nightmare of institutional stagnation and decline began. The ruling elite became corrupt, internally divided, and
sought pleasure instead of Confucian virtues—which proved to be a recipe
for disaster.[4] The Japanese sages were right that the reputation of a thousand years may be determined by the conduct of one hour. China missed
the time in the life of every problem when it is big enough to see, yet small
enough to be solved easily. As a consequence, after its brilliant peak in
the late Song dynasty, the downfall set in with the invasion by the "barbarian" Mongols, first with the fall of the capital of northern Song (1126),
and later with the capture of the southern city of Hangzhou (1276). China
was occupied for the first time in its history. After a short revival in the
Ming, this decline culminated in China's becoming a target of colonial
ambitions and a dumping ground for opium during another foreign-
dominated line of rulers, the Qing dynasty (1644–1912), established by
the Manchu invaders.

As a reflection of these aberrations that led to an unprecedented nadir,
in modern times China started yet another "natural experiment" in organizational theory (Shenkar 1984). In a sense the Great Cultural Revolution
wanted to prove the invalidity of contingency theory.[5] The revolutionaries
claimed that organizations do not need formalization and specialization
under any circumstances, since they are only inherited faces of hidden
power without any functional rationale. Therefore, the Red Guards abolished, for example, sterilization rules in hospitals and claimed that nurses
could easily perform surgery. The resulting loss of life provided strong
evidence for the rejection of this thesis.

Present reforms and development of the domestic private sector: Reasons to celebrate

The contrast between shiny glory, full of innovative organizational forms,
and shameful defeat is startling. But after the Cultural Revolution, China
obtained a new lease on life, moving along a steep path toward a great
cultural and economic revival. To realize this dream of a national renaissance, China's leaders kicked off another organizational experiment. They
created an allegedly new economic system called "socialism with Chinese
characteristics", managing the transition from a centralized planning system to a socialist market economy.

In the aftermath of the "liberation" in 1949, communist revolutionaries
quickly removed the non-governmental individual economy through col-

lectivization in the mid-1950s. Only a few street barbers and other licensed artisans remained as strange relics of times gone by, serving as curious reminders of the "old society." An important pillar of the subsequent reforms that the late paramount leader Deng Xiaoping's started in 1978, was the recreation of a private economy. He intended to achieve this objective by developing special economic zones in China's southeastern coastal areas, and, at the same time, introducing new forms of ownership. After the official endorsement of the "open door policy" during the Communist Party's historic Third Plenum in December 1978, Shekou was established in January 1979 as the first "special economic zone." In 1981, the government encouraged entrepreneurs to set up individually-owned enterprises (*getihu qiye*) in urban centers, followed by collective "township and village enterprises" (TVEs) in rural areas in 1984. Liu Shaoqui's[6] prediction—"If we eliminate it [the private economy] too early, later we'll have to invite it back" (Gao and Chi 1996, p. 23)—thus proved to be right. Apart from these ownership changes, another key element of Chinese economic reforms at the macro-level were changes in the state-business relationship. Through the "director responsibility system", the state separated government functions and officials from enterprise management (see, for example, Schermerhorn 1987 p. 346; Hunt and Yang 1990).

The ownership-related policies caused a boom in nonstate economic activity, which was particularly dramatic in the case of individually-owned enterprises. The nonstate sector became an invaluable driver of growth and employment. Private enterprises developed most rapidly in Guangdong (Gao and Chi 1996, p. 26). They also grew at a fast pace in other booming cities along the coast and in the south. The number of new millionaires in private mainland Chinese enterprises, especially in these areas, increased steadily. In contrast to this rosy picture, the Western hinterland did not fully participate in this entrepreneurial revolution and capitalist bonanza, inspiring tremendous efforts to correct the imbalance (Schlevogt 2000i).

The share of nonstate-owned enterprises in gross industrial output grew from 24% in 1980 to 73.5% in 1998, while the share of state-owned enterprises dropped sharply from 76% in 1980 to 26.5% in 1998. The growth trajectory of the nonstate-owned economy was interrupted only once. After it developed quickly in the first decade of reforms until 1989, the Tian'anmen incident halted its development. In the aftermath of Deng Xiaoping's famous inspection of south China in 1992, it resumed rapid growth, breaking the 50% mark of total industrial output for the first time in 1992. In the five-year period from 1994 to 1998 alone, the share of individually-owned private enterprises in gross industrial output rose from 10.1% to 16% (see Figure 1-1). Output grew at a compounded average rate of 30.2%, significantly exceeding the compounded average growth of GDP in the same time period, which reached only 14.2%. This demonstrates the enormous dynamism of this new class of enterprises. From 1994 to 1998, the share of other private enterprises increased from 14.8% to 21.5%, with output growing by 27.2% annually on average. Private enterprises together produced $575 billion in gross industrial output in 1998. In the five-year period from 1994 to 1998, state-owned enterprises (SOEs) grew at a much slower pace, which led to a decline in their share of industrial output. They recorded a compounded average growth rate in gross industrial output of only 6.4% from 1994 to 1998, with its share in gross industrial output declining from 37.3% in 1994 to 26.5% in 1998, which is equal to $406.1 billion.

In 1998, there were more than six million individually-owned private enterprises, which reveals strong grassroots energy. With a share of 76% in 1998, they accounted for the largest part of the industrial enterprise population in China. Evidently, this share is significantly larger than their share in gross industrial production, mainly due to the average smaller size and capitalization of private firms compared with state-owned enterprises. The total number of private enterprises is likely to be understated, since in the past many entrepreneurs used "red signboads" (*hong paizi*), i.e., they registered a private enterprise as a collective entity in order to receive more benevolent treatment from the government and to hedge themselves against potential political backslash. The amendment in the constitution in March 1999, which enhanced the status of private enterprises, might make the environment less hostile. The number of state-owned enterprises decreased from 102,200 in 1994 to 64,700 in 1998. In contrast to private enterprises, the share of state-owned enterprises in industrial production is still much larger than their share of the enterprise population.

Nonstate-owned enterprises in general, and private enterprises in particular, also turned out to be crucial job creation engines in both rural and

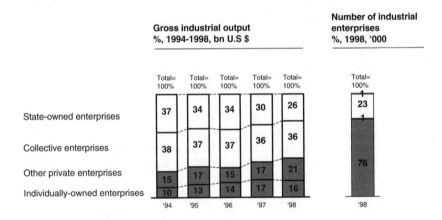

* Figures rounded to next decimal place
**Other private enterprises include: Non individually-owned enterprises; jointly-owned enterprises; shareholding enterprises; foreign-funded enterprises; enterprises funded by entrepreneurs from Hong Kong, Macao and Taiwan; others.

Figure 1-1 Development of private enterprises in China. Source: National Bureau of Statistics (1999)

urban areas, absorbing surplus labor released from the state-owned sector. The total number of people working in private enterprises and self-employed individuals in urban and rural areas increased from 44.2 million in 1994 to 78.2 million in 1998, growing at a compounded average rate of 15% per year. Together, they accounted for 11% of the total workforce in 1998. Total employment in the nonstate-owned sector, i.e., the sum of jobs in urban collective enterprises, TVEs, private enterprises, and self-employed individuals increased from 197.3 million in 1994 to 223.2 million in 1998, growing at a compounded average rate of 3% per year. In 1998, the total number of individuals employed in the nonstate-owned economy amounted to 32% of the total workforce. Together, the sum of these newly created jobs by nonstate enterprises is more than 1.5 times larger than the total *population* of Russia! In contrast, urban state-owned enterprises reduced employment from 112.1 million in 1994 to 90.6 million in 1998, shedding about 5% of their workforce per year on average. In 1998, they employed 12.9% of the total work force. The remainder of the economically active population predominately is rural labor.

The rapid development of output and employment in the private sector is even more astonishing, if one considers that most of the growth is not financed through official sources of capital such as government grants and credits. The bulk of domestic savings (94.1% in 1998) entering the official banking sector is channeled to SOEs, which are often inefficient. Some observers believe that the easy access to underpriced capital explains the predicament in the state-owned sector—a situation that differs sharply from the healthy development of the private economy. In their view, cheap credit encourages overly risky and aggressive strategies, resulting in overproduction and the eventual destruction of economic value.

Witnessing the dramatic surge in private economic activity, one cannot help asking what the sources of this dynamism are and whether this process is related to changes in the way Chinese firms are managed. (Schlevogt 2001f). Such a microeconomic explanation seems to be warranted, given that factors in the macroenvironment, which in the past had been rather constraining and sometimes even outright hostile, cannot be thought of as fueling the rapid growth. A key point of this book is to show that the newly established private Chinese enterprises (re-)adopted a distinctive management model that is similar to overseas Chinese management. It might well explain the inherent dynamism in the private sector and its resulting rapid growth over time. In addition, the problems of the state sector, too, may be traced back primarily to their management practices rather than to macroeconomic causes, such as the supply of cheap credit. If my microeconomic explanatory approach were not correct, it would be difficult to elucidate why there are also efficient and value-creating SOEs in an environment full of incentives that supposedly stimulate opportunistic behavior.

So far, little information about the effectiveness of the new private enterprises is available—one of the objectives of this book is to close this gap—but there is prima facie evidence that a brilliant success story looms behind this rapid growth. Due to the alleged lending bias toward state-owned enterprises, with private enterprises being starved for funds, the dramatic growth often has to be partly financed by informal loans from relatives and friends. They are collectively known as the "informal capital market." But most importantly, it is fueled by high retained earnings that provide significant, internally generated cashflows for future expansion, and are an indicator that significant economic value is created.

China is not an escape route for lack of competitiveness and innovativeness in your core business at home. If you did not succeed at home, you will probably fail miserably in China as well.

Foreign direct investment in China: Growing but failing?

With its growing importance, the last business frontier attracts continuous interest from Western businessmen (Schlevogt, 2000a), in the form of both foreign direct investment (FDI) and international trade. You often hear comments such as: "China is a huge new growth market"; "More than 1 billion customers, just imagine!"; "Our competitors have entered China—so we have to be there as well, otherwise we might be left out"; "It's a *strategic* investment" (in other words, the company has experienced continuous losses since market entry). These are the reasons that serious CEOs of multinational companies use to justify huge investments in China without deep insights into the fundamental characteristics of the market or a realistic view of how it might evolve. They often fail to ask probing questions. Sure, the GDP was growing in double digits for most of the 1990s, but were sales in *your product category* growing as well? Will the future be just an extrapolation of the past? In recent years, a large part of production went to the stockpile. In 1998, involuntary stockbuilding added about 1.2 percentage points to GDP growth. It is true that China's population exceeds 1 billion people, but how many of them live in cities and can be reached easily? The sobering fact is: Only about 30% of the total population is urban. Besides, assuming people need your product (or can be persuaded to need it) and can be reached easily, do they all have the purchasing power to become your *customers*, which will transform potential into real demand? And will the specific target market segments grow in the future? For sure, all your competitors are in China, from all over the world. But this is not a reason to follow them. There is hardly any other place in the world where you will enjoy such strong competition! Virtually every big company is present and struggles for a piece of the same small pie of customers, located mainly in Shanghai, Beijing, and Guangzhou, who can afford your foreign products. Are you certain that all your competitors create economic value and, even if so, will you generate profits as well?

Finally, assuming you are confident that there is at least latent demand for your product, do you have the requisite skills to enter the market and succeed? Step back and ask whether you know which total investments are required—initial *and* continuous cash outflows—what it takes to excel in China, and what sort of bureaucratic harassment you have to overcome. Do you know, for example, that DaimlerChrysler, in the past did not obtain licenses to import Mercedes limousines despite being subjected to a 100% import tariff already? The bureaucrats in charge refused to provide any official justification for the injustice. Do you know in what order the creditors of GITIC—a financial conglomerate that went into receivership—were paid? First, the ordinary people; second, the government; third, Chinese companies; last *and* least, Western companies. A strategic investment sounds good, but when will you know that your losses are not strategic anymore? Think of what you invested in capital and know-how to fulfill the Chinese requirements of technology transfer. Wouldn't this investment have produced higher returns in other markets, maybe helping your own country to accelerate growth and reduce unemployment? Other markets also offer tremendous growth opportunities. Through hard thinking and industry foresight, you may create a *new* market before others, and may possess distinctive leverageable skills to succeed on your new turf. China is not an escape route for lack of competitiveness and innovativeness in your core business at home. If you did not succeed at home, you will probably fail miserably in China as well.

Alas, few people engage in such an imaginary dialogue and ask these crucial questions. The inquiring person is brushed off as "academic," and accused of lacking vision and pioneering spirit. A "bias for action" is the word of the day. You will hear: "If we fight hard enough, we will win"; or: "It's not gonna be cheap, son, but we have to invest to reap the future returns." Many decision-makers prefer a cowboy mentality over hard thinking. An "eyeball to eyeball" iron determination replaces creative insights. They place huge bets, and make no efforts to reduce the risk of such gambles through intelligent analysis and hedging. Oddly, these modern asphalt cowboys follow the herd instead of either leading it or striding on their own lonely ways, which bear the potential of great discoveries.

As a result of the bias for action, the growth of FDI in China, both in the form of wholly foreign-owned enterprises (WFO) and joint-ventures, parallels the rapid development of the domestic private economy. From 1991 to 1999, actually-used FDI in China grew at an average compounded rate of 32% per year, reaching US$ 40.4 billion in 1999 (see Figure 1-2). China has become the largest recipient of FDI in the third world, absorbing nearly half of total foreign investment in developing countries since 1992 (The Economist, 1999). In the past, it ranked among the top three recipients of FDI in the world (after the U.S. and, more recently, Britain).[7] Despite a 11.4% fall in actually-used FDI from 1998 to 1999, China was less hard hit by the Asian economic crisis than most of its neighbors.

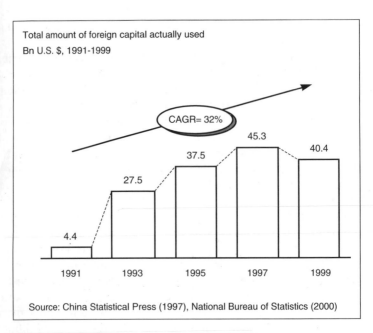

Total amount of foreign capital actually used
Bn U.S. $, 1991-1999

CAGR= 32%

45.3

40.4

37.5

27.5

4.4

1991   1993   1995   1997   1999

Source: China Statistical Press (1997), National Bureau of Statistics (2000)

Figure 1-2   Growth of foreign direct investment in China

FDI has proved important both for Western companies and China's national economy. Apart from providing capital and cutting-edge technology stimulating domestic growth, FDI has been a dynamic engine of China's trade with other countries through intracompany exchanges of goods and services and open market transactions. From 1994 to 1998, gross industrial output from enterprises funded by foreigners or entrepreneurs from Hong Kong, Macao and Taiwan grew at a compounded average rate of 27.8% per year, reaching US$ 214.4 billion in 1998. China's total international trade volume grew at a compounded average rate of 13% per year from 1991 to 1999, totaling US$ 360.7 billion in 1999 (see Figure 1-3). FDI had a positive effect on the balance of trade. In 1998, foreign-funded companies in the P.R.C. generated US$ 81 billion of exports, which is equal to 44% of China's total exports.

However, to put these numbers into perspective, it should be pointed out that long-term national growth in China is driven mainly by domestic forces, among them (a) the highest saving rate in the world, with saving deposits by urban and rural residents reaching US$ 720.1 billion in 1999; (b) the largest population and labor force of any country on earth—in 1999, the population reached 1.26 billion and the total number of employed people in China amounted to 705.9 million; and (c), as I will argue in this book, the dynamism of private Chinese enterprises.

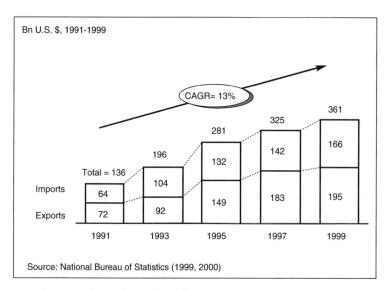

Figure 1-3   Development of trade volume in China

Just following the crowd is not enough, because the crowd is always wrong!

For Western companies, with mature markets at home, China is one of the few perceived remaining opportunities to grow dramatically using existing products. However, despite the huge market potential and the strong desire to do business with China, the track record of foreign companies in the P.R.C. has been mixed at best. Just following the crowd is not enough, because the crowd is always wrong! But at least it takes the pressure off from the CEO for his failure. He can always point to the bad track records of other companies and will not go down in history as the "company's chairman who missed China"—a fear expressed by the Chairman of Ford.

Indeed, there is a significant and growing amount of evidence that, looking at the experiences in their China operations, companies in many instances find that they did not live up to their performance aspirations at the start of their China ventures. What in theory should be a win-win situation has been mainly a one-sided bargain. Whereas FDI has proved to be of great benefit to China, its gains are more questionable for most foreign companies. For example, veteran global players such as Whirlpool, Peugeot, and Caterpillar decided to close factories or scale down their businesses due to poor performance. In the pharmaceutical industry, where one would expect a strong competitive advantage for multinational companies, only four out of the fifty-odd foreign drug companies in China were generating a reasonable return on their investment (*The Economist*

1998, p. 72). Prospects have worsened since the Chinese government introduced price caps, which shift the cost burden to foreign pharmaceutical companies. Similarly, a survey of ninety-six managers of European companies in China showed that most companies performed worse than expected (54%), overestimating the market size (61%), taking longer to achieve profitability than forecast, and suffering from high employee turnover (Harding 1998a). Likewise, research on U.S. businesses in Asia by the American Chamber of Commerce (AmChamb) demonstrated that companies earned the lowest return on investment in China.

At the same time, AmChamb found that the perceived risk of operations was highest in the country of dragons.[8] This contradicts the Nobel Prize-winning "capital asset pricing model" (Lintner 1965; Sharpe 1964), which states that riskier investments demand higher returns. Finance theory and common business sense suggest that such a situation is not sustainable for long. Apart from the disappointing corporate results, many expatriate managers in China did not achieve their *personal* objectives, and left their companies in search of exciting new entrepreneurial challenges. As a result, there is a growing secondary market for expatriate managers in the P.R.C.

In view of the low returns and high risk, Western companies would normally have to terminate their operations and leave China altogether, unless they make major strategic changes. This would be the rational reaction to similarly unsuccessful investments anywhere else in the world. But in China the show goes on, irrational hopes are still fueled, hype and hubris are maintained, even if the consequences are disastrous.

China is the ultimate test ground for leadership skills and a company's ability to excel in other nonstructured situations. . . . If you can make it here, you can make it anywhere!

The imbalance between market potential and realized gains might result from executives not clearly understanding the key success factors in the country and failing to develop the required core competencies and other resources. It is therefore important to study the underlying drivers of high performance in China (Schlevogt, 2000b). This approach seems to be more effective than either completely abandoning China, which despite its unrivaled complexity (Schlevogt 2000a) remains a very promising market, or continuing to suffer bad results. China is also the ultimate test ground for leadership skills and a company's ability to excel in other nonstructured situations, such as mergers and acquisitions and crises (see Schlevogt 2001b). If you can make it here, you can make it anywhere! If you cannot make it here, you cannot make it anywhere! Unfortunately, there is almost no empirical, survey-type field research illuminating how to do business in China. Usually anecdotes are the only "evidence" available. Can they be justified on epistemological grounds?

Importance of further research on China and general research question

Given the dramatic development of private economic activity in China—both new domestic private enterprises and foreign direct investment—combined with the lack of solid empirical evidence, there is a need for further research. To address the interest that academics, businessmen, and policy makers have in China, this book aims at analyzing the nature, causes, and outcomes of Chinese management more closely—this time using a nonintrusive sampling approach instead of a "natural organizational experiment" that requires a cultural revolution. The study aims at answering the following general research question:

Problem statement   "Is there a contextually determined, distinctive Chinese management model in mainland private enterprises that is positively associated with organizational effectiveness?"

I intend to analyze the distinctiveness of the Chinese management model in private, mainly family-based enterprises. I hypothesize that the newly founded private enterprises in the P.R.C. have readopted the distinctive overseas Chinese management style and family-based cultural values. To test for its distinctiveness, I will analyze the model's characteristics, influencing factors, and effectiveness outcomes in private enterprises, and compare these aspects to state enterprises. This will enable me to draw conclusions as to whether private Chinese management is indeed a distinctive art, defined as "the *skill* of doing something *well*" (see Simpson and Weiner 1989, p. 657). By addressing effectiveness issues, I will be in a position to conclude what the key success factors in the Chinese market are, and thus provide important insights and guidance not only for domestic organizations but also for the ailing foreign entities. Figure 1-4 presents the detailed research questions.

Research contributions and benefits for different readership groups

By answering the research questions in figure 1-4, this book will benefit different groups of readers: Scholars, businessmen, and policy makers.

Usefulness for academic readers

This book aims to make distinctive contributions to international management, organizational theory, and economics, and will therefore be use-

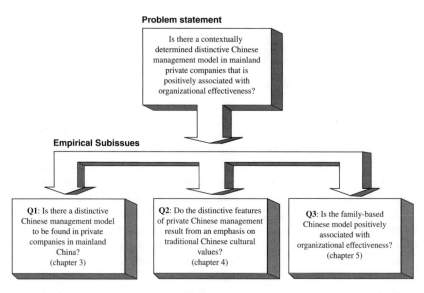

Problem statement

Is there a contextually determined distinctive Chinese management model in mainland private companies that is positively associated with organizational effectiveness?

Empirical Subissues

Q1: Is there a distinctive Chinese management model to be found in private companies in mainland China?
(chapter 3)

Q2: Do the distinctive features of private Chinese management result from an emphasis on traditional Chinese cultural values?
(chapter 4)

Q3: Is the family-based Chinese model positively associated with organizational effectiveness?
(chapter 5)

Figure 1-4 Problem statement for China study

ful for researchers, educators, and students. I will discuss research contributions and hypotheses in more detail in chapter 2. There are three benefits for academic readers:

First I will use survey and case study methodology to examine the nature of a distinctive Chinese management style found in predominantly small, private firms in mainland China. The distinctiveness of Chinese management has occasionally been mentioned in the descriptive literature, but there have been very few empirical studies testing the Chinese management model for its distinctive characteristics, influencing factors, and effectiveness. The key idea here is that the emphasis placed by the entrepreneur on traditional Chinese culture has potent direct and indirect (via its association with small company size) impacts on organizational choices, leading to the distinctive management features. In addition, the management style had been assumed to be practiced only in overseas Chinese communities, but I will show that it has been readopted in mainland China as well, and probably contributes significantly to the dynamic development of the private sector. Moreover, I have developed scales for traditional culture and subcontracting that will enrich the measurement toolbox of organizational researchers in the future. Since the research also employs standardized measurement instruments that have been used in other countries, it is possible to perform cross-national comparisons of different forms of organization. Further, the book adopts an interdisciplinary perspective, avoiding the single focus of many other works about China. It bridges anthropology, political science, economics, management, and psychology. By presenting original insights and data about Chinese management, I hope to act as pioneer opening a new research area and stimulating subsequent research within it.

Second, I have often heard regrets that there are almost no case studies of Chinese companies. Such case studies are enormously important for bringing the real complexity of private and state enterprises to life and engaging students in decision-making situations that will prepare them to deal with emerging markets. By presenting four in-depth case studies, I hope to reduce this gap.

Third, since the core curriculum in business schools increasingly integrates international elements, the book may serve as very useful reading in (post)graduate management and international business courses.

Usefulness for businessmen

Due to the increase in both FDI and trade, foreign companies will transact more frequently with Chinese counterparts. Therefore, foreign businessmen need to acquire a firm understanding of (a) the inner workings of Chinese companies and (b) the Chinese market in general. This book is one of the first attempts to combine scholarly research on Chinese enterprises with practical recommendations for executives. Traditionally, China research in the regional studies field has focused mainly on theoretical issues, and thus has lacked relevance to managers. In contrast, recommendations in the "commercial guide" stream on how to do business in China often have stated the obvious. Those works have explained, for example, how to hand a business card to a Chinese contact. Despite the strong emphasis on "cultural sensitivity" in the literature, this is a question the Chinese does not care about *at all*, as long as he senses a great business opportunity. Apparently, those "handbooks" lack scholarly methods and depth. This study, for the first time, bridges the worlds of scholarship and management. Let's discuss the two contributions, that is, explaining organizations and markets in China.

First, foreign companies that are interested in trade or direct investment in China must know the organizational structure and management practices of Chinese companies, as well as their own strengths and weaknesses. Their Chinese counterparts might be trading partners, customers, suppliers, competitors, distributors, takeover candidates (institutional) investors, and partners in joint ventures or strategic alliances. To deal with them effectively, Western companies need to know, for example, how bureaucratic Chinese companies are, who makes decisions, what are the distinctive features of the decision-making process, which leadership style they practice, how communication flows, and what can be regarded as the main characteristics of Chinese cultural values. This understanding will help them to identify the key leverage points when dealing with Chinese companies. Since in the presence of cultural disparities, organizational practices and their effectiveness may differ from those in the West, the research will also shed light on the usage, applicability, and transferability of Western management techniques to China. If there are indeed such differences, foreign companies in China may have to *adopt* at least parts of Chinese management, such as its leadership style and personnel practices. Even companies that do not intend to enter the Chinese market may learn from Chinese management (as exemplified by the most effective Chinese companies in the sample). They may thus defend themselves against Chinese competitors at home or gain a competitive advantage in other markets, no matter whether Chinese competitors are there or not. Finally, managers might choose or have to work in *Chinese* companies that expand abroad or operate exclusively in China. Thus, they might want to learn more about their prospective employers and their organizational practices.

Second, to conduct business successfully in China, Western companies have to understand the key success factors in the Chinese market. I have described the tidal wave of foreign activity in China, commented on its sometimes dubious reasons, and the resulting failure of many companies. I also have mentioned that despite the high stakes, unfortunately, in many cases anecdotes and guru advice are the only input for decision making, and the single most important source of support for struggling managers. By systematically analyzing the effectiveness of Chinese companies in the context of other factors influencing success, the research will create a fact base and provide best practice recommendations to improve the success in doing business in the Chinese market.

Usefulness for policy makers

China's transition from a centralized planning model of economic organization to a (socialist) market economy is a unique historical experiment. So far it has been one of the most successful economic transformations in the world. Despite the immense historical challenge, there are few empirical studies that explain the reasons for the success of the megaproject in social engineering, in particular the unprecedented boom in private economic activity and amazing entrepreneurial revolution. This gap is particularly large with respect to the microeconomic drivers at the enterprise and management level that have contributed to the enormous changes. Economists are usually suspicious of survey data and in many instances focus only on macroeconomic causes of economic growth.

Since the study will examine these important but neglected aspects of organization structure and management, it will address this research need. Proving the crucial role of organizational design at the microlevel for economic development, the study shows how the new Chinese management model can serve as a framework for economic policy and reforms, including the revitalization of state enterprises. Because it also compares the differences in the organizational effectiveness of private and state enterprises in mainland China, it will shed light on the success of the attempt to introduce capitalist business organizations into a

Communist society. Therefore, at the level of society the findings may have additional important policy implications for China, and also interest policy makers around the world who work in the areas of privatization and transition economies.

Basic research model and theory

Figure 1-5 presents a graphic illustration of the general research model. I will discuss the individual research hypotheses in more detail in chapter 2. The respective individual research models used to operationalize and test them will be introduced together with their findings in part II. The general model posits various effectiveness-induced, optimal structural and managerial responses to external and internal contingency factors, which are moderated through the "strategic choice" (Child 1972b) of managers.[9] "Appropriate" structure, certain management styles, and other contextual factors influence organizational effectiveness, conceptualized as a broad set of financial and other criteria. For the sake of clarity, this model does not show all reciprocal relationships and feedback loops. However, I will analyze certain interaction effects in later chapters.

This underlying model is used to state the theory that one specific configuration of structural choices and managerial practices consistently

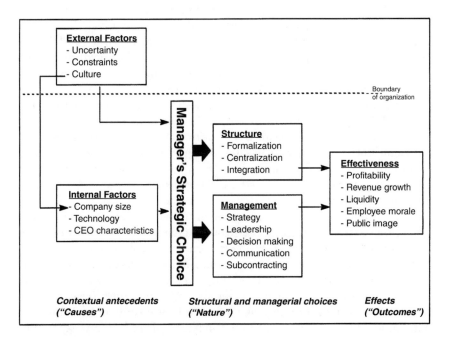

Figure 1-5 General research model

emerges from the influencing factors in private enterprises, which is not found in state enterprises. Most important, the emphasis on traditional Chinese culture directly and indirectly (via its association with small company size) leads to the adoption of what I call web-based Chinese management (WCM) in private enterprises, characterized by centralized and informal structures, entrepreneurial decision making, and extensive enterprise webs. I predict that this family-based model is positively associated with organizational effectiveness.

Research methods: A brief overview

This section provides a very short overview of the methodology used for this research. The interested reader will find more details in the appendix.

Sample

The sample consisted of 124 firms located in mainland China. Half of them were based in Beijing and half in Shanghai. These two cities, apart from Hong Kong, are considered to be China's major "growth engines" (Ou, Shi, and Xu 1996, p. 3). Given that more work has been done on Hong Kong, this study focuses on companies in Beijing and Shanghai. These two cities also represent two very different cultural-geographical areas, the north and south of China (Fitzgerald 1986). About 50% of the companies belonged to the state sector and were randomly sampled from the official *Directory of Enterprises and Institutions* (Ji 1993). The private firms were sampled from the records of local statistical bureaux in Beijing and Shanghai.[10] The overall response rate of 79% far exceeded the extremely low response from the mailed pilot test. This underlines the effectiveness of using personal interviews in China. Higher response rates also were obtained by systematically following up on nonresponses, first by calling the prospective respondent and, in case of further nonresponse, by visiting the company. Many managers were curious about the research, because they had never participated in such a survey before. Furthermore, they hoped to learn from a scholar coming from the West. This increased their readiness to participate in the study. The research thus profited from its pioneering nature.[11]

In addition to the survey, I conducted three in-depth case studies to gather qualitative data full of real-world richness. These case studies included two private enterprises: one corporate image design firm in Beijing and one educational services firm in Shanghai. In addition, I analyzed one SOE, a major industrial bank in Beijing. Personal interviews, participant observation, artifacts, company materials, and newspapers served as data sources. In addition, I undertook an in-depth case study of the American International Group (AIG) in China (Shanghai), based on my experience of dealing with the group and on archival data.

Measures

The relevant research literature guided the selection of independent and dependent variables. Wherever possible, I chose well-validated scales with strong theoretical grounding. Frequent replication had shown their desirable psychometric properties in terms of reliability, validity, and unidimensionality. In particular, I used the Aston scales (Pugh and Hickson 1976) for the measurement of structural properties. They have been developed at the University of Aston (England) as part of an extensive research program aimed at studying macroorganizational features in a systematic fashion, which approaches the rigor and accuracy of the natural sciences. These measures have been applied and tested all over the world and have been shown to be very robust. I also developed measures of traditional Chinese culture and subcontracting for this study.

Procedures

The questionnaire was translated into Chinese and back-translated to ensure the accuracy of the original translation (Brislin, Lonner, and Thorndike 1973). Previous organizational studies in cross-national settings, including China, had demonstrated the validity of this procedure (Adler, Campbell, and Laurent 1989; Baird, Lyles, and Wharton 1990; Tan and Litschert 1994). The questionnaire and administrative procedures were pilot-tested with an effective sample size of $N=10$. The pilot enabled me to compare the effectiveness of different forms of data collection in China, to test and improve scale effectiveness, and to examine the quality of the sampling frame. As a result, some translations were adjusted.

This study applied an "institutional," interorganizational data collection approach. It combined the key informant method (Seidler 1974; Zelditch 1962) and, wherever available, archival records. I conducted face-to-face interviews in Mandarin Chinese with one informant per company (CEO in 85% of the cases, otherwise the most senior vice president).[12] The manager reported on organizational characteristics by responding to the questions of a standardized questionnaire. In some cases the executive brought in staff assistants to answer specific questions in their field of expertise. Archival records included organizational charts, company brochures, and annual reports. They were used to verify the oral information.

Analysis

I used structural equation modeling (SEM) with the program AMOS 3.61 (Arbuckle 1989; 1997) to analyze the Chinese management model, its influencing factors, and its effectiveness. SEM is one of the most sophisticated statistical methods available. It has not yet been widely used in organizational analyses. This book therefore represents a pioneering step to broaden its application. SEM allows the researcher to specify relations between observed variables and latent constructs,[13] such as "Chinese culture," and then to test whether this set of relations is statistically probable, given the observed correlations among the measures (Connell 1987; p. 170). It enables the researcher simultaneously to perform two actions: first, he validates new and existing scales in a *measurement model*. He thus holds measurement error constant, which is usually a severe problem in social science research. Second, he tests his hypotheses in a *theoretical model*. This approach thus integrates measurement and theory, and avoids their artificial split in traditional ordinary least squares (OLS) regression models.

Plan of the book

I will start my journey to the East in the footsteps left by another European more than seven hundred years ago, searching for new truths and ideas—about the social organization of human endeavor, developed by an Oriental culture. John Ruskin once said that there are men of facts, men of design, and men of both. In this book, I want to adopt the spirit and ideals of the men of both. Following this mission and vision. I integrated two perspectives that are usually separated: the analytical view of the scholar and, based on my professional experience in China and elsewhere, the action-oriented view of the practitioner. Managers usually find academic books too "dry" whereas scholars often criticize management bestsellers for their lack of empirical evidence and unscientific treatment of subjects, which often leads to the statement of the obvious and repetition of the trivial.

To realize my aspirations, I divided the book into four parts, with varying perspectives, and an appendix. The academic reader, apart from the introductory part I, will be particularly interested in part II, which presents the individual models and empirical evidence ("know-what"). The practitioner will be eager to read the case studies in part II and to learn about the practical applications in part III ("know-how"). Both types of readers will be interested in the general conclusions in part IV. The book allows the reader to choose the level of detail he desires on his journey of discovery. Let me discuss the four parts in more detail.

Part I. Introduction and development of theory: Laying the groundwork

After the introduction, I will review the present state of accumulated (Western) knowledge about Chinese management. Scholars have commented on individual aspects of Chinese management. They have failed, however, to integrate the individual pieces into a systematic model and to operationalize and test it with empirical data. Furthermore, they have assumed that the management model is used only outside of mainland

China. To address these deficits and further research needs, I will integrate the anecdotal fragments into a coherent theory (web-based Chinese management) and fully operationalize it by specifying individual hypotheses to be tested (chapter 2).

Part II. Empirical findings: Establishing the fact base

In my role as a "man of facts," I will present the findings from my journey to the East: the empirical evidence derived from my survey of 124 companies and several case studies. This fact-based analysis follows the approach of Marco Polo. The Mongol emperor Kublai Khan repeatedly sent Marco Polo on fact-finding missions to distant parts of his empire, such as southwestern and southeastern China. Following this spirit of discovery, I will analyze empirically the nature (chapter 3), causes (chapter 4), and outcomes (chapter 5) of Chinese management in private and state enterprises.

Part III. Practical applications: Using the facts for design.

As a "man of design," I will suggest applications of the findings. To make this section particularly helpful for practitioners, I start the individual chapters with executive summaries. They contain the key "so whats," the "thirty-second-answer" a consultant would give to a client CEO whom he accidentally meets in an elevator and who asks him, "So what's the solution to our problem?" Throughout the book, I highlight important passages in bold print for quick scanning and avoid excessive jargon. In the first application chapter, I present ideas about the organization of the future based on the web-based Chinese management model, synthesizing what international businessmen and investors can learn from WCM to improve their dealings with Chinese enterprises and improve their own operations (chapter 6). Then I will broaden the perspective by discussing what it takes to succeed in China and other emerging markets in general (chapter 7). I will identify key success factors, core competencies, and other resources apart from family ownership and its associated organizational characteristics. They are synthesized into systematic best practice approaches for excellently managing foreign (as well as Chinese) ventures in these markets. I illustrate the resulting new conceptual framework through case studies of high-performing companies and, in the spirit of integrating Western science and Chinese art, several relevant traditional cultural concepts developed in China for leadership and organization.

Part IV. Conclusions and research outlook: A glorious past, challenging present, and bright future for China?

In the last part (chapter 8), I will broaden the perspective once again to paint a broad canvas of China's past, present, and future development, discuss emerging themes from the study, its limitations, and a future research agenda. First, the amazing cultural revival and reunion with the Chinese diaspora will be celebrated. I then will elaborate on the notion of web-based Chinese management as an art. After discussing whether Chinese private firms possess the potential to grow into an international force, I will analyze their impact on domestic economic development. I will suggest how the Chinese government can use the WCM model for making policies in general and reforming state enterprises in particular. Then, I will debate the broader requirements for China's national revival, including the role of Western countries in fostering this amazing renaissance. Next, the circular flow of ideas from East to West to East will be retraced, followed by ideas about how this research can lead to new studies.

Appendixes

The appendixes provide a treasure for researchers who are interested in more details related to the study, perhaps with a view to replicating its findings or building on them. I intentionally have included more material than is found in other books. This avoids the pitfalls of works that do not provide much raw material, and thus make it necessary to rely on interpretations by the authors. This is particularly problematic in the case of qualitative data. Appendix A provides background material on the survey research design in terms of sample, measures, and procedures, and outlines methodological limitations. Appendix B presents the details of the qualitative case study research design. Appendix C contains part of the exploratory data analysis (that is, an examination of sample characteristics). Appendix D includes the standardized English survey questionnaires. The Pearson correlation matrices for the three research models in Appendix E enable researchers to replicate the findings of this study, using the matrices as input in their statistical program. Besides, the electronic files containing the complete raw data for all survey respondents are available from the author. Scholars thus can leverage the huge database for further joint research. A glossary that provides definitions and explanations for all key terms is followed by notes to the chapters and then a bibliography. Finally, an index facilitates easy navigation through the work.

Summary and conclusions

In this introductory chapter, I presented some background on organization in China. I highlighted China's historical connections with organizational developments and its frequent "natural" social experiments. I stressed its growing political and economic importance, which is due mainly to the success of the recent reforms, particularly the large-scale reintroduction of private property in China. The research question aims at understanding the microeconomic causes and lessons of this entrepreneurial renaissance, a distinctive web-based Chinese management model practiced in private Chinese enterprises. Next, I discussed contributions to the world of academe, business, and politics. The basic research model posits that effectiveness-induced constraints tend to narrow managerial strategic choice, which in turn influences organizational effectiveness. In private enterprises, the emphasis on traditional Chinese values is thought to lead to the particular combination of organizational practices encapsulated in WCM theory. The following section briefly outlined the research design in terms of sample, measures, procedures, and analysis. The final part discussed the structure of the book. It is organized around four major parts: theory development, findings, applications, and conclusions. In chapter 2, I will review and synthesize the field of Chinese management, develop WCM theory, and operationalize it into testable hypotheses.

2
The New Theory of Web-based Chinese Management

The main objective of this study is to analyze the nature, causes, and outcomes of the organizational structure and management practices in mainland Chinese companies, including both private and state enterprises. In particular, I will test whether the dynamic, newly established private enterprises have adopted a distinctive web-based Chinese management model. As a first step, it is necessary to introduce the reader to the basic concepts and principles of Chinese management. This discussion provides a basis for the full theoretical research model, since it helps to (a) identify the need for further research, (b) decide which variables to include in the research model, and (c) deduce detailed theoretical hypotheses to be tested. It will thus prepare the ground for chapter 3.

This chapter first presents a short overview of Chinese management, which serves as a backdrop for the ensuing synthesis and analysis. Then, mirroring the individual research questions (see figure 1-4), the three major themes of this book are presented. First, I discuss the distinctiveness of the Chinese management style (nature), integrating the basic building blocks into the new web-based Chinese management theory. The following sections deal with its influencing factors (causes) and its relationship with organizational effectiveness (outcomes).[1] Next, areas for further research will be identified, followed by the detailed research contributions and research hypotheses.

Web-based Chinese management thus contains all elements that I deem necessary for a theory (as opposed to a mere conceptual framework). It has a cohesive gestalt, includes a mechanism with explanatory power, and can be used to make predictions. As a useful theory, it closes a knowledge gap, while still being able to explain phenomena. Like a Russian doll, it explains new things and thus adds a new layer (of knowledge) and covers previous ones. A strong theory such as this is necessary if one wants to test a model with a sample, which is always limited in terms of respondent number.

Overseas Chinese management: A brief overview of the
state of the art

Despite its importance, research on Chinese management is a relatively
recent phenomenon and the literature is still sparse (Leung 1995, p. 6;
Redding and Ng 1982, p. 201). Discussions tend to center exclusively on
overseas Chinese styles. Earlier writers such as Redding (1990) used the
term *Nanyang Huaqiao* to describe the overseas Chinese. *Nanyang* means
South China Sea, and *Huaqiao* literally stands for Chinese *temporarily*
living outside mainland China (including Hong Kong). The historical
magnetism of greater China as the Middle Kingdom, the intermediary
between heaven and the rest of the world, and its unique cultural heritage
led to the linguistically embedded assumption that those living abroad
eventually will return to their mother country—even though in many
cases they have been living overseas for many generations. The term is
quite uncommon in the Mandarin spoken in mainland China (*Putonghua*).
The expression *Haiwai Huaqiao* (overseas Chinese) is more appropriate.
Although this Mandarin expression is not commonly used in the literature, I will introduce it here and hope that future studies adopt this
usage.

Overseas Chinese either have left the mainland to make a living elsewhere or are descendants of such emigrants. They mostly went south, just
as Americans ventured west and Russians penetrated the eastern wilderness. Before the sixteenth century they were mainly non-resident merchants engaging in seasonal overland and seaborne trade. From the sixteenth to the mid-eighteenth century a pattern of long-term settlement
started in Southeast Asia. Emigrants either fled poverty and disaster in
overpopulated southern China or ventured out to establish permanent
trade posts. From the mid-eighteenth century to the 1930s, the rapidly
expanding colonies imported Chinese labor on a large scale and an increasing number of Chinese settlers engaged in small-scale business (Wu
and Wu 1980). Another wave of emigration started after the Communists
"liberated" the mainland in 1949 with many Shanghainese in particular
fleeing to Hong Kong, which served as a business exile.

Most scholars believe that, due to the presence of a communist regime
in mainland China, which originally abolished private property and
scared off entrepreneurs, who fled the mainland, the particular Chinese
management style cannot be found in the P.R.C. anymore and is practiced
only overseas (cf. Hickson and Pugh 1995, p. 170). Redding's (1990) work
is representative in this respect. He delineates it as follows: "It is however
important to draw a line and make clear that this book is not about China
now, and will only make passing reference to what is happening there . . .
our agenda here is the Chinese as capitalists, not as communists or socialists" (p. 3).

In contrast to this view, I argue that private enterprises in mainland
China have readopted the particular Chinese management style and emphasis on Chinese family-based values. Ironically, they were already cap-

italists when Gordon Redding published his book in 1990. Thus, I believe that descriptions of *Haiwai Huaqiao* management apply to private enterprises in mainland China as well, no matter what you call them—perhaps "socialist entrepreneurs"? Deng Xiaoping's famous black-or-white-cat dictum[2] can be restated as follows: it does not matter whether you call them capitalists or socialists; as long as they make money, they are good entrepreneurs.

Apart from missing the changes in mainland China, most accounts focus on individual, fragmented aspects of Chinese management. There is no overarching framework that synthesizes these various ideas, or a theory that explains its effectiveness and allows for predictions. Writers also lack conceptual clarity regarding the distinctiveness of the Chinese management style. They often use words like "comparatively," but do not specify what they compare the Chinese style *with*. Thus, it is almost impossible to test their assertions empirically. It comes to no surprise that writers on overseas Chinese management in private firms have not compared this style with management in state enterprises to test its distinctiveness.

In terms of methodology, most of the literature lacks empirical evidence that supports the diverse ideas and anecdotes—even though writers, such as Shenkar (1989, p. 121), for a long time have urged empirical methods to overcome guesswork about organization in China. At the time the research was undertaken, no single study of mainland China had used a survey, which included, for example, a comprehensive set of standardized scales such as the "Aston" measures of organizational structure. Concepts and measures are not normally linked back to micro-level management theories and the relevant research literature. The few existing empirical studies usually adopt a case study approach with a very limited number of organizations, often restricted to one location. In many instances, they use convenience samples or "invited samples" for which the researcher is directed to enterprises selected by officials (Shenkar 1994, p. 20). Especially frequent are interviews with seminar participants, which are often observed by party cadres and have been shown to yield biased results (Adler, Campbell, and Laurent 1989, p. 67).

Let us now look at some representative studies of private Chinese management. One of the earliest accounts of Chinese "economic psychology" dates back to the 1930s (Wilhelm 1930). Table 2-1 presents a selection of more recent studies, together with their relevant findings and research methodology.

Distinctive characteristics of Chinese management: The new web-based model

To integrate the fragmented accounts, I developed an overarching theory of web-based Chinese management. Its gestalt is graphically illustrated in figure 2-1. The model does not apply to all Chinese business firms, but describes the organizational practices of private, mainly family-owned en-

Table 2-1 State of the art overview of private Chinese management

Authors	Year	Relevant findings	Method
P. H. Cai	1997	Overseas Chinese businesses characterized by lack of formalization, entrepreneurial flexibility (*linghuo ying-bianxing*), and enterprise networks, sharply contrast with the professional, consistent, and transparent management of U.S. companies and well-established management theory.	Only descriptive
W. K. K. Chan	1982	Business history shows that the organizational structure of the traditional privately-owned Chinese firm is characterized by strong centralization and coercive leadership style.	Business historical records
R. Heller	1991	Successful overseas Chinese management model characterized by emphasis on family ties and rule by men instead of rule of law or formalization, as well as strongly founder-dominated culture.	Only descriptive
J. Lee	1996	Distinctive Chinese management model in Singapore, characterized by human-centeredness, family-centeredness, centralization of power, and small size, conflicts with Western management model.	Only descriptive
F. F. L. Leung	1995	Distinctive overseas Chinese management model characterized by lack of hierarchy, low formalization, and dominance by owner.	Only descriptive
J. A. C. Mackie	1992	Entrepreneurial versatility as well as importance of personal relations and familism in overseas Chinese firms.	Literature review
M. Montagu-Pollock	1991	Distinctive overseas Chinese management style, characterized by centralization, importance of relations, and enterprise networks, often leads to high organizational flexibility but may limit growth.	Only descriptive
G. Redding and Y. Y. Wong	1986	Typical overseas Chinese firm characterized by strong centralization, low specialization, low standardization, few staff departments, and strong reliance on personal relations.	Case studies
S. G. Redding	1990	Dominance of centralized leadership, informal structures, and importance of personal network in typical overseas Chinese owner-managed firm.	Conversations with managers
K.-A. Schlevogt	1998	High degree of centralization of decision-making power and importance of personal networks in private enterprise in Taiwan, partly due to emphasis on national cultural values.	Survey based on standardized interviews, case study based on participant observation, interviews, and archival records
D. Turpin	1998	Overseas Chinese businesses feature centralized, paternalistic decision making dominated by the owner, simple business structures, flexibility, and "lean and mean" management. The family business represents the traditional form of Chinese capitalism. Due to the reliance on family capital, firms tend to be very cost-conscious and highly efficient.	Only descriptive
M. Weidenbaum and M. Weidenbaum and S. Hughes	1996	Centralized, authoritarian leadership, flexibility, lack of bureaucracy, and enterprise networks in overseas private Chinese businesses. Family businesses are the dominant organizational form among the overseas Chinese.	Mainly descriptive (and anecdotes)

Note: The main focus here is on organizational practices in overseas Chinese private enterprises, which differ from the Stalinist scientific management style in state enterprises. Therefore, the selection does not include literature on Chinese management that focuses on state enterprises, such as Child (1994), Xu (1992), and Weihrich (1990).

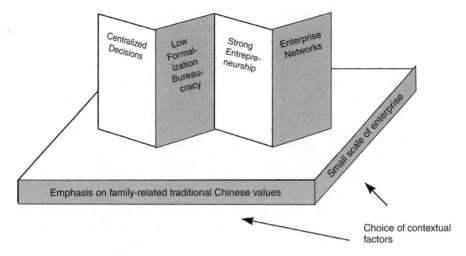

Figure 2-1 Distinctive private web-based Chinese management model

terprises in mainland China. Thus, the term "Chinese management" always refers to this group of enterprises. In fact, an important point of this book is to argue that the style is distinctive when compared to state enterprises. The model probably also applies to small, private overseas Chinese enterprises, but in this book I do not test this assumption. The few large privately-owned overseas Chinese conglomerates may not display all elements of this particular model, but they are exceptions, which resulted from special circumstances in the overseas location. Since I focus on the renaissance of private enterprises in mainland China, and since very few conglomerates exist there, I will not explore the issue of large-scale private enterprises here. One key argument of this book is to show that when the special circumstances do not apply, Chinese private enterprises tend to limit the size of the focal company and to proliferate in intricate enterprise webs instead. Chinese management in private enterprises has the following distinctive characteristics.

Usually a forceful personality—a corporate Hercules—[the Chinese CEO] is the unchallenged captain of his ship.

High centralization

There is a high degree of power centralization in the hands of one autocratic entrepreneur (Turpin 1998, p. 8; Weidenbaum 1996, p. 141), who is usually the founder and owner. This phenomenon can be termed "dictatorship by the owner-manager" (Montagu-Pollock 1991, p. 23). The boss makes all important decisions. Usually a forceful and charismatic personality—a corporate Hercules—he is the unchallenged captain of his ship. Charisma does not necessarily mean that the Chinese leader is an extrovert, but in any case he exerts great power and influence (Schlevogt 2001e). A good example of this structural characteristic is the hub-and-spoke management system of U.S. computer tycoon Wang An, who at times required 136 out of 2000 employees to report directly to him (Cohen 1990, p. 24). In other organizations various branches are required to report directly to the entrepreneur—an arrangement preferred to the adoption of a multidivisional form with relatively independent heads of business units (Kao 1993). Although the CEO makes the final decision, he may ask directly or indirectly for the input of his employees. Good leadership, according to Confucian values, implies that the leader is sensitive to the needs of his subordinates. This is a crucial device for lessening the dangers of power abuse in a hierarchical society. In contrast to the centralized decision making in private firms, enterprises in the state sector tend to be relatively more decentralized (Child 1994, pp. 94–95; Child and Lu 1990, p. 334; Sung and Chan 1987, p. 13).

Low degree of bureaucracy

Chinese private enterprises usually do not develop elaborate bureaucratic controls (Redding 1980; Redding and Wong 1986). Formal means of control are less needed, given that the CEO exerts personal control. The boss usually despises paperwork. He prefers to interact personally with his employees, customers, and suppliers instead of firing memos (or E-mails) at them. This style contrasts with the situation prevalent in Western bureaucracies. The company also lacks specialized roles. The great invention of civilization, division of labor, is not particularly appreciated. Employees are required to do whatever the CEO asks them to do. They quickly become valuable, multiskilled, and versatile contributors, since they are exposed to a wide variety of tasks.

There are few standardized procedures. The CEO ensures that the firm runs smoothly—why bother with rule books? Formal management control systems are also rare. And you won't find an organizational chart in a typical Chinese private enterprise (Leung 1995), since it lacks a well-designed formal hierarchy. The structure is simple: the boss is in the upper box and all employees are at the next level. Do you really need to draw this? Finally, the CEO hates committees, departmental meetings, and other integration devices. He follows the rule that to get something done, a committee should consist of no more than three people, two of whom are absent! The typical Chinese CEO has never heard of "interdepartmental bargaining" or "transfer pricing." Instead, he is the master liaison agent. In contrast, accounts about enterprises in mainland China's state sector have emphasized a high degree of structuredness. For example, Krone et al. (1992) undertook a preliminary investigation of managerial communication practices in state-owned factories. They concluded that Chinese

factories resemble the bureaucratic model in their use of formal information centers. Weihrich (1990) also found that state-owned enterprises are
very bureaucratic.

[The Chinese CEO's] leadership style is pragmatic. As a guiding principle,
reasonableness is more important than reason.

Strong entrepreneurship

Chinese private enterprises tend to pursue proactive and aggressive strategies, and to adopt a flexible leadership style and an entrepreneurial decisionmaking mode (Hickson and Pugh 1995, p. 170; Mackie 1992, p. 53).
The CEO usually spots opportunities quickly and moves faster than the
crowd. He knows, that if you see a bandwagon, it's too late. He decides
on important strategic moves within days, or sometimes hours. The pricing and cash-management skills are superb. Low margins buy market
share and ensure fast turnover and low inventory levels. The volume ensures attractive profits and a constant cash flow. This cash is immediately
injected into new, exciting opportunities, and the money machine rolls
on. The leadership style is pragmatic. As a guiding principle reasonableness is more important than reason (Lin 1977). The CEO prefers seat-of-
the-pants judgment based on well-informed intuition over extensive analysis to derive "optimal" decisions. You usually won't find elaborate
spreadsheets with net present value calculations and sensitivity analyses,
or charts with detailed scenarios stacked on his desk. His problem-solving
technique is intuition, and it works very well. This is because his intuition
is not pure guesswork but well informed foresight, developed by years of
industry experience and long exposure to the specific niche environment
he has chosen for his kingdom. In contrast, studies about the state sector
enterprises have highlighted the importance of planning in decisionmaking (Weihrich 1990). In addition, state-owned enterprises were found to
inhibit the emergence of entrepreneurial managers (Boisot and Liang
1992, p. 180).

CEOs of Chinese private enterprises are personal relations spiders. Incessantly, they spin their enterprise webs.

Intricate enterprise webs

CEOs of Chinese private enterprises are personal relations spiders. Incessantly they spin their enterprise webs. They build large "enterprise cities"

that they glue together through ties based on family lineages and trust. Personal connections (*guanxi*) serve as their linchpin. As a consequence, in overseas Chinese communities extensive (often subcontracting-based) firm networks of small enterprises predominate (Montagu-Pullock 1991, p. 21; P. Williamson 1997). These "centrifugal business systems" (Whitley 1994, p. 173) are characterized by highly personal connections with employees, customers, and suppliers. It is not uncommon for employees to leave the company and set up their own spin-offs. The pragmatism of the Chinese CEO in these circumstances is amazing. He usually seeks to keep a strong connection with the spin-off, offering start-up capital, and placing orders with it. He knows that in the long run, a web of friendship enterprises, even if they are competitors in certain areas, will serve him well—especially if he achieves the network centrality of a system integrator. This cooperative attitude is very different from Western companies' treatment of what they call "traitors." Many lineage-based networks extend internationally (Watson 1975b). Overseas Chinese frequently invest in their hometowns especially in Fujian and Guangdong province. They now represent the most important foreign investor group in China (Fukuyama 1995, p. 92). Many Chinese enterprises are part of the "Hong Kong Business System" (Vogel 1989). Likewise, there are many pan–Asian networks usually owned by one (often undisclosed) overseas Chinese entrepreneur, and managed by overseas Chinese (Cai 1997).

Firm networks protect members in the absence of property rights, legal institutions, and political stability. They also help to deal with the many market imperfections in the region (Child 1994, p. 121). In addition, networks provide useful business intelligence and opportunities. Finally, by "proliferating" or "spawning" through cross-holdings with other companies, instead of growing the size of their own company, many Chinese enterprises can retain close ties with family members. The latter often head spin-offs instead of seeking positions of responsibility in other large companies. In contrast, state enterprises are often vertically integrated and form part of hierarchically organized governmental industry bureaus or ministries.

Influencing factors of Chinese management

In the past, Chinese management was considered to be monolithic. Its relationships with various contingency factors have rarely been explored. However, there are two important factors influencing organizational choices that cannot be ignored: Emphasis on Chinese culture and company size. Differences in their mean levels and correlation with structural and managerial characteristics between private Chinese and state enterprises lead to the distinctive Chinese management model. As shown in figure 2-1, they are the roots of its distinctive structural arrangements and managerial practices.

Emphasis on Chinese cultural elements

Since Max Weber ([1904–1905] 1930) argued that the Protestant ethic fueled the spirit of capitalism in the West, scholars have studied the influence of religion and, more generally, the impact of culture on economic behavior. The Chinese are the world's largest racial, linguistic, and cultural group and are spread all over the world. Researchers believe that, more than in many other countries, in China "culture pervades" (Hall and Xu 1990, p. 574). Despite the influence of communism, neo-traditional values remain pervasive in the P.R.C. (Hall and Xu 1990, p. 574; Laaksonen 1988, p. 7; Walder 1986). Various writers have also highlighted selected elements of Chinese national culture as part of the distinctive Chinese management style. Cai (1997), for example, concluded that overseas Chinese family businesses and Chinese traditional culture are *one* research topic. It therefore seems worthwhile to discuss the impact of culture in China in more detail.

Apart from other factors and to a greater extent than other religions (such as Buddhism or Taoism), Confucianism, with its personal ethical principles, has shaped social relations within the Sinitic culture most profoundly over the last twenty-five hundred years, and has significantly influenced economic development (A. Chan 1996; Hofstede and Bond 1988; Yang 1961). The great Confucian principles that promote wisdom, peace, and harmony still dominate the Chinese mindscape. Its ethics were internalized by members of the community through self-cultivation and socialization. Instead of abstract preaching, Confucians modeled desirable behavior in day-to-day transactions. The moral values instilled through learning and socialization often served as surrogate for laws. The Confucian emphasis on self-cultivation contrasts with the legalist school that motivated the first emperor to build a strong bureaucratic system.

Despite the common emphasis on culture in China, there is some disagreement whether emphasis on cultural elements, especially the importance of personal relations, should be treated as an independent variable influencing the structure and management of Chinese enterprises (Harrison 1994; Solt 1995; G. Wong and Birnbaum-More 1994), or as a dependent variable (that is, one additional organizational characteristic of the distinctive Chinese management style) (Alston 1989; Montagu-Pollock 1991; Wall 1990). This distinction has not been discussed in the literature, mainly because few writers have adopted a contingency perspective. Instead, they have treated Chinese management as one invariable conceptual block. In contrast, I consider emphasis on selected Chinese cultural characteristics a contextual influencing factor of structure and management. The mean level for this contextual factor and its correlation with organizational practices are hypothesized to be higher, and thus distinctive, in Chinese private companies compared to state enterprises.

I will now discuss in greater detail the distinctive elements of Chinese culture and their impact on organizational design. A common underlying thread in the literature on Chinese culture is the emphasis on family-related values in private enterprises. Cai (1997), for example, states that "overseas Chinese enterprises put family capital, traditional customs and Confucianist culture together," which promotes cohesiveness among family members. Whyte (1995, p. 1014) states that in private firms "the dynamics of Chinese families are absolutely central."

Respect for age and hierarchy. Confucianism emphasizes seniority, which leads to a strong hierarchical orientation in China (Davis 1997; Smith, Peterson, and Wang 1996). Authority patterns and legitimization strategies probably explain part of the variations in organizational structure (Hamilton and Biggart Woolsey 1988, p. S87). For example, a strong hierarchical orientation will lead to a relatively high degree of centralization (Hofstede 1980, p. 135). Power distance reinforces a top-down command structure, because it leads to a high value being placed on social control, virtually as a end in itself (Child 1994, p. 31). Despite its importance, so far there is little empirical evidence supporting the impact of this cultural attribute on organizations (Lockett 1988, p. 486).

Group orientation. Confucian doctrine stresses kinship ties and group loyalty (Wilson 1970, p. 20). In private enterprises the most important group is the family. The individual exists for the benefit of the collective. He finds his identity through reference to the group and adopts group objectives and opinions in exchange for protection and care. The Chinese intuitively understand that, to use the words of an Italian author, we are all angels with only one wing—we can fly only while embracing each other. Conflict is generally handled through intragroup mediation rather than the external legal system. The social needs of employees in the workplace will be perceived as more important than autonomy and self-actualization needs (Redding 1980; Xing 1995, p. 17). In addition, it is argued that close ties among family members create strong cohesiveness (*ningjuli*) in private overseas Chinese enterprises (Cai 1997). Whereas at the *family* level, group orientation is very important (in contrast to countries such as Japan), there is a weak collective orientation or public-spiritedness at the societal level (Pye 1985). The Chinese author Lin Yutang compared Japanese society to a piece of granite. In contrast, he likened traditional Chinese society to a loose tray of sand, each grain being an individual family.

Face. Another important policing device of traditional Chinese culture is the importance for a gentleman to "keep face" (Bond and Lee 1981; Ho 1976; Hu 1944; Redding and Ng 1982, p. 203). Group pressure is used to ensure conformity through eliciting shame (loss of face). Losing face is thought to be more consequential for a Chinese manager than for a Western one, leading some social actors in China to become experts in power games based on face (Hwang 1987). Achieving a high position may be more significant than in the West (Lockett 1988, p. 489). In theory, this could have organizational implications, such as more hierarchical and centralized structures, but I believe "face management" (Schlevogt 2001i) is too subtle to have a significant impact.

The importance of relationships. Personal long-term relations, a form of social capital,[3] are important when dealing with internal or external stakeholders[4] (Ambler 1994; Yeung and Tung 1996). Personal connections feature dominantly in the description of Chinese business (Davies 1995). In particular, they are most often cited in the literature on Chinese management (Strange, Kamall, & Tan 1998, p. 3). These *guanxi* are a form of social investment, whereby favors are extended on the basis of expected reciprocity (Pye 1992). Confucians prefer socialization over legalism. Thus, Chinese tradition favors the implicit structuring over the precise formalization of social relations (ECAM 1986). Trust-based personal relations among family members and friends often substitute for written contracts (Barton 1983; Roehrig 1994, p. 83) and, in an even wider sense, replace impersonal bureaucratic and legal controls—often used by Western businessmen as safeguards.

It is important to discuss two objections. First, many people believe that relationships are important all over the world. Nevertheless, most writers agree on the special status of *guanxi* in the Chinese context, since they are so ubiquitous and play such a crucial role in everyday life (Tsang 1998, p. 65). Personal relationships based on trust often are more important than the legal system, company policies, and regular Western business practice. Second, some writers argued that *guanxi* are important in the state sector as well (Child 1994). However, because most private Chinese firms are family-owned, they differ from state enterprises in that the closest relationships are often based on *family* ties (Chu and Ju 1993; Heller 1991), which are less dominant in state enterprises.

One overarching theme that permeated the foregoing discussion on Chinese culture is the importance of familism in private enterprises. Due to the Confucian principle of filial piety (*xiao*), the individual must be most loyal to his family (*jia*). Family loyalty is almost a divine act (Fukuyama 1995, p. 86)—even more important than loyalty to the state (Levy 1949b, p. 1). The family also defines an individual's sense of identity. The concept of *jia* is generally wider than that in the West (Freedman 1979). The ideal type is a five-generation household, but statistics show that the joint family (that is, a three-generation household), or even the nuclear family, is much more common (Hareven 1987). Smaller size often results from wealth constraints or family breakup after intrafamily tensions escalated (Lee 1953).

In a wider sense, the family concept includes lineage or clans. A *jiazu* is "a family of families" based on demonstrated descent from a common ancestor (Baker 1979, p. 67). They often share the same surname and property, such as an ancestral hall. These clans sometimes consist of entire villages and are most common in Guangdong, Fujian, and Hong Kong's New Territories (Freedman 1971). In an even wider interpretation, the notion of "family" comprises people who share an aspect of personal identification, including very good friends, former schoolmates, and other close people (Jacobs 1979). Without unitarian and egalitarian ethical principles, obligations are graded instead of universal. Their intensity declines the farther one moves from the inner family circle. There is a strong separation between members of the family, who can be trusted and are accountable for their deeds in front of other kin members, and nonmembers, who cannot be trusted (Wolf 1968, p. 23).

In the absence of property rights and social protection, the family provided a protecting wall against the arbitrariness of rulers and political instability, including, in the twentieth century, warlords, foreign occupation, collectivization, and the Cultural Revolution. A large number of sons also lessened economic hardship in old age (Jenner 1992, p. 4). Therefore, despite the eroding forces of the modern world and the influence of communism, the patrilineal Chinese family has emerged strongest among all institutions (Hareven 1987; Tien and Lee 1988). Even though it changed over time, it represented one of the only certainties in modern Chinese history—family is the most important social unit for Communist party officials, too (Jenner 1992, p. 13).

Small size

Large overseas Chinese conglomerates or Chinese multinational companies are rare. They usually result from very specific local circumstances, such as special protection by the host government in exchange for various favors. Rather, most Chinese private enterprises are small (J. Lee 1996; Montagu-Pollock 1991, p. 21). There is some confusion as to whether size is an influencing factor of organizational choices, as most contingency theorists would argue, or whether it is a dependent variable forming part of the Chinese management system. In this study, I will treat it as a contextual variable influencing structure and management, but the choice of the level of this contextual variable (that is, the decision to stay small) is a distinctive element of Chinese management. For example, in countries and jurisdictions that allow the Chinese free economic activity,[5] Chinese enterprises are predominantly small (Hicks and Redding 1982, p. 212; Myers 1986, p. 29; Tam 1990, p. 161). This emphasis on small size stems from the desire to keep the ownership of the business within the family circle— within traditional Chinese culture, you trust only close relatives (Berger 1994, p. 72). The family protects the individual against outsiders and widespread uncertainty. Thus, in contrast to the prevailing situation in the West, the family business is the basic economic unit of overseas Chinese society (Weidenbaum 1996, p. 141). Statistics show that most private overseas Chinese firms are family-owned and family-managed (Heller 1991; Redding 1990, p. 3). Ownership is either direct or indirect. An example of indirect holdings are publicly listed companies that are owned by banks controlled by the family (Whitley 1990).

Concluding the overall discussion, there seems to be a strong influence of Chinese culture on organizational structure and management. The emphasis on family-based traditional values does not only have a direct impact on organizational properties, but also influences the choice of another contextual factor, size. Chinese private enterprises decide to stay small to maintain personal relations with important stakeholders or to avoid the inclusion of outsiders, who are not trusted.

Chinese management and organizational effectiveness

Another important theme related to the distinctive web-based model is the performance of family-based Chinese management. There is a moderate number of descriptive and fragmented discussions focusing on partial aspects of overseas Chinese management and its effectiveness. Along with this lack of a unifying model, there are few empirical studies that rigorously analyze the influence of Chinese management and, in particular, family ownership on organizational performance. I will now discuss Chinese management's strengths and weaknesses, and the present empirical evidence related to its effectiveness. The merits and demerits of family-based Chinese management are shown in figure 2-2.

Private Chinese businesses excel at managing social and financial capital.

Merits of family-based Chinese management

On the one hand, the Chinese management style practiced in small, family-based enterprises has certain benefits and may lead to comparatively high performance. The unusually strong loyalties and close ties of Chinese families are a potent source of motivation and performance (Whyte 1995, p. 1003)—private Chinese businesses excel at managing social and financial capital and thus reap high returns.

Valuable social capital. For the sake of the family, the Chinese study hard, work long hours, labor for less, and make more sacrifices than nonfamily members would do (Whyte 1995, p. 1003). Because family members usually participate in the capital and are responsible for their own spin-offs, they have strong incentives to act as entrepreneurs and work hard (Harrel 1985; Whyte 1995, p. 1003). At the same time, the family-based network provides some diversification of risk at the aggregate level and a "group insurance against failure" for the individual member (Greenhalgh 1990, p. 90; Silin 1976). Family members are also very loyal to the company. They are likely either to stay with the firm even when better-paying opportunities arise elsewhere, or at least to support the family firm, even from overseas (Salaff 1981; Watson 1975b). Moreover, trust among family

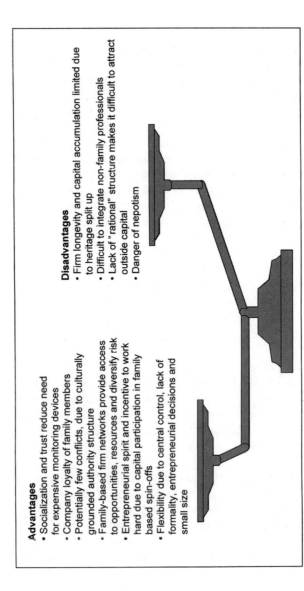

Advantages
- Socialization and trust reduce need for expensive monitoring devices
- Company loyalty of family members
- Potentially few conflicts, due to culturally grounded authority structure
- Family-based firm networks provide access to opportunities, resources and diversify risk
- Entrepreneurial spirit and incentive to work hard due to capital participation in family based spin-offs
- Flexibility due to central control, lack of formality, entrepreneurial decisions and small size

Disadvantages
- Firm longevity and capital accumulation limited due to heritage split up
- Difficult to integrate non-family professionals
- Lack of "rational" structure makes it difficult to attract outside capital
- Danger of nepotism

Figure 2-2 Advantages and disadvantages of Chinese family-based management model

members facilitates a high degree of secrecy, *yinbixing* (Cai 1997), in information-sensitive areas. In addition, the potential for conflicts with the boss is reduced through culturally grounded authority structures in the company, which often reflect positions in the family (Smart and Smart 1993).

Flexibility. Small family businesses with centralized leadership can make decisions flexibly and fast (Montagu-Pollock 1991, p. 21). The CEO enjoys complete sovereignty and usually uses this enormous power and discretion to make decisions quickly, without sophisticated planning instruments or staff assistance. This sharply contrasts with the slow, consensual decision making in more bureaucratic organizations, such as Chinese state enterprises or large Japanese companies. In addition, interorganizational networks based on the extended family make Chinese private companies very responsive to the environment (Whyte 1995, p. 1004). They provide access to scarce visible and invisible resources (including intelligence), business opportunities, and intelligence (Leung 1995, p. 7), enabling Chinese firms to adapt rapidly to changing market conditions.

Cost-efficiency. Subcontracting-based enterprise networks incur low overhead costs and need only a small permanent staff (Montagu-Pollock 1991, p. 21). Web members use the coordinative power of what I call the "socialized market" instead of expensive hierarchies. In addition, firms that rely on internal private capital instead of outside sources of finance tend to be very cost-conscious and highly efficient (Turpin 1998). They have a strong incentive to save resources, since the family capital is at stake. Besides, socialization and trust reduce the need for elaborate incentive systems and monitoring devices, that cause high transaction costs. For example, the CEO does not need complex compensation schemes, expensive accounting systems, and other instruments to ensure that his employees' objectives are aligned with those of the company. There is no separation between family members and the company, since in most cases all capital is owned by the family.

These organizations approach the ideal type assumed in neoclassical theories of perfect competition. Their networked individualism is ideally suited for industries with rapid changes in consumer tastes and other sources of high uncertainty. In those environments, firms need to be sensitive and adapt continuously to changing circumstances. Besides, flexible specialization needs to substitute for mass-production. The model therefore will be most successful in industries in which small size and the associated flexibility are a distinctive advantage. That is why overseas Chinese companies tend to excel in labor-intensive industries and in sectors with fast-changing, highly segmented, and therefore small markets, such as textiles and apparel, trading, timber and other commodities, small-scale metalworking, plastics, furniture, paper products, toys, PC components, and "commodity" PCs (Fukuyama 1995, p. 80). Because of the small size and consequently low start-up costs of private firms, many

sectors in China's economy are characterized by a steady flow of new en-
trants and exits, and thus are pervaded by a highly competitive spirit.
Such an industry structure contrasts sharply with the small number of
oligopolistically organized (and most often capital-intensive) giant firms
sharing certain markets in the West, as well as the large industrial state
conglomerates in the P.R.C. In contrast to their Western counterparts, Chinese private enterprises are lean but not mean (as measured by their results). In conclusion, it might be predicted that "Chinese familism will
fuel the motor of development" (S. Wong 1988, p. 146).

Demerits of family-based Chinese management

In contrast to these positive aspects, the family-based management model
practiced in Chinese private enterprises has certain disadvantages. Company growth is limited for three reasons.

The moment of victory is too short to live for it exclusively—the family is what
lives on.

Limits on capital accumulation. The partrilineal system of equal inheri-
tance for all sons, as opposed to primogeniture, which was formerly practiced in Great Britain and France, limits capital accumulation. It hampers
the growth of Chinese companies, since the family fortune is divided
equally after the death of the founder (Jenner 1992; S. Wong 1988, p. 139).
This makes it almost impossible to build large organizations. In rural
China, plots were partitioned continuously and finally became insufficient for the whole family (Feuerwerker 1969, p. 15). For the Chinese,
wealth is acquired to be shared, not to be hoarded. They believe that the
moment of victory is too short to live for it exclusively—the family is what
lives on.

Lack of integration of professional outsiders. Because of the emphasis on
familism, Chinese private enterprises lack trust toward nonkin members
and a mechanism for adopting outsiders (Berger 1994, p. 72; Watson
1975a). As a consequence, they rarely leverage professional management
talent, which is available in the market (W. Chan 1977, 1982; Whitley
1991). In addition, without professional and rational "Western-style"
structures and transparent forms of governance, it is difficult to attract
nonfamily funding. Both factors further limit growth.[6] Besides, nonfamily
members normally do not aspire to lifetime employment, but try to spin
off their own company after a while (Whyte 1995, p. 1001; S. Wong 1988,
p. 143). Because of their desire to become "boss" (Schlevogt 2001l), they
often are bad team players, which may adversely affect performance.

Moreover, the social distance between them and their Chinese superiors is greater than in other countries (Hamilton and Biggart Woolsey 1988), which may also decrease effectiveness.

Nepotism. Max Weber ([1916] 1951) used the term "sib fetters of the economy" to describe the negative consequences of nepotism. The decline of Wang Laboratories Massachusetts epitomizes its dangers (Brown 1989; Kenney 1992). Private Chinese entrepreneurs who fail to build solid institutions that transcended their family circle depend on the next generation to lead the organization. This gives rise to the "Buddenbrooks" phenomenon of prospering and falling family enterprises, since the skills and motivations to manage differ across generations (Baker 1979, p. 131; Hsu 1967, pp. 5–7). As an example, the wealth of Sheng Xuan-huai, who was one of imperial China's early successful entrepreneurs, dissipated only one generation after the founder's death (Feuerwerker 1958, pp. 84–85). Nevertheless, I believe that the negative consequences of nepotism should not be overemphasized. In many companies several candidates in one family compete for the corporate throne. The Chinese are shrewd businessmen and test these candidates carefully. The father frequently takes his children to his enterprise. They often have ample opportunities to listen to business conversations at the dinner table. The offspring is expected to attend the best schools and universities, often in the United States or Europe, to prepare for future leadership tasks. Those who, after all this grooming and assimilation of "tacit knowledge," do not live up to the gradually more difficult test assignments are mercilessly selected out and left free to pursue other careers. Thus, the lack of quality, as measured by individual leadership ability, is not the most negative aspect of nepotism. More serious are the limits to growth that result from the insufficient quantity of talent, as measured by total leadership capacity, because key managerial positions have to be filled exclusively by family members.

As a consequence of all these factors, Chinese (family-based) private enterprises tend to do less well in industries with indivisible economies of scale and scope, and high capital intensity, such as in steady-state sectors that require mass production and other sectors where small size is not a competitive advantage. Examples include aerospace, semiconductors, automobiles, and petrochemicals. This also applies for mass-marketed consumer brands (Redding 1990, p. 5). Chinese enterprises that want to succeed in these industries usually need strong state sponsorship or even outright state ownership. For example, despite the highly competitive and individualistic industries in the rest of the private economy, the most successful manufacturing companies in China at the start of the modern age, such as those in the porcelain center Jingdezhen, were state-owned and state-operated (Jenner 1992, p. 81). Alternatively, Chinese enterprises may enter these large-scale industries by attracting foreign investment or developing interorganizational networks in sectors with divisible economies of scale and scope. Like networked computer systems, these "webs" leverage the power of individual firms and achieve economies through collective synergy. Using a slightly modified version of Sun Microsystem's slogan, we can state: "The network is the company." Due to the disadvantage pointed out above, *earlier* studies concluded that family enterprises retarded the economic development of China (Feuerwerker 1958; Levy 1949a; Weber [1916] 1951).

Empirical studies analyzing the effectiveness of Chinese management

Empirical evidence on the relationship between Chinese management practices and effectiveness is very sparse. Some macroeconomic estimates or proxies for the performance of the overseas Chinese have occasionally surfaced but they lack statistically validated explanations. There are almost no data for mainland China. Perhaps as a consequence of the advantages of Chinese management, the forty million non-Communist Chinese have managed to produce an unusually large number of billionaires relative to their collective GNP. Nine out of every ten billionaires in Southeast Asia are ethnic Chinese (Chen 1995, p. 69). They also dominate medium- and large-scale corporate capital in all Asian markets except Japan and Korea (Turpin 1998). Other quantitative estimates of their impact have been rather naive. Past accounts emphasized that their aggregate GNP approaches the total GNP for China, which is produced by 1.2 billion people.

However, this comparison is misleading. The overseas Chinese, like almost all emigrants, are the most active and talented elements of the whole people. They are not representative of all Chinese, but instead are a small, successful elite. To compare them with the *total* population of mainland China, most of it rural, is wrong. The erroneous conclusion that the management of mainland Chinese enterprises is completely different from the overseas Chinese style and less effective derives from this inadequate comparison and outdated assumption that communism and entrepreneurship are incompatible. The correct procedure is to compare the overseas Chinese with the new mainland Chinese entrepreneurs. Judged by the estimated large and increasing number of new millionaires in private enterprises in China—especially along the southeastern seaboard—the numbers would be similar to the overseas situation. Apart from these macroeconomic back-of-the–envelope calculations that produce controversial guesstimates, there are almost no empirical data. In particular, there is a lack of studies at the microeconomic level that analyze the relationship between private Chinese management and effectiveness. One reason is the absence of purposefully construed and publicized success stories that serve as (corporate) propaganda. Another explanation is the difficulty of obtaining data. Chinese businesses usually do not strive for glamour and glory. They work efficiently but quietly. Beauty is in their nature—they do not have to be told. And given their secrecy, they do not tell others about its causes.

Critical appraisal of the state of the art of Chinese management

The preceding discussion about Chinese management focused on three areas with further need for research: The nature of the distinctive style, its causes, and outcomes. The present gaps in our knowledge are summarized in the left-hand column of Figure 2-3.

First, previous works are relatively few in number and lack a unifying theoretical model that integrates the elements of Chinese management. I developed a distinctive web-based management model from the fragmented discussions. Further, studies lack conceptual clarity. They do not specify the benchmark to which the style is compared and which dimensions are dependent or independent variables. In addition, it is widely believed that this management style is confined to non–Communist overseas Chinese communities, and does not extend to mainland China. In regards to the empirical evidence, most discussions are purely conceptual and empirically untested. Most authors were unable to operationalize their ideas into testable propositions, or made the epistemic error to conclude that the research subject only lends itself to qualitative analysis or that sufficient knowledge can be gained through such qualitative research alone. Standardized scales, such as the Aston measures, have seldom been used in China in a comprehensive manner. The few empirical studies usually used a case study approach with a very limited number of organ-

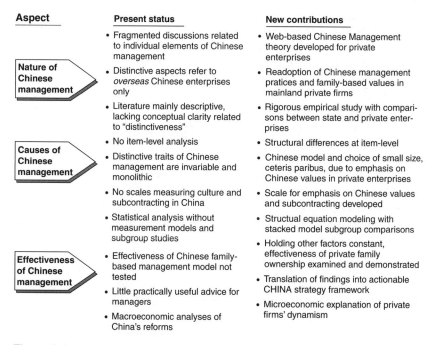

Aspect	Present status	New contributions
Nature of Chinese management	• Fragmented discussions related to individual elements of Chinese management • Distinctive aspects refer to *overseas* Chinese enterprises only • Literature mainly descriptive, lacking conceptual clarity related to "distinctiveness"	• Web-based Chinese Management theory developed for private enterprises • Readoption of Chinese management pratices and family-based values in mainland private firms • Rigorous empirical study with comparisons between state and private enterprises
Causes of Chinese management	• No item-level analysis • Distinctive traits of Chinese management are invariable and monolithic • No scales measuring culture and subcontracting in China • Statistical analysis without measurement models and subgroup studies	• Structural differences at item-level • Chinese model and choice of small size, ceteris paribus, due to emphasis on Chinese values in private enterprises • Scale for emphasis on Chinese values and subcontracting developed • Structual equation modeling with stacked model subgroup comparisons
Effectiveness of Chinese management	• Effectiveness of Chinese family-based management model not tested • Little practically useful advice for managers • Macroeconomic analyses of China's reforms	• Holding other factors constant, effectiveness of private family ownership examined and demonstrated • Translation of findings into actionable CHINA strategy framework • Microeconomic explanation of private firms' dynamism

Figure 2-3 New contributions of China Study

izations and locations. In view of the large number of state enterprises and even greater number of private firms, this narrow sample by necessity provides only a very partial picture of management in China. Furthermore, these studies tended to focus exclusively on public (especially state-owned) enterprises and bypassed the rapidly growing private sector. Given that the share of SOEs in total GDP is already below 50%, and considering that private enterprises form the most dynamic sector of the Chinese economy, are the major beneficiaries of recent reforms, and tend to be managed in a radically different manner, this one-sided focus on one group of companies in the state sector appears to be too narrow a perspective and misses out on one of the most striking features and contrast of Chinese economic reforms. Finally, previous studies did not analyze item-level differences between private enterprises themselves with respect to structural choices. Examples are differences in decision making with respect to individual issues such as hiring and firing and the degree to which different functions are formalized.

Second, most previous works are descriptive, treating Chinese management in a monolithic fashion. They failed to model and explore its relationships with various contextual factors in the task environment, which might influence the individual characteristics. Such an analytical contingency approach would clarify whether the management model is inherently distinctive, resulting from the strong emphasis placed on traditional, family-based values. Some accounts assumed causality, but did not test it. An example is the assumed link between culture and management, which was not tested empirically. They thus could neither prove the causal impact, nor quantify its absolute influencing power, nor rank its importance vis-à-vis other factors. In addition, previous studies usually failed to link their findings to micromanagement theories and concepts, and thus missed the opportunity to exploit synergistic linkages with accumulated knowledge. In regard to measurement, there are no scales that gauge emphasis on selected Chinese cultural characteristics. For the purpose of analysis, most empirical research uses OLS regression, which excludes the measurement model. It thus artificially separates theory from measurement, making it impossible to partial out measurement error.

Third, the differential effectiveness implications of the Chinese management style—particularly family-based private ownership—though occasionally and partially discussed in previous works, were not integrated into a unifying effectiveness model. Without such a model, its effectiveness also could not be empirically tested in a rigorous quantitative and qualitative manner. To do so, it is necessary to measure organizational effectiveness and to compare the differential impact of various structural and managerial choices under different circumstances, while holding constant other key success factors. In addition, there are few microeconomic studies analyzing the reasons for the success of the economic reforms. Empirical studies that use survey data are rare in this respect. Instead, aggregate macroeconomic analysis dominates the field, but lacks convincing explanatory models and practical (as contrasted to statistical) significance. The pre-occupation with *overseas* Chinese management is another reason why the impact of the web-based model on the rapid development of private enterprises in mainland China was overlooked. In addition, previous researchers rarely broke out of narrow academic confines by translating their results into recommendations that managers could act upon to improve the effectiveness of domestic and foreign companies in China and other emerging markets.

Distinctive research contributions of China study

I have identified several areas in which further research is needed to integrate and substantiate previously fragmented conjectures and to gain new knowledge on Chinese management. This book aims at addressing these open issues and stimulating further research in this important new field. By doing so, it clearly enters uncharted waters. This landmark study intends to make theoretical, empirical, and methodological contributions in three distinct areas. I will determine, through surveys, whether a new, integrated model of the distinctive Chinese management style is applied in the newly founded private enterprises in the P.R.C., and will analyze whether it depends on contingency factors and is positively associated with performance. The detailed contributions, which mirror the open issues discussed beforehand, presented in the right-hand column of figure 2-3, are discussed below.

Nature of Chinese management

The first contribution is to examine, through a comprehensive survey that includes 124 standardized face-to-face interviews with Chinese CEOs, and a set of rich case studies, the nature of a distinctive Chinese management style in private enterprises in the P.R.C. As pointed out, some fragments of a distinctive Chinese management style have been described in the theoretical literature, but were thought to be confined to overseas Chinese communities. This study moves one step farther by developing an integrated theoretical model of Chinese management and testing its readoption in mainland China—particularly in the newly founded private Chinese enterprises. Among other things, it tests the hypothesized reemphasis on traditional, family-based Chinese values. One of the distinctive contributions of this study is to show that we witness an amazing managerial and cultural renaissance of private enterprise in the Chinese motherland— a managerial and cultural revolution of entrepreneurship. The study will also analyze item-level structural differences inside private enterprises.

Influencing factors of Chinese management

This book will examine whether the web-based Chinese management style results from the emphasis on traditional Chinese culture. The distinctive structure and management of private Chinese enterprises are thought to be due to the stronger emphasis that their owners put on family values compared to state enterprises. Culture influences structural and managerial choices directly, as well as indirectly by affecting the decision of many private firms to remain small and proliferate into networks instead of growing the focal company itself. Owners desire to maintain personal relations with important stakeholders and avoid the inclusion of outsiders who are not trusted. Previous research has neglected this issue. Because this study uses precise causal modeling with a wide range of influencing factors instead of the usual small set, the impact of culture can be calculated in quantitative terms—both as an absolute number and as a relative position on a ranking of key influencing factors. The inclusion of measurement models controls for the ubiquitous measurement error in social science research. Structural equation modeling has only rarely been used in organizational studies. This book thus intends to promote the greater application of structural equation modeling to organizational problems. It will also suggest new ways of operationalizing culture. I will propose that traditional culture in itself is not necessarily an influencing factor. Instead, the *emphasis* that the CEO places on traditional Chinese values, which varies across different forms of organizations, arguably is significant. The CEO acts as a transmitting device through which deeply embedded cultural values are converted into concrete actions. Through his action, even unconscious and invisible values will reach the surface. To asses the impact of this specific operationalization, apart from other new measures, I will develop and validate a scale that determines the emphasis placed on traditional Chinese cultural values in different forms of organization. Finally, the book will be firmly grounded in contingency theory and other micromanagement theories, such as leadership and decision-making theories.

Effectiveness of Chinese management

This book will analyze empirically the effectiveness of the Chinese management model. Most important, it will examine the influence of private family ownership on performance. By including other drivers of success, apart from its absolute impact, the *relative* strength of association can be determined. In addition, in contrast to other studies, I will build a bridge to the world of practitioners by spelling out several implications and recommendations for businessmen and policy makers. First, I will show that web-based Chinese management is an attractive new organizational paradigm for dealing with many unprecedented organizational challenges in the 21st century and beyond. It is one revolutionary blueprint for the organization of the future. Second, I will develop a model for action. It translates the empirical findings from the analysis of key success factors into detailed practical recommendations for managers of domestic and multinational companies who want to improve the effectiveness of their operations in China and other emerging markets. Third, this book will uncover the reasons for the effectiveness of the new private management model and thus explain part of the dynamism of private economic development in China. I will outline important national and industrial policy implications.

Research hypotheses: Operationalizing web-based Chinese management

After setting up the three-step research agenda of analyzing the nature, causes, and outcomes of Chinese management, it is necessary to operationalize the theoretical concepts and develop testable propositions. Let me recall the overall problem statement of this book: "Is there a contextually determined, distinctive Chinese management model in mainland private enterprises that is positively associated with organizational effectiveness?"

Bearing in mind the specific contributions this book intends to make, I will deduce testable hypotheses from the newly developed model. This operationalization of the theoretical model is the crucial step to examine it empirically. Because previous researchers struggled with this empirical transformation, they could not test their ideas through the statistical analysis of quantitative data. Instead of recognizing their problems with operationalizing the concepts, they suggested that the research subject at best lends itself only to qualitative analysis. However, I will show for the first time that quantitative analysis of the intricate phenomenon of Chinese management is possible.

First, I will derive the individual propositions related to the distinctive characteristics of web-based Chinese management, followed by hypotheses about its influencing factors. The last section will present the proposition for the third empirical theme, the effectiveness of Chinese management. The hypotheses for the individual research questions in the issue tree that disaggregated the overall problem (see figure 1-4) are summarized in figure 2-4 and will be discussed below. The individual detailed research models will be presented in the respective findings chapters (part II, chapters 3–5). More details on definitions and scales for the various elements of Chinese management can be found in appendix A (Detailed Survey Methodology) and appendix D (Company Questionnaire).

Hypotheses related to the distinctiveness of Chinese management

Before deducing the hypotheses, I first had to decide how to operationalize "distinctiveness." The basic idea in this book is to use state enterprises as benchmarks to test whether the management model of private enterprises is distinctive. Distinctiveness implies that the structural and managerial

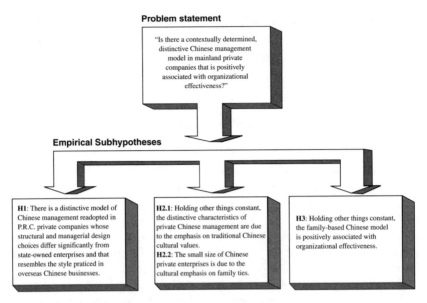

Problem statement

"Is there a contextually determined, distinctive Chinese management model in mainland private companies that is positively associated with organizational effectiveness?"

Empirical Subhypotheses

H1: There is a distinctive model of Chinese management readopted in P.R.C. private companies whose structural and managerial design choices differ significantly from state-owned enterprises and that resembles the style praticed in overseas Chinese businesses.

H2.1: Holding other things constant, the distinctive characteristics of private Chinese management are due to the emphasis on traditional Chinese cultural values.
H2.2: The small size of Chinese private enterprises is due to the cultural emphasis on family ties.

H3: Holding other things constant, the family-based Chinese model is positively associated with organizational effectiveness.

Figure 2-4   Research hypotheses for China study

choices of private enterprises differ significantly from those of state enterprises. As mentioned, one of the weakness of previous studies is the absence of such a benchmark sample. Let me now introduce the individual definitions and operationalizations and deduce the individual propositions. To answer the first research question (in chapter 3), I will analyze the following research hypothesis:

Hypothesis 1   There is a distinctive model of Chinese management readopted in P.R.C. private enterprises whose structural and managerial design choices differ significantly from state enterprises and that resembles the style practiced in overseas Chinese business.

The term "management model" describes the structural and managerial choices of a company. "Organizational structure" refers to distributions, along various lines, of people among social positions that influence their role relations (Blau 1974, p. 12). It includes the degree to which a company is centralized, formalized, and integrated. "Management" is the coordination and motivation of resources toward predetermined goals. To operationalize the four distinctive characteristics of private web-based Chinese management theory developed in chapter 1, the research model can be broken down into two structure-related aspects and two management-related aspects. In this section, I will focus primarily on the distinctiveness of the Chinese style per se without referring extensively to the underlying reasons for its particularity. The next section will focus exclusively on this issue and propose that, holding other factors constant, the distinctive structural and managerial characteristics result from the emphasis that private enterprises place on traditional, family-based values. Let me discuss the first subhypothesis:

Hypothesis 1.1   The structural choices of private Chinese enterprises differ significantly from those of state enterprises.

Private Chinese enterprises have two main structural characteristics that differentiate them from enterprises in the state sector.

Strong centralization. There is a high degree of power centralization in the hands of one autocratic entrepreneur. "Centralization" refers to the degree to which decisions on important business issues are made at the top of the company. Those decisions include, for example, the number of workers required, hiring and firing, production plans, machinery and equipment, and work methods (see appendix D, section 14). I hypothesize that private enterprises score higher on centralization than state enterprises, which tend to be more decentralized.

Low bureaucracy. With extensive personal supervision, there is less need for formal bureaucratic structuring to control or integrate organizational activities. Therefore, I argue that private enterprises, on average, score lower on role formalization, specialization, standardization through control systems, and integration than the more bureaucratic state enterprises. "Role formalization" is the number of written documents defining specific roles and, in some cases, the extent of their distribution or application. These documents include, for example, written operating instructions, job descriptions, and organizational policies. Appendix D, section 13 lists all documents included in the scale that measures role formalization. The company scores one point for each document that it shows to the interviewer. The total degree of formalization is the sum of these points. "Specialization" is the degree to which specialist positions exist in the company. A function is specialized when at least one person performs only that function. Examples of functions include sales and service, public relations, and education and training (see appendix D, section 12). "Standardized Control Systems" are used to gather information about the performance of a company and make procedures uniform. They include, for example, comprehensive management control and information systems, cost and profit centers, and formal appraisal of personnel (see appendix D, section 16). "Integration" is the degree to which a company uses structural and processual liaison devices to coordinate the diverse activities of its members. Examples of structural liaison devices include interdepartmental committees, task forces, and liaison personnel. Processual liaison includes interdepartmental bargaining and planning to coordinate decisions (see Appendix D, section 17).

The detailed hypothesized structural differences between private and state enterprise are summarized in table 2-2.

Table 2-2 Hypothesis for structural differences between private and state enterprises

Aspect	Private enterprises	State enterprises
Centralization	Higher	Lower
Role formalization	Lower	Higher
Specialization	Lower	Higher
Control	Lower	Higher
Integration	Lower	Higher

The following subhypothesis expresses the suggested differences between private and state enterprises with respect to management practices.

Hypothesis 1.2   The managerial choices of private Chinese enterprises differ significantly from those of state enterprises.

I argue that the management practices of private Chinese enterprises differ from those of state enterprises in two respects.

Entrepreneurship. Chinese private firms adopt a more entrepreneurial style than their state counterparts. "Chinese entrepreneurship" can be disaggregated into three distinctive types of strategy, leadership and communication, and decision making. The strategies of private enterprises are more aggressive, proactive, risky, and long-term than those of state enterprises. Companies that pursue aggressive strategies cut prices and sacrifice profitability to increase market share (see appendix D, section 4.1 a–b). Proactive companies constantly seek new opportunities related to present operations and usually introduce new brands or products first in the market (see appendix D, section 4.1 i–j). Another dimension of strategy is riskiness. The operations of private Chinese enterprises can be generally described as high-risk. They have a weaker tendency than state enterprises to support projects for which the expected returns are certain (see appendix D, section 4.1 k–1; the scoring for item 1 is reversed). A long-term strategic orientation involves forecasting key indicators of performance and allocating resources according to criteria that generally reflect long-term considerations (see appendix D, section 4.1 g–h; item h is reversed). In contrast to private enterprises, state enterprises tend to adopt a more analytical strategic posture. They usually engage in thorough analysis and use information systems to reach major decisions (see appendix D, section 4.1 c–d). Their strategies are also more defensive. They prefer to cut costs instead of searching proactively for growth opportunities. For example, to decrease costs, they modify manufacturing technology significantly and use production management techniques (see appendix D, section 4.1 e–f). Many top managers of state enterprises that in recent years have faced economic difficulties talk almost exclusively about cutting labor costs through mass layoffs instead of identifying, entering, shaping, or even creating new markets.[7]

On account of the autocratic nature of their owner-managers, the leadership style of private Chinese enterprises is hypothesized to be more flexible and coercive, and less participative than that of state enterprises. Flexible leaders adapt freely to changing circumstances without too much concern for past practice. They use loose, informal means of control and depend heavily on informal relationships and norms of cooperation to get work done (see appendix D, section 5.2). Coercive leaders use force to resolve disagreements over personal and corporate issues. They issue orders and warnings to implement organizational changes (see appendix D, section 5.3). Participative leaders call for group or democratic decision making on products and services, capital budgeting, and long-term strategy (see appendix D, section 5.1).

Because of their high "power distance" (Hofstede 1980), private entrepreneurs also make strong use of vertical communication. They eschew open channels of communication and rigorously restrict access to important financial and operating information (see appendix D, section 7.1; reversed item).

Private enterprises also adopt a more entrepreneurial decision making style instead of extensive analysis. A charismatic decision maker at the top wields great power. With rapid growth as dominant organizational goal, he actively searches for big new opportunities and makes bold decisions despite the uncertainty of their outcomes (see appendix D, section 6.2). State enterprises, on the other hand, avoid daring moves and adopt a more incremental, adaptive decision making style that makes extensive use of planning. It is marked by a cautious, pragmatic, one small step at a time adjustment to problems. Decisions are generally compromises between the conflicting demands of owners, unions, government, managers, customers, and other stakeholders. They are made locally more often than centrally, and the primary concern is with stability and steady growth (see appendix D, section 6.1). Companies that engage in planning systematically search for opportunities, anticipate problems, consider the costs and benefits of alternatives, and make a conscious attempt to integrate programs of action to achieve specified goals efficiently. The accent is on profit maximization, long-term planning, very careful screening of investments to minimize risks, and expertise and solid research before making decisions (see appendix D, section 6.3).

Enterprise networks. Private enterprises emphasize interorganizational, often subcontracting-based, networks. I introduce the notion of a web to emphasize that these networks vary in formality and that their members are highly interdependent. These webs are held together by family lineages and trust, with personal relations (*guanxi*) constituting their linchpin. In contrast, state enterprises usually are vertically integrated and form part of large, government-run "industry bureaus." For the quantitative analysis, subcontracting is used to operationalize one aspect of these webs. I hypothesize that private enterprises subcontract more than state enterprises. A particular form of interorganizational relationship, subcontracting means that certain activities of a company's value chain are outsourced to other organizations. I developed a scale measuring subcontracting specifically for this study (see appendix D, section 18.4). The case studies will provide richer, grounded evidence on the other forms of interorganizational relations in the enterprise webs. The detailed hypothesized differences with respect to management practices are summarized in table 2-3.

Emphasis on culture. I hypothesize that Chinese private enterprises place greater emphasis on traditional Chinese values than do state enterprises. They attach greater importance to relationships (see appendix D, section 8.1.1, item e), particularly *family* connections. An indication is that the majority of overseas Chinese private enterprises are family-owned. Further, within this context of kinship, members strongly emphasize respect, both respect for seniority in general (see appendix D, section 8.1.1, item b) and family loyalty in particular (see appendix D, section 8.1.1, item c). Private enterprises also emphasize affiliation with lineage-based groups, here termed "collective orientation" (see appendix D, section 8.1.1, item l). This contrasts with the more technocratic, scientifically managed state enterprises. The following hypothesis summarizes the foregoing argument.

Hypothesis 1.3:   In private Chinese enterprises, there is a greater emphasis on family-based relations, respect for seniority and family loyalty, and collective orientation than in state enterprises.

Table 2-3 Hypotheses for managerial differences between private and state enterprises

Aspect	Private enterprises	State enterprises
Aggressive strategy	Higher	Lower
Analytic strategy	Lower	Higher
Defensive strategy	Lower	Higher
Long-term strategy	Higher	Lower
Proactive strategy	Higher	Lower
Risk strategy	Higher	Lower
Flexible leadership	Higher	Lower
Coercive leadership	Higher	Lower
Participative leadership	Lower	Higher
Vertical communication	Higher	Lower
Adaptive decision making	Lower	Higher
Entrepreneurial decision making	Higher	Lower
Planning decision making	Lower	Higher
Subcontracting	Higher	Lower

Small company size. Most private Chinese enterprises are relatively small. Size is operationalized by the number of employees. This notion is expressed in the following hypothesis:

Hypothesis 1.4   Private Chinese enterprises on average are significantly smaller than state enterprises.

Hypotheses related the influencing factors of Chinese management

Most previous research treated Chinese management as a monolithic phenomenon that does not vary with contingencies. The following hypothesis, which is rooted in the discussion of familism in private enterprises, seeks to clarify this issue. It will be analyzed in chapter 3.

Hypothesis 2.1   Holding other things constant, the distinctive characteristics of private Chinese management are due to the emphasis on traditional Chinese cultural values.

When other contingences are controlled, emphasis on traditional family-based values exerts a double impact on structure and management that is not found in state enterprises.

Direct impact. Culture directly affects structural and managerial choices. Let me first discuss its impact on organizational structure. With a strong emphasis on selected characteristics of Chinese culture, such as (family-based) personal relations, collective orientation, and respect, there is less need to specify rules, because informal social controls substitute them in many circumstances. Furthermore, due to the hierarchical nature of seniority, decisions will be more centralized. The decision-making process, though not participative, is likely to be oriented toward consensus among the collective. This requires more interpersonal integrative mechanisms. Culture also directly affects management practices. A CEO with strong personal networks will be less inclined to engage in proactive strategies, because personal connections automatically create new business opportunities. His most important and effective strategy will be to secure friends. Decision making will be pragmatic and adaptive. Further, when great importance is attached to seniority, holding other factors such as size constant, the leadership style will be less participative and possibly more coercive. Managers with high power-distance will probably prefer less horizontal communication in the company, because it might subvert their authority. Finally, the emphasis on personal networking will lead to a stronger emphasis on subcontracting and enterprise web building.

Indirect impact. The choice of mean level for the contextual factor "size" also results from the emphasis that private enterprises place on family values. In order to keep strong family ties, they prefer to proliferate in family-based networks—either through spin offs or by linking up with other players—instead of increasing the company's size. The behavioral patterns of overseas Chinese serve as an indicator of this link between familism and size. In countries where the Chinese enjoy economic freedom, most firms in the private sector are both family-owned and very small.[8] In turn, it is well known that size is strongly related to bureaucracy and other organizational properties. For example, smaller companies usually need fewer bureaucratic controls, such as elaborate rules and procedures, than large ones. Thus, emphasis on familism also contributes indirectly to the low degree of formalization and several other distinctive structural and managerial characteristics of Chinese private firms. The following proposition summarizes this hypothesized indirect path.

Hypothesis 2.2   The small size of Chinese private enterprises is due to the cultural emphasis on family ties in those firms.

Hypotheses related to the effectiveness of Chinese management

After having hypothesized that Chinese management is distinctive, and that this distinctiveness results from the emphasis on familism, the remaining question is whether it is an "art" in the sense of "the *skill* of doing something *well*" (cf. Simpson and Weiner 1989, p. 657). For this to be true the distinctive family-based model must be successful. As has been discussed, when other factors are held constant, private family-based ownership, as contrasted to state ownership, is likely to be positively related to organizational effectiveness for three reasons: First, Chinese family structures provide valuable social capital. Second, small firm size and global, lineage-based networks afford flexibility. Third, family-based networks reduce costs. As one of the major drawbacks, the model limits company size. Thus, I hypothesize that when other factors such as size are held constant, Chinese management based on family private ownership is positively associated with organizational effectiveness. Effectiveness refers to the degree to which an organization achieves its stated purpose and objectives. It is an aggregate measure comprising the firm's profitability, sales growth, liquidity, employee satisfaction, and public image (see appendix D, sections 11.1–11.5).

The following research hypothesis expresses this argument. It will be tested in chapter 5:

Hypothesis 3   Holding other things constant, the family-based private Chinese model is positively associated with organizational effectiveness.

Summary

In this chapter, I developed a new integrated theoretical model of web-based Chinese management (WCM) based on an inventory of the state of the art of research in China. I first discussed its distinctive building blocks: high centralization, low bureaucratization, strong entrepreneurship, and tireless web building. Emphasis on traditional Chinese values and small company size influences these distinctive structural and managerial choices. I also pointed out that the mean level for these factors is higher for private than for state enterprises. They therefore can be seen as a platform that constitutes an integral part of WCM. Further, I discussed WCM's merits in terms of flexible and cost-efficient social capital and its demerits with respect to growth constraints. After drawing some general conclusions on the current state of the field and further research needs, I outlined several new contributions that will emerge from this book.

Next, I transformed web-based Chinese management theory into a set of detailed hypotheses that can be tested empirically with data from the China study. Problems with operationalization constituted a major obstacle for previous studies, blocking researchers from analyzing statistically their fragmented ideas. First, I presented the individual propositions with respect to the distinctive structural, managerial, and contextual characteristics of Chinese management. Private enterprises are deemed distinctive, if they differ significantly from their state counterparts. Second, I developed hypotheses for the influencing factors of the new style. In particular, emphasis on traditional Chinese values is likely to exert both a direct and an indirect (via its association with small company size) impact on structure and management. The last proposition is a positive association between family-based Chinese management and organizational effectiveness. In chapter 3, I will present the findings of the study, starting with the distinctive characteristics of Chinese management.

PART TWO
Empirical Findings: Establishing the Fact Base

3
Distinctive Characteristics of Chinese Management

Overview

The three findings chapters in part II concentrate mainly on the important evidence and facts related to the research hypotheses. A broader discussion of their applications will be presented in part III. Details on sample characteristics are presented in appendix C. The general objective of this chapter is to answer the first research question, "Is there a distinctive Chinese management model in private enterprises in mainland China?" To answer the question, I will test the first hypothesis related to the distinctive nature of organizational structure and management practices in Chinese private firms, comparing the structural and managerial profiles of private enterprises with those of state enterprises. The succeeding chapters will use organizational dynamics models that capture contextual factors in a company's task environment, to explain variations in these organizational properties. This procedure will clarify why companies adopt different forms of structure and management. I hypothesize that the distinctive web-based Chinese management style results from the emphasis that private firms place on family-based traditional Chinese values. Those values directly influence structural and managerial choices, and indirectly affect company size, which in turn influences organizational properties.

This chapter reports quantitative and qualitative research findings. First, in order to determine whether there is a distinctive management model in private enterprises, their structure, management, and context will be compared to those of their state counterparts. I will analyze structure at multiple levels including a comparison of private and state enterprises at the macro-level, and an analysis of intrascale patterns for private enterprises at the micro-level. Next, these quantitative findings will be enriched by qualitative data from the three case studies.

Comparison of structural profiles of private and state enterprises

The objective of this section is to test the following subhypothesis relating to structural differences between companies with contrasting ownership patterns.

Hypothesis 1.1   The structural choices of private Chinese enterprises differ significantly from those of state enterprises.

In order to test this hypothesis, I compared the mean scores of private and state enterprises on the various structural scales (see appendix D, section 2.7). For all profile comparisons of structural and managerial properties, scales were standardized to 100% to allow for inter-scale comparisons. For example, a company with a maximum score on the formalization scale obtained a standardized count of 100% on this measure.[1]

To test whether the observed differences were statistically significant, that is, unlikely to have appeared by chance, mean difference tests were computed. The t-statistic tests the null hypothesis (H_0) of no mean differences between population parameters. Significant t values ($p < .05$) suggest rejection of H_0. Levene's test for equality of variances helped to decide whether to use the equal or unequal variance formula for the t-test. A significant F statistic suggests rejection of the null hypothesis of equal variances. The results of these analyses of organizational structure are shown in table 3-1.

The structural profiles of Chinese private and state enterprises are shown in figure 3-1.

I had hypothesized two distinctive structural characteristics of Chinese private businesses: a comparatively low degree of bureaucracy and rela-

Table 3-1 Mean difference tests for structure of private and state enterprises

Aspect	Hypothesis Private enterprises	Findings from mean comparison					
		$\bar{x}$ Private (%)	$\bar{x}$ State (%)	$\Delta\bar{x}$	t-value	df	Result
Role formalization	Lower	44.2	74.2	−30.0*	−6.4***	81	Supported
Specialization	Lower	62.5	77.7	−15.2	−2.8**	99	Supported
Control	Lower	62.6	66.7	−4.1*	−1.3	96	Supported?
Integration	Lower	47.5	64.7	−17.2	−5.1***	99	Supported
Centralization	Higher	63.2	57.6	5.6	2.2*	99	Supported

*$p < .05$; **$p < .01$; ***$p < .001$ (two tailed).
*Levene's test significant, therefore unequal variance t-test used.
$\bar{x}$ = mean; $\Delta\bar{x}$ = mean difference.
Note: Comparison between Chinese private and state-owned enterprises.

Total score (%)

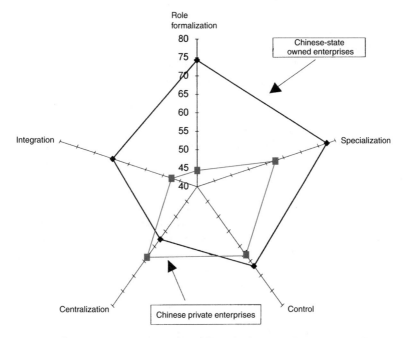

Figure 3-1   Comparison of structural profiles of private and state enterprises

tively high centralization. All differences were as hypothesized. All mean differences were also statistically significant, except for "standardized control systems." This implies that four out of the five hypotheses are strongly supported by the evidence, with the remaining one pointing in the right direction. Thus, Chinese private enterprises on the mainland have (re)adopted the particular structural characteristics described in the literature on overseas Chinese businesses.

Bureaucracy

Bureaucracy structures activities[2]. It includes the degree of role formalization, specialization, standardization through control systems, and integration in a company. I will discuss each aspect in turn.

Role formalization.   The greatest difference was the comparatively low formalization score of private enterprises ($\bar{x} = 44.2$, $\Delta\bar{x} = -30.0$, $df = 81$, $p < .001$). The results from the mainland mirror accounts of overseas Chinese businesses, which usually do not produce a great number of written documents to define desired behavior (Redding 1990; Redding and Wong 1986).

Specialization. The findings also support the hypothesized comparatively low degree of specialization ($\bar{x}$ = 62.5, $\Delta\bar{x}$ = −15.2, *df* = 99, *p* < .01), which is also a distinctive trait of overseas Chinese enterprises (Hickson and Pugh 1995, p. 171). Companies with few written instructions do not need dedicated staff departments that generate formal documents. This may have led to a lower specialization score for private Chinese enterprises compared to their state counterparts.

Integration. As another reflection of their lower degree of structuring, private enterprises utilize fewer integrative devices ($\bar{x}$ = 47.5, $\Delta\bar{x}$ = − 17.2, *df* = 99, *p* <.001) than state enterprises, which make significantly more use of coordinating mechanisms, such as committees, departmental meetings, and liaison personnel.

Standardized control systems. Compared to their state counterparts, private enterprises employ fewer control devices, such as management information systems, cost and profit centers, and other instruments ($\bar{x}$ = 62.6, $\Delta \bar{x}$ = −4.1, *df* = 96, *p* >.05). Yet even though the difference is as hypothesized, it is not statistically significant.

Centralization

As hypothesized, private Chinese enterprises are more centralized ($\bar{x}$ = 63.2, $\Delta\bar{x}$ = 5.6, *df* = 99, *p* <. 05) than state enterprises. The empirical findings support the predominately descriptive work on overseas Chinese businesses, which highlighted that one autocratic entrepreneur concentrates all power in his hands (Montagu-Pollock 1991, p. 23; Weidenbaum 1996, p. 141). By symmetry, the suggested higher degree of decentralization in the state sector (Child and Lu 1990, p. 334; Sung and Chan 1987, p. 13) also was empirically supported.

I conclude this discussion of the observed structural arrangements of private and state enterprises at the aggregate scale level by emphasizing that the differential choices are contingent on culture. Private enterprises in China tend to emphasize family-related traditional values, which exert a direct effect on structure, and an indirect effect by negatively influencing company size—which in turn is strongly related to organizational characteristics.

Item-level patterns of organizational structure in private enterprises

In addition to interorganizational differences at the aggregate level, there may be *intra*organizational variations between the items that make up scales. Ceteris paribus, a distinctive micro*gestalt* could arise from the emphasis placed on family-based values in private Chinese firms. To find out, it is not sufficient to observe that the aggregate score for a scale is high or low for private enterprises, but it is necessary to study additional patterns with respect to the distribution of their responses to the individual items that constitute the scale. However, contingency empiricists do not normally analyze such inter-item differences within individual structural dimensions. In this book, I therefore will perform such an innovative analysis for the three Aston scales, specialization, formalization, and centralization, since they have been the focus of most macrostructural research. I will first analyze specialist positions, then the documents that formalize roles, and finally the decisions made at various levels in the hierarchy.

Specialization

The results of the item-level analysis for specialization in private enterprises are presented in figure 3-2. The findings reveal important patterns in the distribution of specialist roles at the item level. Except for one area (logistics), the distribution of specialist positions differs substantially from the total scale score (62.5%, see table 3-1). In particular, most private enterprises tend to have dedicated positions for basic functions, such as accounting (92% of enterprises), sales (83%), work-flow planning (75%), and administration (72%). Fewer companies engage specialists for the more sophisticated functions of maintenance (38%), training (49%), and production methods (53%).

These findings echo previous arguments and the results of the macroanalysis, and refine them. Some of the relatively low scores seem to reveal a peculiarity of Chinese private entrepreneurs in their emphasis on controlling financial matters and pursuing aggressive strategies through sales specialists. Meanwhile, highly specialized functions such as maintenance and training may be contracted out to other companies, if they are performed at all. The sophisticated managers of cash in private firms avoid investments in expensive fixed assets that require a lot of maintenance by specialists. An example is complex process technology for oil refining, an industry in which there are few private Chinese enterprises. In addition, workers in private Chinese firms often possess multiple skills, and therefore may be able to perform elementary maintenance themselves. There would thus be no need for a specialist who keeps equipment in repair. Finally, private firms may not value maintenance very highly, and thus do not create such specialist positions. Indeed, when doing business in China, you will often observe the extremely high rate of physical wear and tear of real estate and equipment, resulting from the lack of servicing and maintenance. Hotels are a good example. They are often built very quickly and cheaply. The shiny hardware looks like a triumph of capitalism. But once the developer has left, nobody does maintenance—often because the managerial "software" of how to operate the buildings was not imported along with the physical assets. This sin of ommission is compounded by the shortcuts used in the construction process to save

% of companies having specialist roles

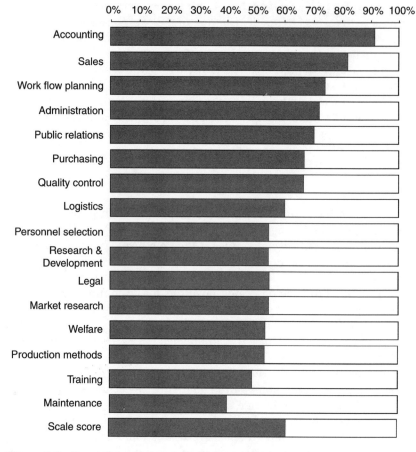

Figure 3-2 Specialist roles in private Chinese companies

time and the use of inferior materials used for the building to save costs. After a surprisingly short time, hotels in China often look very old. Whether this conjecture applies to Chinese private enterprises is yet to be determined.

In addition, relatively few private enterprises (55%) have market research specialists. Much of the market intelligence may be obtained through the CEO's personal contact web without the help of experts. Besides, the future movements of a turbulent market cannot be easily studied through conventional market research. Therefore, the entrepreneur may rather rely on intuition and trial and error. These findings provide some quantitative empirical support for the qualitative observation from overseas communities that Chinese firms lack ancillary departments, such as research and development, labor relations, public relations, and market research (see Redding and Wong, 1986, p. 276).

Moreover, compared to the scale average, few private enterprises (53%) employe worker welfare specialists. Their ownership structure may absolve them from the onerous burdens of many state enterprises, which, owing to their many social responsibilities. serve as welfare agencies or minigovernments. Alternatively, many CEOs may assume direct control over the welfare of their employees and thus do not need a specialist to administer social services.

Finally, comparatively few private Chinese enterprises (55%) have specialists for personnel selection, perhaps because they usually rely on their networks for recruitment.

Role formalization

The item-level analysis for role formalization in private enterprises is presented in figure 3-3. The results again reveal distinctive item-level patterns within the composite scale. Even though their total formalization score is relatively low (44.2%), a comparatively large number of private enter-

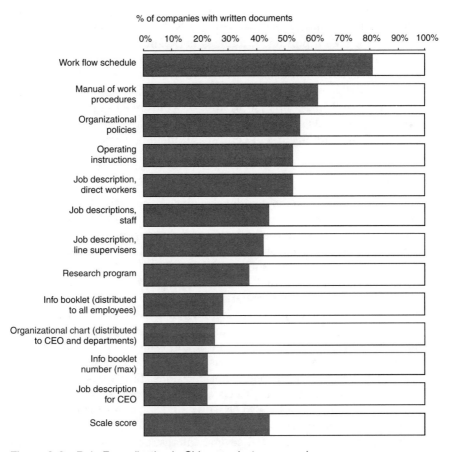

Figure 3-3 Role Formalization in Chinese private companies

prises formalize "scientific management" related areas (see McMillan et al., 1973, p. 43). Written documents for these activities include work flow schedules (81%), manuals of procedures (62%), organizational policies (55%), and operating instructions (51%).

These findings may be explained by the importance the Chinese CEO attaches to technology. In China, the costs of imported technology are very high. They often represent one of the most important cash outflows and a major accounting expense in terms of annual depreciation charges. The CEO may thus want to protect this investment through bureaucratic controls that clearly define desired behavior. In addition, Chinese enterprises often suffer from a lack of highly trained personnel. Written materials help to codify and disseminate knowledge, training employees in how to use the technology and perform other duties. Few private firms have formal job descriptions (ranging from 51% for direct workers to 21% for the CEO) and organizational charts that are distributed throughout the organization (24%). The CEO may want to attain high flexibility by requiring employees to perform a wide range of tasks. Lower levels in the hierarchy are more tightly regulated than higher levels. The lack of a job description for the CEO is conspicuous, perhaps reflecting his authority in the company. Nobody can possibly tell *him* what to do. Like a politician, he does not want to be held accountable for promises and thus clouds himself in vagueness. Only a few enterprises have a comprehensive range of information booklets (21%), which describe, for example, security issues or working conditions. Written research programs (36%) are not widespread either. This is explained by the CEO's distaste for red tape, which he can express freely in small firms without loss of control and inefficiencies.

Centralization

The findings relating to the item-level analysis of centralization in Chinese private enterprises are reported in figure 3-4. The results suggest a dichotomy with respect to the centralization of decision making. Although the total centralization score is very high (63.2%), even more CEOs centralize strategic decisions, such as the priority of orders (83%) and the type of machinery used (60%). This demonstrates the CEO's hands-on involvement in areas that matter most for the business. In most enterprises, the CEO also centralizes personnel management, in particular firing decisions (81%) and the total number of workers employed (68%). Since the CEO wants to stay in control and establish personal relationships which generate valuable "invisible capital" (Schlevogt 2001h), he must keep a tight grip on personnel decisions. In contrast, operational issues are decentralized. Few CEOs allocate work directly (26%), determine the amount of overtime to be worked (28%), or decide on technical production plans (36%).

In conclusion, I discovered several interesting intrascale patterns in private enterprises on the various structural dimensions, which refine the

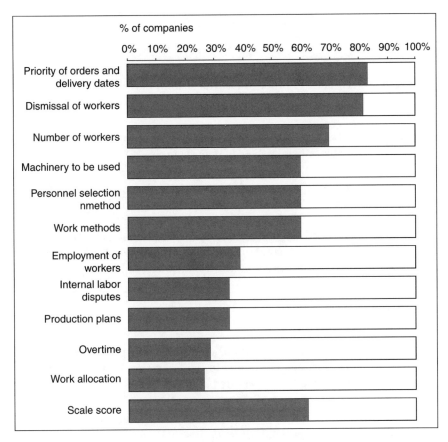

Figure 3-4 Decisions in Chinese private enterprises centralized at CEO level or above

previous evidence and insights from the macrostructural analysis. I speculated that some of these differences might be distinctive for private enterprises and suggested possible explanations. As discussed, it is quite possible that at least some of these inter-item differences result from the direct impact that emphasis on Chinese culture exerts on the structural choices of Chinese private enterprises. It would be interesting to examine this issue rigorously in a future study. In more general terms, these differences are not revealed in the aggregate Aston scores. Researchers who want to gain a more detailed understanding of organizational structure therefore have to take into account these new findings and analyze differences at the item level. Organizational scientists thus can develop a more refined version of contingency theory at the "nano" level. However, it is beyond the scope of this work and will be addressed in the future.

Comparison of managerial profiles of private and
state enterprises

In the next step, I compared the different management practices of private and state enterprises, in order to test the second part of the first research hypothesis:

Hypothesis 1.2   The managerial choices of private Chinese enterprises differ significantly from those of state enterprises.

A comparison of the empirical findings with the research hypotheses is shown in table 3-2. The findings are illustrated graphically in figure 3-5.

I had hypothesized two distinctive managerial characteristics of Chinese private businesses: a comparatively high degree of Chinese entrepreneurship and extensive interorganizational, often subcontracting-based networks.

Chinese entrepreneurship

According to my definition, "Chinese entrepreneurship" consists of three distinctive types of strategy, leadership, and decision making. I will discuss the findings related to these three areas in turn.

Strategic orientation. There is evidence that private enterprises adopt less analytic ($\bar{x} = 72.2$, $\Delta\bar{x} = -8.9$, $df = 83$, $p < .05$) and less defensive ($\bar{x} = 63.2$, $\Delta\bar{x} = -15.5$, $df = 99$, $p < .001$) strategies than their state counterparts. In terms of magnitude, the mean difference on defensive strategic orientation ranks second among all managerial comparisons (after participative leadership). By symmetry, this finding supports the idea that state enterprises tend to adopt cost-cutting strategies in order to survive. They usually conduct thorough analyses supported by information systems to arrive at major decisions. Further, as anecdotal evidence had suggested, private enterprises are more aggressive ($\bar{x} = 61.2$, $\Delta\bar{x} = 5.8$, $df = 99$, $p > .05$). They cut prices and sacrifice profitability to gain market share. However, the mean difference is not significant at conventional levels. Contrary to the research hypothesis, compared to their state counterparts, the strategies of private enterprises focus significantly less on the long-term ($\bar{x} = 61.8$, $\Delta\bar{x} = -6.7$, $df = 95$, $p < .05$), as measured by the use of forecasting techniques and the criteria used for allocating resources. This finding contradicts previous claims (see Montagu Pollock 1991, p. 23). Even though most CEOs of private enterprises are owners, they do not have a more long-term strategic orientation. It also disproves the thesis that managers of state enterprises, because of incentive misalignments arising from the "nonowner feeling" (Mun 1990), favor short-

Table 3-2 Mean difference tests for the managerial practices of private and state enterprises

Aspect	Hypothesis Private enterprises	Findings from mean comparison				
		$\bar{x}$ Private (%)	$\bar{x}$ State (%)	$\Delta\bar{x}$	t-value	df	Result
Aggressive strategy	Higher	61.2	55.4	5.8	1.3	99	Supported?
Analytic strategy	Lower	72.2	81.1	−8.9*	−2.1*	83	Supported
Defensive strategy	Lower	63.2	78.7	−15.5	−3.6***	99	Supported
Long-term strategy	Higher	61.8	68.5	−6.7*	−2.4*	95	Rejected
Proactive strategy	Higher	76.1	81.0	−4.9	−1.3	99	Rejected?
Risk strategy	Higher	44.7	47.5	−2.8	−1.0	99	Rejected?
Flexible leadership	Higher	68.2	66.5	1.7*	0.4	78	Supported?
Coercive leadership	Higher	59.3	48.8	10.5	2.7**	99	Supported
Participative leadership	Lower	50.8	71.1	−20.3*	−4.0***	89	Supported
Vertical communication	Higher	63.2	55.8	7.4*	1.4	85	Supported?
Adaptive decision making	Lower	61.1	65.1	−4.0	−0.7	99	Supported?
Entrepreneurial decision making	Higher	78.1	64.3	13.8	13.8**	99	Supported
Planning decision making	Lower	63.8	72.5	−8.7*	−1.7	87	Supported?
Subcontracting	Higher	34.8	31.3	3.5	1.2	99	Supported?

*p < .05; **p < .01; ***p < .001 (two tailed).

*Levene's test significant, therefore unequal variance t-test used.

$\bar{x}$ = mean; $\Delta\bar{x}$ = mean difference.

Note: Comparison between Chinese private and state-owned enterprises.

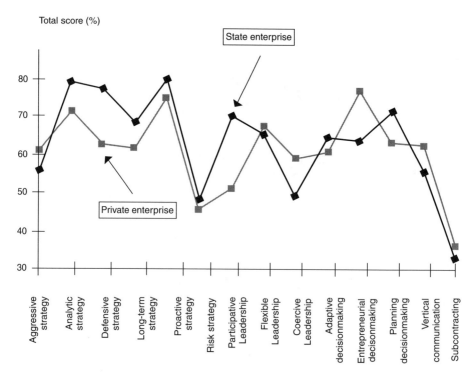

Total score (%)

State enterprise

80

70

60

50

40

30

Private enterprise

Aggressive strategy
Analytic strategy
Defensive strategy
Long-term strategy
Proactive strategy
Risk strategy
Participative Leadership
Flexible Leadership
Coercive Leadership
Adaptive decisionmaking
Entrepreneurial decisionmaking
Planning decisionmaking
Vertical communication
Subcontracting

Figure 3-5 Comparison of managerial practices between private and state enterprises

term benefits over long-term profitability (Tan and Litschert 1994, p. 14). This syndrome is common among mature U.S. organizations (Scholl-hammer 1982). The findings suggest that an aggressive strategic orientation is correlated with a more short-term focus. Quick gains may be obtained at the expense of long-term performance. In the future, researchers perhaps should not treat aggressiveness and long-term orientation as distinctive strategic dimensions, as had originally been suggested by strategy empiricists (see Venkatraman 1989). With the benefit of hindsight, it seems difficult to combine an aggressive posture—slashing margins and thus sacrificing profitability to gain market share—with a long-term outlook.

The empirical evidence did not support the hypotheses about two other strategic dimensions: the strategies of Chinese private enterprises were less proactive ($\bar{x} = 76.1$, $\Delta\bar{x} = -4.9$, $df = 99$, $p > .05$) and less risky ($\bar{x} = 44.7$, $\Delta\bar{x} = -2.8$, $df = 99$, $p > 0.5$) than those of their state counterparts. However, the mean difference was not significant. I will later analyze the cases of several Chinese enterprises to find possible explanations for these startling findings.

Leadership. The leadership style of private entrepreneurs is very flexible, as seen by the high mean level on the respective scale ($\bar{x} = 68.2$). They adapt freely to changing circumstances without too much concern for past practices and control operations only loosely. Private enterprises are also somewhat more flexible than state enterprises. But even though the difference is as expected, it is very tiny and statistically insignificant ($\Delta\bar{x} = 1.7$, $df = 78$, $p > .05$). Besides, leaders of private enterprises use significantly more coercive means than their counterparts in the state sector ($\bar{x} = 59.3$, $\Delta\bar{x} = 10.5$, $df = 99$, $p < .01$). They tend to use force to resolve disagreements, and issue orders and warnings to implement organizational changes. This provides empirical support for claims about the autocratic nature of private owner-managers (Hickson and Pugh 1995 p. 170; Redding and Wong 1986) and their coercive style (W. Chan 1982). Compared to state enterprises, leadership in private enterprises is significantly less participative ($\bar{x} = 50.8$, $\Delta\bar{x} = -20.3$, $df = 89$, $p < .001$). This was the largest mean difference of all managerial comparisons. Chinese private entrepreneurs make less use of group or democratic processes to decide on products and services, capital budgeting, and long-term strategy. Finally, they seem to engage more in vertical communication ($\bar{x} = 63.2$, $\Delta\bar{x} = 7.4$, $df = 85$, $p > .05$), rigorously restricting communication flows and access to important financial and operating information, but again the mean difference was not statistically significant.

Decision making. Executives in Chinese private enterprises, as hypothesized, use a significantly more entrepreneurial decision-making style ($\bar{x} = 78.1$, $\Delta\bar{x} = 13.8$, $df = 99$, $p < .01$). A charismatic decision maker at the top wields great power. He actively searches for big new growth opportunities, and makes bold decisions despite the uncertainty of their outcomes. Entrepreneurial decision making is the dominant managerial trait of private enterprises, because on this dimension, they obtained the highest absolute score. This was the third largest mean difference compared to state enterprises. The findings for the first time empirically substantiate and quantify earlier statements about the entrepreneurial decision-making style of private firms (Hickson and Pugh 1995, p. 170; Mackie 1992, p. 53). Private enterprises, as hypothesized, also seem to make less use of planning as a means of systematic problem solving ($\bar{x} = 63.8$, $\Delta\bar{x} = -8.7$, $df = 87$, $p > .05$), and make decisions less incrementally ($\bar{x} = 61.1$, $\Delta\bar{x} = -4.0$, $df = 99$, $p > .05$). In contrast, state enterprises adjust to problems cautiously, strive for compromises between the stakeholders, and decentralize decision making in the pursuit of stability. The less extensive use of both planning and incrementalism in private enterprises accords with earlier anecdotal evidence, but the differences with state enterprises were neither very large nor statistically significant.

Networks. As hypothesized, private enterprises subcontract more than state enterprises, but the mean difference was tiny and not statistically significant ($\bar{x} = 34.8$, $\Delta\bar{x} = 3.5$, $df = 99$, $p > .05$). In addition, both types of companies outsource very few activities in absolute terms. The findings therefore may not suffice to prove the extensive interorganizational networks of small agile enterprises that were repeatedly mentioned in the literature (see Montagu-Pullock 1991, p. 21; P. Williamson 1997). These webs differ from the more vertically integrated state enterprises that often belong to large governmental "industry bureau." Perhaps subcontracting alone did not capture the full richness of informal enterprise networks, which may be difficult to measure with purely quantitative scales. I will therefore explore *family-based* networks in the case studies.

Finally, it is important to analyze the factors that influence these managerial differences. As for structure, I believe that they can be traced back to the direct and indirect impact of the emphasis on traditional Chinese values in private firms. This analysis will be presented in chapter 4.

Comparison of emphasis on culture in private and state enterprises

So far, I have tested the hypotheses related to the structural and managerial distinctiveness of private Chinese management. I concluded that mainland Chinese private businesses have readopted most organizational aspects of the distinctive style practiced by the overseas Chinese, and conjectured about the sources of these differences.

As discussed in chapter 2, the Chinese management model includes two other distinctive dimensions. However, observers have disagreed whether to treat them as dependent or independent variables. I regard both, emphasis on traditional cultural values and company size, as independent variables, but argue that the absolute mean level of these factors differ between private and state enterprises. In addition, I believe the two factors interact—culture confines size—but this issue will be analyzed in chapter 4. To test the third subhypothesis, this section analyzes mean differences for the first of the two factors, emphasis on family values.

Hypothesis 1.3　In private Chinese enterprises, there is a greater emphasis on family-based relations, respect for seniority and family loyalty, and collective orientation than in state enterprises.

The governing thought is that private enterprises place great emphasis on *family*-related traditional Chinese values. In the first step of the analysis, which triangulated different data points, I compared the mean differences on the standardized emphasis on selected Chinese cultural characteristics scale (see appendix D, section 8.1) between Chinese private and

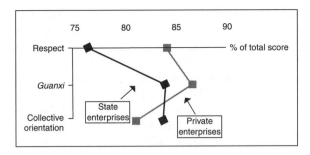

Figure 3-6 Emphasis on Chinese culture

state enterprises. It measured how much importance respondents attached to the various elements of culture in their daily business dealings. The results are graphically illustrated in figure 3-6.

Table 3-3 reports the results of the mean difference tests.

The findings support the first part of the subhypothesis, since private Chinese enterprises place significantly more emphasis on respect for seniority and family loyalty than their state counterparts ($\bar{x} = 84.2$, $\Delta\bar{x} = 7.5$, $df = 90$, $p < .05$). The empirical support for the second part was weaker. The difference was as hypothesized—private enterprises attached slightly more importance to personal relations ($\bar{x} = 86.6$, $\Delta\bar{x} = 2.5$, $df = 99$, $p > .05$)—but lacked statistical and practical significance. In fact, both types of companies strongly emphasize *guanxi*. Managers of state enterprises, too, may need to cultivate relationships, for example, with party officials. However, I will argue later that the *type* of relation differs in private and state enterprises. In particular, Chinese private enterprises attach significantly greater importance to *family*-based relationships. The third part of the subhypothesis was not supported.

Table 3-3 Mean difference tests for emphasis on culture in private and state enterprises

Aspect	Hypothesis Private enterprises	Findings from mean comparison					
		$\bar{x}$ Private (%)	$\bar{x}$ State (%)	$\Delta\bar{x}$	*t*-value	*df*	Result
Respect	Higher	84.2	76.7	7.5*	2.0*	90	Supported
Guanxi	Higher	86.6	84.1	2.5	.8	99	Supported?
Collective orientation	Higher	81.2	83.9	−2.7	−.7	99	Rejected?

*$p < .05$; **$p < .01$; ***$p < .001$ (two tailed).
*Levene's test significant, unequal variance *t*-test used.
$\bar{x}$ = mean; $\Delta\bar{x}$ = mean difference.
Note: Comparison between Chinese private and state-owned enterprises.

Although the difference was not significant, state enterprises tended to value collective orientation more than private enterprises ($\bar{x} = 81.2$, $\Delta\bar{x} = 2.7$, $df = 99$, $p > .05$). Socialist ideology may have an overriding influence in the state sector.

In the next step, I examined the correlation between private ownership and emphasis on selected Chinese cultural values. "Private ownership" was a binary dummy variable with value "1" equal to the state sector and "2" equal to the private sector. The two clusters emerged from summing the first two and last two items in appendix D, section 2.7. The findings of the correlation analysis are reported in Table 3-4.

Even though the coefficients in the first column, which shows the correlation between private ownership and the various dimensions of culture, were small and statistically insignificant, they corroborate with the findings from the preceding analysis. In particular, private ownership was slightly positively associated with emphasis on respect ($r = .10$, $N = 124$, $p > .05$) and personal relations ($r = .05$, $N = 124$, $p > .05$). However, it was slightly negatively associated with collective orientation ($r = -.02$, $N = 124$, $p>.05$). Besides, the significant correlation between respect and collective orientation ($r = .25$, $N = 124$, $p < .01$), and respect and *guanxi* ($r = .21$, $N = 124$, $p < .05$) suggests that the elements form part of one latent construct,[3] emphasis on culture. These results serve as sanity check.

The earlier qualitative literature emphasized that private Chinese entrepreneurs value family affiliation. To test this form of collective orientation, I examined the shareholder structure of Chinese private enterprises. I distinguished family ownership from shareholding by outside private individuals and institutional investors. The results are illustrated in figure 3-7 and show that most Chinese private firms (60%) are fully family-owned. Families own the majority stake in another 27% of private enterprises. In total, families thus control more than three-fourths (87%) of private enterprises. These statistics demonstrate the importance of family relationships in the private sector. Further, they empirically support theoretical conjectures by other researchers. First, even though they have admitted that many private firms in other countries in the initial development stage are family-owned, they believe the

Table 3-4 Correlation between private ownership and emphasis on Chinese culture

	Private ownership	Respect	Guanxi
Respect	.10		
Guanxi	.05	.21*	
Collective orientation	−.02	.25**	.17

Note: "Private ownership" is the focus of the analysis.
*$p < .05$; **$p < .01$; ***$p < .001$ (two tailed).
$N = 124$

family ties in China are unusually strong and durable (see Cai 1997; Whyte 1995, p. 1003). Future studies may compare these international differences in more qualitative detail, and thus confirm close-knit familism as a distinctive aspect of Chinese traditional culture. Second, research about overseas Chinese communities has shown that, in contrast to family business in other countries, which tend to grow, adopt professional structures, and go public, Chinese private enterprises usually remain in the hands of families and do not grow significantly (Hickson and Pugh 1995, pp. 170–71). Instead, they prefer to proliferate through networks. Because of the cross-sectional nature of this research and the recency of private enterprises, a future longitudinal study will have to furnish the final proof of this pattern in the P.R.C.

In the last triangulation step, I calculated the correlation between the private ownership scale and a scale for family ownership ("individ"). It ranked companies according to the percentage share the *family* held in them (appendix D, section 2.8). More details on this scale will be presented in chapter 5. Suffice it to say here that higher scores indicated a larger family share of the capital. The two scales were significantly correlated ($r = .88$, $N = 124$, $p < .001$). These findings confirmed that most private enterprises tend to be family-owned. Partialing out other variables, such as size and industry, to control for potential intervening effects did not significantly affect this positive association. The family-based ownership pattern of Chinese management in sinitic enterprises in Southeast

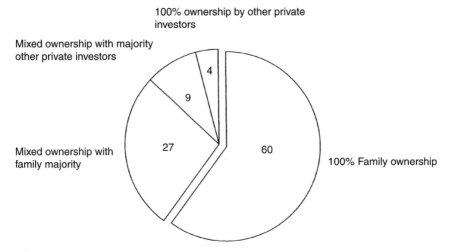

% of private enterprise population

Figure 3-7   Ownership structure of Chinese private enterprises

Asia and elsewhere, suggested in other works, has thus reemerged in the P.R.C. The case studies will illustrate the importance of familism.

Let me summarize the key implications of the foregoing analysis. In general, Chinese private enterprises tend to place more emphasis on certain cultural characteristic than state enterprises. The most important finding was the value placed on family-based relationships, respect for seniority, and family loyalty. This suggests that the newly founded private enterprises on the mainland have readopted traditional Chinese values. Even though in comparison, state enterprises appear to attach slightly more importance to the collective orientation of their employees, in absolute terms, groups, as cognitive and emotive nodal points and sources of identity, played a pivotal role in both the private and state sector. The type of focal group differed in each case. Managers of state enterprises, who are imbued with socialist ideology, tend to emphasize affiliation with the work unit (*danwei*). These results corroborate with previous findings. The descriptive literature has stressed the key role of the *danwei* in state enterprises (Hall and Xu 1990, p. 574; Jackson 1992; Lockett 1988, p. 487; Shenkar and von Glinow 1994, p. 60). The *danwei* is not just the focus of work activity. As a "total institution" (Goffman 1961, p. 17), the worker's entire life depends on it. Apart from work, it controls areas such as birth control, child care, schooling, health care, and housing (see Clayre 1984, p. 162; Littlefield 1996). In contrast, judging from the ownership patterns and correlation analysis, belonging to a *family*-based group is very important in private enterprises, but not crucial for state enterprises. To conclude, as "protective shelter," the family is the equivalent of the work unit in state enterprises.

Comparison of company size of private and state enterprises

Writers on overseas Chinese businesses have stressed small company size as another distinctive characteristic of Chinese management. Like culture, I treat size as a contextual factor, whose mean level is likely to be lower for private enterprises. In this section, I will test the following subhypothesis:

Hypothesis 1.4   Private Chinese enterprises on average are significantly smaller than state enterprises.

To test the hypothesis, I computed the t-statistic for mean comparisons.[4] The findings are reported in table 3-5.

   The results clearly support the hypothesis that private enterprises are significantly smaller than their state counterparts in terms of sales ($\bar{x}$ = 21 million RMB, $\Delta\log\bar{x} = -1.10$, $df = 99$, $p < .001$). They also employ

Table 3-5 Mean difference tests for size of private and state enterprises

Aspect	Private enterprises					State enterprises					$\Delta\bar{x}$ (log)		
	$\bar{x}$	med	s	log $\bar{x}$	s	$\bar{x}$	med	s	log $\bar{x}$	s	$\Delta\bar{x}$	t	df
Sales	21	5	51	6.70	.75	347	95	789	7.80	1.00	−1.1	6.17***	99
Employees	59	20	96	1.46	.47	12,796	702	76,054	2.85	.89	−1.39*	9.95***	82

Notes: Sales are denoted in million renminbi (RMB) yuan, China's national currency. US \$1 = 8.35 RMB (at the time when the major part of the survey was conducted).
$\bar{x}$ = mean; $\Delta\bar{x}$ = mean difference.
med = median; s = standard deviation.
*p < .05; ** p < .01; ***p < .001 (two tailed).
*Levene's test significant, therefore unequal variance t-test used.
Note: comparison between Chinese private and state-owned enterprises.

significant less people than state enterprises ($\bar{x}$ = 59, Δlog$\bar{x}$ = −1.39, *df* = 82, *p* < .001).

The results corroborate with qualitative discussions on overseas Chinese businesses, which highlighted their small size. As mentioned, small size probably can be attributed to the emphasis on familism. Staying small—a deliberate choice that has clear trade offs—may be the only way for private Chinese enterprises to "keep it all in the family" (Heller 1991, p. 31). Small size allows family members to maintain close ties with each other, while networks provide the required structural flexibility and resources to manage their own spun-off businesses within the kinship group.

Overview of case studies

In the previous section, I used quantitative analysis to test the hypotheses related to the distinctive structural, managerial, and contextual choices of private enterprises. I will now ground and enrich some of the findings through case studies, which convey a feeling for the *gestalt* and practical meaning of the somewhat abstract, organizational and contextual properties. The qualitative data also helps to further explore several hypotheses that were rejected or only tentatively supported. The purely quantitative data and computations may have missed some finer points that can neither be reduced to formal mathematical statements, nor be measured through standardized scales. Complex phenomena such as interorganizational networks and national culture are less susceptible to "hard" analysis than company size, for example. The case studies do not formally test hypotheses; the results are not statistically generalizable. Cases are exemplary snapshots, not comprehensive proofs. Like experiments, they allow for *analytical* generalization, if the evidence supports a theory and, ideally, invalidates a rival theory. A second case serves as replication. The theory then becomes a valid generalization of the observed pattern (see Yin 1994).

I will focus on four themes, each relating to one of the distinctive features of Chinese management. Instead of analyzing all insignificant differences, I focused on the most salient ones, especially with signs opposite to those hypothesized.

Enterprise networks

The managerial profile comparison showed that private and state enterprises did not differ significantly in their use of subcontracting. Both groups outsourced relatively few activities in absolute terms. It therefore was important to use case studies to analyze the broader notion of webs spun by private enterprises.

Family-related traditional Chinese values

Even though private enterprises put somewhat more emphasis on *guanxi* than state enterprises, the difference was minimal and statistically insignificant. In addition, both types of enterprises attached a high absolute value on personal connections. To solve this puzzle, I explored the importance of *family*-based relations in private enterprises from a qualitative angle. The case studies also afforded richer insights about the two other dimensions of family-related Chinese cultural values: belonging to a family-based group and respect for seniority in a family context.

Entrepreneurial management style

One of the most distinctive features of Chinese management is the high entrepreneurial intensity in private enterprises. Since "entrepreneurship" is an abstract umbrella term, I grounded it in organizational reality. This helps readers to experience its facets and dynamism on the corporate turf. In addition, the case studies explain the lack of support for the hypotheses about proactive and long-term strategic orientation and flexible leadership.

Informal dictatorial style of owner-manager

The findings showed that the owner-manager in private enterprises leads a dictatorial regime and uses personal controls to secure compliance. An outsider may find this notion of a personal, centralized dictatorship difficult to understand. Westerners, in particular, cannot easily imagine patterns of authority and behavior that differ from their egalitarian culture. The case study illustrates this concept of dictatorial informality in practice. Besides, the example of an impersonal bureaucracy in a large, state-owned enterprise serves as contrast to personal control and low formalization.

I will first present the case studies: Tiger Corporate Identity Company, Magnolia Education Group, and Cathay Industrial Bank.[5] Because of my long field visit to Tiger, this case study is the most extensive. Afterward, I will draw cross-case conclusions.

Tiger Corporate Identity Company

Objectives of the case study

In this case study, I intend to convey real-world richness by focusing on three of the themes related to the distinctive Chinese management style in private enterprises: enterprise webs, emphasis on family-based values, and dictatorship by the owner-manager.

Introduction

Scene I: After sipping his "black dragon" tea, Mr. Wang slowly leans toward the owner of the exquisite Chinese *chaguan* (traditional Chinese teahouse), located in a peaceful suburb of Beijing. Quietly, the two men discuss the fortunes of one of the owner's entrepreneur friends. Suddenly, Mr. Wang rises and says, "Yeah, why can't I do some design work for this guy? By the way, can you introduce me to him . . . ?"

Scene II: With a broad smile, Mr. Wang welcomes his visitors to the small exhibition on the 5th floor of his office in Chaoyang. The guests walk slowly around the room and marvel at the creative talent of the owner. The logos of famous airlines, food companies, and shopping malls, arranged side-by-side, tell a gripping story of how high Mr. Wang's star has risen above the nation's capital, since he first came there, equipped with only his talent and his ambition . . .

Background

Tiger Corporate Identity was founded in 1992 by the current CEO, Mr. Wang. It is registered as a private unlimited company and is 100% owned by the Wang family. The company's offices are located in Beijing's Chaoyang district, which boasts one of the largest concentrations of foreign enterprises in the city. It competes in the following businesses: corporate image design and consulting, advertising, the lumber trade, and property development. The company is very small, which is typical of private family businesses in China. It employs only twenty-five people full-time. For confidentiality reasons, the owner did not disclose revenues and profits. Such secrecy is quite common in Chinese private enterprises.

Mr. Wang has a very humble background. He grew up on Daxing'an Mountain in the far north of China, where his father, a technician from Hunan Province, had been transferred during the Great Cultural Revolution, in order to be "reeducated." After high school, Mr. Wang moved to

Beijing, to try his luck in the nation's capital, believing the slogan (which was originally applied to New York) "If you can make it there, you can make it everywhere." He studied decorative painting and traditional Chinese philosophy at the prestigious Central Institute of Industrial Arts. After graduation, he opened his own business.

Mr. Wang can be called a high achiever—or at least a high flyer. He is driven always to give his best and works extremely hard, including many nights. He has even installed a bedroom in his office. As a guide to success, he tries to follow the path of American industrial pioneers such as Henry Ford, rather than other Chinese entrepreneurs. On his computer, he has designed a new corporate headquarters with a corporate flag on top. He is not worried by the fact that its dimensions and splendor exceed his current financial means. The architecture is strongly reminiscent of the White House in Washington, D.C. His choice of office location also expresses his ambitions. The company shares a building with Siemens, the German industrial giant, in a district that is dominated by foreign businesses. Such a prestigious location is quite uncommon for small Chinese private firms, which often operate from tiny flats.

Networks

I had hypothesized extensive enterprise webs as a distinctive feature of Chinese private enterprises. However, the quantitative analysis, which focused on subcontracting, showed very little differences compared with state enterprises. I therefore explored a broader notion of networks in this case study. The far reaching *guanxi* network that Mr. Wang built up is one of Tiger's most striking features. These webs mainly rest on family ties and other personal connections, which glue the diverse network members together. These highly informal and personalized connections with other enterprises differ from more formal interorganizational networks such as alliances, subcontracting, and joint ventures, which feature less prominently in Mr. Wang's relationship portfolio. The exclusive focus on subcontracting relations in the quantitative analysis missed the richness of these distinctive webs in Chinese private enterprises. Let me now look in more detail at the shape and relationship hierarchy of Mr. Wang's web, which is illustrated in figure 3-8.

Mr. Wang sits like a spider at the center of a complex and flexible web of informal ties. The closeness of these ties declines in concentric circles from the center. The "outside" environment starts where interorganizational boundary-spanning *relations*—a new concept that differs from traditional boundary-spanning roles—end. The outside environment is beyond the reach of the spider and deemed hostile. Caution is justified. In analogy with biology, outside forces can destroy the web, but it is highly elastic and, through its structural design, much more powerful than the individual fine threads.

Let me describe the concentric hierarchy of the webs. Family relations are at the core. This seems to be the most distinctive feature of private

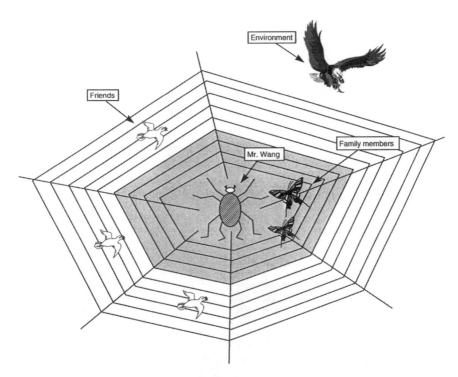

Figure 3-8 General Shape and relationship hierarchy of Mr. Wang's web

Chinese networks compared to those of other enterprises. A positional analysis reveals the sources of power. Family members hold all of the few top management positions. Mr. Wang, the youngest son, is CEO. His elder brother serves as the only vice president in the company and simultaneously functions as chief adviser to the CEO. Further, because the CEO holds a municipal government position, which may lead to conflicts of interest, the CEO's mother-in-law officially is sole owner of the company.

The family is the central hub from which a myriad of linkages depart. Mr. Wang's relationships, which form an intricate enterprise network, are illustrated in figure 3-9. The CEO's father-in-law holds a key editorial position at the very influential newspaper *Industrial Commercial Times Daily*, which is one of Tiger's major clients. The CEO's wife works for Air China, also a very important client. Mr. Wang designed Air China's corporate identity, including the company's logo. I saw this and other logos in the private exhibition of Mr. Wang's designs mentioned in the introduction to this case study. Through her employer, his wife has built major business connection with Air China Food Corporation. Naturally, this company has also become a major client. Informal family-based channels helped Mr. Wang to reach for the stars. He leveraged these airline connections to establish close business links with Germany's Lufthansa Airlines. It offered him the lucrative contract to design the corporate image of its

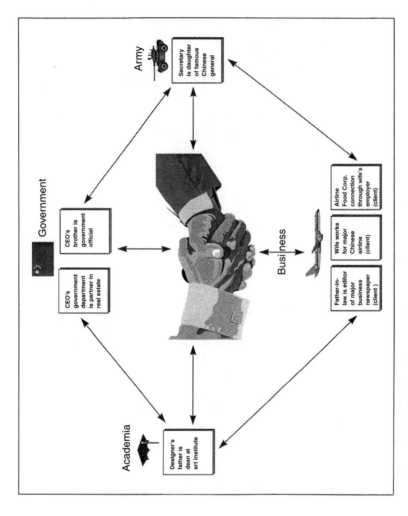

Figure 3-9 Mr. Wang's enterprise network.

Army

Government

Academia

Business

Secretary is daughter of famous Chinese general

CEO's brother is government official

CEO's government department is partner in real estate

Designer's father is dean at art institute

Airline Food Corp. connection through wife's employer (client)

Wife works for major Chinese airline (client)

Father-in-law is editor of major business newspaper (client)

Beijing-based shopping mall, called Yansha (literally meaning "Beijing Lufthansa").

Moving from the center of the web to the outside, there are personal relations based on friendships rich in trust, which have developed over time. First, Mr. Wang has excellent relations with the government, since he is a relatively high municipal government official in the Department of Housing, and because his brother also holds public office. His department is the company's major joint venture partner in real estate development. In addition, his secretary's father is a famous Chinese general. This relationship provides him with vital connections to the People's Liberation Army—a crucial source of power in many spheres of Chinese society. Furthermore, the father of his chief designer, Mr. Kong, is the dean of the Department for Decorative Painting at the Central Institute of Industrial Arts (and claims to be a descendant of Confucius).[6] This is the department from which the CEO graduated—an excellent example of strong path dependencies that afford sustainable competitive advantage based on time, since most new relations depend on older ones and are therefore difficult to replicate by competitors. This connection provides Mr. Wang the best access to new artistic ideas and design talent, a very scarce and valuable resource in China. He attracted his chief designer mainly by offering him a mortgage, which he urgently needed to buy a house. As a token of appreciation for this timely help, Mr. Kong has stayed with the company ever since. Finally, Mr. Wang maintains excellent contacts with other important Chinese entrepreneurs many of whom are his clients and provide him with new (business) contacts. A very good example is his connection with the owner of the only private teahouse in Beijing mentioned in the introduction to this case study. Because many VIPs frequent this teahouse regularly, Tiger can always tap into a stream of potential client leads—a powerful strategic opportunity pipeline.

Mr. Wang's friendships even spread internationally. For example, on his business trips to Japan, he developed close connections with Japanese corporate identity gurus. He thus can absorb very advanced Western design knowledge. As another example, I myself almost became the latest layer in this web. During my site visit, Mr. Wang tried to convince me to introduce him to some of my other respondents, so that he could sell his services to them . . . a suggestion I politely refused. This incident revealed the pattern of network-building through "*guanxi* proliferation." Mr. Wang had to build all these friendship-based relations from scratch, since he came to Beijing with almost no connections.

Tiger outsources all printing jobs to a Taiwanese joint venture in Beijing, whose owner is a good friend of Mr. Wang. Outdoor advertising for his clients also is subcontracted. Thus, even though Tiger is subcontracting extensively, these more formal interorganizational relationships form only part of the more extensive web described above. To summarize the above discussion, it is possible to develop a framework that classifies the different types of enterprise relations on a continuum according to their degree of formality. They range from personal informal enterprise connections to more institutional formal subcontracting and joint-venture arrangements. This notion is graphically illustrated in figure 3-10.

The analysis reveals the major advantages of Tiger's informal, family-based networks with other companies or people. A form of social capital, they are an excellent source of new opportunities and business intelligence about new market developments. Because the business contacts rest on family links, they are very stable, virtually guaranteeing a steady stream of revenue. As a consequence, Tiger does not need to advertise. All client development is through personal relations.

Emphasis on family-based Chinese values

In the quantitative analysis, I found some support for a stronger emphasis on traditional Chinese cultural values in private enterprises compared to state enterprise, particularly in regard to the strong sense of familism. Because the quantitative evidence was derived mainly from the responses to the culture scale and the analysis of ownership patterns, I needed to explore the importance of family-based values in the Tiger case study in more qualitative detail.

As in the quantitative section, the four interconnected elements of familism—family-based relations, respect for older family members, family loyalty, and collective orientation toward the family—carry much weight in Mr. Wang's firm. First, the company is fully family-owned and its top management consists exclusively of family members. Most major business connections are based on family ties, such as his wife's link with Air China. Second, Mr. Wang's great respect for seniority within the family is evidenced by the fact that his mother-in-law has the final word in all major decisions. He also greatly cherishes his family lineage, which is shown by his worshipping at an ancestor shrine in his home. Because of communism, this practice is not very common in modern China. At home, he also treasures the calligraphy (beautiful handwriting) produced by his ancestors. Third, family loyalty outweighs all other obligations. Mr. Wang built the business in order to serve his family. He is unlikely to jump his own ship and abandon the family, in order to pursue a career in a large organization. Fourth, his emphasis on group affiliation illustrates and enriches the discussion on collectiveness in private enterprises. Belonging to the *family* group is of key importance to him. In contrast, because of his independence, belonging to a particular work unit is not significant.

The case study offers a broader understanding of what emphasis on Chinese culture means than the quantitative analysis. Because Mr. Wang had studied Chinese philosophy and decorative painting, and had worked as an artist, he highly values traditional Chinese culture *in general*. Among other classics, he displays Sun Zi's "The Art of War" in his office and freely quotes major passages from it. He avows publicly that he resorts to

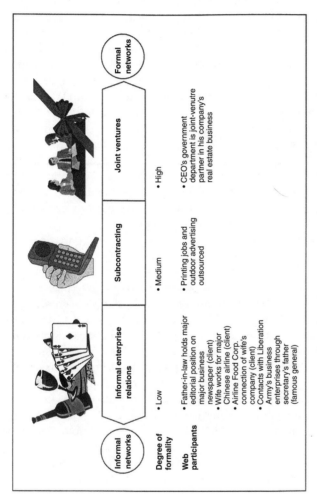

Figure 3-10 Classification of enterprise networks in Tiger case study

ancient Chinese warfare strategies to succeed. In addition, twice a week he lectures his employees—most of whom have just finished art school—on classical Chinese values and requires them to complete home assignments. He thus hopes to root Chinese culture in the hearts and minds of the younger generation. In traditional Confucian terms, he exchanges benevolence for loyalty. Even though in China, highly qualified workers are in high demand and switch jobs often, his employees are fiercely loyal.

More generally, Mr. Wang believes that, as a private entrepreneur, it is his mission to preserve, readopt, and revive China's great cultural heritage, which communists and state industrialists had tried to wreck. To this end, he reconstructed virtual photo images of parts of the old Imperial Summer Palace, Yuan-ming Yuan (Garden of Pure Light), in Beijing. Built in the late 17th century, this imperial summer residence had been annihilated by the Anglo-French armies in 1860 during the second Opium War (1856–60). The Chinese have kept the ruins to remind the world of the foreign aggression. The entrepreneur's great dream is to resurrect these splendid gardens and buildings.

In conclusion, the Tiger case study illustrates the supremacy of family-based traditional Chinese values in private enterprises. It also captured a broader notion of traditionalism—an entrepreneurial mission to reanimate traditional Chinese culture, which would have been difficult to detect and measure only through quantitative means.

Dictatorship by the owner-manager

The quantitative analysis revealed that Chinese private enterprises made decisions at significantly higher hierarchical levels than state enterprises. The case study shows how this phenomenon operates in real business life. Mr. Wang, a charismatic and visionary leader, welcomes suggestions, but usually has the final word on all organizational issues. Occasionally, he decides jointly with his elder brother. The organization consists of only two hierarchical levels: the CEO (and his brother, who plays the role of corporate center) and the rest of the company. The vertical span of control, that is, the number of job positions from the top to the bottom of the organization, thus is minimized. The company is conspicuous for its almost complete lack of formal hierarchical titles. For example, there are no vice presidents except for Mr. Wang's brother. The CEO's horizontal span of control, which is the sum of all direct reports, is maximized: it equals the number of employees. The operational logic excludes any formal delegation. The CEO controls not only strategy, products and services, finance, and personnel, but even resolves operative issues himself. Mr. Wang delegates only tedious accounting matters to his secretary, because his artistic temperament prevents him from developing much interest in these "boring" matters. Even though he reigns supremely, his leadership is very pragmatic and practical. He does not separate intellectual and manual jobs. Instead, he performs the same tasks he requires from all employees, from simple design to complex management.

The high concentration of power partly is attributable to the CEO's belief in his superior capabilities and insights, which he thinks enable him to exercise better judgment than others. It also stems from his emphasis on traditional Chinese values, which prevent him from delegating power to nonfamily members. The family is a protective group of people who can be trusted in a highly uncertain and complex environment. Because of external dangers, outsiders cannot be entrusted with the important operations of the family business. Besides, the CEO knows that his employees are conditioned by traditional Chinese culture. They expect firm leadership from the boss, which he has to provide. These role expectations shaped by socialization are the primary Confucian device for structuring social relations and creating a stable order. If the CEO did not comply with the expectations of his employees, they would not perceive him as a strong leader and would not follow him.

With such strong centralization and personal control, there is little need for bureaucracy. Mr. Wang strongly dislikes structural integration devices such as committees, liaison personnel, or task forces, which aim at building consensus. Instead, he prefers the role of a supreme commander who decides the fate of his troops from his reclusive mountain top. Neither does he take advantage of process liaison devices such as a master plan that coordinates decisions, bargaining among heads of departments, or interactive and mutually reinforcing departmental decision processes. The CEO only calls for informal brainstorming sessions at irregular intervals for artistic purposes, such as designing a corporate logo for a client. In addition, he eschews structural differentiation. The company lacks departments and specialists—employees perform whatever task is required in a given situation. There are no specialist titles. In particular, there is no need for staff departments to analyze problems and draft solutions. The CEO computes even difficult issues in his head, enriching his problem solving with substantial industry expertise, intuition, and foresight, and hands down his verdict. Without specialists who produce written documents, formalization is very low. The CEO prides himself on well designed company brochures, but would shred any organizational charts, job descriptions, operation manuals, organizational policies, or research reports, were they ever produced.

Owing to the high degree of centralization and lack of bureaucracy, decision making is flexible and fast. Nobody has to ask authorities above the CEO for permission, which may delay or impede action. Ownership and control are not separated. In other companies, such a separation leads to conflicts between the "principal" (owner) and his "agent" (manager), since both often pursue different objectives. Mr. Wang unites and personifies the shareholder's meeting, the board of directors, and the executive board. Because of the hands-on approach, he is well informed about latest business developments. He thus makes intelligent decisions, knows what to expect from employees, and more generally, serves as a role model.

In conclusion, this case study conveys a flavor of centralization in action, explains its negative correlation with bureaucracy, and spells out its implications in terms of speedy and flexible decision making. I found that emphasis on familism in private enterprises directly and indirectly drives centralization.

Other observations

As an interesting by-product of my field visit, I made an observation that arguably was possible only because of my relatively long stay at the company. The enterprise was somewhat "loosely coupled" (Meyer, Scott, and Deal 1983). Institutional theorists argue that a company's *management organization* is shaped by norms held in the outside institutional environment. Executives interface with society and display rituals of good management. This facade structure is only loosely coupled to a *work organization* or operating core, which performs the actual operations: transforming inputs into outputs (Thompson 1967). It does not necessarily reflect outside norms and may even conflict with them. Thus, because of strong pressures to adhere to social norms, organizations convey the appearance of conformity, which is a myth, since there are separate structures at the operational level.

The environment treats private Chinese enterprises with suspicion. Banks and other resource owners consider them too small to be reliable. In contrast, the government acts as lender of last resort for their state competitors. Therefore, as a legitimization strategy that satisfies external expectations of solidity, Mr. Wang tries to project an image of professionalism and strength. For example, his firm operates from the same five-story office building as Siemens of Germany. Moreover, he claims to drive a Red Flag limousine, which happens to be the former vehicle of a famous Chinese general. Further, despite the small size of the company, he showcases a strong and modern corporate culture and a well-rounded corporate identity to the outside world. For instance, he meticulously designed a glossy company brochure that rivals the publications of large Western companies. Employees have to wear elegant company uniforms that give them a very formal, armylike appearance. Mr. Wang also crafted stylish visual corporate identity symbols, such as logos and flags.

However, because the core is still a tiny and informal work organization, this external image, which is intended to dispel any fears that Tiger is a small and unreliable company, is a fake. Employees wear the uniforms only when important visitors frequent the office. Once they have left, the employees immediately exchange them for jeans and other informal attire. Despite the glossy brochure, internally there are very few written documents, and communication is informal. Finally, I never saw the Red Flag limousine during my one-month observation period. Does it really exist?

Magnolia Education Group

Objectives of the case study

This case study focuses on two themes related to the distinctive private Chinese management style. First, I will scrutinize unsupported differences related to Chinese entrepreneurship and bring this abstraction to life. Second, because of their importance and weaker support in the quantitative study, I will again delve into private enterprise networks.

Introduction

Looking through the window of the glamorous New Jin Jiang tower on one of the early days of Shanghai's splendid summer, Mr. Li observes the sun setting slowly beyond the glittering skyline of the booming city. Down below, he spots students leaving an education center located close to a five-star hotel. "Yes," he muses to himself, "education has profit potential in China, too."

Background

The Magnolia Education Group is a fully family-owned, private Chinese enterprise with unlimited liability. It was founded in 1983 by the present owner-manager, Mr. Li, and is headquartered in Shanghai's main business district, Luwan. The company started with education and training services, which remain its core business. It originally focused on foreign language and computer classes for adults. Now the company trains a variety of customer groups in a wide array of disciplines, ranging from painting instruction for small children, evening university classes, and tailored in-house training for organizations, to in-depth preparation for students wanting to study abroad. Recently, the company expanded into the hotel business.

Magnolia is a medium-sized company. It reported revenues of 6 million RMB yuan (approximately U.S $0.7 million) in 1995. However, the CEO may have understated revenues, since he fears that the true figures could be leaked to the tax authorities. He currently employs 350 people, including part-time staff and contract professors. The administrative core of full-time staff is significantly smaller (approximately fifty people). Mr. Li is very ambitious. He particularly strives for external recognition. Thanks to his public relations talent and connections with the local media, the company is well known. At the same time, Mr. Li has become a VIP in the Shanghainese society of influential businessmen.

Entrepreneurship

The quantitative analysis confirmed that Chinese entrepreneurship—the triad of strategy, leadership (including communication), and decision-making style—was significantly stronger in private enterprises than in state enterprises. However, the quantitative results did not support the hypotheses on proactive, risky, and long-term strategic orientation. Besides, the difference on flexible leadership was statistically insignificant and represented the smallest absolute gap of all managerial comparisons. Therefore, while illustrating the other well-supported findings, the case study explores broader notions of flexibility in action and thus makes practical sense of Chinese entrepreneurship.

Strategy. Mr. Li pursues highly proactive strategies, with some diversification to reduce risk. He started out with education in China—an industry with strong competition between new private providers and established state universities. With great foresight, he intuitively grasped the urgent need for well-managed institutions that generate valuable human, intellectual, and social capital. This compelling vision motivated waves of expansion into different education markets, both attracting new customers and "mining" existing ones by offering new services to them. In the early 1990s, he spotted a new opportunity and diversified into the hotel business, first entering the upmarket and then the massmarket segments. He acquired a major stake in the large scale New Jin Jiang Hotel, a five-star hotel in one of the most prestigious locations in central Shanghai, and later established a low budget hotel. In view of the high competitive intensity of the hospitality industry in China and the excess capacity, this investment can be considered risky. Whereas in the mass-market hotel segment Mr. Li seeks competitive advantage through aggressive promotional and discounting strategies, in the upmarket accommodation and education segment he differentiates products and services.

In particular, the company prides itself on the quality and innovativeness of its educational services, which leverage "advanced" support systems for effective teaching. For example, it uses white boards, which is quite exceptional in China. This practice differs sharply from large, state educational institutions, such as the Tongji University, where chalk dust is ubiquitous. As part of its distinctive value proposition, the Magnolia Group also deploys relatively advanced technology, such as video-assisted teaching. In addition, the classrooms are fully air-conditioned. This contrasts with Tongji's lecture theatres. Each of them is equipped with only one fan, which, as expected in Confucian culture, is directed at the teacher. The students have to endure the heat and mosquitoes.

These findings enrich our understanding of strategy in private enterprises. They illustrate proactive strategies and reveal that companies at the same time can *combine* risky and aggressive strategies in one business or customer segment with long-term, quality-oriented strategies in other ones. These differences may have averaged out in the quantitative analysis, which explains why private Chinese enterprises were not found to pursue more proactive, risky, and forward-looking strategies than their state counterparts.

Leadership. Mr. Li leads very autocratically and coercively, allowing little participation. Communication, in either vertical or horizontal direction, flows sparsely, since the CEO does not seek the input of his subordinates and discourages interdepartmental "conspiracy." It comes as no surprise that teamwork is rare at the Magnolia Education Group. Likewise, the boss eschews meetings, which promote integration. He coordinates, but intentionally does not integrate the various activities—a machiavellian policy of "divide and rule." For example, he completely separates the three business segments—education, upmarket hotel, and budget guest house—in order to dilute the power of their (assistant) managers. Otherwise, they may join forces to overthrow the leader. This dictatorial owner-manager dislikes paperwork and written rules, and controls directly by monitoring compliance with his orders, and indirectly by implanting values in his followers' heads and exemplifying them in action. He decides all major business issues, delegating only minor operating decisions. Mr. Li believes that he "has to centralize everything related to money, because you never can trust other people in these matters." This high degree of centralization is enshrined in the shape of the organization, which is undifferentiated. The hierarchy consists of only two levels; there are no job titles and specialists. Without intermediate levels, the CEO's span of control equals the number of employees. In other words, all employees are his direct subordinates. There are no vice presidents in the organization; the next level below the CEO is "assistant." Every employee performs a variety of tasks and has to learn new skills when circumstances require.

Mr. Li's leadership style is very flexible. In fact, his agility is one of the most striking findings of this case study. He actively seeks and quickly spots new opportunities. Unlike large companies whose organization can impede action, he commands a sufficiently lean structure to rapidly seize market openings and adjust accordingly. The move into the hotel business, a major shift in direction, proves this point. His power to decide without permission from higher authorities also increases his adaptability. Mr. Li's entry into the *mass-market* hotel segment (after investing in the five-star hotel) illustrates this distinctive quality. Through clues from his business network and his intuition, he suddenly sensed the potential of operating a hotel for Chinese visitors to Shanghai. A "back-of-the-envelope" calculation illustrates his simple business rationale: The total population of Shanghai (thirteen million people) includes two million people who visit the metropolis—a large group of people who need affordable hotel services.

Mr. Li entered the business in an unconventional way, which demonstrated his enormous flexibility and pragmatic attitude. Because he wanted to capture this attractive market segment quickly and without any major additional capital investment, he simply *converted* part of his administrative building into a budget guest house for domestic travelers. An outline of Mr. Li's business complex is presented in figure 3-11. To increase flexibility further, he sometimes accommodates the participants of his training programs in this guest house, which ensures full capacity

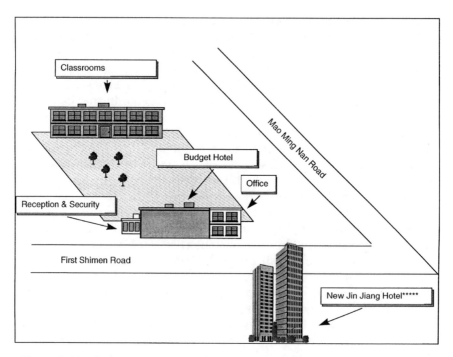

Figure 3-11 Arrangement of Mr. Li's business complex

utilization and smoothes demand. Clearly, the CEO uses common sense instead of complicated theories and analyses to make decisions. Opportunistic, ad hoc, and partial strategies substitute for grand designs and holistic plans. This move is also symbolic, since Mr. Li physically traded administration and bureaucracy for "real production."

Decision making. Mr. Li's decision-making style is highly entrepreneurial. A charismatic leader—his employees esteem him so highly that they hang his portraits in the office and school buildings—he makes big, bold moves, such as entering the hotel business and acquiring a stake in a five-star hotel that operates in a very competitive environment. Undoubtedly, he favors such "bet-the-company" moves over more incremental decisions that are grounded in careful planning.

Networks

The quantitative analysis produced only very limited support for private networks, perhaps because it was confined to subcontracting. As in the Tiger case study, I therefore investigated the broader notions of formal and informal webs in Magnolia.

Mr. Li clearly has readopted the overseas Chinese network style; his connections are essential for success. Let me analyze the core and concentric layers.

The inner web of family ties matters most. Mr. Li controls an extensive web of overseas Chinese contacts that are mainly based on kinship ties. The CEO uses these strong family connections to promote his business, without sacrificing quality by succumbing to nepotism. For example these connections are very useful sources of foreign currency and capital, since he can easily attract web members as (passive) investors for new ventures. The expansion into hotelling could happen only because he convinced his overseas family to contribute funds.

In the next layer, outside the family core, Mr. Li has established an extensive personal network mainly based on friendship ties. For example, he enjoys excellent relations with government officials. Otherwise, he would not obtain licenses for education, a very sensitive area in China. Further, he strongly benefits from academic collaboration and the exchange of befriended professors with renowned universities. For instance, his assistant's sister-in-law, who is highly qualified and lectures at Tongji University, serves as his German professor. Moreover, he relies on friends in the media to create a good image for him.

More formal interorganizational relations also matter. In particular, subcontracting features prominently in the company. The Magnolia Education Group insources many labor-intensive business activities. As mentioned, it hires renowned professors from other universities on a contract basis. By externalizing these activities, Mr. Li keeps the organization lean and overhead low. Without the burden of administration, he can think strategically and move quickly into new markets.

These relationship-based webs have helped the company to manage a very constraining task environment. Because of national security concerns—the protests in 1989 started from universities—the education sector in China is highly regulated. Entrepreneurs find it extremely difficult to obtain government licenses to start an educational institution. Mr. Li disclosed that he needed about fifty seal imprints to get started. Over time, he spun a far-reaching network that enabled him to secure all the vital licenses and the continuing backing of the authorities for his ventures. Mr. Li thus used his web to shape his environment, gaining more control over stakeholders and resources, simplifying it, and making it more predictable. He thus created a protected niche in the entangled and volatile wilderness. The lack of highly qualified teachers is another constraint. Mr. Li's personal and subcontracting network helped to overcome this bottleneck.

Cathay Industrial Bank

Objectives of the case study

Bearing in mind that this study mainly focuses on the distinctive private Chinese management style, I present this case study of the state-owned Cathay Industrial Bank (CIB) merely as a *contrast* to private enterprises.

I will concentrate on the very high degree of bureaucracy in state enterprises in China. Such a high level of structuredness differs sharply from the freewheeling, informal style of Chinese private firms. As in the case of entrepreneurship, the quantitative comparisons yielded clear results: Private enterprises are significantly less bureaucratic than state enterprises, which probably results from the stronger emphasis that entrepreneurs place on familism. Having settled this issue, I use the qualitative case material to paint a more colorful picture of a real-world bureaucracy.

Introduction

The heavy wood-paneled doors open slowly. First only a glimpse of the interior is visible, then the sheer size of the meeting hall overwhelms the visitor. Twenty leather chairs are neatly placed around a table that would make a formidable stage for one of the small theaters in Beijing's suburbs. The foreign interviewer from a venerable English university sits down, surrounded by an army of assistants and note takers. He asks the first question, then a somber voice is heard in the dimly lit room, saying: "Well, let's analyze this question. . . ."

Background

The Cathay Industrial Bank is a wholly state-owned enterprise, whose top management is appointed by the State Council, the highest political body in the country. It is headquartered in Beijing's Haidian district, the financial center of the nation's capital. Founded in January 1984, it has become the largest state-owned commercial bank in China and one of the largest banks in the world, offering a diverse range of financial services. The finance giant employs approximately 560,000 people. In 1994, it reported total revenues of 580 billion RMB (about U.S. $71 billion) and net profits of 4.2 billion RMB yuan (U.S. $0.5 billion). It owned total assets worth 2.96 trillion RMB (U.S. $361 billion) in 1995. The London-based *Banker* magazine ranked it seventh largest in the world in terms of capital in 1994. It was listed as the eleventh largest bank in *Euromoney* magazine's ranking of the top 200 banks in the world in terms of total assets in 1995. It has ranked first among the five-hundred largest service enterprises in China three times since 1991. The bank manages 8.1 million industrial and commercial accounts and 420 million personal savings accounts in urban areas. The number and volume of its transactions account for more than 50% of transactions in the banking industry in China. The company takes pride in its size. It published the number of employees in the section "Major Performance Statistics" at the beginning of the 1994 annual report.

Bureaucracy

Organizational complexity. CIB's organization is highly differentiated. The organizational chart conveys a taste of the myriad hierarchical levels (see figure 3-12). In addition, the company operates a huge number of sites—approximately 30,000 locations (see table 3-6). In addition to its operation in Hong Kong, the organization has started to expand overseas, opening representative offices or wholly owned subsidiaries in Japan, Singapore, Korea, Kazakhstan, and the United Kingdom. The branch levels are so numerous that it is difficult to translate all the names of the administrative units. In the annual report, for example, two levels are called "business offices," supposedly because the translator ran out of English bureaucratic terminology. I translated the entries in table 3-6 directly from the Chinese annual report and company brochure.

This rich bureaucratic vocabulary reminds me of other cultures that have developed an unusual variety of words that describe a phenomenon with special importance in their habitat. Eskimos, for example, use dozens of terms to differentiate snow. Likewise, the Chinese possess a treasure of organizational terms that reflect the size and complexity of their country and their status of master mandarins, which they earned since they developed the world's first bureaucracy. The equivalent in Chinese private enterprises, which cherish familism, is a cornucopia of names that denote kinship ties. Instead of just saying "grandfather" (as Westerners do), the Chinese use a more precise term such as "father-side grandfather."

Like the branch levels, the weight and diversity of titles also betray the hierarchical differentiation of CIB. As evidence from textual analysis, the annual report section introducing the executive directors proliferates in titles. The scope and variety of CIB's business activities increase complexity further. Its financial services include wholesale and retail banking, investment banking, international banking, and trading. The mission statement offers a glimpse of CIB's heroic aspirations: "To serve the national economy by raising funds both at home and abroad, strengthening the management of credit, supporting industrial production and commercial circulation, and promoting technical renovation (*sic*) and upgrade of enterprises" (CIB company brochure 1996, p. 2).

Standardization. CIB standardizes many procedures to govern its diverse business activities, including: production, inspection, finance, people, communication, sales, and marketing. A passage from the annual report highlights the importance of standardization: "In 1994, the Cathay Industrial Bank, by focusing on raising credit quality, reducing credit risk, and guaranteeing the timely satisfaction of fund requirements of State priority projects and priority industries, intensified target management and standardized its credit operation procedures, resulting in a marked increase in its credit quality" (CIB annual report 1994, p. 11).

Control systems. CIB takes full advantage of control systems to manage its diversified organization. Its support systems and applications largely follow Western patterns. Information technology (IT) features prominently in the overall control concept. Textual analysis again proves the point. The otherwise very general company brochure lists the technical details

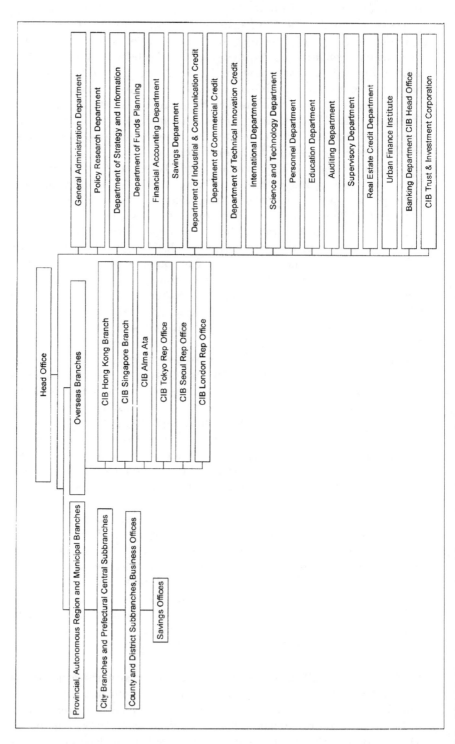

Figure 6.10 Cathay Industrial Bank organizational chart

Table 3-6 Operating sites of Cathay Industrial Bank

Site	Pinyin*	Number
Provincial branches	*shengji fenhang*	29
City (sub)branches	*shifen (zhi)hang*	194
Prefectural central subbranches	*diquzhongxin zhihang*	242
County subbranches	*xian zhihang*	2,336
District subbranches	*chengshi banshichu*	1,134
Branch business offices	*fenlichu*	3,987
Town business offices	*jizhen banshichu*	2,853
Savings offices	*chuxusuo*	21,831
(International) representative offices	*daibiao jigou*	5
(International) wholly owned subsidiaries	*quanzifushu jigou*	1

Source: CIB 1994 annual report; CIB 1996 company brochure.
*Pinyin is the official romanization method for Chinese characters in the People's Republic of China.

of the computer system in a special section on "electronic data-processing implementation" or, to use the literal Chinese translation, "electronization construction." The systems won the first prize for scientific and technological progress awarded by the People's Bank of China. The reach and density of CIB's computer network impresses in the Chinese circumstances (see figure 3-13).

Sixty-five percent of CIB's 37,000 offices are equipped with computers and connected to the network. In addition, 27,000 ATMs and 12,000 POSs have been installed. In May 1995, CIB launched an electronic funds transfer system—at that time the only one in China—which enabled bankwide fund transfers within twenty-four hours. The system handles more than 70,000 transactions, worth 10 billion RMB yuan, every day. The bank proudly proclaims that "the rapid and safe transmission of funds within the bank illustrates that the settlement business of the bank has entered the information superhighway era" (CIB company brochure 1996, p. 9). Table 3-7 presents more details on CIB's IT systems.

Formalization. CIB abounds in written documents. My first encounter provided circumstantial evidence, which served as smoking gun. The managers required me to present some of my requests in written form; I even had to apply for an annual report in writing. Formalization apparently is used to control information flows. The company also distributes stylish brochures, including a "growth chart" that displays CIB's corporate development. The professional color graphics are printed on high quality glossy paper, which is very rare in China. Besides, special assistants noted all details of the interview.

Specialization. As another feature of bureaucracy, specialist roles proliferate. The total number of specialists in each area impresses. For example, about 11,000 technicians serve the computer network. For important tasks, the company groups individual experts into departments, which are

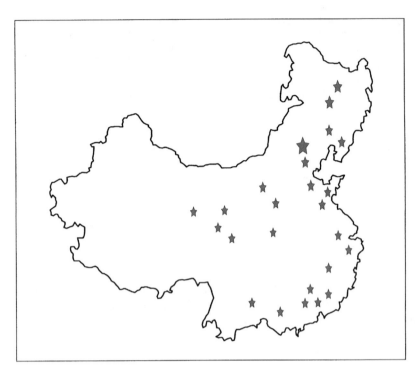

Figure 3-13 Cities with CIB mainframe computers

Source: Adapted from CIB company brochure (1996, pp. 8–9).

"collective specialists," who process the various data streams in the organization. An analysis of the organizational chart uncovers such specialist units as a policy research department, department of strategy and information, science and technology department, and department of technical innovation credit. An entire institute deals with urban finance. A significant number of high-level departments focus on control, including auditing, supervision, financial accounting, and general administration. These major departments are directly attached to the executive board. In addition, there are myriad smaller specialist departments at lower hierarchical levels, which in turn created many expert staff positions.

Integration. CIB utilizes a battery of liaison devices to unite its organizational parts. This response reflects the dilemma that structural differentiation, which pulls the organization apart by creating impermeable layers, functional silos, and specialist islands, necessitates additional expenditure on bureaucracy to counteract centrifugal tendencies and thus achieve a new synthesis. The company heavily emphasizes collective decision making. Consensus-driven committees determine the firm's operating philosophy and long-term strategy. In addition, CIB teems with task forces and other joint decision-making bodies. The gigantic meeting room where

Table 3-7 Deployment and use of information technology at CIB

Item	Number
Cities with mainframe computers	30
Cities with minicomputers	113
Mainframes and midrange systems	85
Minicomputers and microcomputers	300
Single- and multiuser PCs	3,000
ATMs	2,000
EDP outlets	17,000
Coverage of EDP	50%
Computerized over-the-counter business	75%

Source: CIB 1996 company brochure (pp. 8–9).

the interview took place and the adjacent rooms of similar proportions bear dramatic architectural witness. Further, company brochures frequently show the organization's members in various committees. Finally, as additional symptomatic evidence, CIB had to arrange an interdepartmental meeting of the international and strategy units to decide whether to grant me an interview.

To conclude, whereas in private enterprises, the owner-manager exercises personal and informal control, CIB turns to an impersonal bureaucracy, which enforces procedures and standards of work performance, to control and influence its people. Ownership is the basis of power in private enterprises. In contrast, at CIB, one person controls another's activities if his *role* prescribes such behavior. More generally, family values, a key element of Chinese culture, play a subordinate role at the technocratic bank. Kinship ties and personal connections based on friendships usually do not catalyze *business* transactions, which tend to be impersonal, anonymous, and computerized. Most networks are institutional, as evidenced by CIB's close relations with the state, which patronizes its servants.

However, senior corporate appointments depend on personal connections with powerful government officials. The weight of such connections in the political games involved in personal advancement increases in proportion to the position. The State Council, which is the apex structure of China's executive branch, fills positions at the pinnacle of CIB—a mini-government in its own right. As another instance of politics, connections help to access key decision makers in the company—without such hot wires, a call for an audience with the leaders of an organization, which amounts to the size of a medium city, would vanish from sight like a needle in a haystack. Connections improve the odds in a game in which the likelihood of success can be compared to the chances of winning the jackpot in a lottery. These findings explain why the quantitative analysis did not confirm significant difference between private and state enterprises in the use of general *guanxi*. Personal connections matter in both groups. But, as a mark of their distinctiveness, *family* ties are more predominant, stronger, and more influential in private enterprises.

As in the quantitative analysis, I could infer that the top management of the state-owned bank values a collective orientation. Interview respondents frequently referred to the "collective." Likewise, content analysis found that group-related vocabulary featured prominently in written documents. This refines the quantitative findings. Whereas state enterprises, for ideologic reasons, stress social attachments to the *danwei* (work unit), the major focus of group affiliation and source of social identity and meaning in private enterprises is the family.

Cross-case conclusions

I will briefly synthesize the three case studies along the four themes that concern the distinctive management style readopted in the newly founded Chinese private enterprises, and condense the main insights. Findings are analytically generalizable, since observations supported my theory; the results disconfirmed rival theories, that is, the null hypothesis of no differences between private and state enterprises (based on the theory that ownership does not matter); and the findings were replicated in a second case study.

Enterprise networks

The cases of Tiger and Magnolia underscored the salience of mainly informal, family-based enterprise networks in private enterprises. The findings confirmed that mainland enterprises readopted this feature of the particular Chinese management style, mentioned in mostly descriptive and anecdotal accounts about overseas Chinese businesses. Following Miles and Huberman's (1984, p. 221) recommendation to think metaphorically, I introduced the metaphor of a spider's web to illustrate these networks. It might enter Morgan's (1986) collection of metaphors to describe organizations. These webs vary in formality. In the case of Tiger, most connections were informal. This contrasted with Magnolia, which subcontracted various high-value-added activities, a major element in its execution strategy designed to overcome the shortage of skilled labor. In this case, the family-based networks also had greater international reach, with overseas Chinese providing urgently needed (passive) investment funds. In both cases, subcontracting was only one, and not necessarily the most dominant part of the overall network. This might explain why the reductionist quantitative analysis, which zoomed in on subcontracting, did not clearly support the original hypothesis.

The analysis of network architecture also afforded important insights. In both cases, the family formed the inner sanctum of the web. Friends ged to more distant concentric layers from this center. Outside the spider web, Tiger's CEO tried to influence the expectations of his external environment by projecting a professional image, which was only loosely coupled to the reality of the operative core. More generally, the trust-based networks helped these two enterprises shape their environment, reducing constraints, complexity, and uncertainty. They served as buffer against a perplexing variety of potential external shocks that may diminish resources and thus endanger organizational survival. In particular, both types of enterprises developed close personal relations with government officials in order to secure privileges and protect themselves from harmful state intervention and the crimes of mandarins—a prime objective of many private enterprises in a country where anti-corruption campaigns often failed to achieve satisfactory results (see Schlevogt 2001k). Finally, they used webs to capture new business and bond existing clients.

Emphasis on family-based values

The case studies of the two private enterprises illuminated another building block of Chinese management, emphasis on familism. The quantitative analysis confirmed the general importance of family values in private enterprises. For example, it showed that families control most private firms. With respect to certain specific elements of familism, the quantitative evidence was weaker. First, unexpectedly, the statistical analysis did not expose striking differences in the expedience of relationships in private and state enterprises. Instead, both highly esteemed personal connections. The case studies unraveled this conundrum by illustrating the stronger weight of *family*-based relations in private enterprises. For example, family members held all top management positions. The most important contacts, the inner core of the spider web, also centered on the family. In the case of Magnolia, the kinship ties extended overseas. Other types of relations mattered in state enterprises, for example, to secure appointments and access. In addition to friendship-based connections, there was a second layer of impersonal, institutional relationships, safeguarding privileged treatment of the *company*, that is, a legal person, by the government.

Second, quantitative findings showed that a collective orientation means much for both private and state enterprises. Ownership patterns had suggested a stronger family orientation in private firms. The case studies showed how essential affiliation with the family is for private actors. Like the work unit, it serves as a source of identity, meaning, and protection.

Third, I found a strong emphasis on respect for seniority and family loyalty in private enterprises. In the state-owned bank, such values were overshadowed, but arguably not replaced, by pervasive socialist ideology, which is constantly reinforced through indoctrination and propaganda. More generally, the CEO of Tiger in Beijing regarded it as his mission as a private entrepreneur to promote the renaissance of traditional Chinese culture and readopt this great heritage in his company.

Entrepreneurship

The quantitative results demonstrated a significantly stronger degree of entrepreneurship in private firms as compared to state enterprises along most theoretical dimensions. Yet the findings did not support more proactive, risk-taking, and forward looking strategies adopted by private firms. The Magnolia case study possibly solved one puzzle, showing that two different strategic modes can coexist under the conceptual umbrella of a farsighted and compelling vision: long-term strategies of product differentiation, which create sustainable competitive advantage, in some business segments, and aggressive and risky moves with a shorter-term outlook in others. For example, Mr. Li adopted an aggressive strategy in the budget accomodation business, but is renowned for the quality of education, achieved through significant investment in high technology. Likewise, the five-star hotel caters for very discerning guests. Besides, as seen in Magnolia's waves of expansion, companies may pursue different strategies at different stages of organizational development. This spatial and temporal parallelism may have averaged out responses and thus diluted aggregate scores on riskiness and long termism, tipping the balance in the opposite direction. In regards to proactiveness, Mr. Wang focused primarily on developing new personal connections as an indirect vehicle to find new business opportunities instead of seeking for new goldmines on his own and exhibiting a bias for action as an end in itself. Being first in the market, which is one important objective of proactive strategies, was less vital for overall success—at best one of several benefits from these relations—potentially explaining the inconclusive findings from the survey. The case study showed that Mr. Li did not invent the education or hotel markets, but he nevertheless reaped benefits from niche positions and incremental innovation. Unlike these different positioning strategies, the execution strategies were similar across all business segments, taking full advantage of a well-aligned and closely knit network organization and powerful values, occasionally even sharing the same physical assets for different activities.

With respect to leadership style, the autocracy of the pater familliae (father of the family), seen in real life in the cases, confirmed and illustrated the clear quantitative findings. With strong emphasis on familism and without formal rules and procedures, the CEO felt the need to control nonfamily members through coercion. Empowerment was not an option. The difference in flexible leadership between private and state enterprises in the quantitative analysis was tiny and statistically insignificant. However, the case study depicted the high flexibility of Magnolia. Mr. Li converted part of his office building to create space for the new hotel business, thus demonstrating the primacy of dynamic business over slow bureaucratic administration.

Finally, decision making in private enterprises was very entrepreneurial. The charismatic leaders favored intuition over complicated analysis and planning. After spotting rent-creating opportunities, they secured resources and moved boldly into the new arenas. For example, Mr. Li diversified into the hospitality industry by purchasing a stake in a five-star hotel, presumably with overseas Chinese funding.

To conclude, the case studies helped to paint a colorful picture of how private enterprises revived the idiosyncratic entrepreneurial style, known from overseas Chinese businesses, in all its facets on the mainland.

Centralization and lack of bureaucracy

The quantitative findings showed that private enterprises made decisions at significantly higher levels and were significantly less bureaucratic than state enterprises. The case studies offered real-world richness to bring these results to life. Unhampered by red tape in the form of rules or job descriptions, departments, and specialists, Tiger's CEO decided all important issues. His horizontal span of control equaled the number of employees. Many organizational economists consider that such an arrangement exceeds the maximum span that can keep "moral hazards" in check (see Milgrom and Roberts 1992). They result from the opportunistic behavior of employees who pursue their own advantage at the expense of the organization. But, perhaps the powerful values that Mr. Wang indoctrinated into the hearts and minds of his employees and family control mitigate potential damage. Values serve as implicit contracts preventing undesirable action. Diagnostic controls, above all the CEO's personal supervision, monitor behavior and outcomes and facilitates corrective measures. Interactive controls, such as strong practical guidance by the circumspect boss, use the collected information to promote learning.

In addition, the Chinese private entrepreneur prefers hands-on involvement over strategic dreaming in corporate ivory towers. He thus breaks with the old Western view that some men should just think, and others just work, expressed in the traditional difference between a gentleman and an operative. Convinced that no master should be too proud to do the hardest work, he believes, as John Ruskin did, that the thinker should often work and the workman should often think and both should be real gentlemen. For the Chinese entrepreneur it is clear that only labor can make thought healthy, and only thought can make labor happy.

To conclude, the case studies conveyed a rich impression of the autocratic and informal management style in Chinese private enterprises, which anecdotes about overseas Chinese businesses had mentioned. Division of labor, in the entrepreneur's eyes, implies that not labor is divided, but men. The lack of bureaucracy contrasted sharply with the Byzantine structure, featuring numerous hierarchical levels, specialists, written documents, and systems, in the state-owned Cathay Industrial Bank. Its proliferating bureaucracy substantiated earlier conjectures about the structure of state enterprises. CIB struggled hard to synthesize what it had differentiated.

Summary and conclusions

In this chapter, I reported and discussed findings related to the first research hypothesis, the distinctiveness of private Chinese management. In a comparison of private and state enterprises, I found quantitative and qualitative evidence that the structural and managerial choices of private enterprises differ significantly from their state counterparts. Specifically, I tested the six constituent elements of private Chinese management. They characterize their lopsided organization, which is light on formal structure, but heavy on enterprising spirit and cultural values.

Lack of bureaucracy

Chinese private enterprises were significantly less bureaucratic than state enterprises. The findings broadly supported the hypotheses relating to the lower degree of formalization, specialization, standardized control systems, and integration. Except for control, all differences were statistically significant. In addition, an intrascale analysis of formalization revealed differences of structural choices inside private enterprises at the item level, probably resulting from their emphasis on Chinese cultural values.

Centralization

Private enterprises tended to concentrate power significantly more than state enterprises. Many private entrepreneurs decided minor operational issues and directly participated in most business activities. As in the case of formalization, I uncovered intrascale differences showing that some decisions were made at higher levels than others. They probably can be attributed to Chinese culture.

Entrepreneurship

Private enterprises showed a comparatively high degree of Chinese entrepreneurship in terms of distinctive strategies, leadership (including communication), and decision-making styles. Compared to state enterprises, they adopted somewhat more aggressive, less defensive, and less analytical strategies. However, greater proactiveness, long-term orientation, or riskiness could not be shown. The case studies of two private firms potentially explained this fact. These enterprises were shown to adopt both, aggressive, short-term moves and longer-term strategies at the same time in different markets. In the survey, differences might thus have averaged out at the aggregate level. In addition, in the cases, the most important strategy was to secure more personal connections. This might explain the lesser need to follow proactive strategies. In regard to leadership style, Chinese private enterprises adopted a significantly less participative and more coercive style. In terms of flexibility, the difference was not statistically significant, but the case study of Mr. Li's Magnolia Education Group illustrated a very flexible style. Finally, decision making was significantly more entrepreneurial in private enterprises than in the state sector. The case studies also showed that bold moves were favored over incremental planning.

Enterprise webs

The quantitative findings failed to clearly support extensive "enterprise cities" in private enterprises. Even though private enterprises were found to contract more than state enterprises, the difference was small and statistically insignificant. Besides, both types of enterprises outsourced few activities in absolute terms. The case studies unraveled this perplexing phenomenon. The two private enterprises leveraged a complex web of personal connections with other enterprises and individuals in these organizations. These relationships centered on the family and varied in formality. Subcontracting thus represented only *one* dimension of these webs. Even though webs in general proved essential for both enterprises, they differed in their use of subcontracting. The singular focus on subcontracting in the quantitative analysis thus missed the richness of these webs, which only qualitative lenses can capture.

Family-based values

The quantitative analysis showed that private firms strongly emphasize certain family-related values. In particular, respect in terms of family loyalty and importance of seniority carried significantly more weight in private enterprises than in their state counterparts. The evidence on the other two facets of culture at first appeared equivocal. Relations in general mattered more in private enterprises, and state enterprises esteemed collective orientation more highly, but both differences were tiny and statistically insignificant. An analysis of ownership patterns solved the puzzle. It demonstrated the pivotal role of *family* relations in the private sector. Families controlled most private enterprises, either through full ownership or majority stakes. In addition, the case studies shed some light on collective orientation and further buttressed the findings on relationships. Family membership proved vital in private enterprises. In contrast, state managers possibly for ideological reasons, greatly valued inclusion in a different group: the work unit. In addition, whereas managers of both private and state enterprises stressed personal connections, *family*-based relations proved to be the distinctive cornerstone of private Chinese management.

Small size

As hypothesized, private enterprises were significantly smaller than their state counterparts, both in terms of revenues and employees. In a small firm, the entrepreneur can directly control essential decisions and transactions, and economize on bureaucracy. In large companies, such centralization would result in loss of control. Informality would forsake the economies of an efficient bureaucracy.

Throughout the analysis, I suggested that the distinctiveness of private Chinese management, ceteris paribus, stems from the emphasis on family-related traditional Chinese values, which directly and indirectly affect organizational properties. To rationalize the design choices of Chinese managers in chapter 4, I will present the findings from the structural equation modeling of various factors influencing organizational structure and management practices in China.

4

Influencing Factors of Structure and Management in China

This chapter aims to answer the second research question: "Do the distinctive features of private Chinese management result from an emphasis on traditional Chinese cultural values?" To recapitulate, I have found empirical evidence that private Chinese enterprises have readopted the distinctive web-based Chinese management style practiced in overseas Chinese family businesses. Supporting evidence and illustrations from the survey and case studies showed that structural and managerial mean levels differed significantly between private and state enterprises. At this point, most discussions of overseas Chinese management styles would normally stop. But is the Chinese management style monolithic? To find out, I suggest a contingency perspective, which examines whether factors in the task environment affect organizational design. In particular, I will test whether emphasis on traditional Chinese culture, most importantly familism, directly and indirectly (via its impact on size) influences structural and managerial choices in private, but not in state enterprises. This procedure ascertains whether the private web-based Chinese management model is indeed a distinctive cultural artifact. I will test the following hypotheses:

Hypothesis 2.1   (*Related to the direct influence of culture*): Holding other things constant, the distinctive characteristics of private Chinese management are due to the emphasis on traditional Chinese cultural values.

Hypothesis 2.2   (*Related to the indirect influence of culture*): The small size of Chinese private enterprises is due to the cultural emphasis on family ties in those firms.

This chapter is organized into two major sections. The first section presents the quantitative findings relating to the influencing factors of organizational *structure* in private and state enterprises, and compares the results to the hypotheses. The second section examines the influencing factors of *management* practices in China in the same fashion.

Influencing factors of organizational structure in China

The objective of this section is to analyze whether the emphasis on traditional Chinese values directly and indirectly (via its association with small company size) affects the structure of private enterprises, but not of state enterprises. Such a differential impact of culture would prove that the structural features of the web-based Chinese management model are distinctive, compared to state enterprises. After a statistical primer, I will delineate the basic model and report the concomitant findings. Pearson correlation matrices for the individual research models can be found in appendix E.

Structural equation modeling

This chapter is written for readers with little knowledge of advanced statistical techniques. I will explain the various analytical techniques and avoid technical jargon. I used structural equation modeling (SEM), also called "causal modeling," to quantity the impact of independent variables on dependent variables. SEM analyzes a series of equations expressing functional relationships. It processes the raw data from the survey to assess how well the hypothesized equations fit the data. It simultaneously evaluates an empirical (measurement) model and a theoretical (structural) model. The equivalent of factor analysis, a measurement model specifies relationships between observed (manifest) indicators and unobserved (latent) constructs (traits).

Social science researchers cannot directly observe abstractions but infer them from combinations of manifest factors (such as questionnaire answers from a survey). An example is intelligence, defined as the power of learning and understanding. Even though empiricists cannot gather data on this theoretical concept of mental ability directly, they may administer tests on its constituent parts, such as verbal comprehension (measured by the knowledge of vocabulary and reading) and spatial visualization (the ability to visualize mentally and manipulate objects).

A dimension, derived from one or several items (such as individual questions), enters the structural equation model as a manifest indicator. By analyzing the strength of association between the latent construct and the observed variables, the empirical model assesses measurement error, which occurs frequently in complex social science models. Because SEM integrates the measurement model with the theoretical model and assesses them simultaneously, contaminating measurement error can be filtered out. This simultaneous assessment of one integrated model is a great advantage of SEM over other analytical techniques.

The structural model, comparable to Ordinary Least Squares (OLS) regression, tests the operationalized research theory. A set of equations specifies the hypothesized functional relations between dependent (endogenous) constructs, such as centralization, and independent (exogenous) factors, such as emphasis on traditional Chinese values. Path diagrams graphically illustrate these relationships, using arrows to connect the variables. Arrows in the structural model, called regression paths, point at endogenous variables. Traits that are not targeted by regression arrows are exogenous. Arrows that depart from traits and lead to indicators are factor loadings, known from factor analysis. They form part of the measurement model.

Specification of organizational structure research model

After this crash course in SEM, let me introduce the first detailed research model which will be tested later. The path diagram shown in figure 4-2 depicts the model in structural equation format. I will discuss its two constituent parts: (a) the structural model, and (b) the measurement model.

Structural model. I used the structural model to test whether emphasis on traditional Chinese cultural values (independent variable) influences web-based Chinese management (dependent variable set). In this section, I will analyze the first two of the four distinctive characteristics of private Chinese management, bureaucracy and centralization. Bureaucracy subsumes two dimensions: (a) "generic" formalization,[1] including written documents that formalize roles, specialized roles, and standardized control systems, and (b) integration through structural liaison devices, such as committees and departmental meetings, and processual liaison, such as using a master plan and interdepartmental bargaining. Centralization describes the concentration of decision–making power in an organization. The most important exogenous factor, from my point of view, is emphasis on selected characteristics of Chinese culture (called: "Chinese culture" in figure 4-2). It comprises respect for seniority and family loyalty, personal relations, and collective orientation. In private enterprises, it influences structural choices directly (regression paths from Chinese culture to formalization, centralization, and integration), and indirectly through its impact on company size, which in turn affects structure (regression paths from Chinese culture to size, and then from size to formalization, centralization, and integration).

To neutralize spurious and intervening relations,"[2] and thus to isolate the impact of culture, I incorporated other important influencing factors of structure as control variables. They include the traditional contingency variables size, technology, uncertainty, and environmental constraints, and the nontraditional factor CEO need for achievement. Size refers to the number of employees in the company (see appendix D, item 2.4). Technology is the means or processes that the organization uses to transform inputs into outputs. I focused on mass-production technology, since in previous research it had the strongest impact on structure (see appendix D, item 15.4). Environmental uncertainty is the level and unpredictability of change in demand, customer tastes, competitive behavior, technology, product obsolescence, and sources of supply (see appendix D, section 19.1). Constraints are factors in an organization's task environment that limit its access to resources (see appendix D, section 19.2). CEO need for achievement (McClelland 1961; McClelland et al. 1953) is the CEO's degree of striving to meet standards of excellence, to accomplish difficult tasks, and to achieve success (see appendix D, section 10).

Measurement model. The exogenous and endogenous unobserved traits, drawn in ellipses, are measured by indicators, drawn in rectangulars, which were observed in the survey. Each indicator is linked to an error term that models the cumulative effects that excluded variables and purely random measurement error exert on the observed variables. It is comparable to the error term in regression. In the path diagram, these errors are numbered e1–e20. In addition, each endogenous construct is linked to a unique error variance (e21–e23). Following standard procedures, the path from the construct to the indicator that supposedly best measures the latent construct, arranged as the first indicator in the path diagram, was constrained to unity. This approach helps to scale the other indicators. Best practice in structural equation modeling entails including more than one indicator per construct. This avoids framing complex constructs too narrowly and averages out the specificity of individual indicators. It thus reduces unique error and measurement error. Therefore, when possible, I split aggregate scales consisting of several items into several indicators. I applied this procedure to the following variables: need for achievement (three indicators, nach_1, nach_2, nach_3), uncertainty (two indicators, uncert_1, uncert_2), constraints (three indicators, constr_1, constr_2, constr_3), and centralization (three indicators, cent_1, cent_2, cent_3).

Owing to the nature of the scales, the constructs of size and technology had only one indicator, the natural logarithm to base 10 of the number of employees (lg10size) and the mass-technology scale (mstech). The factors respect (respect), collective orientation (collect) and personal relations (guanxi) are subdimensions of a second-order factor, emphasis on selected characteristics of Chinese culture. Likewise, the role formalization (formal), specialization (spec), and control (control), scales are indicators of one generic formalization trait. Following D. Miller and Droege's (1986, p. 547) approach, the integration construct also subsumes two different subscales, structural liaison devices (liastruc) and process liaison (liasdmg).

Having outlined the basic structure of the first detailed research model, I will now present the findings from the analysis of factors influencing the distinctive structural arrangements of Chinese private enterprises, which differ from state enterprises. It seems worthwhile to briefly outline the game plan for analyzing the results (see figure 4–1). I first will test the adequacy of the basic model outlined above, then compare general differences between the private and state enterprise subgroups. I will subsequently zoom in on specific subgroup differences in the direct and indirect impact of culture and then analyze the sign of these individual paths in a comparison between private and state enterprises. In the last part, in order to test the two hypotheses, the strength of association between culture and structure will be analyzed for the private enterprise subgroup. My new "funneling" technique, which moves from the general to the specific, enables the researcher to reject hypotheses at the earliest stage possible and thus avoids unnecessary analyses. For example, if at the total sample level all structural coefficients are equal across both subgroups, it will not be necessary to analyze the significance of the path from culture to size for private firms only.

Findings for basic unconstrained organizational structure model

Let me first outline the findings for a basic model that does not constrain any parameters. This and all constrained models are described in table 4-1. Its basic path structure is illustrated in figure 4-2. It is called a "stacked model" because it includes two subgroups, private and state enterprises. The two subgroups emerged from splitting the sample into halves according to a company's value on the "private ownership" dummy variable derived from item 2.7 in appendix D. The initial step in the analysis of structural equation models is to ascertain whether the distribution of the observed variables corresponds to stipulated re-

Table 4-1 Description of nested subgroup comparisons in organizational structure stacked model

Model name	Description
Model Ia	Stacked model with unconstrained regression path from emphasis on Chinese culture to size
Model Ib	Stacked model with path coefficient between Chinese culture and size fixed to zero
Model Ic	Stacked model with equality constraints for *all* structural parameters between private and state enterprise subgroups
Model Id	Stacked model with equality constraint for regression path from Chinese culture to *formalization* for private and state enterprise subgroups
Model Ie	Stacked model with equality constraint for regression path from Chinese culture to *centralization* for private and state enterprise subgroups
Model If	Stacked model with equality constraint for regression path from Chinese culture to *integration* for private and state enterprise subgroups
Model Ig	Stacked model with equality constraint for regression path from Chinese culture to size for private and state enterprise subgroups

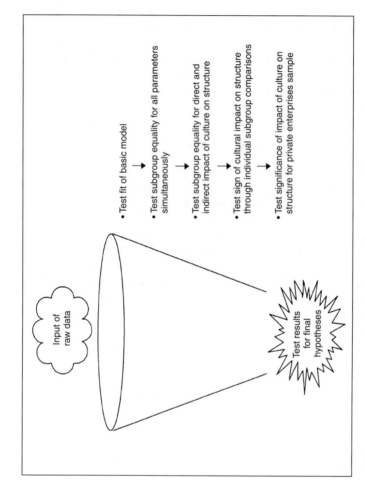

Figure 4-1 Funneling technique used for testing research hypotheses

Input of raw data

- Test fit of basic model
- Test subgroup equality for all parameters simultaneously
- Test subgroup equality for direct and indirect impact of culture on structure
- Test sign of cultural impact on structure through individual subgroup comparisons
- Test significance of impact of culture on structure for private enterprises sample

Test results for final hypotheses

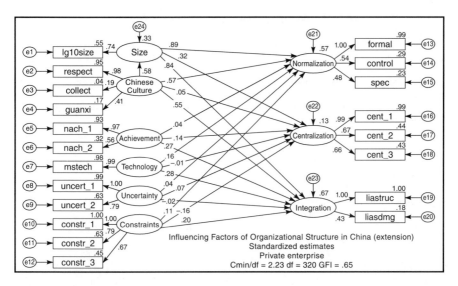

Figure 4-2 Influencing factors of organizational structure in private enterprises ML (standardized estimates)

quirements. Results revealed no problems from a lack of multivariate normal distribution. More statistical details for all analyses are available from the author. Next, the empirical model has to be assessed, to see how well the scales measured the latent constructs. The results confirmed the unidimensionality of measures, convergent and discriminant validity, and reliability.

The theoretical model tests the substantial hypotheses. I first assessed the overall fit of the basic model structure imposed on the raw data. The results for this and all subsequent models are reported in table 4-2. This base model (Ia) shows an acceptable global (absolute) fit as measured by the chi-square statistic, adjusted for the degrees of freedom ($\chi^2/df=2.23$, $df=320$), and other fit indices (GFI = .65, IFI = .62). It meets all recommended conservative cutoff points (see Carmines and McIver 1981, p. 80). This model represented a significantly better fit to the data than another model (Ib) that omitted the regression path between emphasis on Chinese culture and size ($\Delta\chi^2 = 12.51$, $df=2$, $p<.01$).[3]

After establishing the basic adequacy of the research model, I examined subgroup differences between private and state enterprises, for all regression paths together, and the direct and indirect impact of culture on structure in particular. Without significant differences between the two groups, the two research hypotheses could be rejected at this stage. Otherwise, the next analytical step would need to ascertain whether in the private enterprise subgroup the impact of culture moved in the hypothesized direction and was statistically significant.

Table 4-2 Fit indices for organizational structure stacked model nested comparisons

	χ^2/df	df	GFI	AGFI	IFI	$\Delta\chi^{2'}$	p	df
Saturated model (Covariance structure)	.00	0	1.00	n/a	1.00	n/a	n/a	n/a
Model Ia (Base model w/o constraints)	2.23	320	.65	.53	.62	n/a	n/a	n/a
Model Ib (Model w/zero culture→ size path)	2.25	322	.64	.53	.61	12.51**	.00	2
Model Ic (Model w/all equality)	2.20	338	.64	.56	.60	29.79*	.04	18
Model Id (Model w/culture→ formalization path equality)	2.24	321	.65	.54	.61	5.44*	.02	1
Model Ie (Model w/culture→ centralization path equality)	2.22	321	.65	.54	.62	.03	.86	1
Model If (Model w/culture→ integration path equality)	2.23	321	.65	.54	.62	4.06*	.04	1
Model Ig (Model w/culture→size path equality)	2.25	321	.64	.53	.61	8.62**	.01	1
Null model (Independence model)	3.55	380	.44	.38	.00	n/a	n/a	n/a

N = 124.
χ^2 = chi square; $\Delta\chi^2$ = chi square difference; df = degrees of freedom; p = significance level.
*$p < .05$; **$p < .01$; ***$p < .001$.
*Baseline comparison is model Ia.
GFI = Goodness of fit index.
AGFI = Goodness of fit index, adjusted for degrees of freedom.
IFI = Incremental fit index.

General subgroup difference between private and state enterprises in organizational structure model

I first compared *all* regression weights between private and state enterprises. SEM facilitates such a comparison of statistical relations between two data sets, which are *stacked* in one model. The researcher first specifies a general baseline model, then adds various nested models. Each nested model is a constrained version of the baseline model, since it confines all or selected regression paths to be equal for the two subgroups. Next, this nested model is compared with the unconstrained model. If the more constrained model results in a worse fit for the data than the base model, as shown by a significant chi-square difference, it has to be rejected. This means that the subgroups differ with respect to all equality-constrained regression path(s). Significant parameters are marked by one or more "*" signs in the tables, depending on the significance.

The general baseline model that allowed parameters to vary freely within the two subgroups (model Ia) was compared to a nested model that constrained all structural parameters to equality for both subgroups (model Ic; see table 4-1). The significant chi-square statistic for model Ic ($\Delta\chi^2=29.79$, $df=18$, $p<.05$; see table 4-2) suggested that the structural path coefficients for private enterprises deviated significantly from those of their state counterparts.

Subgroup difference related to direct and indirect
impact of culture in organizational structure model

In light of these findings, it was necessary to scrutinize the pivotal regression paths: the direct and indirect impact of emphasis on culture on structure. In regard to the direct path, models Ic–e (see table 4–1) constrained the paths from emphasis on culture to each dimension of structure to equality. The results (see table 4-2) revealed significant subgroup differences for the paths from emphasis on culture to formalization ($\Delta\chi^2=5.44$, $df=1$, $p<.05$; see model Id) and to integration ($\Delta\chi^2=4.06$, $df=1$, $p<.05$; see model If).

In regard to the indirect path, I examined whether private enterprises were distinctive (when compared to state enterprises) in their culturally determined choice of size. Model Ig constrained the path from emphasis on culture to size to equality. The comparison of model Ig to the base model (Ia) showed that the path coefficient between culture and size significantly differed between the two subgroups ($\Delta\chi^2=8.62$, $df=1$, $p<.01$; see table 4-2).

Individual structural subgroup comparisons

These results showed that private enterprises differed significantly from their state counterparts with respect to the direct and indirect impact of culture on structure. Next, it was necessary to assess the sign and significance of this impact for the private enterprise subgroup, thus testing the structure-related part of the sub-hypotheses (2.1 and 2.2). I first computed the individual path coefficients for the private enterprises and, to investigate subgroup differences, juxtaposed them with the results for the state enterprises. Table 4-3 reports the results for the stacked model (Ia). Since it did not constrain the parameters, we could see the true absolute differences. All coefficients for private enterprises are graphically illustrated in the path diagram (see figure 4-2).

Nested model tests for private subgroup in
organizational structure model

To find out which factors were significant, I performed an additional set of nested model comparisons for the private sample only, using the unstacked version of model Ia (called: model I) as a baseline. The results of this analysis are reported in table 4-4.

Let me discuss the findings from these analyses.

Table 4-3 Maximum likelihood standardized path coefficients (gamma) for baseline organizational structure model (Ia)

Independent variable	Private	State
Size		
Formalization	.89***	.19
Centralization	−.32	−.37**
Integration	.84***	.41**
Technology		
Formalization	.16	.26*
Centralization	−.01	.14
Integration	.28**	.05
Uncertainty		
Formalization	−.04	.05
Centralization	.07	−.21
Integration	−.03	.13
Constraints		
Formalization	.11	−.04
Centralization	−.16	−.02
Integration	.20*	−.10
Achievement need		
Formalization	.04	.05
Centralization	.14	−.02
Integration	−.27*	−.06
Chinese culture		
Formalization	.57**	.03
Centralization	−.05	−.12
Integration	.55**	.13
Chinese culture→Size	−.58***	.18

N = 124.
*$p<.05$ (C.R. > 1.98); **p <.01 (C.R. > 2.62); ***p < .001 (C.R.>3.38).
All critical ratios (C.R.) are based on unstandardized coefficients.
→ = Regression path (γ).

Direct impact of cultural emphasis. The findings on organizational structure support sub-hypothesis 2.1. Holding other factors constant, model VIa shows that, emphasis on traditional Chinese cultural values significantly influences the distinctive structural choices of private Chinese enterprises ($\Delta\chi^2=10.02$, $df=3$, $p<.05$). In contrast, as shown in table 4-3, it did not

Table 4-4 Nested comparisons for private subgroup in unstacked organizational structure model

	χ^2/df	df	$\Delta\chi^{2*}$	p	df
Saturated model (Covariance structure)	0.00	0	n/a	n/a	n/a
Model I (Baseline structural model)	2.53	160	n/a	n/a	n/a
Model II (Structural model w/o size)	2.56	163	11.83**	.01	3
Model III (Structural model w/o uncertainty)	2.49	163	.27	.97	3
Model IV (Structural model w/o achievement)	2.52	163	6.16	.10	3
Model V (Structural model w/o constraints)	2.51	163	3.77	.29	3
Model VIa (Structural model w/o culture)	2.55	163	10.02*	.02	3
Model VIb (Structural model w/o culture→formali- zation path)	2.56	161	6.61**	.01	1
Model VIc (Structural model w/o culture→centrali- zation path)	2.52	161	.08	.78	1
Model VId (Structural Model w/o culture→integra- tion path)	2.56	161	7.50**	.01	1
Model VII (Structural model w/o culture→size path)	2.58	161	10.70***	.00	1
Null model (Independence model)	4.04	190	n/a	n/a	n/a

N=61 (private enterprise sample).
*$p < .05$; **$p < .01$; ***$p < .001$.
*Baseline comparison is Model I.

significantly affect the structure of state enterprises. This quantitative analysis has advantages over other qualitative conjectures. Apart from demonstrating the impact of culture in absolute terms, I can also comment on its ranking compared to other influencing factors. The size of individual path coefficients and the significance of these contingencies show that culture is the second most important direct influencing factor of structure after size (which will later be shown also to be influenced by culture).

In regard to the sign of individual coefficients, as hypothesized, emphasis on Chinese cultural values was significantly *positively* associated with integration (γ=.55, p<.01; $\Delta\chi^2$=7.50, $df = 1$, p<.01; see table 4-3). The nested model subgroup comparison using stacked model If (see table 4-2) showed that this path also differed significantly from state enterprises ($\Delta\chi^2$=4.06, df=1, p<.05). Contrary to the original conjecture, emphasis on traditional Chinese values was significantly *positively* associated with for- malization (γ=.57, p<.01; $\Delta\chi^2$=6.61, df=1, p<.01, see table 4-3). This sug- gests that the hierarchy-related aspects of traditional Chinese values, such as respect for seniority, may call for more formalized structures. As shown in the nested stacked model subgroup comparison (model Id in table 4- 2), this path also proved distinctive when compared to state enterprises ($\Delta\chi^2$=5.44, df=1, p<.05). Emphasis on culture did not significantly affect centralization (γ=−.05, p>.05, $\Delta\chi^2$=.08, df=1, p>.05; see table 4-3). The hard empirical evidence substantiates anecdotes from the literature on the overseas Chinese. It also demonstrates that the distinctive structural char- acteristics of the web-based Chinese management model readopted in mainland Chinese private enterprises, are attributable to their emphasis on traditional Chinese culture.

Indirect impact of cultural emphasis. The empirical findings also supported sub-hypothesis 2.2. As reported in table 4-3, there is a significant negative causal relation between emphasis on Chinese culture and company size in private enterprises ($\gamma=-.58$, $p<.001$). A nested comparison for the private enterprise sample confirmed the indirect impact of culture (see model VII in table 4-4). A nested model that constrained the path from culture to size to zero had to be rejected at conventional significance levels ($\Delta\chi^2=10.70$, $df=1$, $p<.001$). In contrast, in state enterprises, the association between emphasis on culture and size was positive and statistically insignificant ($\gamma=.18$, $p<.05$). As mentioned above, the earliest stacked model comparison testing for subgroup equality with respect to the culture-size path (model Ig in table 4-2) confirmed the significant difference between private and state enterprises ($\Delta\chi^2=8.62$, $df=1$, $p<.01$). A nested comparison for the private sample (see table 4-4) showed that company size, in turn, significantly influences structure ($\Delta\chi^2=11.83$, $df=3$, $p<.01$, see table 4-4).

The findings thus rationalize earlier observations in the literature on the overseas Chinese. They explain why in countries that grant the Chinese economic freedom, most firms in the private sector are both family-owned and very small. In order to keep strong family ties, private entrepreneurs prefer to proliferate into networks instead of increasing company size. They thus can both give responsibility to family members who want to head spin-offs and maintain close personal relationships within the family.

To conclude, the structural dimensions of the distinctive private Chinese management model are attributable to the emphasis that Chinese private enterprises place on traditional, often family-oriented values. State enterprises lack such strong and consequential familism. Chinese family values directly and indirectly affect organizational structure in private enterprises. Let me define "potency" as a combination of high mean levels for a contextual factor and the strength of association between this factor and other contextual or structural properties. Using this definition, emphasis on Chinese cultural characteristics turned out to be very potent in private firms in three ways. First, the mean level of emphasis on family values is high (compared to state enterprises). Second, emphasis on culture exerts a strong direct influence on structure in private firms. Third, as an indirect structural effect, culture strongly influences the choice of mean level for the contextual factor "size" in private firms, which in turn significantly affects organizational structure.[4] More generally, these findings disconfirmed the notion of a monolithic Chinese management style, which exists independently of any influencing factors.

Influencing factors of management practices in China

I will now complete the analysis of the second research question related to the influencing factors of the distinctive web-based Chinese model by focusing on management practices. Let me first outline the basic structure of the research model to be tested.

Specification of management practices research model

The basic management model is presented as a structural equation path diagram in figure 4-4. The model formalizes the hypothesis that a set of exogenous contextual traits significantly influences the various managerial practices of Chinese companies. The path diagram shows the structural and empirical model.

Structural model. Having examined the influencing factors of bureaucracy and centralization, in this model, I will focus on the remaining two managerial dimensions of WCM, testing whether strong entrepreneurship and extensive interorganizational enterprise networks are monolithic features or whether they are attributable to the emphasis on cultural values in private firms. The endogenous variables for Chinese entrepreneurship included proactive strategy, participative leadership, adaptive decision making, and horizontal communication (another angle on the communication theme). I operationalized interorganizational networks as subcontracting relationships with other enterprises. Except for technology, I included the same contextual constructs as in the organizational structure model: size, uncertainty, constraints, CEO need for achievement, and emphasis on selected characteristics of Chinese culture. Based on the literature, I concluded that technology does not significantly influence general management practices and therefore did not need to control it. Again, I hypothesized that culture directly and indirectly (via its impact on organizational size) influences managerial choices in private firms. I will outline the operational definitions and indicators for the unobserved traits below.

Empirical model. The exogenous and endogenous traits were measured by different indicators. Proactive strategy is the degree to which companies actively pursue new opportunities (indicator: opport, see appendix D, item 4.1 i) and attempt to be the first to introduce new products to the market (newprod, appendix D, item 4.1 j). Indicators for participative leadership style included the degree to which top levels in the firm use democratic decision making for issues related to products (prodpart), finance (finpart), and strategy (strapart) (appendix D, items 5.1 a–c). Adaptive decision making (adapt, appendix D, item 6.1) adjusts incrementally to problems. Decisions are generally compromises between the conflicting demands of various stakeholders. They are made locally more often than centrally, and the primary concern is stability and steady growth. Horizontal communication is the frequency of departmental meetings, which allow members of the same department to engage in joint decision making (horcom, appendix D, item 7.2). Subcontracting was operationalized as the degree to which a company outsources various functions in the value chain (appendix D, item 18.4 a–k). I randomly split the items (every kth item) into three indicators (subcon_1, subcon_2, and subcon_3) to assess scale measurement properties. An error term modeled the effect of excluded variables and random measurement error of each indicator (e1–e21). Each endogenous construct had a unique error variance term (e22–e26). I constrained the path from the construct to the indicator that supposedly best measured the latent construct to unity.

Having specified the second detailed research model that operationalizes factors influencing the managerial practices of Chinese private and state enterprises, I will once again sketch the strategy for testing the two sub-hypotheses and then outline the findings. To answer the research question, I used the same approach as for the previous structural model. I moved in successive steps along a decision tree, which allowed me to reject hypotheses at the earliest stage possible. The tree is illustrated in figure 4-3.

Findings for basic unconstrained management practices model

Let me first present and discuss the findings for the basic unconstrained model. Table 4-5 describes this stacked model and all nested subgroup comparisons. Its path structure is illustrated in figure 4-4. The maximum likelihood method proved very robust against violations of the multivariate normality assumption. The measurement model supported the unidimensionality, convergent and discriminant validity, and reliability of the measures. Table 4-6 presents the findings for the stacked model and nested comparisons. The base stacked model (Ia) fitted the data reasonably well as confirmed by the chi-square statistic adjusted for degrees of freedom (χ^2/df=1.91, df=346) and other fit indices (GFI = .69, IFI = .69). This model fitted the data significantly better than did another research model (Ib) that omitted the regression path from emphasis on Chinese culture to size ($\Delta\chi^2$=10.52, df=2, p<.01).

Having confirmed its global fit, I could use the research model to analyze subgroup differences between private and state enterprises, first in regard to all regression paths at once and then to the direct and indirect impact of culture on management. To test for between-group equivalence, I computed chi-square difference tests and other fit indices for nested comparisons within the stacked model that subsumed the two subgroups.

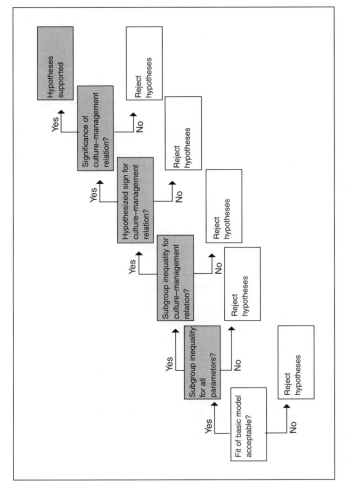

Figure 4-3 Decision tree for testing of management-related sub-hypotheses

127

Table 4-5 Description of nested subgroup comparisons in management practices stacked model

Model name	Description
Model Ia	Stacked model with unconstrained regression path from emphasis on Chinese culture to size
Model Ib	Stacked model with path coefficient between Chinese culture and size fixed at zero
Model Ic	Stacked model with equality constraints for *all* structural parameters between private and state enterprise subgroups
Model Id	Stacked model with equality constraint for regression path from Chinese culture to *proactiveness* for private and state enterprise subgroups
Model Ie	Stacked model with equality constraint for regression path from Chinese culture to *participation* for private and state enterprise subgroups
Model If	Stacked model with equality constraint for regression path from Chinese culture to *adaptation* for private and state enterprise subgroups
Model Ig	Stacked model with equality constraint for regression path from Chinese culture to *communication* for private and state enterprise subgroups
Model Ih	Stacked model with equality constraint for regression path from Chinese culture to *subcontracting* for private and state enterprise subgroups
Model Ii	Stacked model with equality constraint for regression path from Chinese culture to size for private and state enterprise subgroups

General subgroup differences between private and state enterprises in management practices model

As a first decisive test, I compared *all* regression weights between the two types of companies in a nested subgroup comparison. According to the decision tree, I could reject the research hypotheses at this early stage, should I fail to detect significant differences at this level of analysis. To find out, I compared the general baseline model that allowed the parameters to vary freely within the two subgroups (model Ia) to a nested model that constrained all structural parameters to be equal in both subgroups (model Ic, see table 4-5). The significant chi-square statistic for model Ic ($\Delta\chi^2$ =42.24,df=25, p<.05; see table 4-6) suggested that in the stacked model, the structural path coefficients for private enterprises differed significantly from those of state enterprises.

Subgroup difference related to direct and indirect impact of culture in management practices model

In view of these findings, I had to continue by performing a set of nested comparisons within the stacked model to see whether private enterprises were distinctive (when compared to state enterprises) in regard to the relationship between culture and managerial choices, and in their culturally determined choice of small size. The comparison centered on the direct and indirect path from emphasis on culture to management, which plays a pivotal role in this book. As for the direct path, models Ic–h (see

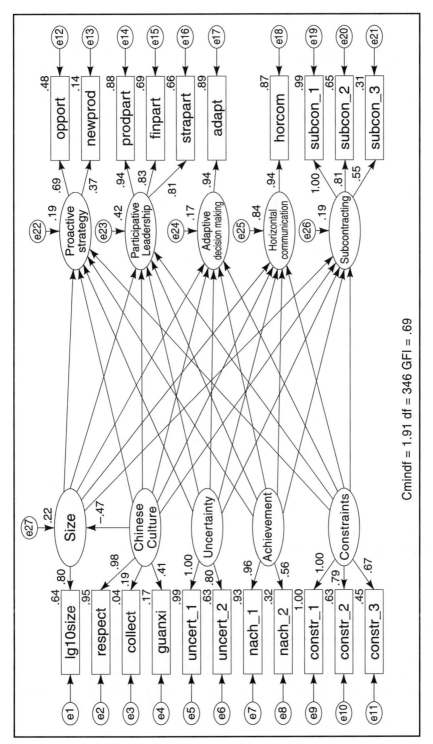

Figure 4-4 Influencing factors of management practices in Chinese private enterprises (standardized ML estimates)

Cmindf = 1.91 df = 346 GFI = .69

Table 4-6 Fit indices for management practices stacked model nested comparisons

	χ^2/df	df	GFI	AGFI	IFI	$\Delta\chi^2$†	p	df
Saturated model (Covariance structure)	.00	0	1.00	n/a	1.00	n/a	n/a	n/a
Model Ia (Base model w/o constraints)	1.91	346	.69	.59	.69	n/a	n/a	n/a
Model Ib (Model w/zero culture→size path)	1.93	348	.69	.58	.68	10.52**	.01	2
Model Ic (Model w/all equality)	1.89	371	.68	.60	.67	42.24*	.02	25
Model Id (Model w/culture→proactiveness equality)	1.90	347	.69	.59	.69	.94	.33	1
Model Ie (Model w/culture→participation equality)	1.91	347	.69	.59	.69	1.32	.25	1
Model If (Model w/culture→adaptation equality)	1.90	347	.69	.59	.69	.42	.52	1
Model Ig (Model w/culture→communication equality)	1.92	347	.69	.59	.69	7.89**	.01	1
Model Ih (Model w/culture→subcontracting equality)	1.90	347	.69	.59	.69	.05	.82	1
Model Ii (Model w/culture→size path equality)	1.92	347	.69	.58	.69	7.87**	.01	1
Null model (Independence model)	3.25	420	.49	.44	.00	n/a	n/a	n/a

N = 124.
*p < .05; **p < .01.
†Baseline comparison is model Ia.
GFI = Goodness of fit index.
AGFI = Goodness of fit index, adjusted for degrees of freedom.
IFI = Incremental fit index.

table 4-5) constrained the coefficients from emphasis on culture to each dimension of management to subgroup equality. The results (see table 4-6) revealed significant subgroup differences for the path from emphasis on culture to horizontal communication ($\Delta\chi^2$=7.89, df=1, p<.01; see model Ig).

I then analyzed subgroup differences for the indirect path from culture to management via the intervening variable organizational size. Model Ii specified that emphasis on traditional Chinese cultural values influences size in the same way in both types of companies. The nested model comparison showed that the path coefficient between culture and size differed significantly between the two subgroups ($\Delta\chi^2$=7.87, df = 1, p=.005; see model Ii).

Individual managerial subgroup comparisons

The results showed that private enterprises differed significantly from their state counterparts with respect to the direct and indirect impact of culture on management. To test the management-related part of the two sub-hypotheses 2.1 and 2.2, I needed to assess the sign and significance of this relationship in the private enterprise subgroup. Therefore, I computed the individual path coefficients for private enterprises and, to an-

Table 4-7 Maximum likelihood standardized path coefficients (gamma) for baseline management practices model (Ia)

Independent variable	Private	State
Size		
Proactive strategy	.42	−.14
Participative leadership	.58***	.37**
Adaptive decision making	.29	−.09
Horizontal communication	.97***	.15
Subcontracting	−.20	−.32*
Uncertainty		
Proactive strategy	.23	.15
Participative leadership	.20	.01
Adaptive decision making	.08	.06
Horizontal communication	−.08	−.03
Subcontracting	.24*	.16
Constraints		
Proactive strategy	−.05	.27
Participative leadership	.16	.25*
Adaptive decision making	.05	.07
Horizontal communication	.27**	.02
Subcontracting	.04	−.04
Achievement need		
Proactive strategy	−.01	.10
Participative leadership	−.30*	.12
Adaptive decision making	−.28*	−.03
Horizontal communication	−.19	.31*
Subcontracting	−.28*	.06
Chinese culture		
Proactive strategy	.22	−.06
Participative leadership	.19	−.03
Adaptive decision making	.26	.20
Horizontal communication	.43**	−.13
Subcontracting	.02	.10
Chinese culture→size	−.47**	.18

N = 124.
*$p < .05$ (C.R. > 1.98); **$p < .01$ (C.R. > 2.62); ***$p < .001$ (C.R. > 3.38).
All critical ratios (C.R.) are based on unstandardized coefficients.
→ = Regression path (γ).

alyze individual subgroup differences, juxtaposed them with the regression coefficients of state enterprises. Table 4-7 reports the results for the unconstrained stacked model (Ia), which revealed the absolute subgroup differences. The path diagram illustrates all coefficients for private enterprises (see figure 4-4).

Nested model tests for private subgroup in management practices model

To find out which factors were significant, I performed an additional set of nested model comparisons for the private sample only, using the unstacked version of model Ia (called: model I) as a baseline. The results of this analysis are reported in table 4-8.

Direct impact of cultural emphasis. The findings supported subhypothesis 2.1. Holding other factors constant, model VIa (see table 4-8) showed that emphasis on traditional Chinese cultural values influenced the managerial choices of private Chinese enterprises ($\Delta\chi^2=9.94$, $df=5$, $p=.077$). It was significant at the slightly less conservative level of $p<.10$ that some researchers use. In contrast, as shown in table 4-7, the path coefficients of state enterprises were not significant at any conventional

Table 4-8 Nested comparisons for private subgroup in unstacked management practices model

	χ^2/df	df	$\Delta\chi^2$†	p	df
Saturated model (Covariance structure)	0.00	0	n/a	n/a	n/a
Model I (Baseline structural model)	2.08	173	n/a	n/a	n/a
Model II (Structural model w/o size)	2.23	178	36.75***	.00	5
Model III (Structural model w/o uncertainty)	2.07	178	7.65	.18	5
Model IV (Structural model w/o constraints)	2.06	178	6.57	.26	5
Model V (Structural model w/o achievement)	2.09	178	12.19*	.03	5
Model VIa (Structural model w/o culture)	2.08	178	9.94	.08	5
Model VIb (Structural model w/o culture→ proactiveness)	2.08	174	.94	.33	1
Model VIc (Structural model w/o culture→ participation)	2.08	174	1.50	.22	1
Model VId (Structural model w/o culture→ adaptation)	2.08	174	2.34	.13	1
Model VIe (Structural model w/o culture→ communication)	2.12	174	7.73**	.01	1
Model VIf (Structural model w/o culture→ subcontracting)	2.07	174	.02	.88	1
Model VII (Structural model w/o culture→size path)	2.12	174	8.70**	.00	1
Null model (Independence model)	3.77	210	n/a	n/a	n/a

N = 61 (private enterprises sample).
*$p < .05$; **$p < .01$; ***$p < .001$.
†Baseline comparison is model I.

level. To draw more detailed conclusions on the significance of emphasis on Chinese culture, I examined individual path coefficients in private enterprises. Contrary to the original conjecture, emphasis on traditional Chinese values was significantly *positively* associated with horizontal communication ($\gamma=.43$, $p<.01$; see table 4-7). But most important, the nested model comparison for the private sample (model VIe in table 4-8) showed that this factor was significant at the more conservative $p<.01$ level ($\Delta\chi^2=7.73$, $df=1$, $p=.005$). The detailed comparison thus clarified the results from the aggregate nested model comparison (model VIa in table 4-8). Nested subgroup comparisons within the stacked model (model 1g in table 4-6) revealed that this path from culture to communication also differed significantly from that of the state enterprise subgroup ($\Delta\chi^2=7.89$, $df=1$, $p=.005$).

Family connections possibly explain the positive association between emphasis on culture and horizontal communication. The owner-manager may encourage or at least tolerate communication between people in the same department, if they are members of his family. He thus caters to the collective orientation and communication needs of his kins, and shows benevolence in general. However, he still makes the final decisions. As in the case of organizational structure, culture turned out to be the second most important direct influencing factor on management practices in private enterprises after size (which, as will be shown below, also is influenced by culture). This holds true for both the size of individual path coefficients and their significance in nested model comparisons.

Indirect impact of cultural emphasis. The empirical evidence supported sub-hypothesis 2.2, suggesting a causal relationship between emphasis on Chinese cultural values and the size of private enterprises. As reported in table 4-7, emphasis on Chinese culture had a significant negative relation with size ($\gamma=-.47$, $p<.01$). A nested comparison for the private enterprise sample (see table 4-8) confirmed these findings. A nested model that fixed the path from culture to size at zero had to be rejected at conventional significance levels ($\Delta\chi^2=8.70$, $df=1$, $p=.003$). In contrast, the association between emphasis on culture and size turned out to be positive and statistically insignificant in state enterprises ($\gamma=.18$, $p>.05$; see table 4-7). This subgroup difference between private and state enterprises with respect to the path from culture to size also proved significant within the stacked model ($\Delta\chi^2=7.87$, $df=1$, $p=.005$; see model Ii in table 4–6). A nested comparison for the private enterprise sample (see model II in table 4-8) showed that company size in turn significantly affects management practices in private enterprises ($\Delta\chi^2=36.75$, $df=5$, $p<.001$).

To conclude, the empirical findings showed that the distinctive managerial characteristics of the new private Chinese model and their readoption in mainland China result from traditional, family-oriented values. Those did not feature prominently in state enterprises. As in the case of organizational structure, Chinese family values influence management practices in private enterprises both directly and indirectly. First, the mean level of emphasis on family values is relatively high (compared to state enterprises). Second, culture significantly affects the contextual factor organizational size. Because of the significance of size as an endogenous contextual factor, culture thus influences managerial practices indirectly. Third, culture also directly influences managerial dimensions.

Summary and conclusions

In this chapter, I used structural equation modeling to analyze the relationships between several contextual factors and organizational properties. I intended to answer the second research question by testing whether the organizational choices, synthesized in the web-based Chinese management model, are rooted in the emphasis that private enterprises place on traditional Chinese culture. If such were the case, WCM would have proved to be distinctive—a cultural artifact produced by private, family enterprises in mainland China that readopted certain organizational practices from overseas Chinese businesses. I will briefly summarize the main findings related to this theme.

Organizational structure

The results of nested subgroup comparisons within the context of a stacked model showed that the two distinctive structural choices of private enterprises, centralization and informality, can be traced back to the emphasis on traditional cultural values in private enterprises. Emphasis on Chinese culture, especially in the form of familism, had a potent impact on structure in three ways: (1) through the higher mean level of the contextual factor culture; (2) through a direct significant association with structure; (3) through an indirect effect in terms of a significant association with company size, which in turn was significantly associated with organizational structure.

Management practices

The two distinctive managerial aspects of the Chinese private model, entrepreneurship and interorganizational networking, also were attributable to the potent, direct and indirect impact of emphasis on traditional cultural values in private firms.

In chapter 5, I will present the research findings related to the effectiveness of Chinese companies, and present a case study that enriches the results from the quantitative survey.

5 Organizational Effectiveness of Chinese Companies

In this last findings chapter, I endeavor to answer the third research question: "Is the family-based Chinese model positively associated with organizational effectiveness?" To determine whether private Chinese management is an art, I will analyze whether Chinese management based on private family ownership leads to high performance. Some anecdotes alleged that private ownership is highly effective, but few empirical studies systematically tested such conjectures. Further, factors influencing performance may vary across regions. Such geographical variations have not been tested extensively either. Localities in China differ dramatically in terms of growth rates, social behavior, and cultural norms. In this chapter, I will analyze differences in key success factors between the north and the south of China. The findings not only will serve as fact base for normative recommendations relating to the new organizational model in the family-based private enterprises (chapter 6), but also will enable me to outline success strategies for the Chinese market in general (chapter 7).

This chapter is organized in two sections. In the first section, after briefly discussing the concept of key success factors, I will present the structural equation model used to analyze the effect of private family-based ownership and other factors on performance. This analysis includes regional comparisons between the north and the south of China. In the second section, I will report more detailed, quantitative and qualitative findings on organizational effectiveness from one case study, which will enrich the statistical results from the survey.

Key success factors revisited

Organizational researchers for a long time have tried to identify key drivers of company success. Key success factors (KSF) are the limited number of areas in which satisfactory results ensure a company's successful competitive performance. In my view, those include both external and internal parameters. Core competencies and other valuable resources, therefore, also count as key success factors. The KSF concept implies that a few levers under managerial control create a disproportionately large impact on company success. A focused approach that uses leverage contrasts with the attempt to perform well on all management fronts. After identifying key success factors for a market or an industry, a company can monitor its effectiveness by analyzing how well it performs on each of these factors, and take corrective action if necessary. This form of strategic control based on KSF scores is more informative than pursuing sales or profit figures or other objectives that might be lower than industry standards or the performance of competitors. Perhaps owing to the difficulties of modeling performance (see Goodman, Atkin, and Schoorman 1983; Quinn and Rohrbaugh 1983; p. 374), empirical work on the correlates of organizational effectiveness is sparse (Judge 1994; p. 1). Those few researchers who dealt with the issue usually singled out individual factors influencing performance (instead of analyzing a large number of key success factors), and failed to analyze regional variations.

Specification of organizational effectiveness model

Figure 5–1 illustrates the research model as a structural equation path diagram. Let me delineate the structural and measurement model, which was tested with the total sample.

Structural model

I used the structural model to test the hypothesis that several exogenous variables explain organizational effectiveness, the endogenous variable. For the purpose of analysis, the most important exogenous variable is family-based ownership. To isolate its effect and assess its relative importance, I added other organizational and contextual factors as controls. The organizational influencing factors, under executive control, include organizational structure that fits the task environment (called appropriate structure), proactive and price-cutting strategy, professional management (Khandwalla 1977), comprised of participative leadership and planning-based decision making, and subcontracting, which enables concentration on core competencies. Contextual factors include the size and age of the company, environmental constraints, and government support in the form of favorable regulations. I did not model industry as an influencing factor. The effectiveness construct held this factor constant, because it measured *intra*industry long-term performance.

The model possibly did not capture *all* factors influencing effectiveness. If so, a portion of explainable variance will remain unexplained. To test confounding effects, the basic model did not specify any co-

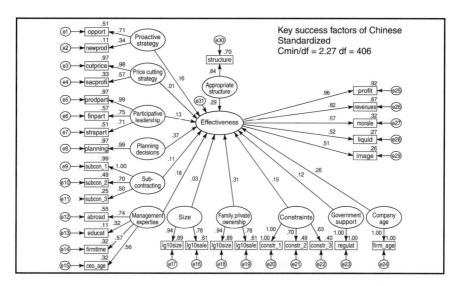

Figure 5-1   Key success factors of Chinese companies (standardized ML estimates)

Note: The path diagram does not display bootstrapped coefficients.

varances between the factors influencing effectiveness. If this model fitted the data reasonably well, I could exclude the possibility of spurious or intervening relations. Besides, rejection of a rival hypothesis serves as powerful replication. Therefore, to confirm the conclusion, I tested an extended model that, based on theory, specified covariances between factors. There were no significant changes in the sign of the structural relationships, which demonstrated the robustness of the research model. For the sake of parsimony, I therefore used the simpler version here.

Measurement model

Several indicators measured the exogenous and endogenous traits. Apart from the measures used in chapter 4, I introduced several scales for the additional traits.

Appropriate structure measures the degree to which a company's structural choices fit its task environment. I used the following detailed procedure to construct the scale (see table 5-1). Companies obtained a score of 1 or 0, depending on whether their degree of formalization, centralization, and integration matched the contingencies size and uncertainty. For example, a large company that formalized many areas to manage its size obtained a score of 1. In contrast, if the same company adopted a low degree of formalization, the structural arrangement was deemed inappropriate, leading to a score of 0. It would be very inefficient to run a large company without codifying at least some past knowledge and best prac-

Table 5-1 Appropriate structure scoring grid

	Formalization		Centralization		Integration	
	High	Low	High	Low	High	Low
Large size	1	0	0	1	1	0
Small size	0	1	1	0	0	1
High uncertainty	0	1	0	1	1	0
Low uncertainty	1	0	1	0	0	1
Maximum score	2	2	2	2	2	2

1 = appropriate structure; 0 = inappropriate structure.

tice into written documents or using formal roles and other controls to govern complex transactions. I split the structural and contextual dimensions at the median. Therefore, "large" or "high" means "greater than the median."

Each pair of adjacent cells for each of the three structural variables formed one variable. For example, the first variable, appropriate formalization, scores large companies with high degrees of formalization as 1 and the remainder as 0. Because each company was either large or small, and operated either in a certain or in an uncertain environment, the maximum total score for each structural dimension was 2. I totalled the scores on all twelve variables to arrive at the final appropriate structure scale (structur). Thus, more instances of fit led to higher scores on the aggregate scale, which ranges from a minimum of 0 (completely inappropriate structural choices) to a maximum of 6 (perfect structural fit with the environment).

As in chapter 4, generic formalization scored all items on the specialization, role formalization, and standardized control scales (see appendix D, sections 12, 13, and 16). Centralization was the composite score for the Aston centralization scale (appendix D, section 14). Integration summed all items of the structural and processual liaison scales (appendix D, section 17). I standardized all structural scales by scaling them to 100%. Size was the log of the number of employees. Uncertainty scored all items of the uncertainty scale (appendix D, section 19.1).

Planning denotes a decision-making style that uses systematic foreward-looking analysis to optimize outcomes for the whole organization. It was measured by one indicator, planning (appendix D, item 6.3).

Management expertise is measured by four indicators: the CEO's international experience (abroad, appendix D, item 1.4); higher education (educat, appendix D, item 1.3); the total time with the company (firmtime, appendix D, item 1.6); and his age (ceo_age, appendix D, item 1.1).

Family-based private ownership was measured by two indicators. The first (private) is a dichotomous dummy variable (aggregated from item 2.7 in appendix D) with 1 equal to "state enterprise" and 2 equal to "private enterprise." The second indicator (individ), a categorical dummy variable (derived from item 2.8 in appendix D), measured the percentage of shares held by the family. It had a maximum of 7 (100% family owned) and a minimum of 1 (100% state-owned). Table 5-2 presents the detailed scoring grid for this variable.

Government support measures the degree to which government regulations positively affected the business. The scale (regulat) scored all items in section 19.3 in appendix D.

Company age, the number of years the company existed, was measured by item 2.5 in appendix D (firm_age).

Company size was measured by two indicators to ensure that the overall model was identified. Besides the log of the number of employees (lg10size) derived from appendix D, item 2.4, I included the log of total revenues (lg10sale), computed from appendix D, item 2.3.

Organizational effectiveness was measured by Khandwalla's (1977) subjective index of intraindustry performance (appendix D, section 11.1–5). Earlier research had confirmed its high reliability and validity. On this scale, respondents evaluate their company's performance in comparison to industry rivals, which controls for industry effects. In contrast to many earlier studies that focused on only one measure of performance, the scale combines five elements, which averages out the specificity of any single item. The scale includes: the company's long-term profitability (profit); the annual growth rate of revenues (revenues); employee morale, job satisfaction, and commitment to the firm's objectives (morale); financial strength, defined as liquidity and ability to raise financial resources (liquid); and public image and goodwill (image). I cross-checked the answers on the subjective index with Khandwalla's index of objective performance (appendix D, section 11.6–7; see Khandwalla 1977 for the formula used to calculate the aggregate scale). It included three components: the firm's absolute level of profitability, the stability of its profitability, and the growth rate of its revenues. The significant correlation between the subjective and absolute index ($r=.32$, two-tailed $p<.01$) confirmed the high reliability and construct validity of the scale, and approaches the results of Khandwalla's original study ($r=.33$, two-tailed $p<.01$).

As in chapter 4, the loading of the indicator that supposedly best measured the latent construct was fixed at 1.0. Each indicator was linked to

Table 5-2 Scoring grid for family-based private ownership scale (individ)

Value	Label
1	100% State ownership
2	100% Collective ownership
3	Majority nonprivate ownership
4	50% State ownership, 50% private ownership
5	Majority private ownership
6	100% Other private investors
7	100% Family ownership

an error term that modeled the effect of excluded variables and random measurement error (e1–e30). In addition, the endogenous construct had a unique error variance term (e31).

Findings for unconstrained organizational effectiveness model

I found no distribution problems in the data, which would have violated the multivariate normality assumption. The empirical model (model I) confirmed the unidimensionality, construct validity, and reliability of the measures. The chi-square statistic adjusted for degrees of freedom (χ^2/df=2.27, df=406) showed acceptable absolute model fit according to all recommended conservative cutoff points. Other indices confirmed the reasonable fit (GFI=.65, IFI=.68). Table 5-4 presents the various fit indices.

The significance and absolute amount of the structural parameter estimates shed additional light on the overall model fit. Both unstandardized and standardized path coefficients (gamma) are reported in table 5-3. The standardized regression coefficients are also displayed in figure 5-1. The analysis revealed several highly significant factors: family-based private ownership (γ=.31, p<.001), planning (γ=.37, p<.001), appropriate structure (γ=.29, p<.01), company age (γ=.26, p<.001), management expertise (γ=.18, p<.05), and environmental constraints (γ=−.15, p<.05).

The model had strong explanatory power (percent of variance explained) as shown by the very high bootstrapped squared multiple correlation (r=.60, SE=.09), the equivalent of R^2 (the coefficient of determination) in Ordinary Least Squares (OLS) regression. This means that the

Table 5-3 Maximum likelihood path coefficients (gamma) for effectiveness model

Independent variable	Unstandardized	Standardized
Appropriate structure	.38**	.29
Proactive strategy	.32	.16
Price-cutting strategy	−.01	−.01
Participative leadership	.10	.13
Planning decisions	.29***	.37
Subcontracting	.04	.11
Management expertise	.74*	.18
Size	.05	.03
Family-based private ownership	.88***	.31
Constraints	−.04*	−.15
Government support	.02	.12
Company age	.02***	.26
Squared multiple correlation	.60***	n/a

N = 124.
*p < .05 (C.R. > 1.98); **p < .01 (C.R. > 2.62); ***p < .001 (C.R. > 3.38).
All critical ratios (C.R.) are based on unstandardized coefficients.
*Bootstrap estimate (ML estimate reported in path diagram).

Table 5-4 Nested model comparisons for organizational effectiveness model

	χ^2/df	df	GFI	AGFI	IFI	$\Delta\chi^2$†	p	df	SMC
Saturated model (Covariance structure)	0.00	0	1.00	n/a	1.00	n/a	n/a	n/a	n/a
Model I (Base structural model)	2.27	406	.65	.59	.68	n/a	n/a	n/a	.60
Model II (Model w/o proactive strategy)	2.27	407	.65	.60	.68	2.43	.12	1	.57
Model III (Model w/o price cutting strategy)	2.26	407	.65	.60	.68	.03	.87	1	.59
Model IV (Model w/o participative leadership)	2.27	407	.65	.59	.68	2.86	.09	1	.58
Model V (Model w/o planning decisions)	2.31	407	.64	.59	.67	20.57***	.00	1	.50
Model VI (Model w/o subcontracting)	2.27	407	.65	.60	.68	2.04	.15	1	.58
Model VII (Model w/o management expertise)	2.27	407	.65	.60	.68	1.77	.18	1	.55
Model VIII (Model w/o size)	2.26	407	.65	.60	.68	.07	.80	1	.59
Model IX (Model w/o family private ownership)	2.28	407	.65	.60	.67	6.99**	.01	1	.49
Model X (Model w/o constraints)	2.27	407	.64	.60	.68	3.56	.06	1	.57
Model XI (Model w/o government support)	2.27	407	.65	.60	.68	2.31	.13	1	.61
Model XII (Model w/o company age)	2.28	407	.65	.60	.68	6.86**	.01	1	.52
Model XIII (Model w/o appropriate structure)	2.29	407	.64	.59	.67	10.87***	.00	1	.49
Null model (Independence model)	4.61	435	.40	.36	.00	n/a	n/a	n/a	n/a

N = 124.
**$p < .01$; ***$p < .001$.
†Baseline comparison is model I.
χ^2 = chi square.
$\Delta\chi^2$ = chi square difference.
df = degrees of freedom.
p = significance level.
GFI = Goodness of fit index.
AGFI = Goodness of fit index, adjusted for degrees of freedom.
IFI = Incremental fit index.
SMC = Squared multiple correlation.

exogenous factors included in the model explained most of the variation in the endogenous effectiveness construct. The high squared multiple correlation and the relatively large and significant path coefficients for several factors showed that the exogenous variables contributed meaningfully to explaining variation in the endogenous structural construct. The large number of significant factors with strong explanatory power reduces the extent to which true effects on effectiveness are misattributed to other factors not included in the model. Such spurious and intervening relationship may have occurred in earlier studies that failed to include such a long list of control variables. Within this well-specified model, the effect of individual factors can be accurately assessed while the other factors are held constant.

Nested model comparisons for organizational effectiveness model

A few earlier writers hinted at the high degree of effectiveness of the distinctive Chinese management model based on private family ownership, but rarely undertook empirical studies to substantiate their conjectures. To close this gap, I scrutinized the following third research hypothesis:

Hypothesis 3   Holding other things constant, the family-based private Chinese model is positively associated with organizational effectiveness.

To test this proposition, I determined the statistical significance of the individual factors influencing effectiveness through a series of nested model comparisons. I compared an unconstrained baseline model with nested models that fixed the regression weight of one of the factors at zero. Significant chi-square statistics suggest that the constrained model should be rejected, indicating that the constrained factor is statistically significant. Table 5-4 reports the findings for this nested model analysis.

The findings support the third research hypothesis. Holding other potential confounds constant, family-based ownership in China resulted in significantly higher performance in terms of growth, profitability, financial strength, morale, and public image. First, the sign of the regression coefficient conformed to my theory: family-based private ownership *increased* organizational performance (γ=.31, p<.001, see table 5-3). Compared with all other variables, ownership was the most important single influencing factor of organizational effectiveness, as measured by the size of the gamma coefficient. Second, rigorous tests within the overall model (the nomological network) confirmed its statistical significance. A nested comparison with a model that constrained the path from family-based private ownership to effectiveness to zero yielded a significant chi-square ($\Delta\chi^2$=6.99, df=1, p=.01; see model IX). This suggests rejection of the nested model and demonstrated that family-based ownership was a significant factor influencing performance.

Because the Chinese management model is confined to private enterprises, the findings imply that this model increases performance and generates better results than the model used in state enterprises. This positive link with performance suggests that Chinese management is an art, the skill of doing something well. The findings confirm anecdotes about overseas Chinese management. The effectiveness of this management model stems from the social capital generated by Chinese family structures, the flexibility of small firms and lineage-based networks, and the economies generated by these family-based networks. As mentioned in chapter 2, this management model also has certain drawbacks. Most important, it may limit the growth of company size. To isolate the positive effects on performance, I held size constant in the organizational effectiveness model. Apart from these conclusions for private enterprises, by symmetry these findings suggest that state ownership is *negatively* related to performance. This confirms earlier conjectures that the "nonowner" feeling depresses long-run performance (Mun 1990).

Let me now briefly discuss the other factors influencing success in mainland China that I included as controls to isolate the impact of private family-based ownership on performance. I will start with the factors that managers directly control.[1]

Organizational structure

The chi-square difference test for a nested model that constrained the influence of appropriate structure to zero was significant ($\Delta\chi^2=10.87$, $df=1$, $p<.001$, see table 5-4), showing that organizational structure significantly influences effectiveness. Table 5-3 shows that it was *positively* associated with performance ($\gamma=.29$, $p<.01$; see table 5-3). It ranks as the second most important success factor in China in terms of regression weight. The findings underscore the importance for companies to consider contingency factors in the task environment and strive for internal and external fit, in order to maximize effectiveness. For example, companies operating in a highly uncertain environment should adopt decentralized and informal structures to deal effectively with rapidly changing customer tastes, technologies, and other factors (see Schlevogt & Donaldson 1999).

Corporate strategy

I analyzed two different types of strategy: proactive and price-cutting strategies.[2]

Proactiveness. A proactive strategy appears to be positively associated with organizational performance ($\gamma=.16$, $p>.05$; $\Delta\chi^2=2.43$, $df=1$, $p>.05$). Though not statistically significant, this result is consistent with earlier empirical studies, such as Schendel and Patton's (1978) general observation that strategy is an important determinant of performance. Even though businessmen and consultants do not doubt its importance—after all, devising strategies is their raison d'être—several research schools question such conventional wisdom. For example, population ecologists stressed the deterministic influence of the environment, which neutralizes the effects of strategy. My study controlled for many of these environmental factors. The results also fit well with the normative strategy literature. Researchers have emphasized the importance of creating competitive advantage based on product differentiation and a bias for action (Peters and Waterman 1982). This posture is epitomized by the "prospector" style of strategizing (Miles and Snow 1978). Differentiated products command a premium price. If cost structures are comparable to those of competitors, the differentiating company generates above average returns. A bias for action helps to implement positioning and execution strategies ahead of competitors.

Price cutting. In contrast, a strategy that relies exclusively on price cutting, aggressively sacrificing profitability to gain market share, is slightly negatively associated with long-run performance ($\gamma=-.01$, $p>.05$; $\Delta\chi^2=.03$, $df=1$, $p>.05$). However, the path coefficient was tiny and statistically insignificant. The negative sign suggests that aggressive price cutting can easily provoke competitors to retaliate, unleashing a price war, which in the long run destroys value in the whole industry. A good example was the devastating price war in the American airline industry after deregulation. To combat its negtive consequences, companies afterward strove to differentiate themselves through innovations such as hub-and-spoke systems, frequent flyer programs, and heavy investment in information technology. All of these measures improved the industry structure, since they decreased competitive rivalry, lowered the bargaining power of customers, and raised entry barriers. Mere price cutting differs from a low cost (or as Emerson Electric calls it, "best cost") strategy, which is a viable option that can be very successful. Low cost producers aim at high profitability by lowering costs while charging prices at the market level or slightly below it. If prices decreased in the same proportion as costs, margins would not improve. The results on price cutting corroborate with studies of mature, low-performing U.S. organizations that sacrificed long-term performance by focusing on short-term profits instead of pursuing proactive strategies (Schollhammer 1982; Tan and Litschert 1994, p. 14).

The findings for the two dimensions suggest that the essence of strategy is to differentiate oneself from competitors—through either superior products, speed, or low costs—and to avoid price wars. Only such strategies create economic rents—returns that exceed the cost of capital, not simply accounting profits. Such results alone justify the existence of companies and managers.

Management style

A professional management style, combining participative leadership (Likert 1961) and planning-based decision making (Lindblom 1959), positively influenced organizational performance.

Participation. Judging from the positive association between participative leadership and performance ($\gamma=.13$, $p>.05$, $\Delta\chi^2=2.86$, $df=1$, $p<.10$), it is efficient for top managers to grant subordinates a say in decisions that affect them vitally. Such participation tends to increase employee morale, motivation, and commitment. It also fully uses local knowledge. The findings resound well with the key ideas of human relations (Mayo 1933) and human resources (Argyris 1956; McGregor 1960). However, participative leadership does not need to be democratic. In China, high power distance prevents empowerment; instead leaders dominate. At best, companies may allow members of the same hierarchical level (the primary decision makers) to influence the final decision, a process of lateral decision making. Vertical "participation" means that a leader *involves* members of a work group in the decision-making process, not that he strives for consensus. If he follows traditional Confucian culture, and thus acts benevolently, he will test and smoothen the waters before declaring and commiting himself publicly. He will sound out the voices of affected "subjects" and ask them to agree to a suggested course of action, even if they do not consider it to be the best choice. But, although he may solicit input from employees, he will still make all final decisions either himself or, especially in state enterprises, together with his leadership group.

Planning. Planning was positively associated with long-term performance ($\gamma=.37$, $p<.001$). The nested model comparisons showed that it was statistically the most significant factor, as measured by the chi-square statistic ($\Delta\chi^2=20.57$, $df=1$, $p<.001$). This finding confirms the literature on decision making, which showed that planning is associated with high performance in the long run (Ansoff et al. 1970; Herold, Thune, and House 1972; Khandwalla 1977, pp. 578–579; Thune and House 1970). Investors in China need to pursue a clear long-term vision that aims at creating economic value instead of acting opportunistically, trying to capture quick gains that will harm corporate health in the future. More generally, the results suggest that scientific management (Taylor 1911), with its emphasis on systematic analysis and the disciplined execution of standardized procedures, might be very effective in many industries and functions in China.

Subcontracting

Subcontracting was slightly positively related to performance ($\gamma=.11$, $p>.05$; $\Delta\chi^2=2.04$, $df=1$, $p>.05$), but this causal path was statistically insignificant. Companies that outsource peripheral activities can focus on their core competencies. They may be leaner, which saves overhead and enables them to adapt flexibly and quickly to changing circumstances. The subcontractor benefits from economies of scale, scope, and specialization. He probably has developed special expertise and continues to move up the learning curve, thus delivering goods and services with consistently higher quality and at lower prices than those produced by generalists. Through subcontracting, organizations may thus achieve "best-in-world" status even if they lack the requisite capabilities. More generally, the findings also highlight the importance of enterprise webs in China. At the level of the whole economy, this gives rise to the phenomenon of network capitalism (see Boisot and Child 1996).

Let me discuss the contextual factors.

Management expertise

A highly skilled and experienced CEO is a very valuable resource in China. His management expertise in terms of education, international exposure, and work experience, was significantly positively associated with corporate performance ($\gamma=.18$, $p<.05$; $\Delta\chi^2=1.77$, $df=1$, $p>.05$). These results reinforce the mainstream organizational literature emphasizing that companies need to manage knowledge and learning to achieve high performance (Huber 1991; Kogut and Zander 1992; Nonaka and Takeuchi 1995). The findings also buttress qualitative research on China with hard empirical evidence. For example, scholars suggested that the lack of well-educated managers stifles performance in China (Dalton 1990, p. 48). This prompted the government to strengthen industrial training (Helburn and Shearer 1984). Because of their relatively low educational level and insufficient experience, Chinese managers find it difficult to master the increased uncertainty and complexity of a market economy in transition, where even many highly educated and experienced western managers fail. I regard the lack of human, intellectual, and social capital as key bottleneck constraining strong qualitative growth and proposed a global network model to develop leaders instead of mere administrators or managers (see Schlevogt 2000).

Size

Size was slightly positively related to organizational performance ($\gamma=.03$, $p>.05$; $\Delta\chi^2=.07$, $df=1$, $p>.05$). However, the effect was tiny and statistically insignificant. I included size mainly as a control to eliminate spurious and intervening effects.

Constraints

Environmental constraints were significantly negatively correlated with organizational effectiveness ($\gamma=-.15$, $p<.05$; $\Delta\chi^2=3.56$, $df=1$, $p<.10$). In an environment with high inflation, poor infrastructure, political instability, difficult access to capital, and shortage of technical manpower, a company will encounter difficulties in securing a constant stream of vital resources and thus to operate effectively. This validates the findings of studies outside China.

Government support

Government support tended to increase organizational effectiveness (γ=.12, p>.05; $\Delta\chi^2$= 2.31, df=1, p>.05), but the relationship was statistically insignificant. Since I held industry constant, I could isolate the effect on performance of an individual company's relations with the government, which determined whether the authorities interpreted laws and directives benevolently. Otherwise, I may have found a positive impact of government intervention for a group of companies simply because they operated in a sector that was favored by the state. As expected, companies that secured privileges such as tax relief, subsidies, special incentives for operations in designated zones, and export aid outperformed competitors that failed to elicit such favorable treatment. Previous studies highlighted the general importance of government regulations but did not empirically test their specific influence on effectiveness. For example, managers mentioned government regulations as the most influential, least predictable, and most complex strategic variable in China. They found it hard to obtain regulatory information and, when they got hold of it, considered it too vague to help business planning. Many top executives in their daily work focused primarily on collecting and interpreting regulatory information (Tan and Litschert 1994, p. 13). My book advanced knowledge in two ways: First, I proposed the theory that supportive regulation directly *increases* performance instead of just being an important input for strategic analysis. For example, subsidies immediately affect the bottom line, without prior filtering through organizational action. Second, I empirically tested and confirmed this theoretical proposition.

Company age

Company age was significantly positively associated with organizational effectiveness (γ=.26, p.<001; $\Delta\chi^2$=6.86, df=1, p=.01). Older companies may have developed wider and stronger *guanxi* networks that help them gather important market information, secure new business, and receive favorable government treatment, which, especially in China increases effectiveness. Old companies also may have accumulated other valuable intangible assets, such as reputation, trust, and goodwill. Those serve as buffers that absorb shocks. In contrast, young companies might suffer from the liability of newness, lacking protective shields and thus being more exposed to negative environmental influences. Therefore, as a general rule, proportionally more new organizations fail than old ones (Stichcombe 1965, p. 148).

Incremental contributions of success factors in China

To assess the relative importance of individual factors, I estimated how they contributed to explaining variance in organizational performance. To this end, I compared incremental changes in the squared multiple correlation (SMC), shown in Table 5-4, resulting from the inclusion of individual factors. Figure 5-2 presents the findings of this analysis.

As shown by the SMC, the structural equation model explained more than half (60%) of the variance in organizational effectiveness. Private family ownership ranked as the most powerful explanatory factor. Specifically, the SMC deteriorated by 11 percentage points from 60% to 49% when the influence of this factor was constrained to zero. The decrease accounted for 21% of the total change in the SMC (overall 53%) attributable to the inclusion of the different influencing factors. This finding further supported the research hypothesis. Family ownership not only was found to increase organizational performance significantly, but it also best explained the performance differences of companies in China. Besides, appropriate structure (20% of total incremental change in the SMC), planning (18%), company age (15%), and CEO expertise (9%) were potent sources of variance in effectiveness. Compared to these key factors, the explanatory power of strategy, leadership style, and other contextual constructs was marginal.

Organizational effectiveness stacked model subgroup comparisons between China's north and south

Writers commenting on China's national characteristics repeatedly emphasized the pronounced differences between its various regions. Most of their anecdotal accounts center on the striking contrast between the north and the south. The Yangtze River, flowing from the Kunlun Mountains in southwestern Qinghai province to the East China Sea, divides the two areas geographically. Faunal differences and paleomagnetic evidence suggest that present-day north and south China originally belonged to separate tectonic plates. The climate, especially in the winter varies widely— Siberian temperatures in the north and subtropical conditions in the south. Apart from these physical features, every visitor to China soon detects marked differences in social behavior in the two areas. One of the most perspicacious observer, Marco Polo, in as early as the 13th century perceived Cathay (north) and Manzi (south, especially Canton) as two separate worlds.

History explains much of the social divide. The Chinese heartland and center of gravity reposed in the dry, dusty plains of the Yellow River in the north. The southern states, such as Chu Guo, did not belong to the united state created by the first emperor, Qin Shi Huang (reign: 221–206 BC) after the Warring States period. For a long time thereafter, China proper could not assimilate them. As a consequence, the south remained an underdeveloped area (Manzi literally means "barbarian"). Driven by an independent and rebellious spirit, it fought many wars with the northern states, which broadened the gulf. Only the short but successful Sui dynasty (AD 581–618), which reunified China after almost four centuries of

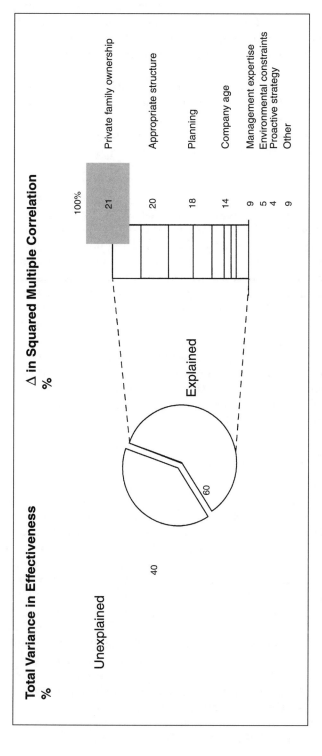

Figure 5-2 Explaining the organizational effectiveness of Chinese companies

fragmentation, managed to integrate the south into the Chinese empire. Yet subsequently economic forces drove China's regions apart. The south was more exposed to western influences because of its active trade with foreign countries. This amplified the differences in the behavioral patterns of the two regions.

This alleged (but not yet empirically tested) divide in terms of social norms and customs implies that business environments differ in the north and the south. Different environments pose distinct requirements for business survival and success—an important aspect so far largely ignored. Few theoretical accounts in the strategic management literature, and even fewer empirical studies focused on differential regional success factors, particularly in China. Therefore, the main contribution of this part of the book is to analyze key success factors in China's two most diverging regions and show empirically that they indeed differ. By highlighting within-country differences, I also refine the general literature on key success factors. The findings matter for multinational and domestic companies that do not yet perceive or agree with the need for tailored geographical approaches *within* China. They may erroneously use the same organizational structures, strategies, and management practices everywhere. Knowledge of the leverage points for success in the north and the south will help them to develop successful, locally adapted corporate and business unit strategies and organizations.

In the following section, I will outline the main differences between the north and south of China, which shows why researchers should not treat them as homogeneous entities. After this theoretical ground work, I will report the findings of the empirical analysis testing the hypothesized differences in success factors in these two parts of China.

Distinctive characteristics of the north

Political, economic, and cultural forces left their traces. Until now, political authorities who strictly control business activities dominated in the north. The influence of the government literally increases with proximity to Beijing. That is why the chairman of a leading private financial group in China located his headquarters in Shenzhen (a city close to Hong Kong), as far away from the political capital as possible. With such strong political influence, close ties with the government and insider information from official sources matter most in the north. In fact, business and government often can be considered as one body (Ou, Shi, and Xu 1996). Many businesses are a byproduct of politics. They spin off the government bureaucracy and maintain close links with it. Adopting the bureaucratic model of their "parents," companies, especially in Beijing, often become miniature governments. Decision making is often highly centralized, dominated by a minor official who "entered the [commercial] sea" (as a Chinese expression puts it), and by Communist party functionaries.

Economic forces also shaped behavioral patterns. In the past, commerce in the north was not well developed. Instead, agricultural traditions pervaded business. The northern "small peasant trader," who was narrow-minded, inflexible, and passive, substituted privileged relations for head-to-head competition.

Further, traditional Chinese culture influenced activities most strongly in the north. This region was the centerpiece of an empire that, starting with the Han dynasty (206 BC–AD 220), promoted Confucianism as state ideology. Confucians believe in the rule of virtuous men and consider scholarship as the only respectable pursuit for a gentleman. Northerners cherish traditional Chinese values, most importantly, seniority, loyalty, kindness, politeness, wisdom, and trust. These values tend to reinforce centralizing tendencies. Family ties and other connections carry much weight. In contrast to virtuous activities such as scholarship, commercial activities do not confer high social status.

Distinctive characteristics of the south

The south prides itself of a sophisticated commercial tradition, which resulted from prolonged political and economic competition. From the tenth to the thirteenth century, the barbarian nomads of Central Asia and present-day Mongolia, pressed continuously at its borders. Perhaps because of a constant sense of urgency and consequently strong performance motivation, the south grew from an underdeveloped wasteland of a vast empire as late as the Tang dynasty (618–907) into a vibrant, prosperous, and densely populated region (Gernet 1962). The ensuing urban mode of life differed sharply from the predominantly rural north.

Owing to its many rivers, the south boasted intensive domestic trade, and with its major sea access points, it participated much more actively in international trade than the north. Southerners thus early on were forced to adopt an aggressive, entrepreneurial, and flexible management style. A book on Chinese cultural history claims: "The northerner is slow, well-balanced, shrewd, but not quick-witted. The *Yangtze* people are nervous and excitable, their minds are agile, but their tempers are short. They are eloquent, adaptable, but perhaps less reliable than the sturdy northern people" (Fitzgerald 1986, p. 5). As a result of frequent international contacts southerners absorbed entrepreneurial attitudes, commercial thinking, and management models from abroad, such as market and customer orientation, advertising, and other promotional techniques. There is a Chinese saying that neatly summarizes the above discussion: "In the south the entrepreneur observes the market, in the north he stares at the officials."

Southerners emphasize traditional culture less, perhaps because of their long independence from the Confucian empire. International influences further diluted and eroded traditional culture in the south. Northerners often accuse southerners—the Shanghainese in particular—of destroying the traditional social structure based on family ties. They criticize them for considering wealth the most important objective in life and for entertaining superficial, temporary, and particularistic relationships. These are considered sure signs that they "lack feeling."

*Empirical findings for differences in success factors
between the north and the south*

To operationalize the theorized regional differences and empirically test their impact on business performance, I built a stacked effectiveness model with companies from Beijing (north) and Shanghai (south).[3] I then performed a nested subgroup comparison to assess whether key success factors differed in the two geographic areas. The results of this analysis are reported in table 5-5.

In the first step of the analysis, I compared an unconstrained stacked baseline model with a nested model in which all pairs of path coefficients in the two geographical subgroups were equal. The chi-square difference test for the nested model comparison was statistically significant ($\Delta\chi^2=23.74$, $df=12$, $p<.05$), which indicates that key success factors differed in northern and southern cities. These differences were hidden in the total sample, which aggregated both subgroups. The study thus shows that researchers must drill deeper into the data and explore finer shadings by analyzing regional differences in key success factors.

In the next step, I examined these differences in more detail, comparing the individual signs and statistical significance of all coefficient pairs. In addition, I performed more detailed nested tests comparing the unconstrained model (Ia) to a battery of models that fixed the coefficient for each individual factor to equality for the two subgroups. Significant chi-square differences show that the difference between the two subgroups with respect to the particular factor was significant. The results of these detailed subgroup comparisons are reported in table 5-6.

The two subgroup models had very strong explanatory power as measured by the squared multiple correlation—.85 for enterprises in Beijing and .68 for enterprises in Shanghai. This means that the factors included in the model explained 85% (north) and 68% (south) of the variance in effectiveness. Except for company size, the sign of the path coefficients in the two subgroups corresponded to the results for the total sample (within

Table 5-5 Organizational effectiveness nested model geographical subgroup comparisons (stacked model)

	χ^2/df	df	GFI	AGFI	IFI	$\Delta\chi^2$†	p	df
Saturated model (Covariance structure)	0	0	1.00	n/a	1.00	n/a	n/a	n/a
Model Ia (Baseline model)	1.94	812	.55	.48	.60	n/a	n/a	n/a
Model Ib (Model w/equality)	1.94	824	.54	.48	.59	23.74*	.02	12
Null model (Independence model)	3.10	870	.34	.30	.00	n/a	n/a	n/a

*$p < .05$.
†Baseline comparison is model Ia.
GFI = Goodness of fit index.
AGFI = Goodness of fit index, adjusted for degrees of freedom.
IFI = Incremental fit index.

Table 5-6 Individual subgroup comparisons for organizational effectiveness model (standardized path coefficients)

Independent variable	Total All†	Region North	Region South	Nested model comparison $\Delta\chi^2$‡	Nested model comparison p	Nested model comparison df
Appropriate structure	.29**	.33**	.32**	.00	.98	1
Proactive strategy	.16	.52	.07	5.71*	.02	1
Price-cutting strategy	−.01	−.14	.03	1.48	.22	1
Participative leadership	.13	.19*	.09	.41	.52	1
Planning decisions	.37***	.15	.33***	.86	.36	1
Subcontracting	.11	.09	.11	.02	.88	1
Management expertise	.18*	.31*	.02	1.44	.23	1
Company size	.03	−.26**	.31***	6.35*	.01	1
Family-based private ownership	.31***	.23*	.47***	1.45	.23	1
Constraints	−.15*	−.16	−.01	.76	.38	1
Government support	.12	.38***	−.04	8.79**	.00	1
Company age	.26***	.10	.35***	2.29	.13	1
Squared multiple correlation	.60	.85†	.68†	n/a	n/a	n/a

Total sample N = 124; north n = 60, south n = 64.
*$p < .05$ (C.R. > 1.98); **$p < .01$ (C.R. > 2.62); ***$p < .001$ (C.R. > 3.38); C.R. = Critical ratio.
†All critical ratios are based on unstandardized coefficients. Squared multiple correlation for total sample obtained through bootstrapping.
‡Baseline comparison is unconstrained model Ia (see table 5-5).
†Maximum likelihood estimate (bootstrapped value not available because of smaller subgroup sample size).

the bounds of conventional confidence intervals). However, their magnitude and statistical significance differed.

The detailed comparison of individual coefficients revealed two significant subgroup differences with respect to government regulation and company size.[4]

Government support. I found the largest significant geographical difference for government regulation ($\Delta\chi^2=8.79$, $df=1$, $p<.01$). It was the most significant success factor in the north ($\gamma=.38$, $p<.001$), but tended to reduce performance in the south, where it also was insignificant ($\gamma=-.04$, $p>.05$). The findings thus correspond to anecdotal evidence that in the north, business and government are strongly intertwined (Ou, Shi, and Xu 1996). These findings explain the paramount importance that northern companies attach to developing close and smooth relations with the authorities, because favorable treatment, such as tax breaks, subsidies, special incentives, and export aid are among the most decisive factors influencing long-term performance. In more general terms, the results support the thesis that the influence of the government decreases as the company's distance from Beijing increases.

Size. Subgroup differences with respect to company size were significant ($\Delta\chi^2=6.35$, $df=1$, $p<.05$). Size was positively related to success in the south (γ=.31, p<.001) but was negatively related to success in the north (γ=−26, p<.01). The two signs averaged out in the aggregate (γ=.03, p>.05), making size nonsignificant at the total sample level. This example demonstrates the importance of analyzing subgroups to discover differences that are diluted or disappear in the aggregate. In regard to the detailed findings, the results underline that companies in the south need to build a buffer against government influence through large organizational scale, which increases their clout and resilience. In contrast, in the north, the government may harm large, conspicuous businesses, which it regards as competitors to its power monopoly. It thus may follow its traditional instinct to suppress commercial activity. Because of the stronger impact of traditional values in the north, the action of government officials often confirms a Chinese saying. It describes a distaste in Chinese culture for people who deviate from group norms, especially when they break new ground and perform exceptionally well: "The gun will hit the bird that first sticks its head out of the nest."

I will now comment on the remaining, statistically insignificant differences.

Ownership. In the south, family-based private ownership influenced effectiveness more strongly (γ=.47, p<.001) than in the north (γ=.23, p<.05), but given the insignificant results from the nested model comparison ($\Delta\chi^2$=1.45, df=1, p=.23), the findings only can be discussed tentatively. In the south, the coefficient for private family ownership also exceeded the total sample average. Further, ownership was the most crucial success factor in absolute terms. It can be inferred that in the more entrepreneurial south, state enterprises, perhaps because of their alleged inflexibility, will find it harder to succeed. The case study at the end of this chapter will illustrate in more detail differences related to the economic value that state and private enterprises create or destroy. Here, I conclude that the web-based Chinese management model of family businesses, which is associated with the private ownership pattern, is most powerful in the south. This is perhaps because the business environment is closer to that of overseas Chinese communities, where the model has already proved its effectiveness. In addition, most overseas Chinese emigrated from the south and invested back into their home towns. One would thus assume a certain affinity and compatibility of the adopted management model, leading to its higher overall effectiveness in the south. The traditional disdain for private activity in the north may have lowered its effectiveness there.

Appropriate structure. The influence of structure-in-fit on effectiveness was almost identical ($\Delta\chi^2$=.00, df=1, p=.98) in terms of absolute size and statistical significance for companies in the north (γ=.33, p<.01) and the south (γ=.32, p<.01). This strongly supports the fundamental importance of organizational structure. It has to follow an "industrial logic," which is similar in the different regions of China and the world in general. Above all, structure needs to fit the task environment. For example, no matter whether the company is located in the north or the south, if it becomes larger, it will probably need more bureaucratic means of control that standardize routine transactions, in order to avoid reinventing the wheel on each occasion. Could you imagine a teller having to think about how best to perform the task of depositing money every time a customer walks in?

Company age. Company age was more important in the south (γ=.35, p<.001) than in the north (γ=.10, p>.05), but again the results have to be treated in an exploratory fashion, because the difference was not statistically significant ($\Delta\chi^2$=2.29, df=1, p=.13). Learning curve effects, which depend on company age, may matter more in a highly competitive environment, such as Shanghai. Likewise, strong relations built over a long time help to shape the competitive environment and secure a steady flow of business deals, which also increases overall performance.

Expertise. The CEO's expertise influences success more in the north (γ=.31, p<.05) than in the South (γ=.02, p>.05), where its association with effectiveness approaches zero. However, the results need to be replicated, because the subgroup difference was statistically insignificant ($\Delta\chi^2$=1.44, df=1, p=.23). In the south, entrepreneurship may pay off greatly, whereas formal credentials do not appear to count much for success. In contrast, in the north, high educational and professional achievement is valued and leads to a high esteem in the community. This emphasis on scholarship and experience may result directly from the stronger emphasis on traditional Confucian values in the north.

Planning. As a somewhat unexpected finding, a planning mode of decision making seems to be more effective in the south (γ=.33, p<.001) than in the north (γ=.15, p>.05), but the difference has to be treated with caution, because it was statistically insignificant ($\Delta\chi^2$=.86, df=1, p=.36). A priori, I expected that in the supposedly freewheeling south, flexible and opportunistic moves would be more successful than in the north and, as a consequence, planning would be less important. In a very tentative way, it might be argued that scientifically managed companies are more distinctive in the south, which is populated by companies pursuing short-term, aggressive moves, and thus may be more effective in the long run. As an alternative line of reasoning, the south, particularly Shanghai, is more sophisticated and competitive than the north. To succeed, companies may require more advanced management techniques. The value of planning in different regions needs more attention in future research.

Participation. Participative leadership was a somewhat more important factor influencing success in the north (γ=.19, p<.05) than in the south (γ=.09, p>.05), but in view of the insignificant results from the nested model comparison ($\Delta\chi^2$=.41, df=1, p=.52), the results can be treated only tentatively. Perhaps because of the strong Confucian values in the north, leaders must show more respect to the will of the collective. They may therefore need to use a more consultative leadership style. The rule of men, however, contrasts sharply with democratic decision making (the rule of numbers), which definitely is not part of the Confucian philosophical makeup.

These findings underlined that key success factors differ strongly between different regions in China. Many foreign companies, which treat China as one market, and even Chinese enterprises need to rethink. They need to adapt strategies, structures, and processes to different geographic circumstances.

This analysis focused on macrodifferences. Future studies need to explore further regional differences at the microlevel, analyzing peculiarities in the values and behavior of individuals and groups. This includes, for example, differences in key buying factors. Further studies also need to examine differences between other regions, including differences between parts of the same city, which in China often is a mini-state with different prices, behavioral patterns, and values in different districts.

Case study: Value destruction by state enterprises and
sectoral comparison

One of the most important findings from the foregoing analysis was that private family-owned enterprises, on average, attained higher organizational effectiveness than state enterprises. This underlined the high performance of web-based Chinese management in private family businesses in China, when other factors, especially the limits to growth inherent in this model, are held constant. In order to examine and illustrate the financial implications of these findings, I analyzed one case study in more detail. Specifically, I focused on the effectiveness of the state-owned Cathay Industrial Bank (CIB). At the macrolevel, this book also compared value creation in the private and state sector for the first time.

On the surface, CIB appears to be a high-performing company, since it grows very rapidly. Figure 5-3 reports average growth rates in different balance sheet items for the period 1990–1995.

The company's compounded average growth rates (CAGR) in total assets, deposits, loans, and equity outstripped national macroeconomic growth (GDP), which amounted to about 9%. In addition, growth in total assets, which ranked first among the indicators, suggests increasing financial strength. External documents such as annual reports and special "growth charts" confirm that growth in size is the most important corporate objective. However, many corporate finance specialists stressed that companies need to grow both their size and profits. Truly high-performing companies, such as Intel, increase revenues dramatically and at the same time also create shareholder value. Those companies, like IBM at the be-

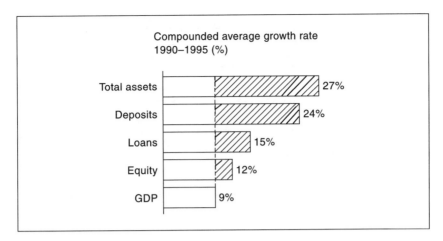

Figure 5-3 CIB growth rates

ginning of the 1990s, which failed to translate revenue growth into economic value creation, subsequently encountered substantial business problems and financial troubles. In the long-run only net present value creation provides a company with the free cash flow necessary to finance future growth and innovation. From the owners' perspective, value creation therefore is accepted as the most important yardstick or acid test for corporate performance.

A more detailed analysis of CIB's other financial performance indicators measuring profit creation showed that past rapid growth destroyed value instead of creating it. This means that the more the company grew, the more it decreased its total value.

As a first "smoking gun," equity growth was significantly slower than growth in total assets. If we assume, for the sake of simplicity, that the shareholders' capital was not markedly increased and the dividend payout ratio was constant, retained earnings were low compared to growth in assets.

A more rigorous analysis of value creation compares the spread between the return on invested capital and the cost of capital. For this case, I used return on equity as a proxy for return on invested capital. Figure 5-4 presents the assumptions for this value analysis.

WACC (weighted average cost of capital) is the weighted cost for both equity and debt. The formula is given in the left-hand box of figure 5-4. It weights the cost of debt according to its share of total capital, and adds it to the costs of equity adjusted for its share of total capital. The cost of debt is the official Bank of China three-month interest rate plus a risk premium for the company. Cost of equity is the return a global investor would expect from his portfolio, adjusted for the riskiness of the specific asset. According to the capital asset pricing model, the riskiness of an asset is assessed by its covariance with the total market portfolio (its beta value). The foregoing analysis is very new for China. Therefore, no exact beta books were

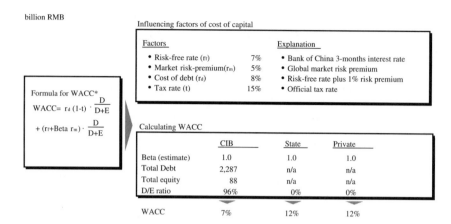

billion RMB

Influencing factors of cost of capital

Factors		Explanation
• Risk-free rate (r_f)	7%	• Bank of China 3-months interest rate
• Market risk-premium(r_m)	5%	• Global market risk premium
• Cost of debt (r_d)	8%	• Risk-free rate plus 1% risk premium
• Tax rate (t)	15%	• Official tax rate

Formula for WACC*

$$WACC = r_d(1-t) \cdot \frac{D}{D+E}$$

$$+ (r_f + Beta \; r_m) \cdot \frac{D}{D+E}$$

Calculating WACC

	CIB	State	Private
Beta (estimate)	1.0	1.0	1.0
Total Debt	2,287	n/a	n/a
Total equity	88	n/a	n/a
D/E ratio	96%	0%	0%
WACC	7%	12%	12%

*WACC=Weighted Average Cost of Capital

Figure 5-4   Assumptions for CIB's value analysis, billion RMB. D = total debt, E = total equity. Source: CIB Annual Report 1994, Datastream, China Study

available. For the sake of simplicity, the beta value was therefore fixed at 1.0, reflecting the assumption that CIB does not increase the riskiness of a well-diversified portfolio very much.

I calculated the cost of capital for CIB, and for China's private and state sectors as a whole. CIB's cost of capital was below the average of private and state enterprises. Most of the capital of a bank is loans (deposits from investors). They are obtained at lower rates than equity. Since the cost of capital is deducted from the return on investment to calculate economic value, holding other factors constant, lower capital costs lead to higher economic value. CIB also enjoys an advantage on the return side, which further increases the spread. Since interest is a tax-deductible expense, a higher debt-to-equity ratio increases free cash flow. But both low cost of capital and high free cash flow come at the expense of a higher risk of bankruptcy, which is not reflected in the economic value formula. To be conservative, I used a 100% equity financing model for the private and state sectors. Because averages for entire economic sectors were compared, the beta weights were equal to 1.0. The results of the comparative value analysis are presented in figure 5-5.

With a return on equity of 3% and a WACC of 7%, CIB's economic spread was *negative* (−4%).[5] In other words, instead of creating economic rents, it massively destroyed value through an economic loss of about 4 billion RMB yuan (approximately U.S. $500 million) in 1994. These figures contrast sharply with the superficial growth in assets, deposits, loans, and equity. Triangulation with results from the content analysis of corporate external relations documents corroborates these findings. The documents highlight organizational growth and strategic milestones, such as the number of credit cards issued or merchants signed up, but never mention profitability or value creation.

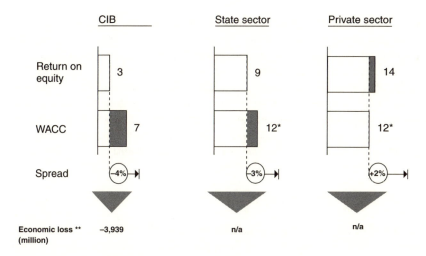

*Assuming 100% equity financed
**Economic profit/loss-invest capital × (ROIC−WACC)
Source: CIB Annual Report 1994, China Study

Figure 5-5   Comparison of value creation in China, 1994 (%)

The questionnaire methodology proved to be very robust and sensitive, since it identified these subtle distinctions. Whereas CIB's CEO rated the company's performance on financial strength higher than industry average, he ranked it lower than average on profitability.

Based on the data from the total sample, the state sector generated a return on equity of 9%. With a WACC of 12%, it, too, produced a negative spread (−3%). In contrast, private enterprises on average achieved a significantly higher return on equity (14%). With a WACC of 12%, they produced a positive spread (2%) and therefore *created* value. This is a very conservative estimate. It is very likely that capital costs of private enterprises are significantly lower than the figure used above. Private owners are satisfied with much lower returns (on their retained earnings for example) as long as they survive. In addition, because of their networks with overseas Chinese and access to other informal credit markets (capital from family and friends), Chinese entrepreneurs can easily tap relatively cheap liquid funds as working capital and long-term capital.

The CIB case and cross-sector comparison, which used an objective measure of organizational effectiveness, thus confirmed and illustrated the results from the structural equation model, which used a subjective index of performance. This additional analysis demonstrated the financial success of private enterprises in absolute and relative terms. Holding constant their cost of capital, they earned a positive spread (or rent) on the invested capital and achieved higher levels of profitability than state enterprises. Free cash flow in turn further strengthens corporate health and provides funds for spin-offs and start-ups, which further enlarge their "worldwide web." The structural and managerial reasons for the higher performance were discussed in the previous chapters, which outlined and tested the web-based Chinese management model. For example, the network increases revenues and decreases costs, and thus increases profitability. The webs also provide low cost capital, which further increases economic value. The comparison in this chapter also provided empirical evidence for the alleged (but untested) inefficiency of the state sector at the macroeconomic level, showing the discrepancy between the appearance of growth and the reality of value destruction on a grand scale.

Summary and conclusions

In this chapter, I focused on the effectiveness of web-based Chinese management. The findings showed that private family-owned enterprises significantly outperformed their state counterparts. Because the private enterprises adopted a distinctive management model, this particular mode of operation thus proved to be more effective than other approaches. Based on a rough estimate in terms of incremental changes in the squared multiple correlation for the endogenous variable effectiveness, private ownership turned out to be the most important factor explaining variation in performance. Its positive association with performance suggests that Chinese management is an art, the skill of doing something well—a point that will be discussed further in chapter 8.

Besides private family-based ownership, several other factors were significantly related to organizational performance. At the total sample level, planning ranked as the most powerful influence on long-run performance in absolute terms. Nested model comparisons revealed that it was also the most significant factor. Further, the strong impact of organizational structure confirmed that everywhere in the world, companies have to choose the right design for their particular task environment. In addition, company age emerged as an important factor, which seems to be a particularly salient feature of China. Older companies enjoy the benefits of path-dependent social capital in the form of *guanxi* that younger companies find difficult to emulate. The results for all other factors, though not statistically significant, empirically confirmed anecdotal evidence in China and studies undertaken in the West. As expected, all of these factors, except for price-cutting strategy, size, and environmental constraints, positively influenced organizational performance.

Further, this study for the first time examined geographical differences in key success factors between the north and south of mainland China. Results from stacked model subgroup comparison showed that the weight of some factors indeed differed significantly in the two regions. The subsequent analysis of detailed differences among pairs of structural path
ients revealed a significant subgroup difference for government
rt (more important in Beijing) and company size (more important

in Shanghai). In contrast, the influence of structure on effectiveness was almost identical in Beijing and Shanghai. This supported the notion that structural choices must follow an industrial logic. In comparison, managerial factors varied more in their importance across the two regions, but the differences were not statistically significant at conventional levels. The results empirically confirm anecdotes about the distinctive characteristics of China's north and south, and highlight the importance for organizational researchers of investigating regional variations that may be hidden in the aggregate sample.

Finally, results from an in-depth case study analyzing the financial performance of the Cathay Industrial Bank (CIB) and a sectoral comparison confirmed and illustrated the research findings from the quantitative structural equation model. In particular, CIB, though growing rapidly in size, incurred a large economic loss in 1994. Its return on equity was significantly lower than its costs of capital. This unleashes a very negative dynamic: The more money is invested in the company, the more its value decreases. The case thus showed in financial terms how state ownership can negatively influence performance. A more general comparative value analysis between the private and state sectors confirmed these findings. Across all industries, the state sector destroyed value, whereas private enterprises, supposedly because of the powerful web-based Chinese model, on average produced economic rents, which would have been even higher, if their lower cost of capital had been figured into the equation. The findings thus provided hard, quantitative support for anecdotes about the comparatively higher financial performance of private enterprises compared to the state sector, and have important implications for privatization policies. More specifically, they underline that the Chinese government needs to promote the growth of the private economy in urban and rural areas. It should remove all remaining ideological bias and practical obstacles, and actively support start-ups and other private activity. Besides, it may revive the moribund state sector through a well-designed privatization or "securitization" program, or by emulating web-based Chinese management through a "virtual privatization" scheme.

In parts I and II, I contributed to the literature by (a) synthesizing the fragments mentioned in previous qualitative narrations into an integrated theory of private Chinese management; (b) conceptualizing distinctiveness (in terms of ownership comparisons); (c) theorizing that the model is readopted in the P.R.C., including the revival of Chinese traditional values, and is positively associated with effectiveness; and (d) operationalizing, testing, and supporting the usually descriptive statements through analytical methods based on empirical data. Apart from case studies, I conducted a representative survey—a technique that, so far, has not often been used in mainland China.

Having established the facts that support the theory, in part III, I will use the evidence to recommend how managers may design effective organizations and strategies. First, I will suggest that web-based Chinese management can serve as a blueprint for the organization of the future (chapter 6). Second, I will develop a strategy framework that translates the findings from the key success factor analysis in China into managerial action (chapter 7).

PART III
Practical Applications: Using the Facts for Design

6
The Organization of the Future:
Chinese Management as a Model
for the Twenty-first Century
and Beyond

Executive summary

An organization is the leader's vehicle and catalyst for implementing strategies but also constrains strategic options. Because of its importance, for thousands of years, leaders have been searching for better organizational ways of coordinating and motivating human endeavors toward the achievement of lofty visions. The dominant organizational model perfectioned in the twentieth century, bureaucracy, proved effective under classical conditions of certainty, when past experience is highly relevant for the present and future. However, because of its rigidity, bureaucracy turned out to be inadequate to deal with the high uncertainty and complexity that result from rapid change and multiplying interdependencies. I suggest the web-based Chinese management model developed and tested in the previous chapters, to excel under these conditions that have emerged in many industries. I propose it as a new management paradigm that advances organizational thought and as a blueprint for the organization of the future. Because of its accumulated social capital, it strongly coordinates and motivates human endeavor at the level of the individual enterprise, and because of its web-based flexibility, it makes the macroeconomy as a whole more resilient to shocks. I suggest practical frameworks to help international businessmen and investors to interact more successfully with Chinese private enterprises, and to decide when and for which divisions of their *own* company the model is appropriate. I also propose concrete ideas on how to implement the model and decision rules for choosing the particular implementation mode that best fits the company's situation.

Overview

So far, I have built a theory of Chinese management in private, family-owned enterprises located in mainland China and have gathered the facts to test its validity in terms of its nature, causes, and outcomes. This is where many empirical studies by "men of facts" or "men of gathering" stop. However, transforming theories and data ("know what") into knowledge that can be acted on ("know how") is of prime importance in a world of increasingly abundant information. Such an environment calls for clear navigation advice for the "men of design" or "men of governing." Know-how replaces guesses and increases the confidence of managers who have previously tapped in the dark. Such a psychological advantage matters for success, especially in an unaccustomed environment. Therefore, it is important to develop recommendations based on the new insights. In this chapter, I will focus on implications and applications that can be derived from the Chinese management model. The governing thought is that the distinctive characteristics of WCM can explain much of the dynamism and growth of the private sector in China and that it can potentially serve as a new management paradigm for the new millennium (and beyond) and as a blueprint for the organization of the future. In chapter 7, I will broaden the perspective and discuss key success factors in the Chinese market besides family ownership and its associated organizational characteristics. I thus will hold constant the structural and managerial characteristics which were distilled in web-based Chinese management theory, tested, and transformed into recommendations. By addressing the key factors influencing organizational performance in China, companies (particularly foreign ones) can turn poor performance into a success story.

This chapter is organized in six sections. First, I will briefly recapitulate the major elements of web-based Chinese management and, on the basis of the empirical results, discuss its strengths and weaknesses. After suggesting it as a new management paradigm for the future, replacing the bureaucratic model in highly uncertain and complex environments, I will explain how international businessmen and investors can use WCM to deal more effectively with Chinese private enterprises. Finally, I will discuss how to determine its appropriateness under different circumstances and ways of implementing it in the executive's own company.

Recapitulating the distinctive characteristics of web-based Chinese management in family enterprises

The main empirical research question dealt with the distinctiveness, influencing factors, and organizational effectiveness of the particular Chinese private management model. The empirical findings provided support for my theory of web-based Chinese management, which is readopted in the new, mostly family-owned enterprises in mainland China and resembles overseas Chinese businesses practices. This model was illustrated in figure 2-1. In particular, the empirical findings showed that private enterprises differed significantly from state enterprises in terms of structure, management, and task context (size and emphasis on culture). When the quantitative findings were less clear-cut, the case studies provided useful additional explanations and illustrations.

To set the stage for the following discussion, I will list the six distinctive characteristics of private Chinese management:

a. *Centralization*: A high degree of centralization of power in the hands of one charismatic entrepreneur (dictatorship by the owner-manager). He calls all the decisive shots and adopts a very hands-on management style.
b. *Lack of bureaucracy*: Little use of paperwork, specialized and narrowly confined roles, standardized control systems, and integration in the form of committees, task forces, and other liaison devices. In addition, there is a distinctive lack of a formal organizational hierarchy.
c. *Chinese entrepreneurship*: Aggressive strategies, autocratic, coercive and flexible leadership, and entrepreneurial decision making.
d. *Enterprise networks*: "Spiderweb" of formal and informal company connections, with the family at the center.

In regard to the choice of contextual factors, there are two further distinctive features:

e. *Readoption of family-related cultural values*: Emphasis on respect for seniority, family loyalty, belonging to the family, and (family-based) personal relations. This emphasis in certain cases results from the CEO's desire to revive traditional Chinese culture.
f. *Small size:* Because of the importance of familism, Chinese private enterprise prefer to proliferate into a large number of small to medium-sized firms instead of enlarging the existing firm.

Effectiveness of Chinese family-based ownership model

Private family ownership as key success factor

Earlier scholars merely assumed that the private family ownership model of Chinese enterprises explains much of the success of Overseas Chinese businesses. I contributed to this debate by (a) operationalizing family-based ownership and (b) empirically testing its effectiveness within the context of a structural equation model that held constant other factors, especially company size. The results showed that enterprises in which families held large shares tended to outperform their state counterparts. Because private enterprises were shown to have adopted a distinctive management model, this particular mode of operation thus was more effective than other models. This analysis enabled me to conclude that Chinese management is an art, a point that will be elaborated in chapter 8.

The findings support qualitative discussions in the theoretical literature on overseas Chinese businesses. For example, scholars maintained that "virtually all accounts of the economic behavior of Overseas Chinese emphasize the versatility and entrepreneurial qualities of their family firms, as well as the particular characteristics of Chinese family structure, as the primary source of socialization and of the transmission of values conducive to business success" (Mackie 1992, p. 53). The findings also confirm reductionist statistical analyses (see Wu 1993) that point to a higher average *productivity* in Chinese private enterprises compared to state enterprises, and substantiate the alleged inefficiency of China's state sector, mentioned in numerous journalistic anecdotes (see Forney 1996, p. 62). WCM's effectiveness and dynamism can thus explain the dramatic development of the private sector in China, which contributed significantly to the overall success of China's economic and overall national revival. This point will be discussed in more detail in chapter 8.

The reasons for the success of the family-based management model include the creation and leverage of assets that are clearly visible on a balance sheet but also of competencies and other intangible capital that are not shown in financial statements. Perhaps in the future, we will use what I term "social capital accounting," "core competence statements," or "knowledge stock audits" to measure and report these crucial assets, which may dramatically increase the valuation of a company, especially a Chinese family business. Let me summarize the individual visible and invisible aspects in turn.

Social capital. The first reason for WCM's success is the strong social capital provided and generated by Chinese family structures. This is a valuable asset both because of its intrinsic value (for example, as a "real option" to get access to resources) and because of its value in use (for example, through positive spillover effects to other areas of management such as improving human relations within the family group). However, despite its value, it does not appear in any balance sheet. Over the last few years interest in social capital has increased. Private Chinese enterprises are one of the best illustrations of its importance. It is surprising that the social capital movement so far has not focused on Chinese family businesses and analyzed its creation, usage, and effectiveness. Perhaps this book will stimulate greater interest in China as a real-life social laboratory. In my view, social capital represents an antithesis to the superiority of the market in many spheres of society. The unhampered spread of market forces, which relentlessly promote (basic) desires and self-interest and atomize social interaction destroy the texture of society. This causes huge social costs that are not directly accounted and paid for. If one considers all these effects—which usually do not enter into business calculations, since they are externalities—the market allocates resources efficiently only in a very limited range of economic activities under special circumstances, such as basic commodity transactions.[1]

Even though social thought is deeply anchored in China, not all Chinese philosophers would agree with my harsh criticism of this decentralized model based on free-market transactions, and my praise for social cooperation. Although the philosopher Lao Zi surely did not have the market economy in mind when he wrote *The Book of Changes*, his remarks are nevertheless highly instructive.[2] He commented, "When the pool dries up, fish makes room for fish upon the dry land, they moisten one another with damp breath, spray one another with foam from their jaws. But how much better are they off when they can forget one another, in the freedom of river or lake" (Waley 1939, p. 14). This example also shows that Chinese philosophy definitely does not constitute one homogeneous block, but incorporates almost any imaginable thought. Thus, when I refer to emphasis on traditional Chinese values, I refer above all to Confucian traditions.

Instead of building empires, Chinese private enterprises spin intricate and intelligent webs.

In broader terms, the family structure appears to alleviate the problems stemming from the separation of ownership and control, which results in moral hazards such as empire-building (Williamson 1970) and residual loss (Fama and Jensen 1983; Jensen and Meckling 1976, p. 308). These concepts refer to the self-interested behavior of agents (in this case managers), who pursue objectives that differ from those of their principals (the owners). The agents sometimes build a large company as an end in itself, constructing headquarters that resemble Germany's Neuschwanstein Castle with art collections rivaling that of the Louvre, acquiring a fleet of corporate airplanes, renting suites in luxury hotels all over the world, and organizing management retreats in the most exotic places. In a word, they attempt to build great empires, with all the attendant power and luxury. Of course, they invent a lot of beautiful fiction to explain these excesses, such as the need for representation and other excuses. Despite their skillfull social construction of reality, the waste of resources is difficult to disguise. We know from the history of leading states, such as Greece, Rome, the Soviet Union, and the present-day United States, that imperial overstretch is always a recipe for eventual disaster.

Obviously, selfish behavior by the agents is not in the interest of the people who invest their capital in the company and, in return for the salaries they pay, expect solid stewardship from the managers. When owners and managers are identical, as in Chinese family businesses, there is no agency problem. Instead of building empires, Chinese private enterprises spin intricate and intelligent webs. We have seen a powerful example of this restless networking activity and web-shaping behavior in the case of Mr. Wang's Tiger Company, whose web members ranged from university deans, newspaper tycoons, and army generals to high-ranking politicians.

The agency problem between managers and their employers also is resolved. After the introduction of Taylorian scientific management, workers had to transfer their knowledge up the hierarchy and could no longer exploit the information monopoly contained in their craftsmanship.[3] As a consequence, they felt they had lost significant power and engaged in class struggles with scientifically managing executives. Web-based Chinese management alleviates such conflict because many employees are dedicated and trusted *family* members. Nothing could be more remote to them than the idea of class struggles. Strikes or other unrest is almost unheard-of in Chinese family businesses throughout the world.

Flexibility. The flexibility associated with small firm size, centralized leadership, and national and international, lineage-based networks also increases performance. Though the ability to deal with changing circumstances in a complex environment is a crucial competence, especially in our fast-moving modern world, it does not figure as an asset in the balance sheet. As seen in this book, a researcher has to uncover this hidden treasure through painstaking empirical studies. WCM's flexibility is particularly valuable in a highly uncertain and complex environment which requires sensitivity to changing consumer tastes, and flexible specialization instead of mass production. In the Chinese family business, the CEO can make decisions quickly, without extensive consensus-building exercises or frustrating authorization processes. He does not need any paperwork, committee sessions, or spreadsheets—he performs calculations in his head using intuition and experience.

The Chinese entrepreneur, even when investing in fixed assets, attempts to make them as flexible as possible. As a rule, he prefers multipurpose machines over narrowly specialized tools. When demand changes or new opportunities emerge, he can quickly convert his production line to manufacture new "hot" products, often within days. Likewise, he requires employees to possess as many skills as possible. Narrow specialization into functional silos is despised. Employees learn to perform different jobs and easily can switch from one task to another. The entrepreneur does not need to search a long time for scarce specialists when the situation requires them.

The entrepreneur can strike deals with members of the network quickly, because he needs no formal contracts. Trust, reputation, and face form a complex nexus of implicit psychological contracts and substitute for tedious paperwork.

Enterprise networks that are based on subcontracting or other types of relations help the Chinese businessman gain access to resources quickly. For example, when demand surges, he easily can locate additional capacity from web participants. When he spots a new opportunity that needs to be seized quickly, before it disappears, he will obtain just-in-time funds from his relatives and friends, even in the form of hard currency. An example was Mr. Li's access to enormous financial leverage through worldwide sources, enabling a medium-size enterprise to acquire a share in a five-star hotel. The entrepreneur can strike deals with members of the network quickly because he needs no formal contracts. Trust, reputation, and face form a complex nexus of implicit psychological contracts and substitute for tedious paperwork, which is so commonplace in the corporate West. Besides, the web members supply ideas and advice—additional important resources that reduce the inherent uncertainty and complexity in the Chinese environment, and help the entrepreneur to deal flexibly with potentially troublesome issues. The webs themselves also reduce complexity and uncertainty. Each part of the web deals with its small portion of uncertainty and its small part of complexity. This division makes the seemingly over-complicated environment manageable, since each web member can adjust quickly to his miniworld, while still leveraging immense visible and invisible resources that even large corporations lack. At the same time, each member operates without the large bureaucracy that large scale requires. Because of its flexibility and the concomitant abundance of real options, the family-based model therefore is most successful in industries with divisible economies of scale and scope where agility is a distinct advantage and small size of operation is not a competitive drawback.

Cost-efficiency. Another reason for the model's success is the cost-efficiency of family–based networks. In contrast to the two intangible assets (social capital and flexibility), which are difficult to measure, these cost savings are visible in the profit-and-loss account and cash-flow statement. They also show on the balance sheet as significant retained earnings. Finally, financial ratios that combine data from the three accounting entities provide the analyst with an even clearer picture.

The cost savings arise from various sources: Because deals with other enterprises in the network are based on good faith, transaction costs are very low. The Chinese entrepreneur can dispense with a legal department that drafts elaborate contracts. He spends little money on litigation. In fact, the Chinese are not famous for extended court battles. Face, for example, serves as a social check and balance that prevents cheating in an environment without strong legal institutions. In this respect, China is fortunate to lack a legal culture. Excessive litigation, which I distinguish from a stable legal framework that is necessary for national development, is always a sign of an aggressive society, which scores low on trust and lacks concern for reputation.

With extensive networks, entrepreneurs can minimize investment in working capital and fixed assets. They do not need to keep extensive inventories, since in many cases goods can be ordered quickly from other web participants. This avoids the embarrassing stock outs that are so characteristic of western companies wanting to manage just in time but fail badly in this endeavor and come to resemble centrally planned agencies known from the Soviet era. The Chinese are also renowned for their efficient management of cash, accepting low margins but turning assets over extremely fast, and thus getting the most out of them.

In regard to fixed assets, Chinese entrepreneurs usually can avoid huge investments in machinery and equipment, since they flexibly source large parts of the value chain's production components from enterprise webs. Because the Chinese entrepreneur is likely to focus on what he can do best, he rarely engages in activities where he lacks the required skills or knowledge. He thus does not need to subsidize loss-making ventures, but will profit from the economies of scale and scope achieved by other web participants that specialize in their core competence. This once again increases cost-efficiency.

There is little excess capacity with soaring fixed costs, which increases the temptation to engage in price wars. Sourcing from web participants, which extends to services, smoothes supply. An example was Mr. Li's education business. Instead of investing in fixed human assets in the form of an expensive standing faculty of demanding and changeable professors, he contracted top experts from other universities on demand, through his extensive network. They served as a virtual pipeline and a human "asset superhighway" in a worldwide web even before the Internet was invented. One call to a friend is more powerful than a mouse click! Without much permanent employment, he could balance demand and supply easily.

The flexible access to capital means that the cost of capital is lower than interest on loans from anonymous financial institutions. A bank is likely to charge a high risk premium when lending to a small business owner—his network power and other invisible assets cannot be easily discerned and quantified and therefore are not valued. Bankers commit the error of thinking that what cannot be valued possesses no value. Without substantial collateral, which may tie up valuable cash, the entrepreneur's lifeblood, he will not obtain credit, except from credit card companies and other sharks. In contrast, the businessman's friends in the network possess better information than a bank. They thus can better assess his character and competence—for venture capitalists, perhaps the single most important decision factor and, because of information asymmetries, normally the most difficult to assess—as well as his business prospects. They thus usually provide capital much more easily and cheaply. They can also be relatively sure that they will get their money back, not only because of their superior information. The tremendous social pressure and reputation effects in these "repeated game" situations ensure that the borrowing entrepreneur will repay the loans. Otherwise, he will be a social outcast even in his own family and lose any basis to do business. This is not an enticing prospect, especially in China, the "relation country." However, capital will never be provided because of friendship alone—cash will flow only if it makes business sense.

The trust embedded in the social capital of Chinese family businesses is a real cost saver.

The private Chinese enterprise incurs few overhead costs, since most transactions are performed outside its organizational boundaries. As a consequence, it does not require elaborate administrative staff. In small firms, the entrepreneur can stamp his personality on the organization. As the captain of a small boat, the Chinese owner thus can force his frugal spirit on the enterprise. He dispenses with expensive headquarters, corporate jets, or similar luxury items. Everywhere economy class substitutes for Ritz-style extravagance. Because of the social capital embedded in family relations, family members work extremely hard, make tremendous sacrifices, and often accept salaries below the going rate. Their goals are perfectly aligned with those of the CEO. Thus, the enterprise does not suffer any moral hazards. Consequentially, the Chinese entrepreneur also does not need expensive monitoring devices. To sum up: The trust embedded in the social capital of Chinese family businesses is a real cost saver.

Another important resource provided by network members is market intelligence, such as advice from overseas Chinese family members about export market conditions, customers tastes, and inexpensive supply sources, which facilitates cost-efficient (and profitable) deals.

Because of the refusal to accept "neutral" capital and hire professional managers, the range and scale of activities that can be undertaken by a single Chinese entrepreneur is limited.

. . . And, alas, its downside

Despite these great advantages, the web-based Chinese management model of family businesses has its drawbacks. The empirical analysis of effectiveness held company size constant, which neutralized one of its alleged major disadvantages: the possibility that it limits internal growth and, in consequence, prevents the exploitation of indivisible economies of scale and scope in steady-state, mass-production industries. This confines it to sectors where small size is most effective.

As a result of their strong traditionalism, private Chinese entrepreneurs want to keep their business in the hands of family members. Outsiders are usually not trusted. Because of the refusal to accept "neutral" capital and hire professional managers, the range and scale of activities that can be undertaken by a single Chinese entrepreneur is limited—his resources and span of control simply cannot be stretched ad finitum. As a way around these limits to the growth of the focal company, the Chinese entrepreneur usually builds up an extensive enterprise web. These webs, though enabling strong resource leverage and control, and allowing for laser-like focus at the same time, do not suit all industries. Although webs, too, can provide strong, decentralized economies of scale and scope, certain industries require a concentration of capital, for example, in indivisible process plants, which cannot be managed through a pre-industrial "putting out" system or its postmodern successor, the subcontracting-based enterprise web.

I tested this argument by analyzing the share of P.R.C.-based private enterprises in gross output for various industries. The findings are presented in figure 6-1.

The findings show clearly that Chinese private enterprises are most

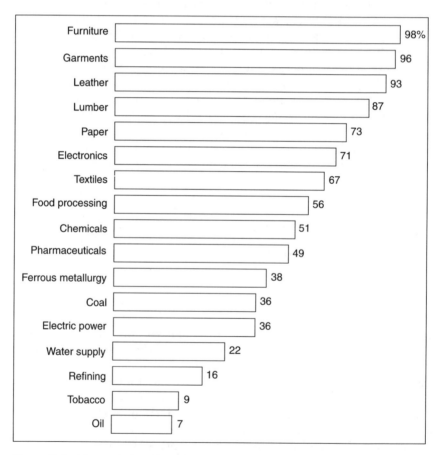

Figure 6-1 Share of private sector in gross output by industry in mainland China (%)
Source: China Statistical Yearbook (1996).

heavily represented in industries that do not require much capital invest-ment and demand rapid adaptation to changing tastes, and thus are suited for small-scale businesses. Examples include furniture (98% share of gross industrial output), garments (96%), electronics (71%), and textiles (67%). This fit between management model and environment explains much of the dynamism of private economic activity in these important sectors in China. Private enterprises are very weakly represented in scale-intensive industries such as oil (7% of gross output), tobacco (9%), refining (16%), utilities (22%), and energy (36%). These scale-intensive sectors may need either strong state involvement, as was the case in the former porcelain center of Jingdezhen, or foreign investment. Foreign involvement might be a less attractive option in sectors deemed strategically important for China, because of close links to national security and development.

An interesting failure and misuse of the private Chinese management model, which has not been discussed in the literature, is the predomi-nance of small cement companies in a fragmented market. The size of most companies is below minimum efficient scale. They usually try to increase production and compete aggressively for market share. However, in the cement business only careful capacity management by a very few players and cooperative strategies ensure profitability levels that allow for rein-vestment. Only a small number of large, professionally managed Western conglomerates has mastered this art and created value. Chinese enter-prises, in contrast, fail to understand that sometimes less means more.

A new business model for the twenty-first century and beyond? Lenin vs. Sun Zi

Based on the findings, I propose my theory of private Chinese management as a new management model or paradigm in organizational studies. It is applicable to a wide range of organizations—from business and non-for-profit organizations, parties, and government agencies to military units (Schlevogt 1999b; 1999h). Because of its distinctiveness, it might continue the pedigree of earlier management models, which, owing to historical and cultural reasons originated in particular countries but later generated worldwide impact, including "German" bureaucracy (Weber 1947/1924), "American" scientific management (Taylor 1911), and "Japanese" man-agement (see Clark 1979; Lambert 1982; Pascale and Athos 1981; Pucik and Hatvany 1983). My model is called web-based Chinese management to stress what may be its most distinguishing feature: the trust-based net-works.

WCM is practiced in private firms located predominantly in mainland China's large "non–Communist" business centers, especially along the coast and in the south, as well as among the overseas Chinese. I discussed its situation-dependent effectiveness. While recognizing the criticism of ideal types in the sense that selected elements invariably reflect the sub-jective choices of the researcher, and acknowledging the incomplete empirical basis for such categorizations—it was the objective of my research to fill some of these gaps—the six dominant features of Chinese private enterprises broadly characterize this business model.[4] It combines hard and soft elements, and stocks and flows: strategy and execution, structural engineering ("statics") and management processes, and the choice and shaping of internal and external context.

Some of these features of Chinese private enterprises also surface in certain Western companies. One example is the tendency toward smaller and more entrepreneurial units. Another is subcontracting-based relationships, such as the cooperation between the textile subcontractors and their *impannatores* in Italy's Emilia Romagna region (Brusco 1982; Lazerson 1995). Other attributes seem to be more distinctive, such as the importance of *trust-based* networks within the extended family and the autocratic and paternalistic leadership style. Those features contrast with modern Western (business) culture, which tends to rely more on formal contracts enforced by the legal system, and increasingly moves toward anonymous organizations that are professionally managed by means of a more participative leadership style, outsourcing to outsiders instead of extended family members.

The emerging Chinese management model is thus not only distinctive in the individual structural and managerial attributes, or their anchoring in private businesses, but most importantly, the above-mentioned elements are *bundled* in the focal Chinese organization and shared across myriad of enterprises with little variability in organizational features. It seems to me that there are no other companies in the world which at the same time are small, rely on extensive personal and enterprise networks, are autocratically, informally, and flexibly managed, and are permeated by strong Confucianist values, in a form unique to Chinese culture and embedded in a family setting, persisting over long time across organizations in different economic and geographic areas and over the organizational life cycle of individual organizations. Figure 6-2 contrasts private Chinese and Western management practices.

Because of the importance of family-based trust and flexible interorganizational networks, the new Chinese management model is significantly more stable than any other model suggested as the organization of the future. Those models emphasize sterile corporate cultural control and self-regulation, which were found to be inherently fragile because of their vulnerability to external shocks and susceptibility to internal power struggles. In the event of outside crises, managers tend to supersede artificially created informal values with formal control mechanisms, which negatively affect knowledge creation and communication. Owing to their fluid internal structures, certain actors try to exploit the power vacuum and introduce latent hierarchies (Robertson and Swan 1998 pp. 561–562).

Besides, the few companies that adopt socially responsible values consciously engineer and intrusively implant them to pursue selfish ends. These values thus will neither create significant impact nor last. They will be swapped for other fads as soon as the gurus tell the managers to do so.

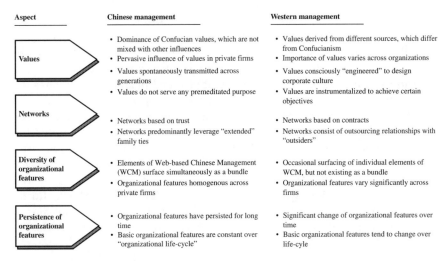

Aspect	Chinese management	Western management
Values	• Dominance of Confucian values, which are not mixed with other influences • Pervasive influence of values in private firms • Values spontaneously transmitted across generations • Values do not serve any premeditated purpose	• Values derived from different sources, which differ from Confucianism • Importance of values varies across organizations • Values consciously "engineered" to design corporate culture • Values are instrumentalized to achieve certain objectives
Networks	• Networks based on trust • Networks predominantly leverage "extended" family ties	• Networks based on contracts • Networks consist of outsourcing relationships with "outsiders"
Diversity of organizational features	• Elements of Web-based Chinese Management (WCM) surface simultaneously as a bundle • Organizational features homogenous across private firms	• Occasional surfacing of individual elements of WCM, but not existing as a bundle • Organizational features vary significantly across firms
Persistence of organizational features	• Organizational features have persisted for long time • Basic organizational features are constant over "organizational life-cycle"	• Significant change of organizational features over time • Basic organizational features tend to change over life-cyle

Figure 6-2   Comparison of private Chinese and Western management practices

And employees know that leaders are not honest and do not believe in the values, and thus adjust their expectations (of future opportunistic changes) accordingly. To be effective and persistent, values need to spring from solid and noble roots (instead of being motivated by greed and ambition), be transmitted spontaneously, and become integrated into daily behavior.

The new web-based Chinese management model might be very appropriate as a blueprint for the organization of the future. Curiously, it fits very well with the prevailing zeitgeist characterized by the importance of the Internet, communitarianism, multipolar (political) alliances, and globalization in general.

Will the organization of the future be based on art or science? In a sense, my model represents an antidote to Weberian bureaucracy and Taylorian management science. I highlighted this juxtaposition in the epigraphs to this book, comparing the theoretical superiority of scientific systems of organization to the practical functionality and efficiency of art, which operationalizes knowledge by means of skill. In figurative terms, I not only contrast science and art, but also Lenin's theoretical principles of collective organization and Sun Zi's practical *Art of War*, or, as applied to this book, state and private enterprises in China.

The new web-based Chinese management model might be very appropriate as a blueprint for the organization of the future. Curiously, it fits very well with the prevailing zeitgeist characterized by the importance of the Internet (see Schlevogt 1999e; 1999n), communitarianism, multipolar (political) alliances, and globalization in general. In all these cases the unifying theme is an emphasis on networks. If it does not achieve this grand success, at least WCM might become one new instrument in the manager's toolbox for achieving success in highly uncertain and complex industries and services. If such were the case, it will be just a new business *model* instead of a new paradigm. Golden Oscar or metal plaque, the choice is for executives to make, they are the jury in this managerial beauty contest.

Possibly the major factor deciding the adoption of WCM as a new paradigm in the West will be the perceived threat from competition by Chinese companies, both in the Chinese market and on Western home turfs. One major reason for the large amount of research on Japanese management and the emulation of the new paradigm by American companies was the exasperation with strong Japanese competitiveness. This book affords an opportunity for Western executives to study the Chinese management paradigm and adopt it *before* the survival of their companies is threatened—at least in the China market.

If Chinese management wins around the globe, the bureaucratic "iron cage" . . . will be replaced by flexible "social webs."

More generally, as an alternative to (state) bureaucracies, the Chinese management model might be the only way to stop the seemingly unstoppable bureaucratization of the planet. By substituting social capital for market forces, it also is an alternative model to the increasing marketization of society. If it is applied widely, I will argue for a slightly changed version of a prediction by Max Weber, the famous German sociologist: I will propose that we witness not an ever bureaucratizing but an ever proliferating or an ever more closely networked model of organization that has to win because of its comparative effectiveness. If Chinese management triumphs around the globe, the bureaucratic "iron cage" and Kafka's nightmarish vision of isolated anonymity will be replaced by flexible "social webs" and enthusiastic cooperation. Iron will be substituted by ideas; material constraints will be dissolved in immaterial connectedness. At an even higher level of analysis, globalization, Westernization, and especially Americanization (with its attendant values), will give way to the spreading of national, Oriental, and especially Chinese values. If these predictions come true, the theory that describes the distinctive private Chinese management style will become a new *paradigm* in the sense of radically breaking with accepted patterns of thinking (Kuhn 1970).

In its potential to cause a paradigm shift, WCM reminds me of the arrival of Chinese traditional medicine in the West. In a sense, it is a Western discovery of ancient Oriental wisdom, this time applied to management. The levers of WCM might help to release the inner energies hidden in Western corporations. Do you remember how the medical profession opposed Chinese medical techniques, calling them "unproven" and "unscientific"? How much the West has changed in this respect! Acupuncture, for example, has become a mainstream treatment for certain ailments. It is even paid for by some insurance companies. I hope the world likewise will accept the holistic Chinese management model, which in its inner operations depends as much on encultured system thinking as Chinese traditional medicine does. It will, however, be a long time before we can fully understand this internal mechanism at a "nanolevel." Fortunately, as in the case of traditional Chinese medicine, our present ignorance does not mean that we will not be able to explain it in the future. In view of the complicated systems elaborated, for example, in the *Book of Changes*, the ancient Chinese might have understood the subtle mechanisms through which the models become so effective. However, they may have been lost on their passage through time and space. This is an alternative explanation contrasting with the somewhat condescending view of Westerners that the Chinese never really understood the scientific underpinnings of their systems, attributing their existence to mere trial and error.

Use WCM to deal more effectively with Chinese private enterprises

So far, I have analyzed the distinctive elements of WCM and assessed its effectiveness and limitations. I then suggested it as a new paradigm for the Global Management Hall of Fame—quite a daring enterprise! This section presents recommendations for practitioners. International managers and investors can potentially derive important lessons from the preceding discussion and leverage the insights for two purposes. Web-based Chinese management might both help them to deal effectively with Chinese enterprises and serve as "best practice" for increasing their own performance.

When investing and managing in the Middle Kingdom, foreign companies may deal with private Chinese enterprises in several ways: as trading partners, customers, (subcontracting) suppliers, competitors, takeover candidates, investors, and partners in joint ventures or strategic alliances. To succeed in these interactions, foreign businessmen need to understand the distinctive Chinese management style. As we have seen, it significantly differs from that of the older state enterprises, which may be more familiar to Western "China veterans." What might have worked well for state enterprises might prove less effective when dealing with private enterprises. The following practical insights can be derived from WCM theory and its empirical evidence.

The owner-manager is the key leverage point

Because decision-making power is heavily centralized in the hands of the CEO, it is of crucial importance to conduct all important transactions through him. This differs from dealings with state enterprises, where significant authority is delegated to specific roles. When getting in touch with a private family enterprise, be sure you first contact the boss (*laoban*). Later, negotiate with him, not with his subordinates. When problems arise with implementing agreements, look to him for resolution—other interventions will yield very low leverage. If you move from the very top to lower levels, subordinates will respect you and not dare to play games with you, because the power of the "Sun King" radiates. L'etat c'est moi (I am the state), or, applied to Chinese private business, the company—that's me. The CEO is like the emperor in the Middle Kingdom. You need to acknowledge his role as the center of the world (in a country that sometimes still believes it is the center) and treat him with respect, even if he does not deserve it! Effectively influencing the owner–manager will open all gates leading to success in the new private business environment.

Unbureaucratic action will be rewarded

In contrast to the state bureaucracies that you may know from past interactions with Chinese companies, the new private enterprises strongly detest rigid rules, formal roles, and elaborate paperwork. You will not make many friends with elaborate discussion agendas, protocols, statements of intent, and contracts. These formalities may be a barrier to getting closer to the top managers and, in very traditional enterprises, may even be regarded as lack of trust. In such a situation, you are better advised to follow the wisdom of "repeated games," where reputation effects will ensure that players do not behave opportunistically. Instead of constant mistrust wrapped into the whole modern weaponry of corporate paperwork, it is better to think hard about unbureaucratic and entrepreneurial means to achieve incentive alignments with the Chinese partner. Win-win arrangements will prevent unwelcome surprises.

Investment in social capital will bear high returns

In view of your rich experience from businesses dealing in the West, you might be afraid of firing all your corporate lawyers, management consultants, and other paper tigers. You probably fear loopholes not covered in contractual agreements. But contracts will not insulate you from danger. First, in a highly uncertain and complex business environment, you will find it impossible to predict all future outcomes. But such forecasts are the basis for writing good contracts. Second, amid all the uncertainty in China, there is one thing you can be sure about: contract law and Chinese courts are very unlikely to help you once your partner has held you up. Because personal contacts matter so much in China, the best way to deal with this legal vacuum is to use reputation and *implicit* contracts that are based on trust. But remember that whereas contracts and physical and financial capital can be transferred from the West, social capital needs to be built on-site, through determined and persistent efforts. In the end, developing long-term relations with your Chinese partners, who may eventually become your friends, will partly protect you from external shocks and unwelcome surprises. The Chinese private entrepreneur will consider it a loss of face to betray his friend. Conversely, it is bad luck if you are *not* considered a member of the "extended family." You may find your partner changeable, unreliable, and in many cases outright deceptive. Finally, it is important to bear in mind that friendship will not help if either partner does not see enough profit in the transaction. Social capital can smooth, but not smooth over, inconsistencies and fractures in the basic business model.

Is your company a candidate for web-based Chinese management?

After explaining how WCM can improve dealings with Chinese private enterprises, you are entitled to ask me, Is it right for me? How can I practice this art? The objective of this section is to answer the first part of this reasonable question. The key idea is that international businessmen and investors can possibly profit from using the model to emulate the successful Chinese management practices for themselves—both in the Middle Kingdom and abroad. These learnings apply mainly to organizations dealing with uncertain and complex environments, which require strong flexibility. The model is less suited for organizations that can perfectly program their operations and must rely on significant, indivisible scale economies.

Organization men do their job, but not more. . . . They search for self-fulfillment in other places, maybe at home, when playing with their toy trains—a field in which they have become world experts and to which they dedicate all their passion.

At first sight, adopting Chinese management practices and applying them to a Western company seems an outrageous suggestion. We all know that Western companies are so much more sophisticated than Oriental firms. The West has transformed management into a science and built sophisticated schools of business administration, which teach the profession of management like medicine or law. But wait a second! Are Western practices really so incredibly efficient? Are the managers confident that they will achieve the greatest dreams with their organizations? Does everybody applaud the highly developed bureaucracies? Are people excited about them? Do they energize them to fulfill grand corporate aspirations and help them to fully develop their human potential? Is the whole economy sparkling with innovation, ideas, and enthusiasm?

Well, perhaps some poets of industrialism might see it that way, but the reality, alas, is different. It has been said that what stands in the way of art is too much satisfaction and too little hope. Our highly developed structures often suppress energies, transforming people into mere functional operatives but do not tap their inner reserves. In a form of modern slavery (and maybe worse than any slavery before), man, as John Ruskin put it, is processed into an animated tool or dehumanized cogwheel integrated into a heap of mechanisms. He is subject to the most sophisticated control systems ever developed in human history. He truly becomes the fuel that is transformed into factory smoke; the dust of his soul runs the machines. Instead of feeling that the work makes him a man, he senses his soul withering within him. These organizations do not divide labor; they divide men, degrading many operatives into office machines whose whole being is sunk into an unrecognized abyss. Even if the worker has inner passions and dreams, organizations are not able to harness them. Western enterprises manufacture everything except men. The whole human gets lost.

Organization men do their job, but not more. Like lava they have inner energy but often flow slowly. To quote John Ruskin (1985, p. 86), who inspired me, "It is not that men are ill fed, but that they have no pleasure in the work by which they make their bread, and therefore look to wealth as the only means of pleasure." They search for self-fulfillment in other places, maybe at home, when playing with their toy trains—a field in which they have become world experts and to which they dedicate all their passion. This is a huge, intangible loss for corporations and societies, never calculated but immensely real. Fortunately, I had the immense privilege of dealing with the exciting art of Chinese management. If instead I had to process bureaucratic files every day, sifting through stacks of claim reports in an process whereby, after I reduced the pile one day, an even higher one appears the next day, I would certainly resort to model trains. But would it not be possible to harness this passion, which is directed to escapist activities, within the context of a collective organization that bonds people together like a family in a spirit of fireside humanity, and strives for a mission full of dignity and honor?

Apart from this stifling effect on individual creativity, are Western organizations capable of dealing with highly uncertain and complex environments, guiding and encouraging pioneering ventures into the unknown? The answer, for most organizations, is negative. A bureaucracy is based on rules that codify past events. It uses the same assumption as the ancient Chinese, who thought that because the supreme ancestors (shang di), first of the ancestral line, knew the whole past of the tribe, they were in a position to calculate its whole future. Each generation practiced augury to retrieve this stock of old knowledge. But simple rules based on the past by definition will not be appropriate in a changing and complex environment. The more the external world changes, the more dramatic the mismatch will be. And the more complex the environment, with different parts of the system being highly interrelated, the more difficult it is to devise effective rules. What sort of ancient misconception did the supposedly modern organizational model perpetrate! The modern Chinese were quicker to realize this superstitious belief!

Thus, any arrogance about the high level of Western development compared to other cultures is absolutely misplaced. The iron cage is not the greatest achievement of mankind. John Ruskin said, "In our dealings with the souls of other men, we are to take care how we check, by severe requirement or narrow caution, efforts which might otherwise lead to a noble issue; and, still more, how we withhold our admiration from great excellencies, because they are mingled with rough fault" (Ruskin 1985, p. 84). We started to realize the iron cage's shortcomings when the Japanese outperformed the West. But now even the highly successful Japanese model has (perhaps somewhat unjustly) come into disrepute. So why not learn from the Chinese, the coming giant of the new millennium? I will show that Western companies indeed can use my theory and findings and apply the web-based Chinese management to their circumstances. As a new global management paradigm, it can be transferred to settings other than its origin.

Would you like to ensure that nobody taps into your war chest without your knowledge? Then there are strong arguments for having some bureaucratic controls in the accounting department. . . . The iron cage would still be there—and serve a good purpose.

Having chastised the bureaucratic model and praised the Chinese way, I have to issue some cautions. I am not saying (as other would-be organizational revolutionaries and prophets of "lean," "mean," "horizontal" and "matrix" structures do) that the bureaucratic model is outdated. It has its place as a reliable tool under specific circumstances and for particular parts of the corporation (Schlevogt 1999d). First, in a stable and reliable environment, it makes sense to economize on constant experimentation by codifying the most efficient way for doing things and then acting according to this blueprint. This is a valuable form of collective, routinized knowledge. Second, even if the environment for the whole corporation is relatively uncertain and complex, it is not automatically true that all parts of the organization face the same unstable and difficult environment. Your thinking needs to be specific and must not succumb to generalizations.

Even if you are a dynamic player in a turbulent environment, you still want to have reliable figures. Then, your accounting department would probably be best organized along functional lines that efficiently divide specialized expertise. Standardized rules leverage the past wisdom of recorded routines and generate administrative economies of scale. Would you like to ensure that nobody taps into your war chest without your knowledge? Then there are strong arguments for putting into place some bureaucratic controls, such as hierarchies, in the accounting department. At the same time, you would also want to reduce creativity in these sensitive financial recording tasks (although you might be a fan of "creative accounting"). The iron cage would still be there—and serve a good purpose. Mindlessly shooting all the middle managers in such areas is a sure recipe for unprofessionalism, communication failure, reduced efficiency, loss of control, and ultimate disaster. There will be no public outcry at this hidden corporate massacre—after all, there is no cable network in the boardrooms and offices—but shareholders *will* eventually take to the streets when they see the dismal results.

Other departments may be more freewheeling and engage in project work, in order to meet the requirements of the external environment and to fit the internal composition and nature of employees. Examples are areas such as marketing, with all its creative geniuses; research and development or other knowledge-intensive departments boasting a great group of "crazy" (rocket) scientists who want to fly high in the corporate orbit; or new business development, full of pioneers, heroes, and champions. These ferocious beasts would escape any iron cage, even if it were golden.

Despite assertions to the contrary, there is no organizational panacea. . . . Being offered this delicious and tantalizing menu of German, American, Japanese, and now even Chinese organizational dishes, how on earth do you choose?

Thus, it is very important to recognize that all organizational models deserve a place in the minds of executives. Designers have not worked in vain; their dedicated efforts are cumulative. Despite assertions to the contrary, there is no organizational panacea. No single design suits all conditions, all types of companies, and all people. Gurus advocating universal models lack this insight, which is their greatest weakness. Being offered this delicious and tantalizing menu of German, American, Japanese, and now even Chinese organizational dishes, how on earth do you choose? How do you, as a practicing manager, decide whether and where to use which model? And which means do you employ to eat the dish? Chopsticks? Forks and knives? How do you implement it?

To answer this intriguing problem of multiculturalism, you first need sophisticated problem solving techniques, starting with solid decision criteria. You can compare your present situation against these criteria and make a choice. There are at least two important dimensions in your task environment that you should consider in order to decide which approach to use: organizational size, and the combination of task uncertainty and complexity. I integrated these criteria into a conceptual framework for managerial decision making that is shown in figure 6-3.

The basic idea of the framework is that, depending on the configuration of the size and "complex uncertainty" parameters, different organizational models are appropriate. Here, I am concerned with dynamic complexity which resembles a game of chess where each move generates a completely new situations. Because of strong interdependencies, one change affects the whole system. I distinguish dynamic complexity from detail complexity which resembles a puzzle game. The distinction is important, since size tends to be correlated with detail complexity, whereas dynamic complexity in my view constitutes an independent dimension.

The old organizational paradigms apply best to classical conditions of certainty and low complexity. The Chinese model is a novel approach to deal with the newly emerging (or proliferating) environmental conditions of uncertainty and complexity in specific industries that no longer fit the classical mold. The framework also allows for internal and external adjustments over time. For example, companies can select, shape, and create environments, which may affect the two decision criteria. After merging with all their competitors, or after amassing global cross-shareholdings that no antitrust official can untangle, they may have made their environment so stable, predictable, and controllable that they can move back to the bureaucratic or, even worse, Stalinist model practiced in a command

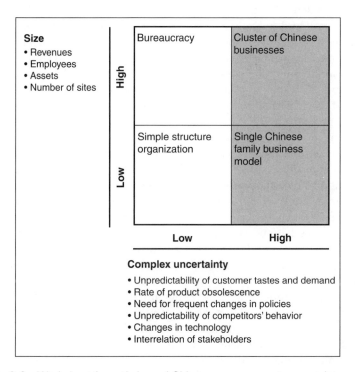

Figure 6-3 Worksheet for web-based Chinese management appropriateness grid

economy. They are disguised oligopolists or monopolists in a superficially free-market economy. Their hierarchical model of organization, in its insensitivity to external circumstances, enervating slowness, and administrative overload, resembles the socialist centrally planned model—with all the dire consequences for helpless (and choiceless) customers. These negative organizational traits are not just the privilege of socialism. They emerge in the "free world" as well, for example in oligopolistic markets. In fact, the essence of strategy is to eradicate competition to create economic rents. Because of intricate cross-holdings and the surface independence of brands and companies, the consumer may be unable to perceive the power concentration.

The new framework, in contrast to other universal best practice recipes, thus addresses not only different contingencies at a certain point in time. To avoid static prescriptions, it also consciously addresses dynamic changes in environments: forces at work and balances of power. To highlight the dichotomy between "classical" and "new age" organizational models, I focused exclusively on these organizational choices and did not include other variants, such as hybrid forms and related species. Bearing in mind the differences in contingency constellations, the message embodied in this dichotomized notion is: Beware, WCM is suitable for very specific applications, not for general use. It fits in where the old models have turned out to be less effective.

Let me discuss the four choices in the framework in detail. If the company is small and operates in a stable environment with low complexity, a simple structure will do—little fuss about hierarchy, specialists, and paperwork. Large companies in an equally predictable and simple context need more bureaucratic control devices in the form of clear lines of command and rules that regulate (deviant) behavior. Routine procedures ensure that the wheel does not have to be reinvented. The work needs to be divided to exploit the efficiencies that Adam Smith described in his famous account of a pin factory. Thus, these companies must recruit experts. To coordinate their work, they need to meet often, so an additional layer of managers is likely to schedule an incessant stream of cross-departmental meetings and committee sessions. When their activity become increasingly dispersed, with all people running in different directions, the CEO must engage liaison persons who pull the strings together. There also needs to be more staff to give advice and assistance to executives who suffocate under their information overload.

And then, as if it is not enough work to run a good old-fashioned bureaucratic (quasi) monopoly, some people start talking about globalization. Consultants, running short of new assignments, push for relentless change (often without reason). Then, as a self-fulfilling prophecy, owing to the high credibility of these change charlatans, change will happen, necessitating more consultants who can "help"—to create more change! Eventually, your company will operate in an environment that has intentionally been made uncertain and complex. The new context requires organizational adjustments. This is where web-based Chinese management comes into play. In the framework, you are about to enter the "WCM zone." My new theory offers ways of dealing with uncertainty and complexity by creating small entrepreneurial units with ownership vested in managers and employees, confederated together in a more or less extensive web sustained and powered by strong social capital.

A small company with limited ambitions in a volatile and complex environment does not need to develop extensive webs (an industry cluster) of networked enterprises, all of which have their own satellites that they often partially own. The traditional Chinese family business model will generate sufficient social capital, flexibility, and cost-efficiency to master the challenges. The company may have many outside relations, but usually does not own stakes in partner firms.

In contrast, large companies in a "new age" environment are best advised to divide their activities among cluster members. For example, being the system integrator and high value added service provider in a network of two thousand enterprises, each of which employs 500 people, is more effective and efficient than managing 1 million people in-house. The affiliated units adopt proactive strategies, are guided by strong and flexible leaders, and make decisions rapidly. The entrepreneurs minimize paperwork. Instead, they achieve control through implicit contracts and socialized, role-modeled behavior. The social capital replaces the plethora of contracts that stifle companies, or at least complements contracts in areas that are difficult to program in advance. It eliminates the need for litigation over small disputes that in any case is too expensive to conduct. Instead of resorting to codified past practice, the extensive webs harness the creative power of humans to develop innovative ideas and solutions to the new problems. Knowledge then is shared and leveraged through the webs. Accountability and authority are clearly vested with certain leaders who command network centrality.

The whole web functions like an extended Chinese family with strong values, mutual obligations, and caring protection, based on intense social cooperation. The webs are flexible, enabling members to adjust to shocks by shifting resources effortlessly to new needs, and create (leadership) training grounds for employees. They thus create and maintain employment, and by absorbing shocks, may even reduce the frequency and length of business cycles and depressions. Those often result from inflexibilities built into the economic system, such as "sticky" prices because of "menu costs" (the expenses involved in printing a new menu, which may deter people from adjusting prices). The webs are very sensitive to changes in the demands of customers and serve them in a very personal manner. Employees rejoice in having freedom and, at the same time, enjoy being integrated into a social community. This is my vision for the future.

Visions are abstract and conceptual frameworks are theoretical. To use them in practice, frameworks have to be operationalized. For example, what do size, uncertainty, and complexity mean? How do you measure these parameters? And how do you implement these intriguing webs and create nuclear or extended corporate families? To answer the question of measurement, I suggest you use a "moon chart" worksheet like that illustrated in figure 6-4.

Let me explain this method. As the first principle, the analysis of whether web-based management is suitable should not be performed at the aggregate corporate level. Instead, you should ask yourself whether there are specific divisions that would benefit from the adoption of this new technique. To do so, you first have to define what your divisions are. They might be organized around customers, products, or geographic markets—or, at an even finer level, be simple departments. Different divisions or departments may need different organizational designs. Then you have to find out what size and complex uncertainty mean for your specific situation, and disaggregate these two dimensions into measurable parameters.

For example, I suggest that size includes revenues, employees, assets, and the number of operating sites, but the components may differ for your business. For example, the size of a steel factory is best measured in the tons of steel it produces—that is the currency of the business. How do you determine whether size is high or low? As a rule of thumb, you might use either industry averages or absolute numbers, such as small = 1–100 employees, medium = 100–1,000, and large = more than 1,000. But these heuristics depend on your assessment of the industry.

Uncertainty could comprise a rapid succession of new products leading to a high rate of obsolescence; frequent and unpredictable changes in customer tastes and demand; the need to frequently change your corporate policies; unpredictability in the behavior of competitors; and major changes in production techniques and technological discontinuities within short periods. Consumer electronics and textiles are examples of industries with high uncertainty. In contrast, glass manufacturers enjoy a more certain environment. There are long breaks between major inventions, and the subsequent implementation of new sophisticated production processes generates further delays. I suggest you use the uncertainty scales in appendix D, section 19.1, to assess the degree of uncertainty your divisions face. If you rank your unit higher than 4, then uncertainty is high; otherwise it is low.

Complexity is measured by the degree of interdependency between stakeholders. Ask yourself, "Does one particular move affect all or most parties, and create a completely new situation?" An example may be the introduction of a new operating system that profoundly will affect suppliers, customers, regulators, and other stakeholders. In the extreme case, your move may even create a new industry.

After you have customized the assessment grid for your specific situation, you can diagnose your divisions and departments and decide which one(s) to convert to Chinese management. To do so, you first have to rate all your individual units according to the customized criteria on the worksheet shown in figure 6-4. You need to derive a total score for each of the

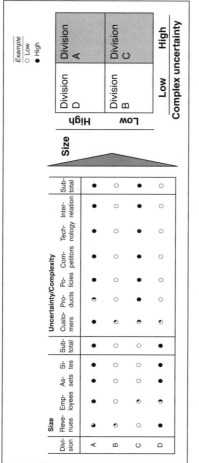

Figure 6-4 Diagnosing WCM suitability in different divisions

two dimensions and enter it into the conceptual framework. The location of the units in the four quadrants gives you an indication of which ones are potential candidates for the new organizational model. It should be emphasized once again that the framework and moon charts do not automatically fit your company. Their main objective is to stimulate your creative thinking, so that after you tailor them to your specific needs, you can determine what is best for your company.

Emulating private family ownership: Ideas for implementation

> *Lease* a man a garden
> And in time he will leave you
> a patch of sand.
> Make a man a full *owner*
> of a patch of sand
> And in time he will grow there
> A garden on the land.[5]

After all the praise for WCM, you possibly took action and singled out those units that need a sense of private family-like ownership (a concept I call "familypreneurship") combined with the desirable structural and managerial characteristics of WCM (accountability, informality, initiative, and collaboration). But how can you implement the new model? What does a manager need to do to harness the full power of Chinese management for his business? How can executives practice this distinctive skill? At this stage, many other works that painted grand visions about the future stop. They do not tell you what to do at 9 A.M. of day 1 of the new organizational life; they will not show you which *specific* action to take. It is like reading a novel that stops before the denouement or a revolution that does not go beyond the destruction of the old system. As a consequence, the manager is usually helpless and cannot act upon the ideas. There is an important leadership maxim: The ideas belong to those who exploit them. After learning great ideas, they can only be considered assets when you can implement them. Impractical learning wastes your time.

Let me discuss several practical ways to create a feeling of connected personal ownership in your company, with the resultant entrepreneurial effects. In all cases, however, changes in structures, systems, and processes do not suffice to unleash the whole power of Chinese management. It is crucial also to emulate the soft aspects, above all the strong emphasis on traditional values. I developed various approaches to implement Chinese management, varying in the degree to which the organizational design is changed.

On one end of the spectrum, an intrusive approach entails designing small, flexible, and entrepreneurial units headed by highly independent general managers or business builders. One method to achieve this goal is to carve out individual divisions. This design implies floating the division on the stock exchange, assigning shares to managers and employees, and making the market responsible for monitoring the performance of the new corporate "family" enterprise. The corporate center might still deliver various services to the carved-out unit, but they would be performed on a contractual basis, monitored by the market, and replaced by other subcontractors in case of unsatisfactory performance. This reverses the authority relation between center and periphery. Using web-based Chinese management, the carved-out units can also be connected horizontally through formal or informal webs, exchanging assets and employees in either strategic or ad hoc fashions. They might be networked externally, drawing on the specialist skills of subcontractors and allies. All three relationships—vertically with the headquarters, horizontally with peer units, and externally with partners—help to reap the benefits of scale and scope, and thus offset the limits of many family enterprises while emulating their powerful social and economic incentives and flexibility.

Another approach is for the headquarters to play the role of a venture capitalist, allocating capital to new ventures within the corporation. It adopts the venture capitalist's sophisticated techniques for screening, nurturing, and evaluating businesses, which in the past helped them to outperform the stock market consistently. The ventures, too, will be very independent, run by entrepreneurs who are free to take risks and responsible for the results. They are thus seedbeds for ideas that in the future might be capitalized on stock markets through Initial Public Offerings (IPOs). They also help corporations to enter activities that are riskier than other operations within the company and that they usually would be reluctant to pursue, partly because they may decrease the valuation of the whole company.

Alternatively, the company can invest in a network of external "seedbeds" for the same purpose. One company, whose name I will not mention, adopted a hideous scheme. It invested in such external "growth options," but when a particular venture developed a profitable idea, it starved the unit of money. The venture then had to declare bankruptcy, and the company bought all the patents. Because of ethical concerns, this is not necessarily an approach to follow.

Another model is to give professional employees the opportunity to leave the company and set up their own businesses, with the corporation's seed money and its promise to contract for their services (cf. Schlevogt 2001m). Using this arrangement, a company can keep a high level of flexibility and avoid layoffs. It also has the advantage of dramatically decreasing overhead for space, transportation, and other items. At the same time, this design creates strong entrepreneurial incentives for the new business owners who manage their own capital.

Using the key elements of web-based Chinese management, even a large company can emulate the strength of private entrepreneurs and retain key performers and business builders.

The carving out, venture capitalist, and professional network routes are attractive for businesses that depend heavily on strong entrepreneurship and flexibility. These are businesses in highly volatile and complex environments with high risk and potentially huge payoffs, which often result from major discontinuities and opacity. Examples include businesses related to information technology (such as Internet startups), sophisticated finance technology, creative projects in the media industry, and pioneering research. These approaches are useful for areas populated by strong personalities—"stars" and "artists" who do not easily fit in as an organization man, or *homo industrialis*. Highly gifted researchers and finance geniuses are examples of people needing such special "structural treatment." Even though they often clash with management and the bureaucracy, they need to be kept in the organization, and must be fully motivated since their pioneering efforts and creativity generate significant value. Leaders need to build the organization around them and produce job descriptions for them instead of trying to force them into narrow templates. The new organizational devices suggested in this book provide talented employees with an independent outlet to pursue creative work and express themselves while strongly bonding them to the corporation.

Using the key elements of web-based Chinese management, even a large company can emulate the strength of private entrepreneurs and retain key performers and business builders who otherwise might lose motivation, produce lackluster performance, and eventually leave the company. Emulating the strong feeling of ownership embedded in the family structure of many private Chinese enterprises creates powerful incentives for the individual to maximize his efforts in pursuit of the organization's objectives, pushing him hard to take entrepreneurial action while being supported by a caring community of interest. This combination of entrepreneurship and family differs from mere profit responsibility and cost control as practiced in Westinghouse, for example. Its CEO expressed his cold management style when he boasted that he would even fire his mother if she did not achieve the budget!

As we have seen, international businessmen can revive the feeling of family ownership in their corporate giants. However, it should be mentioned once again—a fact often overlooked—that some businesses may actually *benefit* from the bureaucratic model. For example, you would not want artistic wizards with changing moods to run a nuclear power station, air traffic control center, hospital, or crucial military installation. When the fallout from errors is huge, impersonal and standardized controls need to complement strong values to guarantee high precision and reliability.

Another way of emulating the social capital of family ownership is to *implant* families in your business. La Quinta, an American motel chain, has a policy of hiring only couples (husband and wife) to run their inns. They live in the motel in a spacious apartment. Being a family themselves, they easily create a home feeling for their guests. They deal with requests quickly and in a flexible manner. For example, through intensive training, they know how to do basic repairs on their own. Thus, they can fix minor problems on the spot, within minutes. Owing to strong financial incentives for the couple, the motels are run as entrepreneurial ventures where responsibility, accountability, and rewards are united in the same persons, who thus strive hard to perform well. The overall setup thus reduces costs and increases revenues. Unlike fragmented family businesses, such an arrangement also leverages the economies of scale and scope of a corporate network (such as joint marketing and shared information technology). This is a very promising model for China, where the family is cherished so much, and for companies in the West that operate in new age environments.

When it is not necessary to separate divisions structurally or import new (family) structures to implement WCM—as in companies with less individualistic personalities—family capital and the feeling of ownership may be replicated via less obtrusive mechanisms. One method is to grant stock ownership or options to the general managers of business units. To build shared ownership among agents who lack sufficient capital to buy large chunks of ownership, companies can make regular deductions from managers' and employees' paychecks that are then used to purchase shares for the individuals—perhaps at preferential prices. This is an alternative to stock options. To re-create the *extended* family of the Chinese business firm, this approach can be expanded to suppliers (and even customers). A certain amount can be deducted from every invoice and later used to purchase shares for the outside stakeholder. In more extreme cases, managers may buy out their companies using strong financial leverage. This is interesting for companies that after restructuring create steady cash flows to service the debt. The complete version of stakeholder ownership is the cooperative, which is owned by its members.

The incentives of private capital can be emulated even less obtrusively through capital allocation policies and the budgetary system (without the need to set up independent divisions). This might be particularly interesting for small entities whose shares are not publicly traded. For example, the owner of a small company may provide the heads of departments with a certain amount of capital and implement a performance-based exit system with two crucial characteristics: First, the department head is completely accountable for the capital and has to earn a certain level of returns; if he does not, he will have to search for other opportunities inside or outside the company. Second, any return higher than the required level goes to the department head. He may either pocket the whole amount himself or distribute some of it to his team. An even less obtrusive version is simple performance-based pay. A manager (or employee) obtains a fixed salary and a variable payment based on the achievement of objectives. The variable part might depend on the spread between the return on capital and the cost of capital for a division (a measure of economic value created). It could be paid as a percentage of profits (profit sharing) or as a lump sum (profit bonus). Pay-outs should not be based on accounting numbers, because they can easily be manipulated. For instance, employees can easily boost revenues by selling goods and services on credit, generating huge accounts receivable that will never be collected. They can reduce expenses by slashing training, R&D, marketing, and advertising. The resulting profits may be huge, but the success short-lived. The division will finally go bankrupt, but the person responsible for the disaster may have been promoted on the basis of his "great performance." In the new position, he will do the same and get promoted again.

As we have seen, there is a continuum of options for emulating and thus re-creating the feeling of private family ownership of Chinese enterprises ("familypreneurship") and the other aspects of WCM. Those options are synthesized in the organizational design framework illustrated in figure 6-5. They differ according to the degree of formal changes in organizational structure and the degree of shared ownership. They represent different stages, building on top of each other, in a move toward a stronger emphasis on capitalistic entrepreneurship (especially suited for large, highly capital-intensive corporations), which I term "capitalpreneurship." These options might also be applied to different *subunits* within the same division. Managers are often unaware of the need for such differential organizational design at the subunit level, and therefore adopt a one-size-fits-all approach that does not address the different contingencies within these subunits.

The effectiveness of the four options varies with contingencies, which therefore must be identified. The following framework, shown in figure 6-6 recommends different approaches depending on two key contextual contingencies: (a) the autonomy need of key employees and (b) the need

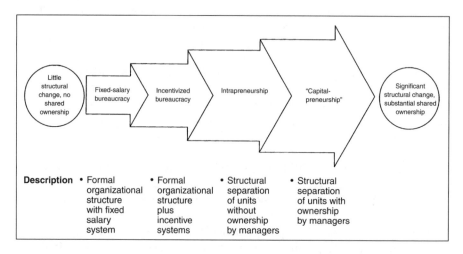

Figure 6-5   Approaches to emulating private family capital

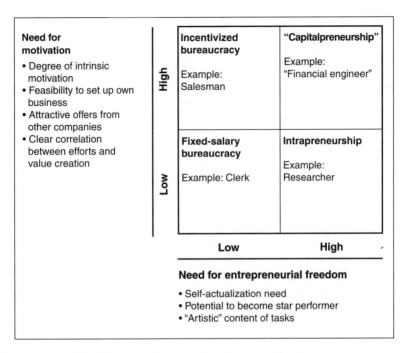

Need for motivation	Incentivized bureaucracy	"Capitalpreneurship"
• Degree of intrinsic motivation • Feasibility to set up own business • Attractive offers from other companies • Clear correlation between efforts and value creation	**High** Example: Salesman	Example: "Financial engineer"
	Fixed-salary bureaucracy	**Intrapreneurship**
	Low Example: Clerk	Example: Researcher

	Low	High

Need for entrepreneurial freedom

• Self-actualization need
• Potential to become star performer
• "Artistic" content of tasks

Figure 6-6   Criteria for selecting capital emulation approach

to motivate these employees (through incentives). With respect to the need for autonomy, artists with strong self-actualization needs and potential high-profile star performers in general may need more space than typical "organization men," who complete routine tasks. Another factor driving the need for autonomy is the "artistic" content of tasks, which requires creativity and experimentation. The need for strong incentives depends on the employee's intrinsic motivation, the difficulty of retaining him, and the strength of association between extra efforts and performance. Intrinsic motivation results from a match between personal motifs and inspiring tasks. The difficulty of retaining key players is a function of the balance between the supply of similar talent and external market demand. The feasibility for a key performer to leave the company and run his own (and possibly more profitable) venture also determines his bargaining power vis-à-vis the company. When the correlation between extra effort and performance is strong and clearly measurable, it might be necessary to reward extra efforts through incentives; otherwise, the individual might not undertake the additional work. An example would be the activities of an insurance agent or piece-rate laborer.

Let me discuss the appropriate implementation options for these contingencies (see figure 6-6). If the person likes to do routine work instead of seeking autonomy and does not need to be motivated to achieve above average performance, then no particular incentives are necessary. A fixed salary will suffice to obtain his steady routine end product (lower left-hand quadrant). An example would be a typical organizational man, such as a clerk who processes claims in an insurance company. To use an analogy from the animal kingdom, these people are like worker bees.

If the employee is no particular highflier and diva, but strongly needs to be motivated, then managers must put in place powerful incentives within the existing structural arrangement (top left-hand quadrant). The appropriate example would be an insurance agent, who might be tempted to set up his own agency but would prefer to be part of a secure body if the payment structure is attractive. The appropriate animal analogy would be that of a sea lion at Sea World. Every time you give it a fish, it will perform its job. Even though it might think that the guardian and audience are silly, it enjoys the fish and is quite happy to live in its pool.

For a person who strongly needs freedom to perform creative work but lacks a particular "greed motive," an intrapreneurship model will work (lower right-hand quadrant). The individual's unit will be structurally separated from the organizational hierarchy, but all capital will still be owned by the corporation (its shareholders, to be precise). A candidate would be a top researcher or "expert consultant,"[6] who does not fit into a hierarchy that mandates routine work and who is driven by strong intrinsic motivation. For him, it might be more important to work with a prestigious company, in a top team, having access to all necessary funds and equipment, than to start his own business or disrupt his career by switching companies often. Taking the insurance example, this model applies to the "rocket scientist," a numerical wunderkind who develops new products based on complicated statistical procedures. His unit would look more like an academic department at a top university than a corporate iron cage. To use the animal analogy, he behaves like a dog: he wants to run in the open fields, but is loyal to his master.

The top gun is the person who needs both freedom and money. . . . He behaves like a cat: he shows temporary allegiance to the food provider, but if the food is not sufficient, he will leave without regrets.

The top gun is the person who needs both freedom and money (top right hand quadrant). An example might be a star trader in a top investment bank. He is a "gold-collar worker" (Kelley 1990). He knows his market value and has shown that he can successfully run his own show. He behaves like a cat: he shows a temporary allegiance to the food provider, but if the food is not sufficient, he will leave without regrets. He knows no loyalties and is ready to switch companies often—the headhunter calls every day and he easily succumbs to the postmodern sirens. At the same time, he could not dream of following anybody's commands. He is successful and clever enough to be the master of his life and destiny. To take the insurance example, he might be the great business builder, setting up new offices in China, Russia, or India, or pioneering with new products in established markets, or raiding undermanaged financial targets. He has many options to pursue other activities beyond his present occupation, since his skills are sought-after and not specific to one particular firm, which makes it easy to sell them in the labor market. He usually has been the captain of his own small warship before, and never wants to be second in command on an aircraft carrier. You had better give such a heroic titan his own show to run and also grant him significant ownership stakes in the capital. He might pay the headquarters a fee for its services, and ask the markets to monitor its performance. In a word, he turns the authority game upside down: it is *you* who has to perform. Times change, my dear reader. Plus ça change, plus c'est une chose *differente*! (The more things change, the more *different* they become.)

Whether you choose the full option of capitalpreneurship (implement family ownership and network new units horizontally, vertically, and externally), or whether you prefer less dramatic moves, the other elements of the web-based Chinese management style will automatically come into being with varying degrees of strength. The captain of his new flagship will surely become a strong leader, truly accountable for his results. This is an example of "good" centralization (remember, in small companies centralization—but not isolation—is effective). As a patriarch, he will care for his workers. In his small unit, he will not tolerate much paperwork, extensive rules and procedures, and boring committee sessions. Anyway, they will not be necessary: the company is small and can be effectively controlled through implicit contracts based on social capital. The mover and shaker will pursue strongly proactive strategies, like a corporate cat that is always on the lookout for new mice. His decision-making style will be charismatic—bold and daring moves serve as big steps toward his mighty vision. Spreadsheets or other analytical tools will be replaced by inspired business-building, almost with an artistic flavor, based on long experience, sound industry foresight, and as intuitive grasp of and focus on the key leverage points in the internal and external environment. He will become a strong networker reaching out to his horizontal peers and external contractors, while pushing the headquarters hard to provide valuable services—at the end of the day, he might fire them if they don't perform! He might prefer extensive webs over a corporate leviathan.

The complete web-based Chinese management model transplanted to Western soil! But wait a second, how about the emphasis on traditional Chinese values? Good question. Believe it or not, I would suggest adopting them as well. View your unit as your family and your web as your extended network of relatives. Work hard to build up trust and cohesion to accumulate valuable social capital. Care for your workers as if they were your beloved family members. Give them a powerful identity and a noble purpose to strive and die for. Never fire anybody to cut costs or to adjust to external business conditions—fire only if a person fails you. You can always move people around within the organization. Even retired people might be kept as consultants. Such respect for seniority within the corporate family is functional, since it makes full use of the increasing pool of (early) retired but "wise" and dynamic experts that results from (socio-) demographic shifts.

In an even more literal sense, think about building a Confucian company—adopt Confucian values, making them part of your corporate culture. This sounds highly unusual, but please think out of the box, learn from the Orientals! If you do something unusual that is effective, and others do not you will enjoy a strong competitive advantage. If you feel comfortable while doing something, this is usually a sign of warmth emanating from the herd which you are closely following. Unfortunately, the herd is always wrong. Even if you move into the right direction, you will not generate above average returns, since you *are* the average. By contrast, when you step out of your comfort zone, it may get cold, you may be alone, but it is a sign that you are probably on the way to the empty summit.

Your strong Confucian culture, in particular, will be very difficult to replicate because, as a result of constant benevolent efforts, the values will be deeply ingrained in the hearts and souls of your corporate sons and daughters. How can anybody entice them away, or quickly change the "soulscape" of his own employees in an attempt to copy you. In China, the values proved so effective that they persisted for several thousand years and even conquered the conquerors (such as the Manchu emperors who adopted Confucianism and wore Chinese dresses). Apart from these path dependencies, there is significant causal ambiguity about the reasons for the success of "Confucian companies." Competitors will find it difficult to emulate them, since they do not know which values are most effective and how to implant them. These are powerful reasons for learning from Confucians. I believe that value-in-use is the litmus test for ideas whose effectiveness by definition cannot be assessed a priori.

Because Confucian culture has so much to offer, you will see its wonders once you dare to venture out into this unknown territory. In particular, it is a philosophy that has proven its worth and adaptability through times of change, instability, and complexity. Despite frequent claims that Confucianism promoted the status quo and thus ossified motion through rigid structure, it is highly appropriate for managing turbulence and interconnectedness. In fact, the doctrines were developed as a response to those complex changes which nowadays re-emerge. Confucianism teaches you humble leadership, the importance of social cohesion and collective effort, reciprocal obligations and caring for your troops, harmony instead of conflicts, subtleness instead of harsh attacks, tireless learning, role modeling, and much more. Values fill the gaps in contracts that result from change. Trust-based relations help to leverage complexity, and thus turn difficulty into opportunity.

Chapter 7 will combine this ancient wisdom with the new empirical results to show in more detail the relevance of this time-proven thought. And on that basis, you might think about it and decide for yourself whether or not it is appropriate for you, your company, and your corporate culture, and whether you want to study it more deeply. And then, its effectiveness in practice will determine its value.

Summary and conclusions

In this chapter, I first reviewed the distinctive characteristics of web-based Chinese management (WCM), and then discussed its strengths and weaknesses. Statistical data showed that it was most prominent in industries that required flexible adaption to ever-changing customer needs and other shocks, but did not require indivisible economies of scale and scope. I mentioned that *decentralized* economies can be achieved through enterprise webs.

Next, I suggested WCM as a new management paradigm in business administration and organizational studies in general, complementing established models. After German, American, and Japanese management, we may witness the millennium of Chinese management. It is one blueprint for the organization of the future, harnessing the full power of humans and enabling flexible adaptation to change. It strengthens the macroeconomy as a whole, making it more resilient and more robust. Because of its flexibility and dynamism, it not only creates and maintains employment, but also cushions economic shocks better than rigid state and corporate bureaucracies. Resources can be shifted easily within the web, so that there is no need to lay off workers. Supply can easily be adjusted to demand, and there is no stickiness in management processes, which is often blamed for recessions. Its flexibility thus might lessen the occurrence and impact of business cycles and depressions and lead to sustained high-quality growth. WCM is thus a great design for an organization and an economy, a great vision for both the microeconomy and the macroeconomy. It represents a revolutionary breakthrough, because the macro- and microlevel (together with the mesolevel of industrial clusters) have never been linked in one great blueprint.

Then, I proposed that international managers and investors can learn from WCM both to improve their dealings with private Chinese enterprises and to increase the performance of their own organizations. In regard to cross-cultural management, WCM teaches Western businessmen to identify key leverage points when working with their Chinese counterparts. Those include targeting the CEO directly in all major negotiations, a bias for unbureaucratic action, and building up strong social capital with the Chinese.

With respect to the adoption of the new model on the home turf, I cautioned the practitioner that WCM is appropriate only in certain circumstances. The bureaucratic model produces reliable and efficient end products under classical conditions of certainty and low dynamic complexity. In contrast, WCM proves highly effective for real-time adjustments to rapidly changing conditions that cannot be mastered by resorting to codified experience. Webs in particular serve as excellent tools for managing and leveraging complexity to create value. WCM thus represents a new generation of business models for a turbulent and interconnected world.

I then suggested a screening framework to single out divisions, departments, and other units that might be suitable for WCM, and operationalized it through a worksheet for unit assessment. Depending on the configuration of parameters in the *external* task environment, managers must choose between (a) simple structures (small size, low complex uncertainty), (b) bureaucracy (large size, low complex uncertainty), (c) the single Chinese business model (small size, high complex uncertainty), and (d) the cluster of Chinese businesses (large size, high complex uncertainty).

Next, I suggested practical approaches for creating a sense of private "family" ownership in the company ("familypreneurship") and building up strong webs, with all the resulting elements of WCM. Leaders need to develop and nurture a Confucian-type corporate nuclear family, consisting of the company father and his entrepreneurial sons and daughters, networked into an extended family with outside "relative enterprises." Approaches differ in the need for structural changes and the degree to which ownership is vested in the key players. I suggested two internal criteria for deciding which of these four organizational stages is appropriate: the need for entrepreneurial freedom and the motivation of key employees. The four options were: existing bureaucratic structures with fixed salaries (low motivation, low autonomy), incentivized bureaucracies (high motivation, low autonomy), intrapreneurship (low motivation, high autonomy), and a new form of ownership (high motivation, high autonomy), christened "capitalpreneurship," which structurally separated newly created units that are owned by managers. I ended the chapter with an appeal to adopt truly Confucian values as an unrivaled competitive weapon. Owing to path dependencies and causal ambiguity, it cannot easily be copied or neutralized.

In chapter 7, I will use the empirical results and Confucian wisdom to embed WCM, the new organizational paradigm, in a larger set of other key success factors apart from family ownership, which is held constant. They enable executives to achieve high organizational performance in China.

7

Achieving Excellence in China: Key Success Factors in the Land of Dragons

Executive summary

Foreign direct investment (FDI) in China increased steadily in the 1990s, and there is no sign of an imminent dramatic change in this trend. Despite occasional declines in capital inflows, worldwide investors remain very interested in the long-term prospects of the market. However, looking back at the experience in their China operations, company executives often find that they did not live up to their performance targets. To turn the disappointing performance around and start running a profitable business in China, managers need to know the key success factors in the market. Instead of analyzing best practice from a limited number of arbitrarily selected foreign companies, as is common in the "airport management literature," this chapter derives lessons from successful *Chinese* companies, based on extensive face-to-face interviews with 124 randomly sampled Chinese CEOs, enriched by several in-depth case studies. The CHINA framework integrates five generic success factors in the P.R.C. and suggests specific best practice process steps and ten "Golden Rules" of implementing them to build companies with high organizational effectiveness in China (and other emerging markets). I also discuss necessary regional adaptations of strategies in the north and south of China.

Objective of this chapter: The keys for uncovering success in China

The objective of this chapter is to develop practical recommendations on how to achieve high(er) performance in mainland China, based on the empirical analysis of the drivers of effectiveness reported in chapter 5. By analyzing key success factors (KSFs), I explain the underlying causes of performance differences of companies operating in China. Executives who understand and leverage these key success factors can assure that the risk–return balance is in their favor. They will outperform companies that do not firmly grasp and manage the fundamental drivers of success. The learnings from China also help foreign companies successfully lead their ventures in other emerging markets: India (Schlevogt 2001e; 2001g), Russia (Schlevogt 2000c), and elsewhere. Apart from benefitting Western companies, the insights are potentially important for domestic Chinese companies, and may have significant implications for China's national political economy. Improving the profitability of foreign companies is crucial for keeping investors bullish on China and maintaining FDI flows, thereby contributing to a continuous increase in exports (by foreign firms operating in China) and overall *short-term* (demand-side) economic growth. The accumulation of capital, upgrading of labor through training by foreign companies, and increased total factor productivity will promote *long-term* (supply side) economic growth.

Concentrating on high-impact areas: The importance of key success factors and focused leverage

To achieve focus, leverage, and control, the first and most important step is to identify the critical drivers of success in a market. In view of the high perceived uncertainty and complexity, this exercise is extremely important in China (see Schlevogt 2000a; 2000b). These key success factors are the limited number of areas in which excellent performance ensures a company's survival, competitiveness, and prosperity. Managers have to detect the few levers under their control that produce a disproportionately strong impact on performance. This notion reminds us of what Archimedes, the ancient Greek philosopher, told us: "Give me a lever long enough . . . and single-handed I can move the world." This focused approach contrasts with an attitude of trying to "boil the ocean," an attempt to perform well on *all* management fronts. This idea of what I call "focused leverage" is expressed in the "80/20 rule," the notion that by concentrating on the 20% that counts, managers can achieve 80% of the result.

Knowledge of the key success factors helps a company to focus on the essential levers and quickly achieve high levels of performance.

In the development of a company's business in China and other emerging countries, the relationship between input and outcome usually is shaped like a S-curve (see figure 7-1). After some initial efforts that get the

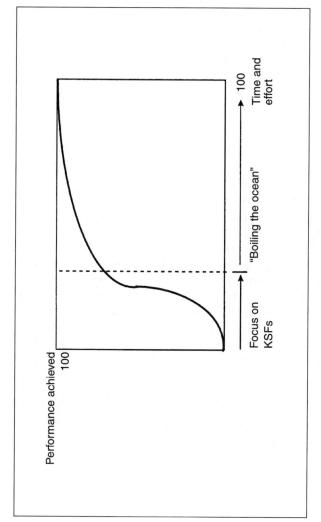

Figure 7-1 Impact of key success factor (KSF) focus on performance

company started and yield limited results, the knowledge of the key success factors helps managers focus on the essential levers and quickly achieve high levels of performance. In contrast, by "boiling the ocean," the company cannot achieve quantum leaps in performance.

Besides this important function of shaping strategic focus and creating leverage, key success factors can also be used for performance control. After identifying key effectiveness drivers for a specific industry, market, or situation, a company may monitor its success by analyzing how well it performs on each of these factors, and take corrective action if necessary. This form of strategic control based on KSF scores is more informative than a simple emphasis on sales or profit figures or other objectives that might be lower than industry averages, the standards set by leading competitors, or other benchmarks.

The need for fact-based recommendations in China:
Adopting a Chinese perspective

One of the key contributions of this book is to take one of the first steps toward replacing "guesstimates" about the drivers of success in China, based on vague experience or a limited number of case studies that usually feature foreign companies, with comprehensive theories supported by scientific evidence. Surveying a large number of randomly selected companies, and grounding the results in case studies, lowers the risk of relying on spontaneous "guru advice" supported only by anecdotes. Their "evidence" is often arbitrarily selected to support a certain point. Yet it is almost always possible to find some supporting examples for a thesis— the key test of any theory is whether it can be *falsified.* These stories also tend to be postmortems based on hindsight. Succumbing to reductionism, some commentators use short-term performance as a litmus test (Yan 1998). This advice is often faddish. Prescriptions change almost according to the seasons. Writers periodically recycle ideas that often date back several years, decades, or longer. Unfortunately, they disguise their origin declaring them "brand-new" and revolutionary. Yet instead of inventing new ideas or revolutionizing the world, at best they remind us of earlier work.

The crucial message is that I not only insisted on uncovering the real facts, but also set out to learn from excellent and weak *Chinese* companies through rigorous empirical analysis, instead of merely describing the actions of Western multinational companies in China.

In contrast, the statistical method has the advantage of deriving key success factors *analytically*, which avoids the need to ask other people what they *think* are the key success factors. The causal link leading from key structural, managerial, and contextual variables to performance is thus free from opinion or bias.[1] Instead of just recommending best practice, I analyze forces at work and uncover the mechanism of creating value. My empirical research design also avoids the pitfall of studying only "excellent" companies. Such an approach cannot demonstrate that the highlighted traits are indeed associated only with high performance. Less successful companies may follow the same strategies, which are labeled "excellent." The real reasons for success would thus remain concealed. My research includes both highly effective and less effective companies, as well as private and state enterprises. The less successful organizations act as a control group, which every experiment in the natural sciences requires. Through the sample composition (which includes sufficient variance in performance) and the analytical design (which models factors leading to success) I reveal the underlying causes of performance differences, resting assured that companies which do not address these factor are less successful. I performed the analysis for the total sample, holding family ownership constant. It thus shows which factors beyond WCM, outlined in chapter 6, influence success in China, irrespectively of ownership.

The crucial message is that I not only insisted on uncovering the real facts but also set out to learn from excellent and weak *Chinese* companies, through rigorous empirical analysis instead of merely describing the actions of Western multinational companies in China. Such an approach requires a shift in the perspective of Western executives and management writers, whose natural instinct is to follow the easier road, preferring to learn from foreign colleagues who are members of the same expatriate clubs, or studying corporations familiar from thousands of case studies in the West, hand-picked through convenience sampling. The dismal record of most foreign businesses in China, the limited pool of "excellent" foreign companies to be examined, and the resulting limited variance in performance suggest that this traditional method of studying foreign companies may end up in an impasse (Schlevogt 2000u).

Understanding and learning from other, especially Oriental, cultures might well become an important advantage in our increasingly integrated world. In the competition for the future, success will depend on a synthesis of East and West, and so far the East has been in a much better position to achieve this than the West.

In contrast to the ailing foreign companies, there are many high-performing Chinese companies, especially private firms (Schlevogt 1999i; 1999k; 2000f; 2001c)—not only because the owners or managers happen to be Deng Xiao-ping's sons or form part of secret triads. In addition, learning from the "enemy"—his past and present (intellectual) treasures—is more in tune with undertaking and acting upon powerful business intelligence. Its importance is stressed by ancient warfare strategists and evidenced by the successful inroads of foreign companies into new markets. For example, when Japanese companies expanded into the United States, they did not primarily focus on the operations of other Japanese firms that had entered before them, but studied and learned from excellent (and supposedly less successful) U.S. companies in their home market. An example was the frequent Japanese fact-finding missions and inroads into Silicon Valley.

In general, understanding and learning from other, especially Oriental, cultures might well become an important advantage in our increasingly integrated world. In the competition for the future, success will depend on a synthesis of East and West, and so far the East has been in a much better position to achieve this than the West. I hope that my book is the first step in reversing this trend and preparing Westerners for the coming Oriental challenge in the new millennium. Sun Zi, the famous Chinese warfare strategist, said, "Only he who, fully prepared, waits for the unprepared will be victorious" (Schlevogt, 1999b p. 685).

What really counts in China: Recalling the empirical evidence

There is some advice in the literature explaining how to do business in China, but only very limited empirical evidence on a comprehensive range of relevant performance drivers to back up the partial recommendations. Case studies normally describe Western companies. However, scholars need to establish conceptual "know-what" before they can derive and teach normative "know-how." To address this issue, I set out to study Chinese companies with rigorous methods, conducting standardized face-to-face interviews at 124 Chinese private and state enterprises in Beijing and Shanghai, and analyzing several cases in great depth. I used structural equation modeling, an advanced statistical technique to test my hypotheses relating to the key drivers of success in China. The results were reported in chapter 5. Traditional case studies alone, even if they analyze key success factors, do not allow the research to draw valid and reliable conclusions on the absolute importance and relative weight of the various performance drivers. In contrast, a quantitative survey provides the basis for compiling a ranking of what counts in China. It is shown in Figure 7-2.

The results for the total sample showed that management style in the form of (a) planning and (b) participation significantly influenced organizational effectiveness. Private ownership also was positively associated with performance. Somewhat surprisingly, appropriate structure, a measure of structure that is in "fit" with the contingencies of size and uncertainty, proved to be more potent than corporate strategy in the form of proactiveness and aggressiveness (price-cutting). Company age, manage-

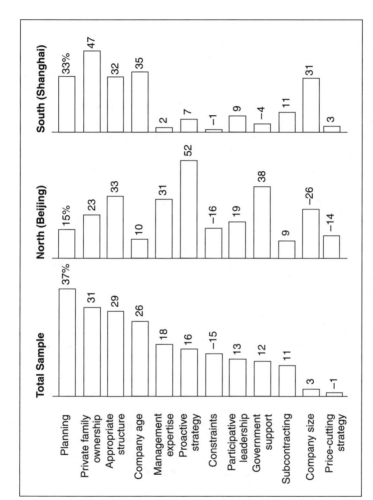

Figure 7-2 Ranking of key success factors in China (regression coefficient)

ment expertise, government support (achieved mainly through *guanxi*), and subcontracting turned out to be additional drivers of performance. A constraining environment tended to depress performance. Company size acted as a control.

The CHINA framework: Strategic recommendations for managers

After empirically testing various theoretical propositions and deriving the statistical raw results from the organizational effectiveness model, it is crucial to translate the empirical findings into recommendations that managers can act upon. Scholars undertaking traditional academic studies often omit this step. Owing to their fascination and obsession with "pure," positive research, they are unable or unwilling to provide concrete, practical advice to managers. However, because managers, especially in China, commonly are very interested in increasing organizational performance (which is seen in their desire to increase shareholder value) I decided to bridge this gap. To provide such normative guidance based on positive results, a researcher first needs to critically evaluate factors influencing organizational effectiveness and discern significant patterns in the data, then synthesize the insights into key success factors, and finally suggest best practice[2] in terms of effective organizational architecture and management practices for companies operating in China and elsewhere.

It must be pointed out that the quantitative results are based on one study only. Even though they are grounded in real-world cases, future studies of this important new subject need to replicate the findings. In addition, all frameworks serve as tools for analyzing, synthesizing, and communicating key ideas. In this book, the components are clearly derived from the empirical analysis, but the particular way of presenting them can take various forms.

Bearing in mind these requirements, I first analyzed in more detail the various factors in the effectiveness model. Some of them can be controlled, others cannot. To deal successfully with both types, I propose an executive "control panel" and an environmental "radar screen." A manager operating in China should view the controllable factors as levers on a panel that he can pull to increase organizational effectiveness. The size of the regression coefficients reported in figure 7-2 indicates the absolute and relative impact of these levers. In contrast, contextual factors, such as environmental constraints, should be monitored on a radar screen that is fed by strategic intelligence. In the short run, managers can adjust according to such input. In the long run, they can also shape these factors, or even create new environments.

To aggregate and structure the controllable factors, I designed a conceptual framework for high organizational effectiveness which operationalizes the key insights from the empirically tested effectiveness model. This CHINA framework (see figure 7-3) integrates five generic success fac-

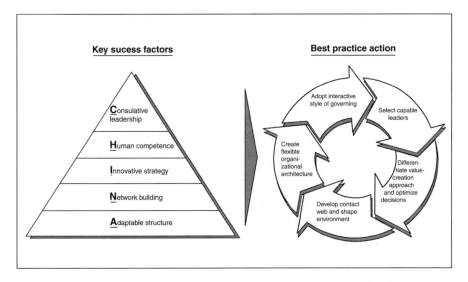

Key sucess factors

Best practice action

Pyramid:
- **C**onsulative leadership
- **H**uman competence
- **I**nnovative strategy
- **N**etwork building
- **A**daptable structure

Process cycle:
- Adopt interactive style of governing
- Select capable leaders
- Differentiate value-creation approach and optimize decisions
- Develop contact web and shape environment
- Create flexible organizational architecture

Figure 7-3   CHINA framework for high organizational effectiveness

tors in the Middle Kingdom and, by extension, in many other unstructured environments and situations. The acronym CHINA consists of the first letters of the five strategic factors. I then suggest a process model (right hand side of figure 7-3) that features best practice steps for leveraging and acting upon the key success factors, and mitigate the negative impact of factors that cannot be directly controlled.

The framework is based on the learnings from high-performing Chinese companies, including both private and state enterprises. Since it deals with generic success factors, it does not only apply to those groups but to foreign companies as well. Because action always needs to be parsimonious, the advice is simplified to some extent. Good recommendations answer the question "What do I have to do on Monday morning?"[3]

The ten golden rules: Learning from Chinese best
practice how to take powerful action

Operationalizing the key insights from the organizational effectiveness model, the CHINA framework suggests five generic success factors in China and strategic steps that lead to high performance. The following ten interrelated "Golden Rules" (see figure 7-4) specify in more detail how to manage the key success factors and implement the best practice process steps through specific corporate action. I will discuss case studies of Western companies to illustrate how foreign companies may leverage the insights from the empirical study of Chinese companies. Because of the pervasive influence of traditional Chinese culture in many aspects of life in China, I enriched the empirical evidence and case studies with insights

1. Use a flexible and consensus-building leadership style
2. Select China leaders with high general management skills and intergrity
3. Proactively search for differentation strategies and avoid price wars
4. Optimize decision through planning
5. Establish *guanxi*, especially with the government
6. Build enterprise networks
7. Select and shape your environment to avoid constraints
8. Flexibly adapt your organization to the task contingencies
9. Create small entrepreneurial units with private capital
10. Build a protective and caring culture with strong Chinese values

Figure 7-4   The ten Golden Rules for success in China

from traditional Chinese wisdom. Even though it often dates back more than a thousand years, it has lost nothing of its significance. It is a gold mine of precious thought, distilling the essence of very complicated topics into concise advice.

The Ten Golden Rules form a bundle of important areas in which a company needs to perform well in order to succeed. It certainly helps to follow selected rules independently, but because of synergies, a company achieves maximum success only when it follows all rules at the same time. In many instances, it is difficult to perform well in one area without excelling in the others. For example, the company cannot generate smart game plans without capable leaders or without a decision-making style that elicits creative ideas from many of its members. Similarly, local leaders will find it difficult to develop broad contact networks if they are tightly controlled by overly centralized structures that give them little freedom of action. Let me now discuss the individual Golden Rules.

*Consultative leadership: Adopt an interactive
style of governing*

Rule 1. Use a flexible and consensus-building leadership style. International businessmen may well learn from China and adopt the Confucian leadership approach. Importing such spiritual software might be more useful than importing textiles and electronics. Because "hard" imports usually replace domestic goods, they usually are accompanied by the destruction or exporting of capital and labor with devastating effects for local communities. We know from the web-based Chinese management model that the leader of a Chinese private enterprise is a tough "dictator." He is not the coach and team player everybody talks about in the West when describing the ideal person at the top of twenty-first-century organizations. But he succeeds and his employees are happy. The explanation is subtle.

Be democratic in discussions and authoritarian in decision making.

Let us start with the facts. Results showed that it is effective for companies to allow employees to participate in decisions relating to long-term growth strategy, capital budgeting, and product and service issues. In China participation, however, does not mean democracy. The leadership style can be termed "consultative centralization." Managers should demonstrate benevolence by asking their subordinates for opinions and ideas, but, in view of the peculiar expectations of what constitutes effective leadership, are best advised to show strength by making important decisions themselves. Put simply: Be democratic in discussions and authoritarian in decision making. Before deciding, the Chinese leader uses subtle ways of testing the waters, scanning his environment, collecting ideas, and gauging potential reactions to the decision. He then uses colorful metaphors ("the great leap forward") and catchy slogans ("the four modernizations"), often expressed as four character phrases, to communicate the idea swiftly and efficiently throughout the organization, and align and energize his people. Through this two-pronged approach, he uses local knowledge, while still reaping the benefits of centralization in terms of speed and flexibility. Traditional Confucian thought expresses this notion of balance, which reconciles apparent opposites in a "golden mean," suggesting that leaders be "gentle yet firm, dignified but not harsh, respectful yet well at ease" (Ying 1995, p. 125, citation 7:38; translated from Chinese).

This implies that simply transplanting decentralized decision making and empowerment *without leadership from the top* is not likely to work in China. The structure of society and groups is hierarchical—with power usually being based on seniority or ownership—and employees expect leadership. This situation should not be confused with lack of freedom. As John Ruskin (1985, p. 86) said, "To obey another man, to labor for him, yield reverence to him or to his place, is not slavery. It is often the best kind of liberty,—liberty from care . . . To yield reverence . . . often is the noblest state in which a man can live in this world." Indeed, the leader in China often has a greater sense of restraint and faces a more difficult task than the man who follows his orders. His obligations are also more onerous than those of leaders in the West, who can easily evade their responsibility for society and their people. They can use "shareholder value" as a pretext for selfish behavior and openly act immorally even at the presidential level. In China, failure to provide high-level guidance is seen as a sign of weak leadership and is unlikely to be rewarded. In contrast, as a great leader, you will become a powerful role model for Chinese employees, who will strongly desire to imitate your behavior. Thus, you will be able to develop strong social capital, embedded in your people.

At the same time, leaders should be open-minded. According to traditional culture, they must avoid four things: arbitrariness of opinion, dogmatism, obstinacy, and egotism. Confucius once said, "I am not one who was born with knowledge; I love ancient [teaching] and earnestly seek it. . . . When walking in a party of three, I always have teachers. I can select the good qualities of the one for imitation, and the bad ones of the other and correct them in myself" (Ying 1995, p. 121, citations 7:20 and 7:22; translated from Chinese). Gathering input from others is different from an attitude expressed by former U.S. Secretary of State Henry Kissinger, who was overheard asking confidently, "Does anyone have any questions for my answers?" Openness to new ideas, and constant learning from employees and other stakeholders, will help to reduce uncertainty and to devise creative strategies for dealing with complexity in China and other emerging markets. The CEO should learn by asking, not just talk. He should serve as a catalyst, clearing the way for people to live up to their potential, and stirring up the powers for better things that reside in every human being. He can thus tap into the collective intellect and energy of his organization, which, no matter how intelligent, experienced, and strong he might be, is more potent than his mind and books alone. The good leader realizes that "none of us is as smart and powerful as all of us."

Humility is an important part of this equation. The leadership philosophy needs to embody the following spirit: "I will not be afflicted at men's not knowing me. I will be afflicted that I do not know men" (Ying 1995, p. 69, citation 1:16). Engaging in hands-on "dirty work," as we have seen in the case studies of Chinese private entrepreneurs, vividly expresses such an attitude. In the absence of other corrective mechanisms known from other cultures, such as democratic institutions and processes, benevolence and humility are important cultural devices for avoiding the misuse of power by superiors, which is not deemed socially acceptable. Western observers often focus only on the "despotism" of China's earlier "autocracy"—they miss the point that it proved to be a workable model with checks and balances. In fact, the "soft" safeguards were less crude and primitive than the "hard" measures based on law nowadays. They relied on subtle role modeling and sophisticated socialization to encourage self-cultivated moral behavior in the first place, instead of accepting immorality and then punishing it, which is how the Western system works. When the socialization of the leader did not work, resulting in behavior that ran counter the will of the people and was detrimental to its well-being, a rebel was always granted the divine right to overthrow the emperor and establish a new dynasty. Role modeling, socialization, and self-cultivation proved much more effective and efficient than the current Western system, since strong and pervasive ethics and morality *prevent* bad behavior from happening. With this model, people do the right thing (effectiveness) in the right way (efficiency). Legal systems only can punish behavior after the damage has been done. Because of the difficulty of devising perfect laws under conditions of uncertainty, change, and complexity—the same conditions many companies face—the individual might even still be able to escape punishment by using one of myriad loopholes. Or the crime might not be detected, or the perpetrator not be caught. I therefore prefer the rule of *noble* men and intelligent social processes over the rule of law alone.

It is crucial to adopt the contingency style of successful Chinese leaders. Instead of using only one approach, they adjust their style to fit different people and circumstances. Such versatility also enables foreign managers to transfer Chinese leadership to their companies and their home countries. This technique can be traced back to ancient times. One of Confucius' pupils (You) once asked the master, "Should one immediately practice what one has heard?" Confucius replied, "There are father and elder brother to be consulted. Why immediately practice what one has heard?" Then another disciple (Qiu) inquired, "Should one immediately practice what one has heard?" Confucius said, "One should immediately practice what one has heard." Another disciple who overheard the exchange was confused. He challenged the master, asking why he gave two different answers to the same question. Confucius said, "Qiu is retiring; therefore I urged him forward. You has more than one man's energy; therefore I kept him back."

Here is a real-world example. Through his constant studies and practice of ancient Chinese warfare, the late Communist "emperor," Mao Zedong became a master at using the consultative strategy. We know from the accounts of his private physician that whenever somebody visited him in his secluded palace, Mao, usually lying in his bed, would ask, "What is new?" He thus used his visitors as sensitive antennae to the outside world in which he could not participate. In meetings he would always encourage everybody to speak up and express their opinions. He then synthesized the input and made a decision that he communicated through vivid language. People were likely to implement the new policy because they felt they had a personal stake in the vital events affecting them. They thus were motivated to act and to work hard for the (party) organization. In a more Machiavellian sense, this approach helped Mao to identify the "weeds" among the hundred flowers, which he then could reeducate or chop down. To be sure, this aspect of the story is not recommended for implementation in corporate life!

Human competence: Select capable leaders

Rule 2. Select China leaders with high general management skills and integrity. Strategic planners need to recognize how much the country manager and other leaders matter for overall success in China. Finding the right person to grow your China operations decides corporate destinies in China. An old Chinese expression praises the virtue of a man who could identify great talent: "Bo Le was skilled in judging and selecting good horses." Key dimensions of winners derived from the empirical results included among other things, the Chinese manager's education, his time with the company, and his foreign experience. The university serves as a first talent screen, since admission depends on outstanding performance in a ferocious nationwide competition among millions of youngsters. In his university studies, an aspiring manager probably learned analytical techniques, which help him to solve problems effectively. During his time with the company and visits to foreign countries, a manager probably absorbed sophisticated, modern management approaches. Perhaps he developed important business contacts that might contribute, for example, to increasing export volume.

These are some of the factors that companies might consider, especially when choosing ethnic Chinese for the top leadership positions in their China operations, because foreign managers may find it difficult to ascertain their aptitude in advance. A balanced set of factors needs to be analyzed, since inborn characteristics ("indices") alone lack differentiating power in a fairly homogenous population (92 percent of China's population are Han). Besides, acquired formal credentials ("signals") are less reliable than in the developed world because of the underdeveloped institutional infrastructure (Schlevogt 2001).

As regards the desired profile of the key leader in China, a combination of both general management competence and area expertise (including cross-cultural skills) is the ideal. I recommend that companies, if at all possible, try not to compromise but strive for the ideal combination of generalist and local capabilities, perhaps reflecting the outlined priorities in different weights attached to screening criteria. However if a company needs to trade off the two sets of capabilities, it is advisable to select experienced individuals with strong general management skills instead of area specialists or "culture experts" without a proven business track record. For example, the management consulting firm McKinsey & Co. implemented recruitment guidelines for Greater China that attach greater value to general leadership potential than specific local knowledge. Similarly, Shell developed a special leadership program for China, which rotated people between jobs every three years to enhance their generalist perspective. The measure proved effective. Whereas annual employee turnover for the industry frequently exceeds 40%, Shell thus lost only eight people (out of 100) in three years (*World Executive's Digest* 1996, p. 19).

I recommend the following supreme maxim for the selection of personnel, especially top executives: Honesty is more important than smartness.

In China, unethical behavior by both foreigners and the Chinese is rampant and not always punished by law. If there is a law at all in a specific area, it often has many loopholes and is subject to discretionary implementation policies. Besides technical aptitude, I therefore recommend the following supreme maxim for the selection of personnel, especially top executives: Honesty is more important than smartness.

In a broader sense, ethical behavior matters also because many stakeholders around the world, including the new species of "vigilant consumers," watch corporate action closely, particularly in China. They often put ethics first, which thus becomes a necessary condition for doing business. For example, customers may not purchase clothes they believe were produced by children, even if they are cheaper and better.

Confucius said, "He who exercises government by means of his virtue may be compared to the north polar star, which keeps its place and all the stars turn towards it" (Ying 1995, p. 71, citation 2:1; translated from the Chinese). The classical Chinese ideal of the superior man is thus the most desirable leadership profile. He combines nine qualities reflecting above all integrity, and could well serve as a screening checklist for applicants: "In seeing, he wishes to see clearly, in hearing, he wishes to hear distinctly. In his expression, he wishes to be warm. In his appearance, he wishes to be respectful. In his speech, he wishes to be sincere. In handling affairs, he wishes to be serious. When in doubt, he wishes to ask. When he is angry, he wishes to think of the resultant difficulties. And when he sees an opportunity for gain, he wishes to think of righteousness" (Ying 1995, p. 223, citation 16:10; translated from the Chinese).

Talented, educated, experienced, competent and trustworthy executives are a scarce resource in China. They are the company's most valuable asset and a crucial competitive advantage for its China operations. In view of strong path dependencies (complex hiring and nurturing over time) and causal ambiguity (the relationship between cause and effect is difficult to understand), it perhaps is the most difficult advantage to replicate. In the short run, competitors who lack this competitive weapon, at best can poach key leaders. But this is a difficult and expensive undertaking, and does not supply leadership capacity continuously.

Therefore, a company's ability to identify, attract, grow, integrate, and retain a pool of suitable candidates is vital. Tailored human resource processes, energized through a strong interface between the corporate CEO, his headquarters, and the China operations, have to be put in place to grow the key leaders for China and other emerging markets and opportunities. First, the company needs to devise and implement effective screening mechanisms to select the persons with the right profile. After hiring key talents, an effective training and coaching environment ensures their continuous nurturing. Even when leaders are sent to China, they must remain in touch with the whole organization back home and elsewhere. This helps them to move from one challenging task to another within the company, which will decrease the likelihood that they will leave because they lack growth opportunities. It ensures that leaders do not become overly specialized in China, but continue to upgrade their generalist skills. This enables the corporate center to leverage their pioneering talent throughout the organization, instead of isolating this crucial capability in one spot and losing it eventually. Ideally, the CEO in the headquarters should be personally involved in the selection, on-site support, and reintegration of these "China heroes," once they have returned to their home base.

Innovative strategy: Differentiate value-creation
approach and optimize decisions

Rule 3. Proactively search for rent-creating differentiation strategies and avoid price wars. The growing number of low-cost local competitors and foreign companies means that many sectors are heavily oversupplied in China. Apart from the high competitive intensity, there are many sudden shifts and discontinuities in the environment causing disequilibria in the market. Though these radical breaks with the past make the environment highly uncertain, they create unique new opportunities that have to be seized very quickly. The Chinese expression for crisis consists of two characters, one signifying danger and the other, opportunity. It is usually in these times of (complex) discontinuites, be they political (as in Germany after the second world war or the fall of the Berlin Wall) or technological (such as the advent of the Internet), that great fortunes are created (and destroyed). It is very difficult to find similar upside potential (and the accompanying risk) in times of stability. Results showed that to thrive in the challenging environment, successful Chinese companies follow ingenious strategies that give them an edge over their competitors. Likewise, high-performing foreign companies constantly look for emerging opportunities, adapt their products to the market, and even redefine their value propositions in order to be more successful in China.

For example, American Standard's (AS) plumbing division, which manufactures bathtubs, basins, toilets, and other fittings, faced low-quality, low-cost local producers selling well below its price and commanding an 85% market share. AS therefore made a conscious decision to concentrate on the premium market, such as bathroom fittings for five-star hotels. To differentiate its offerings, it produced an upmarket glazed porcelain toilet under its own name that was specially designed for the

Chinese market. The success vindicates its strategy. In 1997, its China operations generated revenues of roughly $100 million, resulting in a 15% return on sales (Harding 1998b). It has become the largest foreign producer of toilets in China. Most of the 60% growth in 1997 came from products made exclusively for the Chinese market.

"Bringing plain vanilla banking service to the [Chinese] public is something they know all about. You have to ask yourself why the authorities would encourage foreign banks to come in."—HSBC general manager

---

In contrast, simply slashing prices will not lead to high organizational effectiveness in the long-run. Likewise, dumping outdated products on the market will result in failure. Hong Kong and Shanghai Banking Corporation (HSBC) general manager in China puts it this way: "Bringing plain vanilla banking service to the [Chinese] public is something they know all about. You have to ask yourself why the authorities would encourage foreign banks to come in" (*Far Eastern Economic Review* 1997, p. 66). HSBC cannot teach the Chinese much about basic branch banking. Instead, it intends to use its image of technical sophistication and financial expertise as a ticket to Chinese acceptance. Its decision not to move back into its stately old China head office on Shanghai's Bund is an important symbol of not wanting to go backward and use old-fashioned products. In contrast, it is a sign of "looking forward," demonstrating its commitment to introduce innovative products, such as structured corporate finance and smart cards. For these purposes, a new state-of-the art building was necessary.

It is not enough for the leader to develop grand visions, display "a bias for action," and, looking deep into his employees' eyes, full of confidence, to cry, "Run, guys, you will make it."

Rule 4. Optimize decisions through planning. My study showed that in China, an analytical, rational, comprehensive, and forward-looking problem-solving approach is more effective than "seat of the pants" judgment. Excellent companies in China develop a long-term vision for their business and implement it in their everyday operations through thorough planning. They use expertise and research to search for opportunities systematically, try to anticipate problems, consider the costs and benefits of alternatives, and design integrated action programs to achieve specified goals efficiently. In private enterprises, this insightful foresight is less formalized, but equally powerful. The entrepreneur performs calculations in his head and blends them with expertise, experience, and intuition.

It is not enough for the leader to develop grand visions, display "a bias for action," and, looking deep into his employees' eyes, full of confidence, to cry, "Run guys, you will make it, I'm damn sure you will." And then, when problems happen: "Come on, guys, work harder." Or to say, "Hi, John. I hired you as country manager. Go and build our China venture so that it will be a beacon of hope and strength for the rest of the corporation." Likewise, referring back to the example in chapter 1, can you imagine the project leader in the Shang dynasty assembling his artists and workers, and announcing: "Hi, subjects, I am the leader. I have this great vision of a tetrapod vessel. Go ahead and create it." What would have happened? Chaos—nobody would have had a clue of what to do!

Never guess . . . unless you have to. There is enough uncertainty in the universe.

Sure, intelligent leaders need to create a vision. The helmsman must convince people that they have the potential to achieve more than they believe, and exhort them never to rest on what they have already accomplished. But even though the vision represents a great, almost inhumane, stretch, it has to be feasible. And determining what is feasible requires great understanding of fundamentals, especially the situation on the ground. Strong leaders also need to point out how to realize the vision, even if they leave it to collective wisdom to work out the details. Simply promising the stars and cheering up the troops is not enough. The Bible says, "Make thy way plain before my face" (Psalm 5:8).

Therefore, I recommend analyzing emerging trends and thinking hard about real opportunities and threats in China before defining strategic milestones, and following up with flexible action plans.

Forecasting developments. Even though changes in the environment may be difficult to predict, it is better to think intensively and systematically about future outcomes than just to give up. The advice is: Never guess . . . unless you have to. There is enough uncertainty in the universe. For example, the strategic and financial implications of specific actions should be evaluated under different scenarios (best case, base case, worst case), and sensitivity analysis ("what-if" analysis) should be performed on key parameters. This dynamic approach should replace static investment appraisal methods based solely on financial input instead of a host of strategic and other factors. They use sophisticated templates from the West but do not sufficiently address the uncertainty and complexity in China. Another approach is to design and use computer simulations, such as microworlds. They encourage system thinking to master the complex dynamics that they capture. Using clever and robust approaches to manage the dynamic and complex challenge is vital, since even a small amount of fog can easily blur a manager's vision. Lao Zi said, "Chaff from the winnower's fan can so blear our eyes that we do not know if we are looking north, south, east, or west; at heaven or at the earth. One gnat or mosquito can be more than enough to keep us awake a whole night" (Waley 1939, p. 14).

You also can prepare for "the future that has already happened." Look at crucial events that have occurred, or are currently taking place, and that definitely will have important ramifications for the future. For example, managers may closely observe key laws passed in mainland China and think through all the future consequences in terms of opportunities and threats, which they then can exploit with their company's core resources. They should watch for distinctive patterns, view the information from a different angle, and drill deeper than competitors. Anti-cyclical and anti-mainstream insights and action differentiate a company and may create above-average returns. It is also interesting to watch which issues the authorities particularly emphasize at present that will bear fruits in the future. For example, the Chinese government's western campaign, despite its intrinsic problems and dangers (Schlevogt 2000d; 2000i; 2001a), may well create specific opportunities in China's vast hinterland in the long-run (Schlevogt 2000b).

In addition, strategists may analyze new technologies currently under development that will have a great impact, particularly for China. An example would be upcoming innovations in Chinese character software that might revolutionize certain applications. Or, the fuel cell would be ideally suited for a large market with significant economies of scale and a government that can set and enforce industrial standards. Similarly, executives should closely observe which new "requests for proposals" (RFPs) are posted by companies and the government, indicating new technologies that will be developed and applied in China.

Sociodemographics and other proxies are also sources of future developments. The increasing dependency ratio hints at future changes that can be exploited. It is defined as the ratio of the number of people over 65 (pensioners) to those aged 15–64 years (people of working age). It signals the future need for private pension funds, for example. Further, the tastes and skills of Chinese children might tell us something about their behavior and activities when they grow up and emerge as a new market segment of grown-ups. For example, the "little emperors" (only children) of today may behave differently as adults than the preceding generation, which was used to a large number of kin. Similarly, a surge in the number of driver licences may generate higher demand for cars. This case can be used to show the power of a "derivative logic" to forecast market potential: More cars will also increase the demand for tires and other components.

Strategic planning. There is a Chinese saying that if you do not change the path along which you are walking, you are likely to arrive where the present path is leading. Excellent companies want to avoid making just incremental extrapolations from a (maybe not very inspiring) present state—which, given all the uncertainty and complexity, might prove very difficult and inaccurate anyway—and mindlessly walking the path to nowhere. They aim at quantum leaps in performance, leapfrogging into a bright future that they themselves create. Based on their industry foresight, they first determine what they aspire to achieve, for example, in ten years, and thus develop an energizing dream. It consists of a mission (why), vision (what) and values. The leaders know that the only limits to what can be accomplished are those set by their own dreams. They then roll back the future, identifying obstacles along the way, and decide which action to take to overcome the bottlenecks and realize their mission, vision, and values. Successful companies, at any given point in time, manage different time horizons simultaneously. They pursue strategic milestones (not necessarily only short-term financial results) in the short run, leveraging existing resources in their core business. *At the same time,* they plant options that may lead to future business opportunities in new areas, which entails building new resources.

At the start of a venture, it might be more important to achieve certain qualitative milestones than general "satisfactory" profits starting from the first year which are evaluated against inflexible financial yardsticks and hurdle rates used by the headquarters. For example, the main objective for McDonald's in the first decade in China was to build up as many restaurants as possible, and to establish a strong brand name in the minds of as many consumers as possible. It particularly aimed at gaining children's mind share. Whether free cash flows were positive at this stage is irrelevant. After some time, when the spiderweb of outlets is in place, McDonald's can start catching the flies. But once again, a contingency approach matters. It recognizes that strategic objectives depend on the situation. Managers in industries that do not require high investment in stable and sustainable networks or brand equity might have to focus on profitability right away. In these cases, the lack of profits now is a sure sign of lacking profits in the future.

In general, companies should not increase their discount rate to reflect higher perceived risk. Instead, they may adjust the *expected* cash flows (the average cash flows weighted for the probabilities of different outcomes), while trying hard to reduce the various types of risk and transfer them to those parties that have a comparative advantage in handling them. For example, a power generator may sign a long-term contract with a power distributor, which transfers the demand risk.

American Standard is an excellent example of a company with a well-grounded vision and clear game plan for China through which it minimized risk and maximized returns. Anticipating the boom in new buildings, it first created value by focusing on the premium toilet market while preparing to penetrate the mass market segment by designing specialized products for it. This entailed changing the specifications of their sit-on toilets so that they could be installed in the space formerly occupied by squat toilets.

Focus, stretch, and control went hand in hand: While embracing a challenging target—the strategy aimed at tripling turnover to $300 million (from 1997 to 2003)—it carefully screened investments and minimized risk exposure. It increased commitments based on the accumulation of experience. This approach resembles the way the Chinese government pursues its reforms: It first develops and operates a test site, such as a special economic zone, and then, when the experiment has succeeded, extends it to other areas.

In the early 1980s, AS produced and sold its products to the Chinese market using existing plants and distributors in the United States, Korea, and Southeast Asia, without any large new capital expenditure. To get a foot in the door, it subsequently set up a small joint-venture factory in south China in 1984. When demand finally took off in the early 1990s, it quickly proliferated its manufacturing plants. To minimize risk, it asked Peregrine, an investment bank in Hong Kong, to arrange private placements. Using this approach, it managed to sell approximately 70% of the shares to outsiders. When AS became convinced that the business would succeed, it gradually increased its share in the ventures to about 55%.

Flexible action. Apart from developing foresight and planning ahead, a company must keep aware of future changes in the industry and the broader environment. It should not mindlessly stick to one grand plan based on past predictions, but constantly learn and incrementally adapt its strategy and implementation. Confucius expressed this notion of constant learning and adaptation, paired with hard thinking, in the following remark: "Learning without thought is labor lost, thought without learning is perilous" (Ying 1995, p. 75, citation 2:15, translated from the Chinese). Managers who keep the visionary game plan in mind while constantly remaining sensitive to future changes in the competitive landscape, recognize early on when a key success factor that in the past led to competitive advantage has become a disadvantage.

For example, Volkswagen became the most successful player in China partly because of its strategy to localize much of its production input, purchasing parts from local Chinese manufactures. However, the strong government protection that these local players enjoyed stifled competition. With China's accession to the World Trade Organization (WTO), cheaper imported supplies become available. But Volkswagen is stuck with the agreements that it had concluded with the local government in Shanghai. It needs to therefore source from essentially uncompetitive suppliers.

Similarly, risk reduction now can decrease future upside potential as in the case of presold goods and services and heavy sunk investment into fixed assets. In contrast, nurturing many options at the same time spreads risk and keeps a company flexible to capitalize on new opportunities in a rapidly changing and complex environment. Under such circumstances, the relationship between cause and effect often becomes clear only after a company has progressed on its development path—a classical case of path dependency and causal ambiguity which are so characteristic of China and other emerging markets and situations.

> Establishing government relations does not mean mindlessly spending money on vague displays of corporate citizenship, bribing officials, or visiting the prime minister once a year.

Network building: Develop a contact web and shape the environment

Rule 5. Establish guanxi, especially with the government. You have to become a brilliant external and internal networker. In China, it is of paramount importance to develop strong connections to influential stakeholders, which are a form of invisible assets. Once established and institutionalized, they are a source of sustainable competitive advantage. Because of significant path dependency they cannot easily be copied by competitors. I found that excellent relations especially with local, regional, and national authorities serve as powerful catalysts. They help managers obtain up-to-date insider information on new regulations, crucial licenses, and approvals, ensure that all incentives and subsidies are applied to the company and fully used, and secure general goodwill that guarantees favorable treatment. Besides, excellent government relations can avoid extensive legal wrangles in China's infant market economy, such as those of Kimberly-Clark, the U.S. paper products group. Apart from such domestic links, international relations, for example, with the World Bank and other supranational bodies, increase a company's clout and bargaining power in China, since people understand that the company cannot be pushed around lightheartedly.

However, establishing government relations does not mean mindlessly spending money on vague displays of corporate citizenship, bribing officials, or visiting the prime minister once a year. Instead, to build goodwill, companies must demonstrate sincere and enduring concern for China's long-term national development and target their efforts with the precision of a laser beam. Confucian wisdom tells us that the relations between gentlemen are like water, whereas those between petty men are like sweet wine. Waterlike relations beget friendliness, whereas profit-based friendship does not last long. Once the profit is gone, the relationship will be terminated. Those putting profit first will abandon one another when they encounter disasters. In contrast, righteous men will continue to look after one another under such conditions, as if nothing has happened. Interactions between business and government should equal friendships between gentlemen—the relationship should be like water.

In an environment of universal greed, falseness, and deceit, managers will find that compassion, generosity, truth, and sincerity are perceived as truly revolutionary and serve as effective weapons! For American International Group (AIG), one of the leading insurance companies in the world, demonstrated sincere commitment to promote China's national ascent and the welfare of its people (see Best practice corner: Applying the learnings from Chinese companies). For example, it set up a $1 billion Asian infrastructure fund with the promise of investing half of it in China. It also spent $500,000 to acquire pieces of a bronze pagoda from a European collector and return them to the mainland (Smith 1996). These were sincere signs of concern for China's culture, not simply monetary gifts. As a result, AIG became one of the few foreign companies to obtain an insurance license in China while seventy-odd other international companies were still lining up.

Building relations does not mean, as is commonly assumed, bribing officials—no matter whether they rank high or low or work for the center or localities. *Guanxi* have to be legal. Bribery, despite its widespread use, is *not* acceptable. Just because others are doing it, that does not mean you have to do it as well. Remember, the crowd is always wrong. You should follow the example of Fan Zhongyan (989–1052), a Chinese official in the Northern Song dynasty who insisted on refraining from corruption in an environment where everybody else used and succumbed to bribery. For centuries people revered and celebrated him for his honesty (Yuan 1999). Thus, avoiding corruption literally pays—maybe not in the short term, but definitely in the long term. Even if these moral imperatives are brushed away, one thing is worth keeping in mind: A high-flying foreign manager can spend his time more productively than sitting in a Chinese jail (which is not famous for its comfort), or worse, awaiting his execution (it is worth remembering that, in China, the family of the executed criminal has to pay for the bullet). The company should also design value statements and produce ethical guidelines for selecting partners and countries to ensure that ethical judgments are made and implemented consistently. Such policies and procedures also help managers behave ethically under profit pressure. Levi-Strauss, the jeans company, used its guiding principles and "principled reasoning approach" to decide not to source or invest in China, because of alleged fundamental human rights violations in the country.

Some CEOs believe that visiting the country's prime minister once a year—alone or in a large government delegation—will promote their business. Some executives work hard to secure such encounters, because they make them feel important. However, if the Chinese leaders do not perceive the meeting to be important and therefore do not initiate it themselves, they will just treat it as an official duty and sit through it as through all boring committee sessions. In China organizations hold many meetings, training officials in the art of sleeping with their eyes open. Even when the German chancellor visits China, the Chinese president usually only discusses Goethe's work with him, since erroneously he does not deem Germany to be a pivotal world player. Only if an assistant tells him that the visit matters, will he pay attention.

Thus, CEOs need to elicit leaders' interest by offering something very valuable to China, but ensure a balanced win-win deal instead of sacrificing themselves. Ideally, the Chinese side should be tempted to call for the meeting. This happened—albeit at a large scale—in 1999 at a meeting of the CEO's of the 500 largest corporations in the world, ranked by Fortune magazine (Schlevogt, 1999c; 2001d). In this case, China viewed the gathering, which in the past went largely unnoticed in other countries, as a means of fostering its international prestige and connections, similarly to Germany's discovery of the Olympic Games (in 1936) as powerful display of national might.

It is equally important to build extensive connections at lower levels, for example, with the gatekeepers and the opinion makers of government officials (who alert them not to talk about Goethe!). They enjoy similiar, often informal influence, as the eunuchs at the imperial court. Apart from central strongmen, CEOs should meet leaders in the provinces and other stakeholders, such as customers, employees at all levels of the organization, partners, suppliers, and journalists.

Even though well-selected *guanxi* pay off, managers need to avoid building *guanxi* everywhere, allowing guanxi considerations to dictate business decisions, and relying exclusively on connections to succeed. The principle of focusing on the key impact areas that count most, creating leverage, and maintaining control also applies to *guanxi*. For example, many foreign managers in China believe that joint-venture partners provide invaluable local contacts. Or, they think that overseas or mainland Chinese managers work more effectively in China than foreigners. However, many Chinese government officials and businessmen prefer to deal with "big noses" (white Westerners) and hate to deal with both their compatriots in China, whom, ironically, they do not trust (the Chinese themselves will tell you so!), and overseas Chinese, who are often regarded as arrogant traitors, having left China in times of national difficulties and returning just to make big profits. Because they are westernized, they are called "bananas" (yellow on the outside and white inside). A foreigner can usually build relations with any type of Chinese stakeholder from scratch. The vaguely defined connections of potential partners alone do not justify a joint-venture. On the contrary, local partners can become a liability, making it more difficult and expensive to operate in China. For example, they may monopolize key relationships, barring the foreign partner from the vital information that flow from these relations and other sources, and limiting his freedom of action and reducing his control. Developing one's own *guanxi* web avoids this total dependence on the partner.

As an alternative to the organic internal growth of connections, a company may use the acquisition route to gain access to *guanxi*. Such a move has a dynamic, strategic impact on the environment: while it increases the company's own resources, it reduces the resources of the competition in equal measure. Acquisition can take the form of hiring pivotal individuals with a great treasure of connections or purchasing entire companies that I view as "bundles of *guanxi*." Then, institutional mechanisms need to be put in place for transferring key *guanxi* to the new employer or acquisitor. For example, new hires and the people from the acquired company may be required to take the foreign executives to meetings with key contacts and introduce them.

Even if managers do not acquire other companies, they need to multiply, diversify, and anchor connections within the company. This is crucial to transform the *guanxi* portfolio into an intangible resource that cannot easily devalue, disappear, or be eroded by competitors. Otherwise, the rival might simply poach your best people and thus take away all corporate contacts. The manager should ensure that the relations are spread among many people instead of a small number of individual star performers. Structures, systems, and processes should cement relations inside the company. Access to certain contacts may be vested in roles, not persons. For example, the sales manager may be allowed ex officio to participate in activities organized by the government. When he leaves this position, he must transfer this networking opportunity to his successor. Besides, reward systems should provide strong incentives to transfer relations internally. This way, the company is much more likely to sustain this important source of competitive advantage. Without poaching, a competitor will find it very difficult to replicate the *guanxi* web, which requires long time and tremendous efforts to build. The company is thus protected against imitation and competitive inroads by significant path dependencies and high "barriers to entry."

Even legal relationship-building can be a risky or at least nerve-racking affair. *Guanxi*, though established to provide stability, in certain respects are inherently unstable. Companies therefore need to diversify external contacts in addition to the internal diversification. A diversified contact portolio eliminates unique risk. For example, after some crucial contacts have been built with top government officials, they might suddenly be demoted. Thus, it is smart to build many contacts in one department, so that when the boss is removed, you will still have relations with his former subordinates, who may be promoted to replace him.

A web of relations also puts a lot of pressure on the individual manager to juggle all *guanxi* at once, keeping them in the air while fulfilling myriad expectations, meeting numerous obligations, and saving many "faces." For some managers, this is simply too much. A sad story of what can go wrong is the tragic end of a VW general manager. One day, he flew out of a seventh-floor window, presumably because he failed in the *guanxi* game.

Finally, *guanxi* are also meaningless without a solid business model and distinctive business competencies and other valuable resources. Even if they procure short-term gain, a business environment that becomes more professional may decrease their value in certain cases, since people and roles become separated. They are at best necessary, but not sufficient conditions for success.

Having outlined the key issues in building *guanxi*, it is important to elaborate briefly on the nature of personal relations in Chinese business. This will help the foreign manager to avoid some tricky pitfalls and navigate his corporate ship with ease and confidence in seemingly stormy waters. According to Chinese customs, contacts matter more than contracts. In fact, they often substitute written agreements. Relationships are thus an efficient cultural device for dealing with uncertainty and complexity, reducing the potential of "moral hazards" when contracts cannot be enforced by a legal system and other institutions. If you deal only with your friends, you are less likely to be cheated. Therefore, the Chinese, whom I call a "relationship-intensive people," require you to be a friend before doing business with you. They will drive you around on sightseeing tours and entertain you lavishly, expecting the same treatment when they visit you. The worst mistake is to leave them alone or asking professional tour organizers to take care of them, when they reciprocate your visit.

Westerners, who are used to a clear separation between business and private affairs, sometimes find this difficult to understand. Apart from wanting to remain professional and neutral, they are likely to ask for written agreements—"just in case." The Chinese might see this demand as a lack of trust. They believe that their words, backed up with reputation, should suffice as a guarantee. Insistence on a contract under these circumstances would cause loss of face. Legal documents also might be seen as destroying "warmth," "feeling," and "closeness"—words that in the West do not usually surface in business discussions, and potentially estrange the foreigner even more. Besides, even if a contract has been signed, the Chinese side might explain subsequent deviant behavior by the "fact" that written agreements in Chinese culture do not carry much weight. Naïve cross-cultural management scholars may erroneously confirm the reasons for this excuse.

These are difficult moments for a Western businessman, I can assure you. There are potentially three reactions to such a situation, which I have encountered when operating in China and other emerging markets. The first approach can be termed "provincial." It is the worst case. Under this scenario, the Western businessman visits China and behaves like an alien from Mars. He perceives everything he sees and hears as strange—another planet. If he is arrogant, he might even feel that these things are signs of a primitive and inferior society, not up to the high standards of his advanced civilization. Finally, because of his lack of international experience and parochial outlook, he may do away with all the "nonsense" or "soft stuff," and start to talk business. A battle is a battle, after all, whether fought on Mars or on Earth. The relationship most likely will be damaged beyond repair.

Sophistication, at the end of the game, is measured in dollar (or yuan) terms, not in "degrees of cosmopolitanism."

The second reaction can be called "cosmopolitan." The basic approach can be characterized as follows. Because of his "good upbringing" as a world citizen and since many MBA courses indoctrinated him about the importance of multicultural and multiracial sensitivity, the Westerner accepts the Chinese demands as a manifestation of a different culture that has to be respected. The driving force is the fear of being perceived as rude and unsophisticated. But fear is never a good motive for action. And sophistication, at the end of the game, is measured in dollar (or yuan) terms, not in "degrees of cosmopolitanism."

The third approach, a sure sign of "masterclass," can be labeled "enlightened." In this case, the Westerner is not an ignorant, passive victim of the foreign culture, but a smart, proactive player on an equal footing with his Oriental counterparts. Under this scenario, first of all, the Western businessman knows Chinese customs and has extensive experience in dealing with the Chinese. But secondly, he also understands a deeper layer in this "game." Words like "face" and "feeling" are sometimes evoked as a negotiation strategy. The proof is that many Chinese, when dealing with each other or with foreigners, may ask for written agreements, when they believe this to be in their best interest. They may be the first to insist on a written contract and later on observing certain clauses if this is favorable to them. As a litmus test, you may ask to renegotiate specific terms on the basis that contracts are not important in Chinese culture and therefore should be replaced by friendships. I have also encountered many Chinese entrepreneurs who were very anxious about *their* copyrights and feared pirating by other Chinese companies.

Bearing in mind these subtleties, the enlightened Western businessman distinguishes between (a) real friendship, which in China like elsewhere usually takes a very long time to develop, involving much interaction ("repeated games") and giving and taking, and (b) opportunistic game-playing and maneuvering. If the latter strategy is played, insistence on written agreements and "Western-style" business conduct is not only acceptable but strongly recommended as a means of survival. Meanwhile, I advise the Western businessman to show his respect for Chinese culture, explaining the business case that motivates his behavior instead of just playing tough (which would really be *un*sophisticated). This does not mean that he surrenders his principles. Sincerity and openness are the best strategies, because if you are honest, you do not have to act, rehearse, or remember what you said to whom. Besides, as mentioned before, incentive alignment in a win-win situation is more powerful than any law or institution. It prevents damage whereas contracts at best provide post-hoc relief after the damage has already occurred.

Rule 6. Build enterprise networks. As in the West, companies should focus on their core competencies in areas that create high value and search for opportunities to outsource less pivotal activities. But in China, this imperative becomes more complex. Chinese best practice companies develop diversified networks consisting of different types of institutional relationships with other companies—subcontracting is only one option. These networks provide important business intelligence and serve as pipelines full of new business opportunities. Their elasticity also absorbs the frequent shocks in the rapidly changing environment. Apart from reducing uncertainty, they also divide complexity among network members. Foreigners can reap the same benefits as their Chinese counterparts. Developing such networks takes time and the stamina to endure the difficulties of the moment. My research showed that in China it is often advantageous to move early and persist because it allows companies to build relationships and advance on a learning trajectory in an unknown and difficult environment. This advantage is difficult for newcomers to replicate, because they often suffer from the "liability of newness" (Stichcombe, 1965).

But once again, you have to analyze whether in *your* industry the networking and learning effects are a key success factor. Otherwise, you would be better advised to wait and then exploit "late mover advantages" with plentiful resources. Perhaps you may even acquire companies that depleted their resources while acting as pioneers and creating a better environment for you. Further, a bias for early action should not mean overcommitting resources on big gambles. American Standard, for example, faced the dilemma that it could not possibly sell directly to every potential customer in China without enormous costs and time delays in the buildup process. It achieved instant focus, leverage, and control by developing a countrywide network of hand-picked "good local wholesalers," which helped it to penetrate the national market quickly, without heavy capital investments. Similarly, Volkswagen gained a solid foothold in the Shanghai market by building up a strong network of local suppliers with significant political clout. The promotion of domestic companies pleased the local government, keen to develop its industrial base by increasing the local content in foreign cars.

The two case studies of winning private Chinese enterprises, analyzed in chapter 3, impressively demonstrated how important extensive networks are to secure critical scarce resources. Magnolia, the medium-sized private enterprise in Shanghai that provide educational services, encountered great difficulties signing up high-profile and reputable academics on a permanent basis, since they preferred to be affiliated with prestigious state universities. To overcome this obstacle, it developed an extensive institutional network of professors who contracted their services to the company while remaining formally attached to their institutions. Tiger, a private medium-sized enterprise in Beijing specializing in corporate image design, developed a spider web of (enterprise) relations that guaranteed a constant supply of new information, business opportunities and other advantages (see figure 3-9). As in many private Chinese firms, the entrepreneur maintained the closest relations with members of the nuclear family, and relations declined in importance in proportion to the degree that kinship became weaker (see figure 3-8). The linkages in the enterprise web also varied in terms of formality (see figure 3-10).

Western businessmen can learn valuable lessons from the success of these enterprises in spinning strong interorganizational webs. The crucial characteristic of these networks is that, in contrast to often opportunistic subcontractor relationships in the West, they are mainly based on social capital—most importantly trust, reputation, reciprocity, and shared values. These aspects, which confer to Chinese networks a rare combination of high fluidity and strong cohesiveness, are often neglected or underestimated by Westerners. The "networking society" often is understood only in economic and technical, not in social, ethical, and spiritual terms.

There are many different approaches to building these special enterprise webs. Much can be learned from the Chinese in this regard, too. For example, managers can encourage former employees to build interorganizational linkages with their "alma mater" rather than treating them as "traitors" who have jumped ship. And certain highly entrepreneurial *current* employees might be encouraged to spin off their own enterprises with the promise of continued relationships. This will cut overhead costs and provide strong incentives for the new entrepreneurs. As another option, companies can build interlocking equity stakes through the exchange of shares with newly founded or existing companies. This provides them with strong leverage and control in return for a limited amount of capital that is targeted in the right spots.

When the large-scale production of counterfeit bathroom products threatened American Standard, it took its destiny in its own hands and . . . started raiding a couple of suspected sites each month.

Rule 7. Select and shape your environment to avoid constraints. Constraints abound in China. Because my empirical study showed that they negatively influence performance, managers should select a protected niche for their companies and make their environment as livable and supportive as possible. In a difficult environment, companies can make a difference by handling the challenges better than competitors. For example, if skilled human resources are scarce in the market, they might set up a dedicated company training facility in China or use a corporate university to build up human capital (cf. Schlevogt 2001j). On your next flight to China, talk to your Singapore Airlines (SA) stewardess; she probably originates from mainland China. This is quite surprising, because China is not known for an abundant pool of well-educated and gracious service personnel. Yet SA proactively shaped its environment, turning an apparent disadvantage into a source of strength. Faced with a lack of well-trained human resources but an abundant pool of labor to choose from, it implemented in China one of the toughest selection and preparation processes on earth, identifying young women with the potential to become great flight attendants. It then molds them to SA requirements through several weeks of training and socialization, reminiscent of West Point, the U.S.

military academy. The training scheme does not only develop their mind. Swimming and aerobics form part of the program to shape the body, so that not only their behavior but also their appearance fits the SA template. This is environmental shaping, taken literally! Besides, socialization helps to indoctrinate desirable values.

Similarly, when the large-scale production of counterfeit bathroom products threatened American Standard, it took its destiny in its own hands and, probably with the help of local security forces, started raiding a couple of suspected pirate sites each month. This led to severe jail sentences for repeated offenders. The company earned a strong reputation, which is also a valuable invisible asset. Its enemies understood that "American Standard is not going to be messed with" (Harding 1998b).

To shape the uncertain and complex distribution environment in China, companies may acquire wholesale and retail distribution channels, which enable them to eliminate unwanted intermediaries and filters, control quality, and communicate directly with customers in their own outlets.

Shaping the environment also means that companies actively remove "derivative" bottlenecks in the end-user market. For example, Boeing decreased China's shortage of commercial pilots by donating two 737-300 full-flight simulators with software and visual systems (price tag: $18 million each) to China's Civil Aviation Flying College in Sichuan Province (Mecham 1995). It thus stimulated derivative demand for its airframes. Boeing's top-ten position in the ranking of two hundred leading companies in Asia and its pole position among aircraft makers (*Far Eastern Economic Review* 1997) proves that its strategy pays off.

Adaptable structure: Create flexible organizational architecture

Rule 8. Flexibly adapt your organization to the task contingencies. My research shows clearly that companies whose organizational structure fits their task environment outperform those in misfit. There is no one best way of designing organizations for all circumstances, whatever fancy names might be invented for allegedly new structural devices in the market for management ideas. Lean, mean, and horizontal organizations all have their weaknesses. The environment poses efficiency requirements to which the organization must adapt in order to survive and succeed. Different environments pose different requirements and thus favor different organizational archetypes.

Because of misaligned structures, systems, and processes, the CEO misses many opportunities, places big bets when he suddenly awakes to perceived new market potential in China, and makes unexpected U-turns thereafter.

In China's highly volatile and complex environment with ever-changing regulations and a constant influx of new competitors and products, the best structural response is to reduce bureaucracy and decentralize decision making in order to use local knowledge in real time. Large companies should be more decentralized than small firms. This avoids over-taxing the information-processing capacity of their top leaders. Without such delegation, they would require a plethora of expensive staff functions to assist them processing the information overload.

However, foreign companies operating in China do not always heed this advice. Even though the headquarters often grant nominal responsibility to the China country manager, they still make all strategic decisions. This is a striking case of misfit, because centralized structures do not match with high uncertainty and complexity. The center often uses bureaucratic means of control. For example, the headquarters staff—ignorant of China and other emerging markets—often requires country managers to meet all reporting standards that apply in the home country (which even at home may be excessive). They ask them regularly to submit myriad detailed financial indicators, which are often meaningless or even misleading in China. They may request five- to ten-year forecasts of market trends, which are impossible in an emerging market. I really would like to see a comparison between numbers that were projected five to ten years ago and the outcome now. And these are the data used to make crucial decisions about how to commit millions and billions of dollars! For investments, they mechanically require the use of net present value calculations, although the crucial inputs such as expected cash flows and discount rates are unknown. They often make up for the risk by using an excessively high cost of capital, which makes almost any investment uneconomic. Most likely, the parent company did not use these techniques at its start-up stage at home, which often dates back several decades—yet the company became a success or at least a going concern, capable of investing in China.

It is more meaningful to require reports on factors that matter when building up a business, such as new stores and other strategic milestones. Headquarters should complement or replace rigid investment appraisal methods with disciplined qualitative thinking about future trends and development scenarios, aiming at avoiding big gambles. The input of local managers is crucial for this exercise. Risk can then be better conceptualized. Fear of political risk at the aggregate level is not very helpful, nor is its generic analysis informative. What counts is whether and how this risk affects the particular business opportunity under consideration. Adopting this perspective, many managers find that risk is minor and manageable. I am not advocating less sophisticated techniques. On the contrary, these approaches demand *more* sophistication, since classical models will not necessarily work in China, which requires managers to design innovative analytical tools.

Because of misaligned structures, systems, and processes the CEO misses many opportunities, places big bets when he suddenly awakes to perceived new market potential in China, and makes unexpected U-turns thereafter. I predict the next extreme measure when many CEOs finally wake up from the delirium of a new heavenly market kingdom in China, full of angels asking for their products and services. They will suddenly realize the disastrous performance of their company in China, and the high opportunity costs in terms of foregone growth initiatives elsewhere, and decide to withdraw completely instead of nurturing some valuable options at low costs. Because of their inappropriate organizational design, they will miss local knowledge, such as the insight that despite low average revenue growth and returns in the country as a whole, clever managers can achieve above average company performance. Maybe worst of all, the organizational misalignment and the concomitant poor communication, information asymmetries, and mental distance, frustrate country managers. As a result, they often underperform and leave the company during or after their China assignment, thus depriving the corporation of strong "emerging business managers." These companies thus lose change agents and champions who could inject into the headquarters a more entrepreneurial spirit, competence in dealing with unstructured situations, and a general understanding of and empathy for pioneering and heroic missions.

In this respect, the organizational design of governments sometimes is more effective than that of companies. For example, many foreign offices require their top diplomats to return at regular intervals or to assume permanent senior positions at home. Apart from being re-indoctrinated in national policies and customs, they add considerable expertise about dealing with countries that, because of inherent turbulence and interdependency, outsiders may find difficult to understand.

CEOs in particular can play a pivotal role in radically improving the dismal performance of their corporations in China, which partly results from misfit. This requires better suited and mutually reinforcing structures, systems, and processes. CEOs should properly select, prepare, nurture, and integrate their "China heroes"—an example of appropriate systems and processes—so that they can delegate decision-making authority (including the choice of key managers and capital assets and the design and conclusion of key contracts in China) to the country level—a case of appropriate structures. The organizational interface between headquarters, regional center, and country operation also needs to be improved. The CEO should demonstrate his concern by visiting China frequently, avoid micromanagement, simplify reporting requirements, support the country manager in conflicts with the headquarters, and re-integrate him after his return.

Rule 9. Create small entrepreneurial units with private capital. The book showed that family ownership creates powerful incentives especially in China, where many people are tired of "eating rice from a big bowl" (everybody gets the same, usually low pay). It results in desirable structural and managerial changes, manifested in the WCM model, with positive effectiveness implications. Apart from powerful incentives—the "agent" becomes a "principal" who works on his own account and is free to pursue his own interests—family ownership generates strong social capital in the form of trust embedded in relations. In the case of the Beijing-based corporate image design enterprise, family connections created a constant flow of resources. In addition, small size, the bundling of power, lack of bureaucracy, strong entrepreneurship, and extensive networks also make the family businesses very flexible and cost-efficient. A strong emphasis on traditional Chinese values tends to reinforce the positive outcomes. An example: The CEO of the Shanghai-based education service company spotted the opportunity to provide budget hotel accommodations for the many Chinese visitors to Shanghai. Many five-star hotels had been built, but the budget market had been neglected. He knew that the window of opportunity was very narrow, so he single-handedly decided to convert half of his administrative office building into a budget hotel, literally trading bureaucracy for action (see figure 3-11). It is hard to imagine a company like General Electric doing something comparable.

Large companies tend to destroy an entrepreneurial spirit. The "non-owner" feeling depresses long-term performance. Large corporations are dinosaurs. Through their market power and accumulated resources they survive for a long time, but shocks eventually can eliminate them. They need more rules, documents, procedures, control systems, and division of labor to govern the organization.[4] This might explain why, in my survey, large size in itself was not associated with high performance. "Critical mass" thus matters less than predators suggested in an attempt to justify mergers.

Even if the company is large and, for efficiency reasons therefore needs to structure its activities more extensively than small firms, I advise them to return to their roots, which gave rise to the good old times, encouraging entrepreneurial risk taking, and, at the same time emulating the social capital, above all trust, of Chinese family businesses. Freedom and responsibility thus will go hand in hand, which is rather unusual, in a free-wheeling market economic wilderness. This is more intelligent than firing all middle managers and when you realize that these control layers are necessary to govern the large corporation, hiring mercenary consultants as a replacement for the competence and networks that have been destroyed (Schlevogt 2000m). The range of creative solutions is wide, once you start thinking about new possibilities to become a family again. They were outlined in chapter 6.

For example, the company may design small, flexible, and entrepreneurial units headed by independent general managers. One particular method is to carve out individual divisions. This entails floating them on the stock exchange and entrusting the market with monitoring. The corporate center might still deliver services to the carved-out unit on a contractual basis. This design leverages the scale and scope of large companies and thus offsets the limits of many family enterprises, but still emulates their powerful incentives and other desirable attributes. Complementary to this design, family capital might be replicated in the form of stock ownership or options granted to the managers of business units.

Rule 10. Build a protective and caring culture with strong Chinese values. An ancient Chinese saying tells us: "If there be righteousness in the heart, there will be beauty in the character. If there is beauty in the character, there will be harmony in the home. If there is harmony in the home, there will be order in the nation. When there is order in each nation, there will be peace in the world." A great organization starts with great atoms, the mental programs and maps in people's minds. To create and nurture a strong corporate culture, Western and Chinese leaders alike first must deeply understand traditional Chinese values such as respect for the elderly, concern for the group, and the importance of harmony and trust embedded in warm relations. National culture has to infuse or even supersede corporate culture, not, as anti-national globalists who are keen on sterile standardization usually argue, the other way around. To this end, managers should go back to the origins and read the classics, perhaps starting with the Four Books and Five Classics, the ancient canon for scholars who wanted to pass the imperial exams. I occasionally used this collection of timeless wisdom, which the CEO of a mainland Chinese insurance company presented to me, to inform my analysis of traditional Chinese culture in this book. Based on the knowledge of Chinese classics, managers can develop a culture that instills values of hard work, loyalty, and honesty, and in return offers paternalistic protection to the individual. Then, the company grows into a true community with a living soul, not a mere piece of legal property, a bundle of contracts, or a collection of anonymous shareholders, as many modern economists want us to believe.

Western managers and investors might learn from the caring attitude that the Chinese CEO and the rest of top management adopt towards their employees. As the "company father," the CEO is personally responsible for each individual and receives strong loyalty in return (see Schlevogt 2001m). This differs strongly from the "symbolic manipulation" (Reich 1991) and opportunistic leadership approach of many Western CEOs, who treat their employees as "human resources," not family members. Unlike capital, which they often regard as fixed, they take the liberty to cut personnel at will. It may be healthier to treat people as fixed assets and capital as a flexible quantity! Internalizing and, through role modelling and socialization, promoting the classical Confucian moral values of respect (*gong*), generosity (*kuang*), trust (*xin*), sensitivity (*min*), and kindness (*hui*) will help Western managers to develop better "soft" leadership skills in themselves and others, complementing the existing "hard" scientific management techniques.

In this context, I need to point out that Chinese values are often misinterpreted and misunderstood. Originally, respect for the elderly did not contradict a meritocracy in which capable young people could move faster and assume more responsibility than older people. In fact, as we can read in his work, Confucius always promoted humility, learning, and progress, advocating a dynamic contingency theory rather than static social "cages." As part of a noble spirit of openness and benevolence, he suggested to respect the wisdom and advice of older people and care for them. However, as occurred frequently in human history—the manipulated and contaminated legacy of Jesus and Mohammed serve as examples—ambitious people subsequently deliberately misinterpreted the master's doctrine to cement their power on the basis of age, which among other factors caused China to stagnate. Outsiders erroneously believe that such an inflexible arrangement results from Confucian philosophy. As with Christianity, a "protestant" spirit (which I call "Confucian protestantism") will enlighten us. People should engage in philosophical archaeology, read Confucius' work and rediscover the pure, shining, and empowering truth!

The CEO of [a Chinese company] heavily emphasizes Chinese traditional culture. He symbolized this importance by placing a sculpture of Confucius . . . in his entrance hallway.

The airline Cathay Pacific recognizes the value of a protective and caring corporate culture in China. Initially, the company conveyed a high-energy family touch to its stakeholders. But it grew into a complex and stifling organization with fifteen thousand people and encountered a series of personnel problems. Top management's struggle with cabin crews over pay and conditions exemplified the growing tensions. Faced with such a precarious situation, the company successfully launched a new leadership program for one thousand employees. It rebuilt the corporate culture by emphasizing themes such as encouraging the heart, communicating the vision, enabling others, modeling the way, and challenging the bureaucratic process (*World Executive's Digest* 1996). The resulting strong corporate culture helped to build social capital such as trust and reputation. Employees thought beyond their narrow personal interests and needs, cared for the company as a whole, and interacted exceptionally well with the public. To remain successful after this transformation and continue to grow internally and externally, the company will need to incessantly feed and reinforce this virtuous circle.

As another example, the CEO of the corporate image design enterprise in Beijing held weekly lessons in Chinese traditional culture for his employees. The shared values and joint activities bonded them together. The spirited climate also gave the company an edge in creating innovative designs for its clients. As in a nation, where national prosperity, peace, and harmony start with the values, intentions, and actions of individuals and families, the company's internal (mental) health projects a positive energizing image to outsiders.

> Foreigners do not have to re-create Chinese traditional elements perfectly . . . Chinese employees will strongly reward the sincerity of their intention and respect for China's heritage with their enthusiasm and diligence.

Instilling a sense of Chinese moral purpose can be a powerful approach for motivating and educating one's employees. Sun Zi, in his *Art of War*, elevated morale (*dao*) to the most important principle of governance, which in his view makes all the difference between success and failure. This is the meaning of "To assess the outcome of a war, we need to examine the belligerent parties and compare them in terms of the following five fundamental factors: The first is the way; the second, heaven; the third, earth; the fourth, command; and the fifth, rules and regulations. By 'the way,' I mean moral influence, or that which causes the people to think in line with their sovereign so that they will follow him through every vicissitude, whether to live or to die, without fear of mortal peril" (Sunzi 1999/written about 500 B.C., p. 3).

Especially for the Chinese, rebuilding China's cultural heritage and national glory after a long period of defeat and shame is an extremely powerful motivating engine. They are an inherently patriotic people, which explains its capacity for survival and its longevity. The CEO of Pingan, the most successful nonstate insurance company in China, heavily emphasizes Chinese traditional culture. He symbolized this importance by placing a sculpture of Confucius (next to one of Sir Isaac Newton!) in the entrance hallway of his offices. Paintings of Chinese sages can be found all over the place. He wrote booklets for his managers and agents, telling them about traditional Chinese customs and etiquette, and asked them to respect these norms in all business transactions.

Such an immersion in Chinese culture (or even his own national culture) normally would not enter the mind of typical foreign executives of a multinational company in China. They often are rootless cosmopolitans without country and national pride, part of a globally minded executive circle. Foreign companies that use "culture-free" scientific management techniques, brainwashing and programing employees in the same way everywhere in the world, may at best succeed only partially in China (and elsewhere). They will fail to build crucial social capital and miss out on powerful intrinsic motivation both of which result from reaching and touching deeper levels of the Chinese psyche. Foreigners do not have to re-create Chinese traditional elements perfectly. No matter how clumsy the efforts of the "big noses" may appear, Chinese employees will strongly reward the sincerity of their intention and respect for China's heritage with their own enthusiasm and diligence. Sincere respect lights the spark of collective magic.

Building a strong Chinese corporate culture is significantly more effective in combating problems such as high employee turnover in China than mindlessly introducing extra financial incentives and other perks such as housing allowances, interest-free loans, and overseas training trips. By stressing extrinsic factors, they tend to decrease intrinsic motivation and destroy social capital. And besides, there are always other companies that will pay more, initiating a spiral of increasing compensation, which is as harmful on the expense side as price wars are on the revenue side. Figure 7-5 depicts the organizational dynamics, which includes two reinforcing vicious circles (shown with a plus sign): internal incentive inflation (A) and external incentive war (B). Their interaction makes the problem increasingly more serious. Building a strong Chinese corporate culture is the focused lever that helps to regain control and initiate a virtuous circle of steadily increasing performance and happiness. Such spiritual management based on Eastern traditions avoids the viciousness and vicissitudes of what I call "materialistic management" practiced in many places in the West.

Best practice corner: Applying the learning from
Chinese companies—the case of AIU in Shanghai

The management approach of American International Underwriters (AIU) in China illustrates the Golden Rules that can be learned from Chinese companies. It demonstrates their dramatic impact on performance in China and other emerging markets and unstructured situations, especially when they are used in a bundle.

AIU is the international branch of American International Group (AIG), a world leader in insurance and financial services with an impressive global network and brand. In 1919, the young American entrepreneur C. V. Starr set up a small insurance agency in Shanghai, American Asiatic Underwriters. He first represented American insurance companies in Shanghai, focusing on property insurance. Then, the pioneer established Asia Life Insurance Company and innovated in an industry in which revolutions are rare. The new company marketed life insurance products to the Chinese population, a radical new approach for a Western company. He rapidly expanded his business into other Asian countries, hiring locals for management positions. Starr set up a subsidiary in New York in 1926, which he called AIU. It insured the foreign risks of American companies. In the 1930s, he further expanded his business interests into Latin America. Because of the political turmoil in Asia, Starr moved the company's headquarters to New York in 1939. He transferred his regional headquarters to Hong Kong in 1949 and finally closed the office in China in 1950, one year after the Communists had seized power. After the Second World War, AIU exploited major discontinuities on the European continent (such as an acute insurance capacity shortage), leveraged American political clout, and accompanied U.S. foreign investment to expand into Western Europe. It also entered the Middle East, North Africa, and Australia. In 1970, it became part of American International Group, which had been established in 1967 to manage the American domestic business.

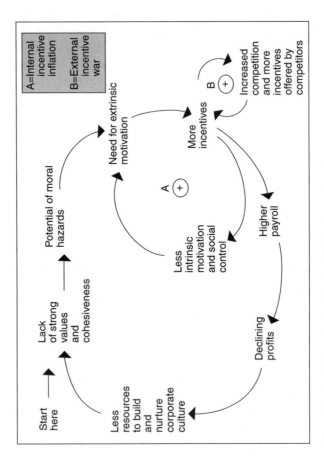

Figure 7-5 Vicious circle of materialistic management

Start → here

Lack of strong values and cohesiveness

Potential of moral hazards

Need for extrinsic motivation

More incentives

Increased competition and more incentives offered by competitors

B +

A +

Less intrinsic motivation and social control

Higher payroll

Less resources to build and nurture corporate culture

Declining profits

A=Internal incentive inflation

B=External incentive war

238

In the wake of China's opening and reform policies, AIU became the first Western insurance company to obtain a license to do business on the mainland. Seventy-odd other international companies were still lining up to secure this precious prize. Starting business in Shanghai, it quickly reached individual life premiums of $50 million. This represented a staggering 90% of the city's market for life insurance (Smith 1996).

AIU's operation in Shanghai illustrates all the Golden Rules. By combining these factors, it created a very strong competitive advantage that is difficult for foreign and domestic competitors to emulate. The company not only is constantly one step ahead of competitors (which in itself is a valuable source of competitive advantage), but also builds strong positions and competencies that would be very difficult for competitors to emulate even if they had sufficient time.

Establish guanxi, especially with the government. AIU managed relations with the government very conscientiously and effectively. The resulting goodwill, a form of social capital, became the key to a license. Even if a company has sophisticated managers, great organizational arrangements, and excellent products, it will not progress in China if it does not pay attention to this crucial success factor. AIG's CEO, M. R. Greenberg, frequently visited national leaders and developed deep relations, which differ from the superficial contacts of other foreign managers. Besides, the company helped to build Shanghai's premier office complex, Shanghai Center, set up a $1 billion Asian infrastructure fund and promised to invest half of it in China, and spent $500,000 to acquire pieces of a bronze pagoda from a European collector and returned them to the mainland. AIG continues a strategy that has paid off in the past, when AIG's excellent relations with the U.S. government opened lucrative business opportunities. For example, after the Second World War, the U.S. military invited it to insure the property of its troops in Japan, which afforded AIG with a bridgehead to this country.

Design rent-creating strategies. At the outset, AIU faced a very constraining environment. The state-owned People's Insurance Company of China (PICC) dominated the market as a quasi-monopoly. Customers were deeply suspicious of a foreign company that had fled the country before. Instead of doing what all other companies did—following PICC, which, at the time, sold only group life policies to big state-owned enterprises—AIU differentiated its offers. It redefined the rules of the game in the Chinese insurance market by single-handedly creating an individual life insurance market. It outsmarted its competitors by sensing and leveraging political and social trends in China, which resulted in a major discontinuity: the withdrawal of the state from cradle-to-grave social protection and its promotion of private insurance to ease the heavy social obligation and financial burden. Ironically the new generation of AIU managers replicated the strategy that had helped Starr to succeed in the 1920s, despite the lack of precedents and the scarcity of loss statistics.

Adopt consultative leadership style and select high-potential China leaders. Early on, Starr adopted a policy of hiring and training local personnel with strong business-building skills and promoting them to managerial positions. The group followed this principle ever since, contributing significantly to the growth of its business. It actively involved the front-line people, who possessed local knowledge and were most affected by decisions, in corporate deliberations. This strongly motivated the competent local managers. Unlike other companies, AIU did not prefer Western "area specialists" (concentrating on Asia) without general management skills over local talent. The personnel processes were tailored to finding, developing, and retaining key business builders. With coaching from western colleagues at the headquarters (including a strong personal commitment by the CEO) and on the ground, this arrangement represented an ideal marriage between East and West.

Apart from Starr's management policies, the company institutionalized his pioneering spirit and leadership style. Once enshrined and fostered through structures, systems, and processes, such invisible capital serves as an incessant engine and unlimited fountain of new ideas and groundbreaking action. AIG thus clearly differs from the many companies that declined after the charismatic founder or other strong leaders left. The official company history states: "The AIG story is more than just the history of an international commercial enterprise. It's a record of how people with vision and determination built a worldwide business organization based on the talents and skills of local people. The entrepreneurial spirit still pervades AIG today."

Plan ahead. AIG re-entered China with a clear long-term vision. In 1980, in a pioneering move, AIG established a joint-venture with the People's Insurance Company of China. Through this venture it built valuable relations, knowledge, and experience that enabled it to become an independent player in China a decade later. After obtaining a license, AIU developed a long-term game plan to exploit fully the market potential without jeopardizing future success. It focused first on the most developed and sophisticated urban market, Shanghai, and then expanded step-by-step into other major cities, such as Guangzhou, where it opened an office in 1998. In each market, the company avoided "imperial overstretch" at any cost. Usually, it first sold relatively simple personal accident insurance. Only when the agents and staff became sufficiently competent, it started selling more complex life insurance products. Managers at AIU thus think hard in the war rooms to develop insightful plans and move ahead incrementally on the ground adapting to new learning. They match opportunities and commitments with the increasing sophistication of their people and accumulated resources.

Build enterprise networks. In view of the huge market potential, one of the most important tasks for AIU was to gain control over distribution so as to reach the customer quickly and directly. The arithmetic appeared deceptively easy: the more agents it could hire, train, and retain, the more policies it could sell. AIU therefore created a large network of high-quality agents for the life insurance market, selling door-to-door to individuals and companies, another novelty in China. Even though other companies also have built agent networks, AIU still enjoys a strong competitive advantage. It paid great attention to the quality of agents who were trained systematically in evening classes, which complemented their sales activities during the day. Because of the unrelenting focus on quality, AIU had to expand its sales force slowly; it took four years to develop a network of 5,000 agents in Shanghai. By doing so it avoided the large-volume, low-quality image (and reality) of other companies, which destroys value in the long run. AIU's enterprise networks in China form part of AIG's worldwide webs, which helped it to earn more than half of its pretax income from abroad.

Shape the environment. AIU's success in Shanghai shaped the environment. Authorities in Beijing, worried about the potential market dominance of foreign players, in the short-run become reluctant to issue many more licenses to sell insurance policies in China. Thus most of AIG's 70-odd foreign competitors were de facto locked out, until China's accession to the WTO brought about supranationally induced changes.

Flexible structure and entrepreneurial units. Despite its huge size, AIG has avoided stagnation due to excessively formalized structures. It set up very entrepreneurial subsidiaries in more than 130 countries and jurisdictions. In China, it delegates significant decision-making authority to the country manager and further down to the city level. The company's managers recognize that in a highly uncertain environment, they need to adopt decentralized structures that allow them rapidly to adapt to ever changing circumstances. Such a structure also helps to deal with complexity, which abounds in China. Complex tasks are disaggregated into small pieces, which can be managed by lower-level executives instead of a supercomputer in the center.

The China manager is supported by a small headquarters staff headed by the CEO. He is very supportive, knowledgeable, and committed to China. He meets frequently with national leaders and, most important, regularly visits the grassroots—his China operations on the ground. In contrast to such a hands-on approach, many CEOs of foreign companies, if they visit China at all, often talk only to a small number of high-ranking officials, enjoy the glamour of splendid banquets and well-staged press conferences, and fly home full of pride—with empty hands. It is of key importance that the CEO shows interest and concern for his men on the ground. They deserve his personal attention, time, and energy. The Middle Kingdom is the ultimate testing ground of leadership. If you can make it here, you can make it everywhere. If you cannot make it here, you cannot make it anywhere.

Caring culture. Inspired by Starr's spirit, AIG developed a strong and caring culture with marked local characteristics, which further reinforced indigenous entrepreneurship and corporate intrapreneurship. It grew into a large, extended family with nuclear families in the various countries. One key initiative to building such a cohesive "family culture with local flavor," as I call it, was AIU's policy of promoting Chinese local managers to high leadership positions. The company thus showed its respect for the indigenous people and national distinctiveness of China, which are so dear to all Chinese. Every visitor will hear that China possesses its particular national characteristics, *guoqing*, which usually serves as a justification to reject foreign approaches.

Key success factors for different regions: Implications for strategists

An important part of the effectiveness analysis (presented in chapter 5) was a comparison of regional differences in key success factors between the north (Beijing) and south (Shanghai) of China. Key success factors for the total sample, and the north and south separately, were shown in figure 7-2. Since I discussed the empirical findings before, here I will concentrate on a few key practical messages for foreign and Chinese managers and policy-makers.

Realize and act upon regional differences. Executives need to realize that differences in key success factors across regions, not only countries, do exist and that it is important to take these regional variations into account when formulating strategies (for the corporate center, business units, and functions), designing organizational structures, systems, and processes, choosing leadership styles, and monitoring performance along critical success factors. As simple as it might sound, many managers are not aware of regional differences *within* a country, or, if they have heard about them, do not adjust their approaches. My consulting and managerial experience shows that this applies to both foreign and Chinese players. In view of this widespread ignorance and reluctance, managers who generate and use knowledge of subcultural differences to adjust their operation to the regional particularities will create a particularly distinctive competitive advantage in terms of strategic positioning and execution.

At the same time, the need to adapt to intranational differences at the subcultural level varies in importance, which should caution advocates of both unconditional feminine cross-cultural sensitivity and a masculine Rambo mentality that ignores cultural differences. "Regional vigilance" is particularly crucial for environmental factors and soft management practices, less so for internal technical decisions, such as the choice of appropriate structure. For example, companies may need to adopt their marketing strategies and practices to cater for regional tastes and customs.

Following the overall trend of branding (Schlevogt, 2000f), companies might not only need to build a Chinese image nationally, but possibly need to develop regional brands. Likewise, politicians who design the institutions and laws in subculturally diverse countries first must understand the different regional environments and then adjust their policies accordingly. The findings apply not only to China, but also to other countries with different subcultures, such as India and Russia.

Figure 7-2 can be read both horizontally and vertically. Chapter 5 presented the results from the horizontal comparison of differences between regions. Here, I will focus on the implications of the ranking of key success factors within one region and discuss their absolute strength in comparison to other factors. I will thus comment on action points derived from the vertical axes of the chart, indicating what it takes to succeed in the different regions. Several factors are significantly correlated with effectiveness in both geographic areas. This shows that the intra-group prioritization does not necessarily mean that the factors are not important in the other region in absolute terms. Let me start with the north.

The government is king in the north. The key to success in the north is the ability to secure government support.[5] Therefore, especially in Beijing, companies have to focus on managing this crucial interface, which can mean the difference between success and failure—no matter which grand strategies executives have devised and how perfectly managed the company is in all other respects. Executive who lack this knowledge might well focus all their energies on the wrong points, which, because of their management education and experience, they paradoxically might consider absolutely crucial.

I have outlined and illustrated various approaches to winning over powerful external constituencies such as the Chinese government. Instead of only pursuing narrow self-interests, foreign investors should demonstrate their sincere commitment to helping China's development, by localizing production, transferring technology, and showing goodwill gestures. American International Group undertook tremendous efforts to demonstrate that it cared for China. As a result, it obtained one of the very few insurance licenses.

The government influences other strategic factors. Large size can undermine success in the north, if it arouses the suspicion of officials that the company will compete for its power monopoly. This does not mean executives should not build large companies in the north; it means they should be aware of the implications for relations with the government and act carefully. Most importantly, they need to remain humble in the face of success. There is an old Chinese saying: "Man is afraid of becoming famous, the pig fears getting fat" (because it will be slaughtered when it is in a nice shape!).

Management expertise is the second most important factor in the north. This can be explained by the value that Confucian culture, supposedly stronger in the north, places on education and seniority. Confucianism espouses the ideal of the scholar-administrator, a king who is a philosopher. As a complementary explanation, stronger government regulation might call for more formal credentials of executives. In any case, human resource managers need to identify, recruit, select, develop, and retain highly competent and well-respected leaders for the company's operations.

There is a third facet to the importance of the government in the north. Environmental constraints strongly influence performance. Companies therefore need to shape the environment actively. For example, they may develop close links with the government to access "sticky" resources and design strategies that—while taking care of the government's interest—create protected niches. I mentioned that managers can educate personnel to overcome the human resource bottleneck, chase pirates, acquire distribution channels, and influence derivative demand.

Networks are the name of the game in the south. Instead of support from an outside body, in the south, the company's proprietary relationship network is the key to success. The strongest influencing factor of performance in absolute terms is private, family-based ownership—the inner sanctum of the relationship web. Companies in the south thus are well-advised to use the toolbox for creating or emulating private ownership and thus to harness its full power. Chinese executives are painfully aware that southerners in particular want to set up their own firms after having been trained by large companies. Once they have left, they usually refuse to be bought back even after having failed on their own. Giving them a feeling of ownership early on and locking them into networks might prevent, or at least leverage, the exodus of talent. High fliers will never know when it is the right time to leave, since the future in the company promises greater growth than the past—a classical case of increasing marginal returns.

Relationships also influence other aspects. For example, company age was shown to be crucial in the South. A manager obviously cannot control the age of his company directly, but the knowledge that age matters might influence acquisition decisions. The findings underline the pivotal role of relational networks, reputation, and learning effects, which are often a corollary of age. Foreign and Chinese managers in the south need to pay great attention to developing and leveraging a strong reputation and a well-diversified and extensive, personal and institutional portfolio of contacts. By doing so, they will gather valuable business intelligence, learn from web participants, and tap the opportunity pipeline and other resources, and thus manage the abundant environment with great effectiveness and efficiency.

Likewise, company size matters in the south, maybe because it gives a company more clout, bargaining power, and benefits to offer in exchange for new relations and cooperation (both vis-à-vis authorities and companies). Size thus helps to control a highly competitive, fast-changing, and complex environment. It enables companies to exploit fully the great opportunities in a less constrained environment with more resources than in the north. Another important factor is planning. In a demanding environment with experienced and sophisticated players, which are often joined together in networks, it is crucial to develop a clear view of the future, design a visionary game plan, and adapt it to new learnings.

If organizational structure is not effectively synchronized with the task environment, visions and strategies are just bubbles. Dreams need structure in order to be realized.

Appropriate structure matters everywhere. Another interesting angle was to examine which factors are universally important (or which are universally unimportant). Appropriate structure turned out to be the one factor that matters for success both in the north and south. This is a good reason for sharpening this tool, which serves as the vehicle for implementing all great ideas (Schlevogt 1999d). If organizational structure is not effectively synchronized with the task environment, visions and strategies are just bubbles. Dreams need structure in order to be realized. In contrast to this universal importance of organizational structure, there are no factors that equally lack importance for both groups (that is, occupy the same bottom position in the ranking of key success factors in both north and south).

I kept the foregoing analysis highly parsimonious, highlighting just a few key insights. It is a first step toward better understanding regional differences in key success factors and addressing them through skilfull strategic management. I hope this analysis will stimulate new research that deepens our understanding of these geographical differences and required adaptations, not only in different parts of China but also in other parts of the world.

Summary and conclusions

This chapter highlighted lessons that foreign (and Chinese) companies can learn from Chinese winners (and losers) to steer their operations into a profitable direction, both in China and in other emerging and unstructured markets and situations. They will help them to capitalize on the market potential now instead of continuing to suffer losses and hoping for a bright future. Discouraging as the results of many foreign companies may be, it is not a good idea to abandon ship. China, apart from its real market attraction, is the ultimate testing ground for a manager's leadership skills and ability to pioneer and learn rapidly in a highly uncertain and complex environment. If he fails here, he will fail in other unstructured situations with tough challenges, such as leading a corporate restructuring, merger and acquisition, and postmerger integration, expanding into new geographical and product markets and customers segments, developing and mastering new technologies, and managing crises in general. A company's success matters for China as well. Only if international investors and managers remain excited about its prospects will foreign capital, people, technology ideas, and passion continue to flow into the country. Keeping such material and immaterial assets flowing is an important corporate mission, too.

Throughout the chapter, I emphasized the great importance and opportunity of learning from the Chinese, and the great benefits from blending their ancient and new secrets of success with Western management techniques—some of which were shown to work in China, too. Instead of just telling stories, I presented quantitative evidence that singled out key success factors and indicated their absolute and relative weight. I thus aimed at building bridges between academic research and managerial action, integrating positive and normative science. I synthesized the recommendations in a CHINA framework for high performance and ten "Golden Rules" for implementation. They emphasized that executives need to manage simultaneously a bundle of empirically tested fundamentals. Case studies illustrated how this focus on the key leverage points strengthens control over the environment and enhances competitiveness, thus increasing not only efficiency but also effectiveness. The combination of factors create a sustainable advantage based on positions, competence, ambiguity, time, and other tangible and intangible resources that competitors will find difficult to imitate.

AIG exemplified such spacial, temporal, and intellectual advantages. Imagine you want to enter the Chinese insurance market and compete to take away some of AIG's market share. You first need a license. A simple bureaucratic process? Your legal experts will fill out the forms? No, as a prospective entrant you will join the queue of seventy-odd other prestigious players. By the time you read this, you might be close to being number 100—a truly sad achievement! AIG's success will further lengthen the waiting time, since officials may fear that too many successful foreign players will dominate the market. Then, perhaps because of the intervention of the WTO, not because of your own strength, let us assume you finally obtained the license. You will dance with joy, a broad smile all over your face. A license to print money . . . or so they say.

But how about the competition, maybe the fiercest in any insurance market on earth? Both a handful of brilliant foreign players and a group of capable domestic actors are biting lustfully into the market cake, leveraging their formidable armies of greedy salesmen. How long will it take for you to build up a strong agent network renowned for its sales effectiveness and, above all, enjoying a strong reputation for quality and fairness? To be honest, it is a long and windy road, if you do not follow the value-destroying path of some players. They pushed relentlessly for rapid growth, hiring anybody as an agent, economizing on training, and slashing prices. But even this chance of mindless aggressiveness diminishes over time, because there are few potential new agents (and customers) left. The resources have been thoroughly depleted. It will be tough to create a new Grand Army of successful salesmen and strong customer loyalty.

And will you be able to develop enough industry foresight and understand the Chinese market sufficiently well to design a clever game plan, better than that already devised by the superb and experienced general staff of AIG strategists? Will you emerge with breakthrough strategies, organizational designs, and revolutionary new products after the revolution has taken place? And remember, the capacity for great transformations and upheavals in insurance is limited. Imagine somebody traveled to St. Petersburg in 1917 with the intention of leading a second proletarian revolution, just after Lenin had become head of the new soviet government. Certain opportunities emerge as narrow windows and do not repeat themselves. Once captured, they turn into an unassailable competitive stronghold, until mismanagement and external pressures turns them to ashes— but this can take more than seventy years!

Further, when you face problems in the highly volatile, complex, and competitive environment of China, especially in the financial sector, will you be sufficiently well connected to access superior information, opportunities, and other resources, and to shape the environment? Will you have the key business builders in place to deal with these issues? This is unlikely if you have not developed local talent or, worse, lack experience in doing so. Suppose you somehow have attracted key talents—maybe by paying headhunters enormous sums of money (for what you might have achieved with an intelligent recruitment drive or simply through your reputation, had you built one). Will you be able to develop and retain them? Do you decentralize decisions, which would be the appropriate structural response to the turbulent and complex environment? Are headquarters personnel comfortable with or able to grant freedom to local managers? Are there supportive processes to nurture the "China heroes" and re-integrate them after they return home? Does the interface between center and periphery function well? If so, does the culture foster the spirit of a nuclear and extended corporate family, effectively bonding key local and foreign talents?

Many ifs and question marks! And many lost opportunities. AIG's position, intuitively based on the effective management of the fundamentals outlined in the CHINA framework and implemented through the ten "Golden Rules," resembles a fortress. Of course, things can change. But the position is likely to remain strong, not only because AIG got the intrinsics right, but also because its competence will allow it to move faster than competitors. The best bet for a potential entrant thus might be to start buying shares in AIG! But even this will not be easy, or at least not inexpensive, since the share price already incorporates future expected cashflows.

Perhaps you still are contemplating entering China—going through myriad feasibility studies, planning rounds, committee sessions with all stakeholders, internal power struggles and, after preparing the grand master plan, waiting for the all-encompassing democratic vote that takes into account everybody's rights and opinions (after all, your employees are empowered and you are a team player making decisions on the basis of consensus). By the time you could start your China venture, AIG will already be active in remote areas of China, India, Vietnam, and other exotic places, learning step by step by acting on the spot and building new money-creating engines that further enlarge its resources. Then you can start catching up again.

In this oriental land of opportunity, the sky is literally the limit, but only if you master the fundamentals for success in China and take action, brushing aside all the bureaucratic chains in your home office. And there is another key lesson: once you have put the key skills and other resources in place, you not only will succeed in China, but also will be able to leverage these tangible and intangible assets in other emerging markets or unstructured situations with high unreduceable uncertainty and dynamic complexity. These settings require the ability to build businesses, above all a pioneering spirit and heroic action.

Apart from the analysis for the total China sample, I identified geographic differences in key success factors between the north (Beijing) and the south (Shanghai). Regional difference are rarely examined in the strategic management literature, particularly with respect to China. In my recommendations, I stressed the importance of realizing that regional differences do exist and adapting strategies and organizational designs at multiple levels. In the north, the most important task is successfully to manage the interface with the government. In the south, the key to success is a large and diversified portfolio of relations and an intricate enterprise web, powered by private ownership incentives. Appropriate structure is a technical universal, equally important in both Beijing and Shanghai.

Let me conclude by sharing with you a Chinese expression that describes the relentless selection process involved in singling out the best: "a carp leaps into the Dragon Gate." In the past, it depicted success in the imperial examination, which determined access to civil service positions. According to an old story, several carps swam against the current of the wild Yellow River during the spring, climbing up the Dragon Gate Mountain. Suddenly, a huge fire struck from heaven, hitting the carps from behind and burning their tails. Facing instant death, they tried to save themselves by jumping into the Dragon Gate. Most failed in the difficult enterprise and drowned. The few that passed the Dragon Gate, miraculously became dragons.

The story symbolizes the extremely tough competition among the best and the brightest. For centuries carps have been the most excellent, and most expensive, fish in China. Students were like carps making their way upriver, hoping to become a dragon. They worked hard to improve their knowledge and skills in order to achieve rapid promotion. Their struggle was like swimming against a mighty river, requiring almost superhuman energy.

The process is full of dangers. At certain points in time, crises with extremely high leverage opportunities emerge whose skillfull seizure guarantees survival and prosperity. But only the chosen few with particularly rich talents, intelligent strategies, and heroic courage will be able to capture them.

The Chinese market offers such a huge window of opportunity fraught with extreme dangers and strong competition. Succeeding in the West and struggling hard in China is not enough—only the very best will become dragons. I hope that by following the lessons derived from the best-performing Chinese companies, more foreign companies will use focus, leverage, and control and make it through the Dragon Gate, where we shall meet again.

In chapter 8, I will synthesize several emerging perspectives and issues related to China's past, present, and future that flow from this study.

PART IV

Conclusions and Research Outlook:
A Glorious Past, Challenging
Present, and Bright Future
Ahead for China?

8
The Art of Chinese Management? Change the Present to Restore the Past and Create the Future

This last chapter affords the opportunity once again to broaden the perspective and pull together the threads and themes emerging from the previous discussion. And please, forgive me these broad strokes of the painter's brush, the object and canvass are too enticing! The journey on a long and windy road from theory through facts and design ends in the Valhalla of all thought, that is, intellectual synthesis through which gathering and governing unite. I will start my integrative mission by commenting on the relationship between overseas Chinese management and the management of private businesses in mainland China, proposing that we are witnessing the closure of a circle. Then, based on all the necessary groundwork in the preceding chapters, I will explore whether Chinese management is indeed an art—as the title of the book suggests. I will ask whether this artistic quality can explain the dynamism of private and general economic development in China, and, on an even grander scale, whether it might signal the development of a new global force of Chinese companies—a Grand Army of Chinese businessmen invading the West. I will propose policies on how to use WCM theory to further stimulate private enterprises, to reform state enterprises, and to keep foreign companies bullish on China. Next, I will broaden the horizon once again, discussing the interplay between this dramatic revival of past organizational practices in the present and China's future, and the continuous reversal in the flows of sophisticated ideas between East and West. I will include some comments on how Western "big noses" can help China become a grand nation once again. The last part will map out some future directions for research in this new, exciting, and promising area of private management in mainland China.

Mainland Chinese and overseas Chinese management

The similarity in styles of mainland and overseas Chinese private businesses

The empirical findings from the interviews with 124 Chinese CEOs and intensive case studies supported my theory of web-based Chinese management. These structural design choices and management practices are very similar to the organizational choices of overseas Chinese (*Haiwai Huaqiao*) family businesses described in casual anecdotes and fragmented qualitative research. Those accounts also singled out particular aspects of the management style practiced by overseas private Chinese businesses as distinctive (though they never systematically explained and operationalized the notion of distinctiveness).

One distinctive structural design choice that resounds well with overseas Chinese descriptions is the autocratic "godfather" style—the personalistic and paternalistic rule by the owner. There is also a strong similarity in the owner's disdain for written documents, rules, procedures, organizational charts, and other "German inventions." It has been said that what the world needs is more love and less paperwork. This is the living principle of the Chinese on the mainland and overseas. Love is extended in the form of the owner-manager's cherishing of family traditions and family relations built on Confucian principles. There is also a great deal of affection (and social capital in general) invested in the personal and enterprise networks spun by the great webmaster, both on the mainland and abroad. The Chinese webscape was in place before the netscape. However, the boss exhibits less love and mercy for competitors, whom he eagerly fights. To this end, he uses entrepreneurial strategies developed through a flexible and charismatic leadership style, epitomizing what we previously thought were the traits exclusively of the "typical" overseas Chinese manager.

Back to the mainland Chinese origin

We thus witness the completion of a full circle. The traditional Chinese management model, including the emphasis on traditional family-based values, that left China to be spread across the Chinese diaspora has returned to the mainland. Whereas previous discussions suggested that this management model is applicable to the overseas Chinese only, this study, for the first time, showed that it also can be found once again in mainland China, in the newly founded private Chinese (family) enterprises. Earlier writers proposed that because the Communists had taken over the mainland and suppressed private economic activity, the traditional management model had vanished from the Chinese motherland. Those accounts, however, missed the dramatic changes in the wake of the economic reforms that once again legalized private economic activity. The new businesses in turn readopted the age-old Chinese management practices and values and used them for modern economic warfare.

This did not happen by default. Other scenarios would have been imaginable. For example, the knowledge of the old management style might have been lost. Or, overseas practices could have been used in a radically changed form. Alternatively, after years of Communist influence on the mainland, people might have brushed away the family-based leadership model as "reactionary." They might have looked exclusively to other Communist countries or the Capitalist West for the nirvana of management. That this did not happen, dramatically testifies the eternal springs of the Chinese cultural treasure and the confidence and belief the Chinese have in it. Even though their loyalty to the (great) China ideal borders on obstinacy, it is one of their greatest assets.

The spirit of Chinese capitalism . . . [was] like a sleeping beauty waiting for the right conditions and incentives to arise again. Deng Xiao-ping was the prince who woke her up; the kiss was his economic reforms.

A great cultural revival in the making

We thus are watching an amazing cultural revival in mainland China. In contrast to the sad story of its predecessor, this "cultural revolution" really deserves the epithet "great." Culture consists of different layers, starting with the visible, external artifacts and moving down to deep strata of internalized, unconscious values. In most cases, we witness a renaissance of traditional values that are not necessarily visible. Often, because of long-time brainwashing and forgetting, and limited resources, the desire for a resurrection is still greater than the knowledge of the subject to be resurrected and the means for doing so. The renaissance gathers strength in the deepest places of the souls of entrepreneurs, and will therefore be stronger than mere external "plug-ins," such as Chinese-style rooftops or receptionists in traditional Chinese dresses. Its most important focus and springboard is the deeply ingrained reverence for family values and the longing for unshakeable authority. I believe that the depth of these beliefs explains why otherwise very vigilant observers have missed this silent revolution. In some cases, the Chinese entrepreneur pushes the revival to the highly visible level, formally declaring that his mission is to give rebirth to traditional Chinese culture. He may lead culture classes for employees, write books about traditional etiquette and distribute them to managers and staff, or engage in other highly visible and symbolic action.

To sum up, on the mainland the inner spirit of Chinese capitalism—its work ethic, inspired leadership, and dynamic entrepreneurship, together with ancient cultural values cherishing the family—were like a sleeping beauty waiting for the right conditions and incentives to arise again. Mao was the sorcerer who put the beauty to sleep. Deng Xiao-ping emerged as the prince who woke her up; the kiss was his economic reforms.

Uniting the Chinese diaspora

To give this circle of escape and revival another spin, it is quite possible that the readoption of the traditional Chinese management style and cultural values in the P.R.C. in part results from the influence of overseas Chinese companies, the most important "foreign" investor group in mainland China. The Chinese government uses smart strategies and tactics, which may serve as example for other countries to follow (Schlevogt 2000e; 2000g; 2000h), to attract Chinese who were born overseas or emigrated. Many Chinese come back even when they are not offered incentives.

There is an enchanting story of an Indian who was actively involved in the American green movement. He had been invited to speak at a seminar about ecology in Europe. After picking him up at the airport, the host started to elaborate on the details of the upcoming seminar, such as the venue and schedule. The Indian did not utter a word, sat motionless and stared into the night. The host, somewhat perplexed, changed the topic, asking the Indian about the flight and the food on the plane. Once again, complete silence ensued. After more than half an hour of this monologue, the host finally asked why the Indian did not speak. His guest answered, composed and quietly: "You know, my dear friend, my soul and spirit are still traveling across the Atlantic. They will need time to catch up with my body. I will tell you when they have arrived; then I will be all there for you."

Although the bodies of the overseas Chinese left the mainland, their souls and spirits often did not accompany them.

Even though the bodies of the overseas Chinese left the mainland, their souls and spirits often did not accompany them. The Indian was fortunate; for him it was merely a question of time until he was reunited with his internal spark. For the overseas Chinese, it was not a matter of catching up. Their souls and spirits did not reunite with their masters' bodies even after several generations. My research shows that the Chinese were right to call their compatriots in the diaspora "Huaqiao," Chinese who had temporarily left the mainland and would come back later.

Indeed, they finally returned to the motherland, many of them in person. And an important flow was reversed, one that is significant in our commercial world—money. The greatest part of foreign direct investment in the mainland comes from overseas Chinese who set up joint ventures or wholly foreign-owned enterprises, or bought equity stakes in mainland companies. In the vicinity of Hong Kong alone, entrepreneurs from the former crown colony employ millions of people. The Taiwanese are equally active, engaging in economic integration before the eventual po-litical reunion—which, based on the reviving national and cultural val-ues, including surging outright race-based nationalism, could happen very soon—peacefully or by force.

When the overseas Chinese did not come back physically, or did not transfer tangible capital, often something even more important came back to China: their ideas—above all their management model—together with their enthusiasm, energy, patriotism, and love. As one important piece of software that complements the hardware, the overseas Chinese brought the age-old cultural values about family and other social relations, thus contributing significantly to the great cultural revival.

If they do not behave arrogantly and thus are repelled, the overseas Chinese can become very effective, since they share common cultural roots with the host. Mainland China thus has an advantage over other developing countries that need to rely more on foreign mercenaries from different ethnic groups.

We thus witness a reunion of the worldwide Chinese diaspora on the soil of the motherland. It is a physical, financial, and spiritual reunion, a shared focus of common allegiances and emotional attachments to this great human idea—the eternal Chinese civilization. A new, grand, and invisible Chinese empire is taking shape—a virtual Middle Kingdom that spans the world from its epicenter in China. Changes of epic proportion lie ahead. When the empire emerges, the world will hold its breath.

The art of Chinese management?

It is now time to refer back to the title of this book, which states that Chinese management is an art. Let us first search for an appropriate defi-nition of "art." The following definition can be found in The *Oxford English Dictionary*: "skill in doing anything as the result of knowledge and practice." At the beginning of the twentieth century, *Webster's International Dictionary of the English Language* produced two somewhat richer definitions: (1) "a system of rules serving to facilitate the performance of certain actions; a system of principles and rules for attaining a desired end; method of doing well some special work; often contradistinguished from science or speculative principles; as the art of building, the art of war" and (2) "skill, *dexterity*, or the power of performing certain *actions*, acquired by *experience*, study, or observation; knack; as, a man has the art of managing his business to advantage." John Ruskin, the great Oxford art critic, conceptualized (fine) art as "that in which the *hand*, the *head*, and the *heart* of man go together" (Cook and Wedderburn, vol. 16, p. 294).

Adopting Webster's second definition, I believe that private Chinese management is indeed an "art" and, as will be shown later, even a "fine art," since it meets the emphasized words in the definitions.

> Apart from shaping webs, another unique skill is [the private Chinese man-
> ager's] ability to accumulate and manage financial capital, and to create and
> nurture social capital.

Dexterity

It is fair to say that private Chinese management constitutes a particular
skill of doing something well, because as outlined above, (a) it is characterized by distinctive structural, managerial, and contextual choices
(chapters 3 and 4) and (b) has proved to be effective (chapter 5).

In regards to the first point, I believe that perhaps the most important
and distinctive skill is the ability of many private Chinese businessmen
to craft or spin their own family-based webs. An interesting feature of
these webs is that they allow the Chinese entrepreneur to shape his environment or, at least, partly insulate himself from uncertainty and reduce
complexity. Apart from shaping webs, another unique skill is his ability
to accumulate and manage financial capital, and to create and nurture
social capital, giving birth to a collective magic in his enterprise, with
organizational members creating and sharing powerful knowledge, learning together, and, in general, sparking greatness in each other. Of course,
the great Chinese philosophers, who aimed at building the ideal society
and devised principles to achieve this aim, must be acknowledged as
(fore-) fathers of this particular skill.

John Ruskin once suggested that man is an engine whose motive power
is the soul. I believe that humans are not primarily motivated by material
incentives, which can tap only superficial resources. Constructing, prop-
agating, and using (scientific) management models that for reasons of simplicity ignore this point, and concentrate only on material gain, leads to
grave errors. Once the idealist human element is introduced into the management equation, a chemical reaction takes place, not a mathematical
transformation in the sense of adding a new variable. (Romantic) idealism
generates quantum leaps in performance, radically shifting the production
possibility frontier outward. What moves man is a sense of mission and
affection. As Friedrich Nietzsche said, the person who has a "why" to live
will endure almost any "how." The Chinese family-based model creates a
strong purpose, mighty emotions, and an almost religious zeal, which harnesses human potential and releases its power to a stronger degree than
an atomized, contractual free-market system or an anonymous, bureaucratic hierarchy—the two choices for coordination and motivation we
have been offered before.

Second, I conclude that by applying their distinctive management skill,
the private Chinese entrepreneurs do very well. This is shown by the effectiveness of the model in my study and the number of millionaires (in
both absolute numbers and relative to their population) it produced overseas and in mainland China. More generally, I observed that in certain
business areas, Chinese private businesses, such as Tiger and Magnolia,

adopt differentiation strategies that create unique value based on innovative, high-quality products and services. This contradicts the thesis developed for other Southeast Asian countries, that Chinese businessmen function as ersatz capitalists (Clad 1989; Yoshihara 1988)—mere rent seekers rather than truly productive entrepreneurs. These earlier researchers assumed that Chinese businessmen mainly pursue trading and other nonproductive activities. They also claimed that those who do produce largely depend on external sources of capital and technology.

Action

Private Chinese management is geared toward powerful action. I found that instead of excessive analysis and overcomplicated planning, there is a distinctive urge to make bold entrepreneurial decisions and get things done in a short period of time. Reasonableness is definitely more important than reason (Lin 1977, p. 86). We saw quite powerful examples of this bias for action. Memorable was Mr. Li's single-handed decision to acquire a stake in a luxury hotel without the necessary "financial clout" and then, within a couple of months, to move into the mass-market hotel business. In both cases, he found solutions through action, such as tapping the overseas network for funds to overcome the capital constraint. He also converted part of his office building into a hotel. This avoided huge time lags that might have neutralized the benefits of quickly seizing the attractive opportunity and occupying the market niche. This action-driven decision making and urge to achieve targets quickly can be traced back to ancient roots. The Chinese warfare strategist Sun Zi, who wrote about 500 B.C., warned that "complacency is perhaps the greatest danger that could hasten the ruin of a successful operation."

[Chinese management] draws its strength from experimentation, observation, and the willingness to learn from other web participants.

Experience

Chinese management is not a science or a system—just the opposite. The lack of formal analytical tools and bureaucracy, ascertained in my empirical study, supported this conclusion. Its practice is based on uncodified experience, which resembles tacit knowledge or *knowing* (Polanyi 1967). It draws its strength from experimentation, observation, and the willingness to learn from other web participants, including contractors, suppliers, partners, customers, and other stakeholders. Incremental learning that leverages feedback from the environment is an effective means of managing uncertainty and complexity. Sun Zi emphasized the importance of rapidly learning from situational experience: "He who wins modifies his tactics in accordance with the changing enemy situation and this works miracles" (Sun Zi 1999/written about 500 B.C., p. 45).

The idea of tacit knowledge is intriguing for my purposes. I observed that many excellent organizations rely on it to create knowledge through action. Tacit knowledge creation implies that certain things cannot be learned from books, or be taught by teachers. Codifying knowledge in writing and transmitting it through education has its limits. Certain things have to be learned by each successive generation through experience. Because of the powerful influence of culture on Chinese management, it comes to no surprise that the aversion against explicit knowledge has ancient precedents. Lao Zi referred to ancient scriptures as "dim footprints of ancient kings." He criticized Confucius, stating, "All your lectures are concerned with things that are no better than footprints in the dust. Footprints are made by shoes; but they are far from being shoes" (Waley 1939, p. 15). Because of his skepticism about Confucius' educational approach, he expressed relief that Confucius never met a prince who was anxious to reform the world.

There is another story, related by Chuang Zi, that epitomizes the value of experience, which I stressed as a particular feature of the art of Chinese management, for mastering difficult tasks. A wheelwright talked to a nobleman who was reading a book. When the craftsman heard that the book had been written by somebody who was dead, he declared it completely useless. The nobleman, outraged, demanded an explanation, threatening that if it was not convincing, he would put the blasphemer to death. The wheelwright replied, "When I am making a wheel, if my stroke is too slow, then it bites deep but is not steady; if my stroke is too fast, then it is steady, but does not go deep. The right pace, neither slow nor fast, cannot get into the hand unless it comes from the heart. It is a thing that cannot be put into words; there is an *art* in it that I cannot explain to my son. That is why it is impossible for me to let him take over my work, and here I am at the age of seventy, still making wheels. In my opinion, it must have been the same with the men of old. All that was worth handing on, died with them; the rest, they put into their books. That is why I said that what you were reading was the lees and scum of bygone men" (Waley 1939, pp. 15–16).

The heart is described as the repository of the craftsman's skill. Experience that is to lead to constant improvement has to resonate with internal nature. In the Chinese case, it needs to build on the foundation of traditional culture, which is almost genetically programmed into everybody's internal makeup. Learning from experience develops in subtle, intuitive ways, which are not necessarily obvious to the outsider who tries to understand Chinese management. According to Chinese wisdom, the swan does not need a daily bath to remain white, and the crow does not need a daily inking to maintain its black color. We have to learn step by step in order to understand Chinese practices. In certain instances, we will have to observe and work with Chinese role models who can help us discover the secret of success ourselves.

The private Chinese businessman has his heart in the right place—the family.

A fine *art?*

Having shown that Chinese management is an art, I also conclude that it is a *fine* art. According to John Ruskin, fine art is "that in which the *hand*, the *head*, and the *heart* of man go together." It is the joint action of body and soul, "the energy—neither of the human body alone, nor of the human soul alone, but of both united, one guiding the other: good craftsmanship and work of the fingers joined with good emotion and work of the heart" as Ruskin put it.[1] I have discussed the Chinese entrepreneur's "hand" in terms of dexterity and action, and the "head" as reflected in the working of his experience. To cross the Grand Canyon between gifted technician and truly inspired genius, and enter the pantheon of his vocation, an individual needs to add the heart, soul, and spirit to the work of hand and head. In *The Two Paths* Ruskin explained, "Without mingling of heart-passion with hand-power, no art is possible. The highest art unites both in their intensest degrees: the action of the hand at its finest, with that of the heart at its fullest."

The private Chinese businessman has his heart in the right place—the family. All his battles—his sweat, schemes, intrigues, and sacrifices—are not for petty material motives, even though those might be the only purpose visible in his actions. The whirlwind created by his activism disguises the ultimate noble driving force at the deepest level: the well-being and prosperity of his family and lineage. The Chinese entrepreneur truly wants his ancestors to be proud of him as a steward who takes care of the great family tradition, and promotes its development.

Fine art can assume different forms. Western art aims at representing facts; Eastern art strives for the harmony of colors and shapes. The same applies to management—a technical, analytical, and deductive craft in the West, and a social, synthesized, and inductive art in the East.

Not only art, but also artifact

The distinctive Chinese management style also can be said to be a cultural artifact, since it is shaped by values that are deeply embedded in Chinese culture. The Confucian heritage emphasized a clear hierarchy based on seniority, and strong but benevolent leadership at the top. This explains the high degree of "caring centralization" in private Chinese enterprises. Since Chinese entrepreneurs appreciate belonging to a (kinship-based) group and social obligations, they constantly spin relations based on reciprocity. The value of the social capital accumulated in these enterprises derives to a large extent from trust and faithfulness. Above all, the dominant position of the family, as the elementary building block of society that promotes heavenly peace on earth, clearly motivates many private

Chinese businessmen to keep their enterprises small. Small size enables him to manage and guard all business within this social unit, in its nuclear or extended version.

Web-based Chinese management is like a precious stone shaped to near perfection by a gifted artist.

Web-based Chinese management is like a precious stone shaped to near perfection by a gifted artist. I say "near perfection" because true art is never perfect. It is like a rare mineral, defined by its external crystalline form, as well as its internal chemical elements and atoms, which escape the eye. The external shape is the organization as a whole, as we see it. The chemical elements that make up the stone are the distinctive structural and managerial practices. At the deepest level, the atoms are the ancient Chinese values transmitted from the first Chinese community, under the legendary rulers of *Yao* and *Shun*, stable in their intricate arrangement. The distinctiveness of Chinese management lies both in its form and in its life. It is defined as much in its constituent parts as in their unique combination and interaction. It is not one of the elements that alone makes the mineral and the social model, but the dynamic union of all.

As in the case of a mineral, which is made up of parts that are also found in other minerals, elements of Chinese management can be found in non–Chinese companies as well. But the soul of Chinese management is the harmony of structural, managerial, and contextual elements in the right quantities. Taking away any single part would destroy it. Remove the sense of familism and social responsibility for this entity, and everything else will evaporate. The entrepreneur will lack a powerful mission that drives him relentlessly and social capital that creates value. Eliminate the (pro)activism, and the family will not survive. Take away the webs, and the enterprise will crumble, smashed by merciless competitors and, in certain countries, ruthless political rulers as well. But, bundled and bonded together, its distinctive elements make Chinese management strong and unique, a piece of (fine) art and an artifact preserved and handed from generation to generation, ever revitalizing itself.

Chinese management does not need to be artificially preserved in museums or other heritage sites—it is a living art! People only start to get extremely preoccupied with preservation when the present, "modern" generation cannot create anything that is worth preserving. They then must hold on to old things. They clutch at the straw of old things in a race against time, which in a more creative society would be a force of improvement. Innovation is an act of creative destruction, which contrasts with sterile preservation. How many ancient treasures were destroyed, for example, to build the Palace of Heaven in Beijing? But who worries—something more splendid replaced it, which would never have been created if all the old things had been preserved. Likewise, Chinese management does not require active preservation efforts. Because of its intrinsic strengths, it preserves and refines itself in perpetuity, even when the mighty bulldozers of Western (scientific) management arrive. In this world of Goliaths, Davids enjoy a distinctive advantage!

Which form of art? The gothicness of Chinese management

I concluded that Chinese management is both a (fine) art and an artifact. This begets the question: What particular form and style of art is it? Though the analogy is derived from a Western context, in my view, Chinese management embodies the Gothic[2] spirit of architecture. I am strongly influenced by John Ruskin, whose fire of genius, flame of life, and divine spark I might have caught in the old vaults of Christ Church, Oxford. Because he is perhaps the most eloquent writer on the Gothic style, and bearing in mind that while writing about art, he created art, I have quoted extensively from his work.

Why did I choose architecture as the form of art for my analogy? It fits philosophically and technically. As Ruskin recognized, "architecture is the work of the whole race." Other forms of art, such as painting or sculpture are the work of one individual, who often is more talented than other artists. Architecture expresses "some great truths commonly belonging to the whole race." The same holds true for Chinese management. It does not only reflect the thinking of one highly gifted individual, such as the inventor of scientific management, Frederic Taylor. Instead, it draws its strength from the links with ancient Chinese culture, revived and practiced in a great worldwide community. It is thus an artifact produced by the whole people. Another more cynical architectural parallel in certain private Chinese businesses springs to my mind. Ruskin said that the best architecture is "the expression of the mind of manhood by the hands of childhood." Alas, in some Chinese factories, this description applies literally! At a more technical level, creating unique value propositions and developing effective and efficient organizations to deliver the promised benefit constitute the art of building in management—they can be described as strategic and organizational architecture.

[The private Chinese entrepreneur] is the managerial engineer of his family's well-being, a cathedral builder of love and compassion. . . .

Now, let me explain my statement about the inner Gothic spirit of Chinese management. The following story conveys a taste of this spirit. A traveling nobleman met a poor worker on his way to Cologne. After discussing the weather and other light topics, the nobleman asked, "What do you do for a living?" The worker's reply made the nobleman gasp, and left him standing, bewildered, on the dusty road. What had the worker said that so puzzled our poor friend? He had remarked rather casually, "I build cathedrals."

The Chinese businessman does not build cathedrals in a literal sense, nor does he give birth to great empires. But still he builds, and creates something grand. He is the managerial engineer of his family's well-being, a cathedral builder of love and compassion within this precious community. He also builds great webs. In addition, he has a sense of mission, of doing something worthwhile—maybe the most valuable thing in the world—caring for his *jia* (family). And he is a worker, often from a rather humble background and frequently, throughout his life, pursues activities that are not particularly glamorous, such as doing (or at least overseeing) the "sweat" jobs for the great brands in his OEM (original equipment manufacturing) factories.[3]

He certainly is not choosy—that is one of the reasons for his success. The Chinese entrepreneur certainly would agree with Ruskin that there should be less pride felt in the peculiarity of employment, and more in the excellence of achievement. He would confirm that the distinction between one man and another is only in experience and skill, and the authority and wealth that these must naturally and justly obtain. For him, therefore, it does not matter whether he works in a glamorous investment bank or runs a pin factory. The Chinese entrepreneur usually continues to be unpretentious even after becoming rich. Like the Gothic style, Chinese management in this pragmatic sense is the only rational strategic and organizational architecture, because it "can fit itself most easily to all services, vulgar or noble."

Apart from this unusual marriage of noble purpose and humble occupation, what else makes me think that the Gothic style epitomizes the spirit of Chinese entrepreneurship? Let me use Ruskin's definition of Gothicness to explain my point beyond this ethical meta-level. He argues that the Gothic style consists of both external and internal elements. It combines external form and internal power and life, mingling many ideas that can consist only in their union. I will focus here on the internal elements, which give rise to external forms. The distinctive internal elements include savageness, changefulness, naturalism, grotesqueness, rigidity (obstinacy), and redundance (generosity).

To start, let us listen to Ruskin's voice in a beautiful and fitting narration in what can be called a sermon in stones, *The Nature of Gothic* (1853). It summarizes the distinctive elements of the Gothic style.

> The inferior rank of the workman is often shown as much in the
> richness, as the roughness, of his work; and if the cooperation of
> every hand, and the sympathy of every heart, are to be received,
> we must be content to allow the redundance which disguises the
> failure of the feeble, and wins the heart of the inattentive. There

are, however, far nobler interests mingling, in the Gothic heart, with the rude love of decorative accumulation: a magnificent enthusiasm, which feels as if it never could do enough to reach the fullness of its ideal; an unselfishness of sacrifice, which would rather cast fruitless labor before the altar than stand idle in the market; and, finally, a profound sympathy with the fullness and wealth of the material universe, rising out of that Naturalism whose operation we have already endeavored to define. (Ruskin 1985, p. 108)

Let me now discuss the similarity in the constituent elements of the Gothic style and Chinese management both of which are forms of art. I will refer back to parts of the above quotation in the process.

Savageness. The Chinese management style is savage in the sense that it does not fit any textbook categories of management. It is indeed 'Full of wolfish life, fierce as the winds that beat.' Like the Goths' energetic simplicity which contrasted sharply with the impotence of Roman luxury, the Chinese enterprise stands out in its 'sturdy power', modesty and sternness, 'breaking the rock for bread', 'cleaving the forest for fire.' It differs from many Western corporate empires that "bask in the dreamy benignity of sunshine" and "gather redundant fruitage from the earth." There is a strong contrast both in temper and in thought. Like the northern tribes of Europe, Chinese entrepreneurs are accustomed to working hard and fast, quickened by the lack of resources in a country that overall has experienced little kindness from earth or heaven. Chinese entrepreneurs 'rejoice in the leafless as well as in the shady forest.' They "give an expression of sharp energy to all they do"—strength of will matching resoluteness of purpose.

Indeed, Chinese management at times can be rude and wild. No doubt, it is unorthodox. This style is not taught in MBA courses geared mainly to Western students, partly because the people and environment in the West differ from China, resembling rather the sunny south than the cold north in my analogy. The other reason for this neglect was Western ignorance. But Westerners should not condemn the distinctive style because it is unusual and unfamiliar. Diversity of ideas and processes enlarges the portfolio of creative solutions, reduces the risk of error, and increases the viability and longevity of a system. Chinese management creates value, especially when it remains unorthodox and thus does not lose its uniqueness and sharpness because of "herding" which would erode profits. Its wildness is the best promise that this will not happen. Perhaps after this book and several subsequent studies, the art of Chinese management will become part of the core curriculum on (international) strategy and organization in business schools around the world.

Wildness has many forms and consequences. The wild determination of the Chinese entrepreneur is similar to that of the Gothic worker: "The years of his life passed away before his task was accomplished; but generation succeeded generation with unwearied enthusiasm, and the cathedral front was at last lost in the tapestry of its traceries, like a rock among the thickets and herbage of spring." Does this remind us of the Chinese family enterprise and the CEO's desire to create a fountain of wealth for later generations, each of which builds on the work of its ancestors and, alas, in certain cases destroys it?

Wildness of thought is often accompanied by roughness of work. Savageness therefore is associated with imperfection, which may be looked down upon. I vividly remember a discussion with the chairman of a new private management school in China. After he asked me about my research topic, I replied that I analyzed Chinese management. He laughed, then remarked rather condescendingly: "There is no Chinese management." He was correct—Chinese management had not been pressed into a convenient standardized mold. Before this book, it had neither been transformed into a comprehensive theory, nor been analyzed systematically, nor been translated into managerial recommendations that others can follow. But it may also be true that the best things are least often seen in their best form. We should not prefer the perfection of the lower nature to the imperfection of the higher. As in architecture, where we can choose between individual freedom of thought and creativity, and perfect control over design and execution, so in management we cannot standardize and individualize management at the same time. "A new design for every glass" contradicts the system of bureaucracy, which aims at repeating codified experience, often by leveling the work to "a slave's capacity."

For example, employees at United Parcel Service (UPS) are perfectly programmed and incentivized human robots (or animated tools). Rules tell them exactly what to do and how much time they have for each activity, such as talking to a customer. For reasons of efficiency, the doors of their delivery vans have been opened so workers do not waste time operating them. In contrast, the family members of a typical private Chinese enterprise are freewheeling entrepreneurs—with all their faults and genius. The Taylorite brown uniforms of UPS contrast sharply with the rolled-up sleeves—and, alas, white socks—of the Chinese entrepreneur. Scientific management cannot be reconciled with the art of Chinese management. Nor are the results comparable. The contributions of employees who are "free" family members are more valuable than those of "organization men."

As we saw in the case of the visionary founder of Tiger, the Beijing corporate image design firm, who designed his grand headquarters on the computer before any realistic chance of building it, the Chinese entrepreneur's mind is often far ahead of his imperfect powers of execution. Ruskin said, "If we are to have great men working at all, or less men doing their best, the work will be imperfect, however beautiful." Put differently, "No great man ever stops working till he has reached his point of failure." We thus should not prefer "smooth minuteness above shattered majesty," nor withhold our admiration from great excellencies because they are mingled with rough faults. No living and free creation can be rigidly perfect. The principal admirable quality of Chinese management and Gothic architecture is that "Out of fragments full of imperfection, and betraying that imperfection in every touch, indulgently raises up a stately and unaccusable whole." Like the subtle pinnacle reaching its fearless height, the enterprise built by the Chinese entrepreneur is sent like an "unperplexed question up to Heaven," challenging conventional wisdom in the pursuit of greatness and excellence. If we do not allow for art in management, "the mass of society will be made up of morbid thinkers, and miserable workers."

Changefulness. Because the wild Gothic heart never reaches the perfection it can imagine, it cannot rest in the condition it has attained. The talent of the artist lies not in monotony, but in change. His genius shines through invention or "creative destruction" not through sameness. Ruskin said, "It is that strange disquietude of the Gothic spirit that is its greatness, that restlessness of the dreaming mind, that wanders hither and thither among the niches, and flickers feverishly around the pinnacles . . . and yet is not satisfied, nor shall be satisfied." The same applies to the Chinese businessman, who is always on the lookout for new opportunities and tirelessly searches for great breakthroughs that will enlarge his fortune. He is like the first dove sent by Noah, which "found no rest upon the face of the waters." The entrepreneur is as changeful as the clouds that shade the sun. Like the Gothic style he "can shrink into a turret, expand into a hall, spring into a spire." He is "subtle and flexible like a fiery serpent" and "never suffer[s] ideas of outside symmetries and consistencies to interfere with the real use and value of what he does."

The Chinese pragmatist prefers reasonableness over reason and adaptation to new challenges over conformity to old standards. If he "wants a window, he opens one; a room, he adds one, a buttress, he builds one; utterly regardless of any established conventionalities of external appearance" or accepted management wisdom. He starts with a blank sheet. Does this remind us of Mr. Li's conversion of part of his office building into a hotel? Like the Gothic builder, he might open a useless window in an unexpected place to surprise his competitors, rather than "forbid a useful one for sake of symmetry!" There will always be various changes in one part of his value proposition and value chain—to the distress of those who want to catch up with this serpent-like manager.

The variety of every (external) feature of his business, the perpetual change both in design and in execution, bears witness that the Chinese family manager never repeats himself, never engages in routine work. Like a Gothic artist he never says or does the same thing over and over again. His heart and head call for variety and change, which are a measure of his (economic) freedom. A genius of business, he sparkles with new ideas.

His entrepreneurial spirit is noble in its disquietude; irregularity is his trademark.

Many people hate modern (functionalist) buildings and because of a spirit of rebellion and for aesthetical reasons prefer gothic exoticness. Likewise, the Chinese family manager takes no pleasure in modern management techniques as ends in themselves. He does not just copy what all the MBAs do, irrespective of the value. Even if some standardized techniques are functional, they may limit his freedom and creativity. "Nothing is a great work of art, for the production of which rules can be given." Love of order and routine is not love of art, but Chinese management is an art. Wherever there are rules, there is no art, only manufacturing. In contrast, the living spirit of Chinese management, unconstrained by analytical tools, rules, paperwork, functional boundaries, and self-styled "experts" promotes vitality through *positive* change and thus constant progress.

Like the Gothic builder, the Chinese management artist invents new forms, and those in turn perpetuate novelty. In the Gothic case, the use of tracery not only was an innovation in the treatment of window lights, but also enabled countless changes in the interlacement of the tracery bars. Similarly, the creation of enterprise webs grounded in social capital not only was a startling change in the governance of businesses but also admitted endless changes in the myriad linkages between the web participants, a great source of irregularity and variation.

But change always must serve a purpose; it should aim for improvement, though perfection need not be sought. Change might also aim at confusing competitors or outsmarting them through sudden moves. Ruskin said, "Change in the best schools is subtle and delicate, and rendered more delightful by intermingling of a noble monotony. . . . Love of change becomes morbid and feverish in following the haste of the hunter and the rage of the combatant." Why cannot all our change consultants and change managers hear these words? "Those who will not submit to the temporary sameness, but rush from one change to another, gradually dull the edge of change itself, and bring a shadow and weariness over the whole world from which there is no more escape." Man is driven "to seek delight in extreme and fantastic degree of change, when change becomes itself monotonous." This is a "diseased love of change." In many cases, a value is attached to stability and a huge cost associated with change for its own sake.

The Chinese businessman realizes that "too much change is in itself monotonous," and strives for the golden mean, the right balance between change and stability. While he flexibly adapts his shell, the inner values do not change; his family is a source of the stability that he actively seeks (Schlevogt 2000q). He will never pursue change management programs, only because a new management fashion has emerged, which needs to be reversed afterwards (through another change management program). He understands that best change is continuous incremental adaptation and improvement ahead of needs when change action is not intrusive and not visible. Constant small efforts can move mountains.

Naturalism. Naturalism is the "love for natural objects for their own sake, and the effort to represent them frankly, unconstrained by artistical laws." Gothic architecture looks back at a "history of rural and thoughtful life, influenced by habitual tenderness, and devoted to subtle inquiry." As we know from Ruskin, the Gothic builder's power of artistic invention did not surpass that of the Byzantine workman. He accepted the received types, "but he could not rest with them." He discovered that "there was no veracity in them, no knowledge, no vitality." He liked the true leaves better than the artificial Greek and Roman foilage. Thus, cautiously, "He put more of nature into his work, until at last it was all true."

Does this remind us of the Chinese family businessman? He usually knows Western management models—Chinese in the south and overseas have been exposed to them for more than a century. But the Chinese management artist found no truth in them, he disliked the bureaucratic model, and thus removed its mental chains, and created his webs, true to nature, free from artificiality. This distate for established artificial norms and his act of creation and subsequent persistence also suggest that in the future, Chinese management, unlike the management styles of other countries, will not be westernized—at best hybrid forms will emerge.

"The Gothic artist is as firm in rendering of imaginative as of actual truth," and "does not leave the sign in need of interpretation; he makes the fire as like real fire as he can." The Chinese businessman does not need nice boxes for empty concepts either; he hates the myriad Christos in management consulting who make money only by packaging things.[4] He usually only accepts those consulting services that through efficiency improvements pay for themselves. He will not accept long-term "strategic" work where the payoffs are highly uncertain, but the upfront fees certainly very high. Love of truth (and true results) replace an empty sense of beauty. Therefore, I consider the Chinese the most sophisticated and demanding consulting clients in the world. Anybody who thinks that, because they are citizens of a third world country, it will be easy and profitable to dump old consulting frameworks (or old products in general) on them is completely wrong (Schlevogt 2000n; 2000o).

The Gothic artist has no respect for laws. And how about the Chinese businessman? I suggest we interpret "law" in the sense of *business* laws! And in this case, he breaks the law wherever possible. In his quest for freedom of creation and innovation he constantly infringes every depowering principle, transgresses the laws of design, and disguises his limited material. For example, management textbooks recommend that in order to control upstream suppliers or downstream distributors, companies should integrate them under one roof rather than engage in arm's-length transactions. What does the "lawbreaker" do? He creates webs based on implicit contracts that are filled by social capital. How about rules and other formal devices for internal control and coordination? The Chinese entrepreneur chooses other means to achieve the same or better results. He generates loyalty and attracts resources through his charismatic leadership and family ties. For example, the Chinese owner-manager of Magnolia was possessed of limited material resources, which, according to conventional wisdom should have prevented him from acquiring a stake in a five-star hotel. But he presented himself as a big and resourceful boss, and thus successfully attracted overseas capital and implemented the necessary changes in his organization to accommodate the new business.

Naturalism creates the same results in management as in Gothic architecture—"the new direction of mental interest marks an infinite change in the means and the habits of life." Naturalness inspires the entrepreneur and his partners to rebel against management theories and fashions "which fix a form for everything, and forbid variation from it." They always summarize past best practice without anticipating future excellent approaches—literally representing the *state* of the art, a static quantity (or stock), not the future development of the art, a flow. In Gothic architecture, this originality is reflected in slopes of roofs, heights of shafts, breadths of arches, or dispositions of ground plans, which defy established conventionalities of external appearance. "These disturbances of the formal plan rather tend to give additional interest to its symmetry than injure it." To achieve these natural breakthroughs, the Chinese entrepreneur resorts to strong common sense and streetsmartness that insulate him from the conventional wisdom that has been taught in business schools and textbooks for a long time. Spontaneous breakthroughs also emanate from the feelings and habits of free but networked organization members who are shareholders or other stakeholders in the social (and often the financial) capital.

The merit of art, in architecture as in management, consists in saying new and different things which create value. We do not derive any "pleasure out of a universe in which the clouds are all of one shape, and the trees all of one size, from an architecture whose ornaments are of one pattern, and whose pillars are of one proportion." The tight rules of scientific management, reminiscent of the Renaissance style, contrast sharply with the free spirit of Chinese management and Gothic architecture. It resembles the difference between St. Peter's (Renaissance style) and the Cologne cathedral (Gothic style). Repetition is no more characteristic of genius in marble than it is of genius in management. This fundamental truth is sometimes hidden by false teaching that substitutes inflexible theories for natural intuition.

The natural deviation from rules can be seen not only across different Chinese private enterprises at one point of time, but also within the same enterprise over time. In Gothic works, every successive architect, employed upon a great work, added his own pieces, regardless of the style adopted by his colleagues and predecessors. The same casual disregard for superficial precedents that stands in the way of progress applies to Chinese entrepreneurs, who are flexible in designing strategies and organizations, while being imbued with the same spirit as their compatriots and ancestors.

In addition, like the Gothic architect, the Chinese private businessman discovers beauty in natural forms; his spirit is noble in its hold on nature. The artist looks at the nature around him for material. Likewise, the Chinese manager looks at the spiderweb outside his house and copies it, and looks at his competitors for new ideas, always learning from the natural environment. Using Ruskin's words, "The sculptor who sought for his models among the forest leaves, could not but quickly and deeply feel that complexity need not involve the loss of grace, nor richness that of repose; . . . nor is it to be wondered at that, seeing [nature's] perfect and exquisite creations poured forth in a profusion which conception could not grasp nor calculation sum, he should think that it ill became him to be niggardly of his own rude craftsmanship." He thus grudged "his poor and imperfect labor to the few stones that he had raised one upon another, for habitation or memorial." The Chinese manager's webs, though crude in comparison with nature, are great devices to deal with uncertainty and complexity "which conception could not grasp nor calculation sum." This is an important lesson for all management scientists who aim at developing artificial mathematical approaches to deal with challenging tasks and environments. Uncertainty and complexity outside do not involve the loss of internal control and grace.

The Chinese entrepreneur's preference for naturalness is also seen in the importance he attaches to personal relations with other human beings (especially his kins), which replace inhuman systems. In addition, it shows in his desire to remain true to his distinctive cultural roots instead of submitting to the standardizing forces driving toward synthetic globalization in the pursuit of "one world." Undisturbed by outside artificial pressures, he flows spontaneously with eternal nature instead of trying to combat it—his love for cohabitation with nature and nations is stronger than his "love for hunting."

The Gothic artist shines in his frankness, unconstrained by artistic laws; he never seeks to disguise the roughness of work, or his object's roughness of make. Using rougher material, this workman is compelled "to seek for vigour of effect rather than refinement of texture or accuracy of form." The Chinese businessman, too, stands for what he is doing, however humble and unglamorous it might be. He is interested in end products. Subject to the unalterable laws of human nature and materials, he works hard to achieve his purpose, combining the "monk's enthusiasm with the soldier's force." With great aspirations but limited resources, he needs to develop innovative solutions, which create value beyond their original application. Frankness in business negotiations with outsiders (the "enemy") is another matter—here, alas, often the end justifies the means.

In private Chinese businesses, nothing is unthinkable—business life is a perpetual brainstorming session.

Grotesqueness. Ruskin mentioned that the "tendency to delight in fantastic and ludicrous, as well as in sublime, images, is a universal instinct of the Gothic imagination." The latter is described as having a "curious and subtle character," rejecting any notion of simple shapes in repeated formats. Ruskin reminds us that "no architecture is so haughty as that which is simple, which refuses to address the eye, except in a few clear and forceful lines, which implies, in offering so little to our regards, that all it has offered is perfect." Of course, Ruskin referred to renaissance architecture, which still is aesthetically pleasant. What would he have said about modern buildings? In my view, sterile functionalism in architecture and management alike lacks creative power and inspiring richness.

At times, the Chinese management style, with all its fancifulness and richness, seems very odd to the Western observer. For example, how can anybody ask an academic interviewer to refer other interviewees to him for business purposes? How can a CEO convert his office building into a hotel? Who would think of linking up at the same time with army generals, university deans, and government officials to engage in myriad ventures? What a grotesque melting pot and cauldron of magic ideas and idiosyncratic people! The oddness is its charm—and secret competitive weapon. In private Chinese businesses, nothing is unthinkable—business life is a perpetual brainstorming session. In contrast, Western businessmen set themselves many limits through unquestioned assumptions and theories and waste many resources in activities that are accepted as necessary, without investigation.

The business practices and habits of the Chinese manager are unorthodox. That should not surprise us. Love of order, though extremely important, differs from love of art. Ruskin says that experience "teaches us that accurate and methodical habits in daily life are seldom characteristic of those who either quickly perceive, or richly possess, the creative powers of art." There is, however, "nothing to hinder us from retaining our business habits, and yet fully allowing and enjoying the noblest gifts of invention." Similarly, some of the unorthodoxies in later times will become mainstream practices, which create substantial value. In a Chinese insurance company in Shenzhen, employees need to sleep a few minutes during noon time, which might seem a stupid waste of time. Yet latest research in the West has shown that short sleep breaks are very effective, since they refresh the brain. These findings will inspire Western companies to introduce this innovation as a standard business practice. Of course, they could have done so earlier, if they had been willing to learn from the Chinese. I hope that this book will prevent similar delays.

Rather oddly, the Chinese management style combines external modernity with internal antiquity. On the one hand, the quest for innovation drives the entrepreneur to develop and apply (post-)modern management principles. These principles may be avant-garde, potentially serving as a new generation of business paradigms. For example, the question of how to deal with uncertainty and complexity is at the top of the agenda of the most advanced and famous organizational researchers and management consulting firms.

An integrated network organization, with the center and periphery spontaneously switching roles and resources, and the peripheral units initiating activities and exchanging resources among themselves, all powered by self-multiplying social capital and endless human energy, is the most sophisticated and difficult organizational entity to design, implement, and run—once initiated by an entrepreneur with strong values and ties, it needs to evolve naturally as a web.

On the other hand, as I have shown, the Chinese entrepreneur heavily emphasizes traditional values engrained in Chinese culture. These values are the entrepreneur's soul food and glue him to the community, leading to a healthy spiritual (and material) life. Once again this synthesis of modernity and antiquity finds its parallels in Ruskin's ideas. He believed that all good art is full of the most frank anachronism. In my view, art everywhere creates something new based on the past, and thus serves as a bridge across time and space.

Rigidity. Greek and Roman buildings stand passively by their pure weight, stones put one on top of the other. The same applies to the Eiffel Tower in Paris, which is not fixed to the ground, but remains stable because of the weight of the steel. The Gothic style, in contrast, uses "active rigidity." In its vaults and traceries "there is a stiffness analogous to that of the bones of a limb or fibres of a tree; an elastic tension and communication of force from part to part." What a great image to describe the Chinese enterprise web and its embedded social capital! Each unit in the web stabilizes the next one by exchanging resources. Bundled together through strong trust-based relations, the emerging architecture proves incredibly resistant to shocks and threats. The web also divides environmental and internal complexity; like the limbs and organs of a body, each of its parts deals with one aspect of complexity. The networks possess the "peculiar energy that gives tension to movement, and stiffness to resistance, which makes the fiercest lightning forked rather than curved, and the stoutest oak-branch angular rather than bending; and is as much seen in the quivering of the lance as in the glittering of the icicle." Like traditional Chinese architecture, complex interwoven structures hold together without a single intrusive nail replacing the headquarters and its orders. The ideas and values that enabled this arrangement serve as glue, exemplifying how the flexible immaterial can effortlessly unite and govern the rigid material.

Contrast this to the "stable fixedness" of the bureaucratic colossus— one giant company that tries to master and rule the complex world. In an arrangement that resembles Greek and Roman buildings, we find mechanically divided roles in boxes, passively recumbent one on the other. They stand by their own mass and weight. But give me a lever (or let me use Chinese martial art), and I will use their own mass to bring them down. Can you try to use a lever against a web? It will probably get stuck. In the bureaucratic model, there is "no expression of energy in the framework of the ornament itself." It is like a "surface engraving," without "studious expression of elastic tension and communication of force throughout every visible line of the building." As a consequence, internally, the bureaucratic structure does not inspire heroic deeds. In contrast, the Chinese web "stands out in prickly independence, and frosty fortitude, jutting into crockets, and freezing into pinnacles; here starting up into a monster, there germinating into a blossom, anon knitting itself into a branch, alternately thorny, bossy, and bristly, or writhed into every form of nervous entanglement; but even when most graceful, never for an instant languid, always quickset." What better description could be found for the unorthodox, naturally developing, at the same time strong and fluid enterprise webs, built to last by family members and friends, that are one of the hallmarks of Chinese management?

Redundancy. The last, and least important, element of the inner spirit of Gothic architecture is the uncalculating bestowal of the wealth of labor. The accumulation of ornament in certain Gothic styles results from the workman's creative savageness and freedom—flowing from the lack of formalization described above—his enthusiasm, selfless sacrifice in the name of work, and naturalism, which drive him to represent the full richness of his living environment.

In Chinese management, a similar redundancy can sometimes be noticed. Without formalized coordination mechanisms, employees are likely to engage in activities that overlap to a certain degree. Because they also are relatively free from organizational control, they have ample space to be creative but also imperfect. "Admitting the aid, and appealing to the admiration, of the rudest as well as the most refined minds," Chinese management's richness "is, paradoxical as the statement may appear, a part of its humility." In other words, "if the co-operation of every hand, and the sympathy of every heart, are to be received, we must be content to allow the redundancy which disguises the failure of the feeble, and wins the regard of the inattentive." Besides, the frequent spin-offs from Chinese enterprises, which later compete (and cooperate) with the former employer, are an additional source of repetition.

Further, the CEO's enthusiasm, which "feels as if it never could do enough to reach the fullness of its ideal," and his humility lead him to perform many jobs himself. When other employees do the same work as the CEO, hands-on involvement duplicates efforts. He often thinks that mind and hand should not be separated, and that manual labor is not a sign of degradation. In a more artistic sense, as we have seen in the case of Tiger, the CEO is aware that in the case of designs that cannot be exactly formalized, one person's ideas can never be expressed by someone else.

As Ruskin said, "The difference between the spirit of touch of the man who is inventing, and of the man who is obeying directions, is often all the difference between a great and a common work of art." Moreover, we heard that driven by his strong work ethic, the CEO "would rather cast fruitless labor before the altar than stand idle in the market." Some CEOs work extremely long hours, but their average productivity is low. They might be better advised occasionally to take a break during the day, or even a vacation instead of generating decreasing marginal returns. Besides, Ruskin understood redundancy as a sign of generosity. The head of the Chinese business family may appear stingy in his dealings with outsiders and minimizes his personal consumption, but is usually very generous to his family and friends.

As is almost inevitable in an idealized comparison and interpretive account that involves two races, occidental and oriental, draws an analogy between art and management, and bridges different time periods, some elements depart from the close parallel. I also acknowledge the danger of forcing the research object into the analogy mold, as into a straitjacket. However, in this book I mitigated this danger by first gathering the empirical evidence to test a theory and then starting the interpretive and narrative process—a journey of sense making, social construction, and "world making" (Chia and King 1998, p. 463). I thus attempted to stabilize what is essentially a changeable reality.

Maybe the greatest difference in the individual elements that make up the inner spirit of Chinese management and Gothicness is the sense of individualism and independence of the Gothic artist—viewed from a religious angle. This is a conjecture, since, though the Gothic works remain, the spirits that produced them have left. In contrast to the collective emphasis of the Chinese, Christianity cherishes the individual value of every soul. Christians independently tend to God's greater glory in a "face-to-face" dialogue, which, in its pure form, needs no intermediary.

But in wordly terms there are strong parallels with respect to this independence and individualism and their relation to collective efforts. The Chinese manager, consciously or unconsciously, often sets his individual reason against authorities in the field of standard management teaching. This is a clear sign of an individualistic and independently-minded character that does not tolerate undue manipulation and control, which is a classical impulse of the Gothic heart and protestantism. Further, in the social context, if the Gothic heart is individualistically independent, the Chinese heart is collectively so. It is group-oriented within the family but independent to serve the family when dealing with the environment. Each family (or extended version) is an island in a rough sea. At an even higher level, the Middle Kingdom's independence as a nation, achieved through domestic seclusion and stern self-reliance, is symbolized by the Great Wall which separated it from the outside barbarian world. It bears further witness of this "collective individualism." As a result of a similar "dialectic reaction," many individualistic and independent Gothic artist together created a collective magic—a cathedral that stands as lonely in the skies as an island in the sea. Like emissaries from other nations who came to old China and absorbed Confucian values, people visit the cathedral to pay tribute and are assimilated to the belief system in the process.

As for the overall analogy between art and management—using Ruskin's words in a slightly different context—the idea of reading a management model as we would read Milton or Dante, and getting the same kind of delight out of the management techniques as out of the stanzas, never entered my mind before I wrote this book. But, as seen, inspired individual and social activity can produce very artistic results indeed.

Chinese private enterprises on the international stage: A new global force?

No Grand Army

Having praised the web-based Chinese management model in such high terms—elevating it to a lofty artistic stature, giving it the status of precious cultural artifact, and daring to compare the Chinese entrepreneur to the Gothic artist and builder of cathedrals—do we have to prepare for an invasion of Western countries by Chinese private firms comparable to the Japanese takeover of corporate America—fueled by the unquenchable spirit of Chinese entrepreneurship? Imagine the headlines, "The Chinese Empire Strikes Back"! Please, dear reader, do not worry! Let me reassure you. If it is an army, it rather resembles that of the first emperor's trustworthy friends—the Terra Cotta army that was placed in his tomb.

I strongly believe that there is no imminent threat of a business invasion for three reasons. First, because of economic fundamentals, many Chinese enterprises feel no particular urge to expand abroad. It comes to no surprise that their international growth track-record is negative. Despite more than twenty years of reforms, so far very few companies from mainland China have made successful inroads into Western markets by means of foreign direct investment. China offered abundant resources of capital and labor especially for state enterprises, boasting the highest saving rate in the world and a huge pool of inexpensive labor. Companies certainly needed to concentrate their resources to grow in the huge, seemingly unlimited battleground at home. Outsourcing production when most Western companies entered China to profit from production factor-driven cost advantages would have seemed irrational. In contrast, the scarce resources and limited opportunity space in Japan motivated many companies early in their development to search for new sources of inputs, production facilities, and markets abroad.

Second, if my prediction is correct, most family-based private enterprises will not grow sufficiently to be able to fund and manage a foreign campaign. The desire to keep business in the family may constrain expansion. The lack of valuable outside resources, such as professional management and strong brands, which appears to explain why many private enterprises refrain from entering foreign markets, is thus only a symptom, not the root cause. In fact, the real reason for limited growth are deep cultural values.

Third, in contrast to Japan and Korea, private enterprises in the P.R.C. in the past did not receive strong government support. They had to raise their funds from private sources of capital instead of national banks, which in China did not constitute a well-functioning savings system. Even though the informal capital market is liquid, its size and access is limited.

Nevertheless, I predict that certain exceptional private enterprises (but normally not family-owned ones) will become successful international players. Potential candidates are the Shenzhen-based financial service company Pingan, which in less than twenty years has grown into the second largest insurance company in China (after the state-owned People's Insurance Company of China), the fast growing China International Trust and Investment Corporation (CITIC); and China Everbright. To grow internationally, private enterprises need to attract outside talent and other resources, form hybrid professionally and family-managed organizations using, for example, a multidivisional structure (or other fitting designs) and adopt universally successful management techniques, such as strong brand management and international marketing. The development of Acer, the Taiwanese computer maker, from humble beginnings to an international powerhouse, exemplifies the strategic and organizational changes needed to succeed in the global market place. New Hope in China went public to be monitored by the market and attract outside talent and capital. Such a company has the right structure to diversify and expand quickly, at home and abroad. Another group of candidates for international expansion are state enterprises that because of their connections with high-ranking officials, can leverage strong political clout and financial resources. They will seek listings, for example, on the New York or London stock exchange in order to secure funding for international expansion.

WCM is not suitable for managing nuclear power plants, hospitals, or other high-reliability organizations.

. . . but formidable guerrilla fighters

Even though I have argued for their intrinsic limits to international expansion, I still think that in mainland China, the new generation of private enterprises will become very strong competitors to multinational corporations by occupying niche positions and gaining advantage through quick adaptations to uncertain, complex, and competitive markets. For example, in less than two years, China's Legend Group has become number 3 in the Chinese computer market (from number 6), just behind IBM and Compaq (Turpin 1998). Now, after China's accession to the World Trade Organization, many private enterprises (but not many state enterprises) are well-positioned to stand their ground among the influx of new foreign players and existing competitors. But once again, web-based Chinese management is likely to succeed only in sectors that favor small scale and flexibility rather than the predictability of organizational outcomes. WCM is not suitable for managing nuclear power plants, hospitals, or other high-reliability organizations.

Chinese management and the development of China's economy

Chinese management and the development of the private economy

Witnessing the significant rise in private economic activity that I analyzed in chapter 1, one cannot help asking what caused this dynamism. Above all, I need to determine whether this process is related to changes in the way Chinese firms are managed. Such a microeconomic explanation seems necessary, since the macro-environment in the past was rather constraining or outright hostile, and thus did not fuel the rapid growth. One key point of this book is to show that after Deng Xiao-ping's "reform and opening" policy, significant changes in enterprise management occurred. We are watching a great entrepreneurial and managerial revolution in the making. According to my research, the distinctive new management style—readopted in the newly established private Chinese enterprises and reminiscent of overseas Chinese management—explains the inherent dynamism in the private sector and accounts for much of its rapid growth. It clarifies how private enterprises were able to satisfy pent-up demand in the Chinese market quickly, growing tall like a cactus in the desert with little outside water. I thus advocate a microeconomic explanation of private firms' development, demonstrating the importance of management for economic development.

This study shows clearly that the distinctive features of web-based Chinese management create enterprises and jobs, and make these enterprises and employees prosperous. It helps with navigation in unstructured, uncertain, and complex situations, and effectively harnesses the power of human potential. Let me give you some examples. Centralized charismatic leadership by the owner-dictator results in speedy decision making, great flexibility, and razor-sharp accountability. Informal structures and entrepreneurial leadership allow for dynamic adaptation to new opportunities. Small company size reinforces this agility. Extensive enterprise webs enable entrepreneurs to leverage visible and invisible resources from other participants, and serve as seedbed for new enterprises and jobs. The emphasis on traditional Chinese values, especially familism, creates valuable social capital, which helps to reduce costs and boost revenues. The powerful ownership incentives focus entrepreneurs on profitability, achieved through responsible housekeeping, efficient cash management and prudent revenue growth. Implicit contracts fill the holes in formal contracts in uncertain and complex situations.

Thus, even though private enterprises are not likely to become a major force internationally, they will be the major engine of domestic economic growth and job creation in the future. Their efforts will make China a political, economic, and military powerhouse and a new strategic force in the world. I expect that private Chinese enterprises will become even more influential in the future. One development that favors this trend is the spread of the Internet in China. A great economic demoncratizer, it levels the playing field and empowers individuals and small firms. The latter are in a very good position flexibly to take advantage of the new opportunities and to become the major players on the virtual battleground.

Chinese management and the development of the macroeconomy

The intricate coordination and control devices of WCM enable entrepreneurs to flexibly and rapidly adapt to a changing environment. This also makes the macroeconomy, the aggregate of individual economic activity, more adaptable, and more robust. Through their decentralized resource allocation mechanisms embedded in social capital, private Chinese enterprises absorb and overcome external economic shocks quickly, increasing the resilience of the national economy as a whole. Because of its dynamism and flexibility, WCM thus not only creates and maintains employment, but also cushions economic shocks better than rigid bureaucracies.

Entrepreneurs can switch resources easily within the networks. For example, they do not need to dismiss workers every time a crisis happens, but can assign them to different tasks within the web. Supply can easily be adjusted to demand, since there is no "stickiness" in the management processes. Private enterprise neither underinvest which would lead to stagnation and decline, nor do they overinvest and build up overcapacity which results in destructive price wars. With few loans on their balance sheet, private enterprises are unlikely to fall into debt traps and suffer liquidity crunches, which caused many economic crises.

WCM's lack of structural and managerial rigidity and inertia, and balanced approaches towards investment and other decisions thus might lessen the occurrence and impact of business cycles and depressions, and lead to sustained, high-quality growth. It is thus a great blueprint not only for an organization but also for entire sectors and the whole economy, a great vision for both the microeconomic level, the mesolevel, and the macroeconomic level.

The short-term economic crisis in Asia (1997–1998) did not change the fundamental economic reality underlying the success of WCM. On the contrary, the distinctive characteristics of private enterprises—apart from macroeconomic factors in China such as controls on capital flows and on exchange rates—may have protected China from this highly infectious disease. First, their flexibility helped them to absorb the external shocks and adjust, for example, their product portfolio to changing demand in export markets. In view of their ability to spot new opportunities, I am sure that many firms even profited from the discontinuity and rent-creating potential. Second, the private sector, because it is mainly self-financed, did not carry huge (short-term foreign) loan burdens, which would have endangered the economy if currency devaluation inflated foreign interest obligations and nervous investors called in their funds. The private sector thus offset the high (long-term and domestic) loan exposure of state enterprises. Third, the enthusiasm spread by the successful development of private enterprises may have sustained consumers' and investors' confidence, avoiding runs on banks and slumps in consumption and investment. This way, China gained time to deal with structural problems, such as rampant excess capacity—and its corollary, deflation (Schlevogt 1999j)—and bad debt. These challenges are similar to the problems of other Asian countries and would have been sufficient to serve as "dry wood" that speculators could ignite into a forest fire. But WCM and the resulting confidence served as built-in macro-economic stabilizer at the microeconomic level neutralizing negative structural effects or at least holding negative temporary effects in check.

If anything stops China's long-term growth, in my view, it will be the lack of sufficient skilled managers and workers, innovations, and institutions—path-dependent and causally ambiguous human, intellectual, and systemic social capital—not short-term economic disruptions. Perhaps private enterprises will even improve these macroeconomic fundamentals through grass roots initiatives, especially by blending social and digital webs. A small firm has already started to tackle the human bottleneck through electronic means. Zhaopin.com (*zhaopin* means "recruitment") helps companies and individuals to match skills with opportunities in a virtual labor market.

Dynamic implications for Chinese economic development and policy making: The need to focus on the micro level

Explaining the malaise of SOEs: Introducing a new perspective and approach

Modern macroeconomists could argue that many of China's economic problems, especially of the state sector, result from an inefficient financial system. Because of political power considerations and the underdeveloped financial and legal infrastructure and processes, SOEs, in particular, get the lion's share of the abundant national savings, at very low interest rates, without the disciplining force of bankruptcy risk. Politicians need to subsidize their power base, which backs and implements their action. At the same time, China lacks efficient credit rating mechanisms, and investment appraisal methods which signal "lemon" borrowers and projects. Especially for loans granted by the state, there is a lack of close scrutiny by smart bankers and markets and an effectively enforced bankruptcy law.

The incentive misalignment is expected to cause moral hazard problems resulting from easy access to credit and subsidized interest. SOEs are thought to pursue overly risky and aggressive strategies, leading to overproduction and big bets. They do not have to pay for the downside but reap all potential fruits. This chain of reasoning implies that the political, financial, and legal macroenvironment distorts the allocation of scarce resources, diverting them from their best, that is, most efficient, uses. Such an explanation reminds me of the "tragedy of the commons" phenomenon. Free goods tend to be exploited without respect for the social costs (externalities) that have to be paid by parties other than the incurring one, as happened when commons (public grass land) were overused in centuries past.

Despite the elegance of this possible macroeconomic argument, researchers must look at the microlevel to see whether the theorized managerial behavior *actually takes place*. Alas, economists very seldom conduct organizational surveys, and instead prefer to manipulate aggregate secondary data from their armchairs. In contrast, I left the coziness of my Harvard office and ventured out to collect real-world data through personal interviews with Chinese CEOs. This enabled me to test the assumptions and hypotheses of the armchair economists. In this context, one of the interesting findings of this study was which differences between private and state enterprises were *not* statistically significant. Contrary to macroeconomic beliefs, my survey showed that state enterprises did *not* pursue significantly more risky or aggressive strategies than their private counterparts. State enterprises actually pursued significantly more longterm, defensive, and analytical strategies than private firms. This seriously undermines the macroeconomic explanation for their problems.

In addition, results revealed cases of effective and efficient state-owned enterprises that outperformed some private enterprises. Given that all SOEs are exposed to the same environment with an abundant supply of cheap credit, it is difficult to explain why certain SOEs still effectively and efficiently allocate their resources. Further, the lack of a well-functioning financial and legal system in general also affects private enterprises. But nevertheless on average they attain comparatively high performance levels. Similarly, why are there examples of low-performing private enterprises that do not obtain easy credit? Why do especially some large private enterprises adopt aggressive strategies and overstretch resources, pursuing unhealthy, low-quality growth that results in excess capacity and financial disasters (Schlevogt 1999c; 2001d)? Why do these exceptions to the positive examples of private resource stewardship in family businesses occur? To sum up the argument, a quantity that does not change, such as the macroenvironment, cannot account for variation.

In view of the failure of the aggregate explanation, the difficulties of SOEs, and state enterprises in general, have to be explained primarily by their management at the microlevel rather than by general macroeconomic causes, such as the supply of cheap credit. And the sophistication of management is an outcome of the quality of managers. If the macroeconomic explanatory approach were correct, it would be very difficult to explain why there are also efficient SOEs in an environment that supposedly stimulates opportunistic behavior. In contrast, my microeconomic approach solves the conundrum. The reason for the efficiency of individual SOEs is good management.

The macroeconomists neither explain the activities and performance of private enterprises—a subject that has so far been overlooked. After having outlined the reasons for the success of private enterprises, let me explain why a few entrepreneurs fail. Some large private enterprises lack well-crafted corporate and business strategies, which match the company's strengths and weaknesses with environmental opportunities and threats. The CEO of a large company may not be able to devise smart strategies for all units alone and through mere intuition. Perhaps the company also operates without an effective organizational architecture, such as a corporate center with subordinated divisions. It may lack solid management control systems, which, based on key performance indicators, issue early warnings, signaling potential problems before it is too late. These are all examples of strategic and organizational misfit. WCM entails small size and growth through networks. If the focal company grows itself (instead of proliferating into webs), it needs more formal and informal structuring and processing of activities to remain in internal and external fit. If it does not adapt internally, at least it needs to shape the environment to suit its needs.

Paralysis in SOEs often comes from overanalysis.

Having outlined my innovative microeconomic method, let me elaborate on the microeconomic factors influencing the performance of state enterprises in general, and SOEs in particular. As in the case of private firms, my study sheds some light on the causes leading to the problems of state enterprises, which were shown on average to create less value than their private counterparts. Many SOEs are highly bureaucratic. Of course, larger companies need more control mechanisms, but they can choose between rigid formal controls and more subtle culture controls. Myriad rules and extensive paperwork will be antifunctional in a highly uncertain environment that requires flexible adaptation to constantly changing contingencies. It is also very difficult to formalize best practice in a very complex setting in which system parts are strongly interconnected, with one move affecting the whole system. Further, SOEs are significantly less entrepreneurial than private enterprises. This is actually the largest overall difference. The comparative lack of entrepreneurship makes it difficult for SOEs to seize new opportunities quickly. Paralysis in SOEs often comes from overanalysis. The strategies of SOEs also are significantly more defensive, with an emphasis on cutting costs instead of generating innovations (which may increase revenues, among other things). Moreover, they lack the intricate enterprise webs that radically improve the performance of many private enterprises. Large size further inhibits flexibility and reduces the speed of decision making. Finally, SOEs do not strongly emphasize Chinese traditional cultural values that create valuable social capital. The lack of familism and individualized ownership reduces managerial incentives to work hard. The combination of values and ownership makes the difference. It would not suffice to emulate private ownership alone or even to privatize state-owned enterprises—another microeconomic insight that refines or replaces broad macroeconomic brushes.

The failure of classical macroeconomic cures in China

Only if we recognize the real sources of a disease, we can identify the cure. As a result of their wrong diagnoses, macroeconomists recommend the wrong policies for China—if they make any practical suggestions at all. And their inability to learn is very frightening. (Mis-)using Russia as a real world laboratory for their social experiments, they made costly mistakes paid by the Russian people. They essentially destroyed a whole nation (Schlevogt 2000c), which now needs to be rebuilt, while carefully handling the revanchism and nationalism that the abuse sparked. Now, similar recipes are advocated for China. Fortunately, the country so far has proved largely resilient and rejected all the "smart" Western advisers who lack management knowledge, practical experience, and a basic culturally grounded understanding of the Middle Kingdom, but are keen to use China to promote themselves at the expense of others. Such knowledge is essential—economics is a social science that needs to be rooted in the social context.

What are the suggestions of Western macroeconomists? They advocate an explosive mix indeed, which combines supply-side and demand-side policies in an ecclectic, opportunistic, and short-termist fashion. First, economists advocate the hardly innovative and constructive idea of tightening bankruptcy laws and forcing companies into receivership, thus kicking off a process of Darwinian selection in which the fittest survive. Bad news for the majority of state enterprises and their employees, which would fail. Another approach is financial reengineering, swapping the debt of state enterprises for equity (see Schlevogt 2000r). But how will the new asset management organizations administer or sell their shares? Besides, they are unlikely to improve microeconomic fundamentals. The case of the German Treuhand, which took over Eastern Germany's state assets, showed at a much smaller scale how difficult state management of essentially private activities is.

Further, financial institutions may change their credit practices and channel loans to high net present value companies and projects, which are identified through sophisticated credit-rating systems and investment appraisal methods. But future cash flows and discount rates are inherently difficult to estimate under situations of uncertainty and complexity. It is questionable whether such financial appraisal is more objective. And finally there are the worn-out exhortations: in regards to fiscal policy, a call for lean budgets through cuts in government expenditure, making it possible to cut taxes which stimulates demand, plus a restrained monetary policy that keeps inflation at a low level. We have heard it all thousands of times, and rarely saw cases where macroeconomic tinkering alone increased the wealth of nations.

Will the policies proposed by the macroeconomists solve the problem? At best, I could say that their recommendations are necessary, but not sufficient, conditions. At worst, and more likely, in many cases they will produce the opposite effects from what they set out to achieve, because system dynamics are not recognized. Let me take one example to illustrate the point. On the surface, more bankruptcies seem to be good—as a disciplining device for market players, which serves as prevention and as punishment for bad management. Economic theory implies that bankruptcy helps to optimize capital allocation. It frees up capital, moving it from inefficient projects to the most efficient uses in a process of market self-regulation. But which deeper, complex chain reactions follow? In the first instance, there will be more unemployed people. This unleashes a set of negative effects. First, it will increase government expenditure. The state will have to pay out more social benefits and spend more on law and order to combat widespread crime and social unrest. If jobs are cut in rural areas, people will migrate to the cities, leaving behind shattered communities, overstretching urban resources, and eventually spreading crime (and disease). We are now witnessing my predictions coming true.

At the same time, central and local governments will collect less revenues in the form of corporate and personal taxes. They thus will have less funds to invest into transport, communication, and health care, for example. Without such hard and soft infrastructure, the nation will generate less visible and invisible assets. Besides, because of the increasing instability and decline of the country, the national market will become less attractive to investors. This will lead to a decrease in foreign direct investment and an exodus of domestic investors, further reducing the capital base and tax revenues. The combination of higher expenses and lower revenues leads to a shrinking budget and eventually high budget deficits. Thus, without new loans (which would increase the interest burden and finally result in a debt trap, where most revenues are consumed by interest payments), and without printing more money than productivity increases warrant (which leads to inflation) less funds will be available, for example, to invest in education and research. As a consequence, the quality of managers and workers will decrease and talents emigrate in search of greater development opportunities. Thus, products will worsen, resulting in more bankruptcies. The vicious circle is closed.

As a result of the interdependent forces at work, both long-term and short-term growth will be negatively affected. Long-term, supply-driven growth depends on capital, labor, and a residual called technological progress (or total factor productivity), which determines production possibilities. In the above scenario, the amount of available capital will most probably decrease because of the decline in foreign direct investment and dwindling domestic sources; the amount of high-quality labor will decrease owing to cuts in education spending; total factor productivity will go down due to deflated government research budgets, less technology transferred by foreign companies, the general upheaval, and the decay of the system, its institutions, and processes. As a result, the country's pool of tangible and intangible resources will be further depleted leading to a further decline in individual living standards, collective welfare, and general confidence and happiness.

Short-term, demand-driven growth, which determines whether what is produced will be sold, depends on consumption, investment, government expenditure, and net exports (the difference between total exports and imports). It, too, most likely will be negatively affected. Lower consumer confidence and disposable income decrease consumption. Lower business confidence and higher nominal interest rates in the wake of inflation might crowd out investment. Because of reduced tax revenues, there will also be less funds for government expenditure. Finally, net exports might suffer as a consequence of declining product attractiveness in the world market. This might result from curtailed research budgets and poorer quality of management and labor, and potentially higher imports (financed by debt), since essential goods cannot be produced by the country itself anymore. Most of the quantitative effects will be visible in hard statistics, but some of the more subtle, qualitative effects, which often are more powerful, will be seen only in real life when it is too late.

Macroeconomists often do not see these complicated dynamic interconnections. One important reason is the simplicity of their mathematical and econometric models. Owing to their abstract nature, they do not fully capture real-world richness. Otherwise, if models become more complex and closer to reality, they lose their value of abstracted simplicity that allows researchers to analyze complex phenomena. Another reason is time lags, which separate cause and effect. They make it difficult to learn—by observing the impact of action. If the water gets not hot quickly after we turn the switch in the shower, we probably will turn further and get burnt eventually. Moreover, economists fall prey to ideological dogmatism and rigid thinking that is boxed in a universe of conventional wisdom and unchallenged beliefs and assumptions, and they dislike analyzing the real world. They often forget that the principles and benefits of market economics apply only in a perfectly competitive market. But such a setup is rare, since carefully selected and highly paid executives strive hard to decrease competition by forming alliances, building brands, and pursue other rent-creating strategies. And even if such idealized conditions apply, the market does not care about social issues, and the theory does not capture complex human interaction, which can have profound economic consequences.

In addition, many macroeconomists who focus exclusively on SOE reforms, overlook the important role of the private sector and its even greater significance in the future. Their only advice in most cases is to channel more savings to the private sector through loans. Based on the results of my study, I do not think that such action alone would have a great impact on the development of private enterprises. So far, lack of capital does not seem to be the greatest problem of private enterprises. They can obtain funds from the informal credit sector, such as family members and friends in SOEs and banks, and can finance projects from the retained earnings of their business.

In fact, I would predict that, because of the inherent limits to growth that result from the emphasis on familism in private Chinese enterprises, they would not be able to "digest" most of the additional capital provided through loans. It would act like excessive artificial vitamins that are rejected by the body. Besides, owing to their frugal nature, financial conservatism and concomitant fear of financial risks, and emphasis on trust-based relations with insiders, there will be cultural barriers to borrowing large sums of money, especially from outsiders. I would thus predict that if they really need capital, private firms are more likely to resort to *minority* equity financing through web members or venture capital or private equity firms, without losing control over the business. Thus, an activist policy, channeling more financial resources to the private sector, is unlikely to produce any significant impact. Instead, the most important help for private enterprises would be a laissez-faire policy that removes obstacles in their environment which inhibit their flourishing.

As regards foreign-funded private economic activity, it is not sufficient to improve incentives for foreign companies, by reducing corporate taxes or offering tax exemptions for a limited number of years. The real success factor and make-or-break issue is whether foreign companies can achieve *long-term* profitability in China by building up a workable business model. After all the years of losses sustained by most foreign companies, and with no changes in sight (in many industries, markets will become even more competitive, partly because of China's accession to the WTO and concomitant lower barriers to entry and action), I would not be surprised if many managers of foreign companies, after reading this book, finally become rational and pull the plug. They might invest their money elsewhere and maybe come back to China when the time is right, buying up the companies that exhausted themselves in a quixotic battle.

Targeting economic growth and reform policies at the micro level: The applicability of WCM to policy making

In view of the theoretical fallacy of Western macroeconomic suggestions and their historical failure, as well as the new theories and empirical evidence from this study, it is time to rethink which growth and reform policies should be chosen. The heightened domestic competition and further increase in competitive intensity from foreign players in the wake of China's accession to the World Trade Organization (WTO) pose real danger to the survival and well-being of many companies and for the development and prosperity of the economy as a whole. Here, I will suggest some ideas that need to be elaborated upon later.

At the macro level, a stable protective framework should be maintained. Despite the self-interested criticism by foreign governments and businesses, which are keen to open new markets while protecting their home turfs, and by ideologically blinded economists, it proved tremendously successful in China and other developing countries. Within this stable macroeconomic framework, reforms at the micro level will yield a high impact. Thus, I advise the Chinese government to keep control over the fundamental factors of the economy, such as capital flows, exchange rates, and the number of short-term (foreign) loans issued, in order to insulate itself against attacks from speculators who operate in concert with the international media like those that triggerred the Asian meltdown. This does not mean that the macroeconomic framework should not be improved and structural problems not be solved, so that any attempts to shake the country will be neutralized. If somebody spread negative propaganda about Germany's economy for example, a meltdown would be unlikely. Further, some sort of protectionism will be crucial to give Chinese companies a chance to develop before the seeds or the field where seeds could be planted are rolled over by Western multinational companies, which will stay forever and ensure that no new domestic competitors develop.

This protectionism has proved a key success factor in the past, and will continue to be vital in the future. Despite economic theories predicting the contrary, protectionism (like authoritarian systems) has not deterred foreign companies, which have less comparable investment opportunities and bargaining power than commonly assumed, from investing in China. On the contrary, many companies had to invest in China, because trade barriers made it difficult for them to export to it.

This is why it is questionable whether entry into the World Trade Organization was desirable at the present time. The downside is substantial, but the global power elite probably will ensure that negative consequences are not attributed to this supranational institution. The WTO demands a phased removal of all protectionist measures, thus taking important policy control levers from the government and making China (above all, the state sector) very vulnerable to foreign attacks. This could increase the plight of SOEs in particular and lead to major social dislocations. In the short-run, consumer demand will fall even if prices fall (one of the alleged advantages of free trade), because many people will lose their jobs and income, and government expenditure will also decrease because of reduced personal income tax revenues. Even net investment may decline if more companies are forced into bankruptcy than are newly created. It is not clear whether the increase in exports will exceed the surge in imports.

What China gets in return for WTO membership is not worth this tremendous sacrifice, and could be achieved through its own efforts or less intrusive and less risky methods. As we have seen, innovation can be driven by domestic private enterprises. In addition, most technology that initially is not developed at home, can be sourced through strategic alliances or licenses and can then be further developed and applied at home. Capital and labor in any case predominantly originate from domestic sources.

Through bilateral treaties, China could better leverage its bargaining power than in a multilateral, supranational organization—a playing field that requires subtle international political games still unknown to China, but mastered to perfection by the country that dominates any international organization if it is to join it—the U.S. (Schlevogt 1999l). China allowed the pursuit of international recognition and prestige associated with WTO membership to blind its view of economic fundamentals, a classical case of political and ideological considerations overriding technical realities, which always results in failure (see Schlevogt i). The uncritical quest for international approval also undermines China's national interests, since the Middle Kingdom will no longer fully control its own destiny and occupy the center stage that its name implies.

Let me now discuss my most important economic cure: policies targeted at the enterprise level. I suggest to use web-based Chinese management theory to deal with China's macro-economic challenges at the micro level. WCM can serve as a model for policy making. As we have seen, it is an important tool for creating companies and jobs, leading to prosperity. The Chinese government should encourage WCM by letting the private economy flourish and multiply (together with its management model)—a first step has been taken by amending the constitution to recognize the legitimacy of nonstate enterprises. It should also encourage the spread of WCM to state enterprises, and suggest its application to foreign companies and organizations in general. The combined WCM elements, which are worth being nurtured in private enterprise and transferred to state enterprises, have been discussed in more detail in previous chapters, which also showed how to implant them in foreign organizations. I will focus here on advice regarding their application to Chinese entities.

Instill entrepreneurial leadership. One of the main virtues of private enterprises, which accounts for their dynamism and profitability, are their strong, charismatic leaders and their high degree of entrepreneurship. Thus, one of China's key economic reforms would be not only to foster the further growth of private economic firms by removing political constraints, but also to inject more *intra*preneurship into state enterprises in general and SOEs in particular, which then could become as dynamic as private firms. We have seen how entrepreneurship can be infused into companies that are not family-owned. The advice given to foreign managers applies to their Chinese counterparts as well and probably will be even more easily absorbed.

Further, the quality and accountability of managers is another very important element in the success equation. The evaluation of their competence is more important than any sophisticated spreadsheet analysis of net present values to predict success—this is the experience of venture capitalists investing in new, uncertain, and complex technologies and businesses. Alas, excellent managers are the scarcest resource in China (Schlevogt 2000t). Systematic selection, competence sourcing through alliances and joint ventures, best practice codification, in-house and external management training, mentorship programs, role modeling, and job rotation, will help state enterprises to attract, develop, nurture, and retain these invaluable business leaders, capable of developing smart strategies, designing excellent organizations, managing and inspiring others. One of the key reasons for Acer's success was its ability to attract entrepreneurial people who were given much freedom and care to develop innovative technologies and other sources of competitive advantage that lifted the company above the noise level created by hundreds of computers makers in Taiwan.

Mastering the principles of effective leadership is of key importance for certain private enterprises in China as well. Even private enterprises sometimes pursue unwise expansion projects because they neither know how to assess opportunities in the environment, nor how to appraise investment projects, nor how to develop appropriate strategies and organizations. The rampant excess capacity in privately developed office space and residential housing memorializes this failure in concrete.

Create strong enterprise webs. Another important aspect of private Chinese management—proliferation into enterprise webs instead of growth in company size—is more difficult for state enterprises in general, and SOEs in particular, to emulate, since they lack the social capital embedded in family structures. It also involves more intrusive structural changes. A potential approach would be to carve out the various divisions of large integrated conglomerates, list them on the stock exchange, and expose them to outside market controls. The corporate center could still sell its services to the carved-out units. Like family-owned private Chinese enterprises, the individual units would be small and unbureaucratic. They might link up with each other in webs and integrate with outside companies and other webs to form industrial clusters or communities of interest in competive landscapes that cross traditional industry boundaries and constantly reshape themselves. On different occasions, the role may vary between web-creator, web-builder, web-shaper, system integrator, and web-member. The common interest and shared purpose may be their only stable quantity. Web participants may be connected horizontally (at the same value chain stage) and vertically (at different value chain stages).

Integrated state enterprises will still have their place. Owing to economies of scale and scope, certain industries require a large minimum efficient scale. Sometimes, the economies cannot be achieved by atomized units working in concert. For technical reasons, it may be impossible to break up conglomerates into individual units and, as a consequence, webs will not be feasible. Besides, because of the inherent limits on growth of private enterprises, state sponsorship might be necessary to provide the large amount of capital required for these businesses. These companies might thus best be state-owned. The same applies for sectors that are strategically important for national security, such as defense and energy. Moreover, in cases of rampant excess capacity, it might be necessary for the state to merge businesses into large units through horizontal integration.

Accumulate valuable social capital. A very distinctive feature of WCM is the network of implicit contracts based on traditional cultural values. They form an excellent control and motivating device, enabling companies to dispense with many formal, intrusive and expensive, structural arrangements. This important element needs to be transferred to state enterprises. Without strong family legacies and ties, the creation and inculcation of values in state enterprises has to be a more conscious human and social engineering effort. One approach is to build a strong corporate culture that replicates traditional Confucian values. In view of large company size, unlike small private enterprises, the culture cannot be rolled out and nurtured by one charismatic leader alone. After the design stage, the culture might be implemented through centers of excellence that disseminate corporate identity symbols and codified best practice, and role-model and reward desirable behavior.

Singapore serves as an excellent country example of how Chinese values can be reimplanted in the minds of the Chinese and other races. Further, Shenzhen-based Pingan Insurance is a large shareholders' company in which the visionary leader has designed a complete Chinese-style corporate culture system, which ranges from highly visible artifacts and rituals, to deeply held assumptions, beliefs, and values. Since such an invisible asset involves strong path dependencies and causal ambiguity, it creates sustainable resource- and time-dependent competitive advantage.

Policies for foreign enterprises primarily should focus on increasing their profitability, maybe by offering them government advice or domestic role models on how to do business in China. I have shown how the WCM business model, as a new generation of strategic and organizational approaches for an uncertain and complex environment, can help build a company buzzling with "familypreneurship" or "capitalpreneurship" at a larger scale. I also have pointed out generic and regionally-differentiated key success factors in the Chinese market. These new insights might help to turn around the dismal performance of many foreign companies, keep them bullish on the Chinese market, and thus ensure the continued flow of visible and invisible resources to China.

In conclusion, just changing the macroeconomic environment and hoping to achieve wide-ranging changes probably will not be very effective if micro-level managerial practices—above all strategy and organization—are not affected. The experience in Russia has shown that simple tinkering with macroeconomic policy variables, without changing the fundamentals of management practices, will not suffice to promote sound economic (and social) development. Likewise, letting companies "exit" through bankruptcy is not desirable from an economic or from a social standpoint, especially if one considers the existing high latent and real unemployment. The number of exit candidates would be enormous, and probably would involve *most* state enterprises. A Russian situation should be avoided at all costs. It should be remembered that there is a premium on avoiding bankruptcies and maintaining stability even if the (direct) costs are apparently high. So far China's success is based on stable incrementalism, and this path should be maintained. Reforms should be evaluated against the value they create and destroy. A destabilized and disintegrated society, where only the mafia holds the anarchy in check and performs the vital functions of the state (such as collecting taxes, providing security, and mediating conflict), is a sign of failure. This holds true even if some macroeconomic indicators improve and a manipulated, oligarchy-ruled system of democracy is introduced.

The key to the success of Chinese economic reforms lies in upgrading the human capital embodied by the Chinese enterprise leadership and in creating strategies and organizations that emulate the ingenious dynamics of private firms, thus creating valuable intellectual and social capital. Instead of dumping unsuccessful state enterprises and SOEs in particular to industrial graveyards, reformers need to reposition their strategies, restructure their organizations, inject an energetic spirit of entrepreneurship into managers and workers, and convert their products into best-sellers.

A change (or better: improvement) management program is needed that develops inspiring visions, collects best practice from China and abroad and codifies it into a database and manuals, empower well-positioned and well-connected change champions, and roll out the blueprint in successive waves through local change centers and change agents that visit the grassroots, discuss solutions, and implement them jointly with local leaders. The whole process should be highly adaptive, emphasizing constant learning. It must start with quick wins in targeted areas and then institutionalize the changes and put in place continuous improvement mechanisms (Schlevogt 2000j; 2000k; 2000l).

All this means taking charge, rolling up the sleeves, and doing real things instead of remote-controlling from Harvard or MIT. Only in that way can China control its destiny, finding the right solutions to its specific problems and avoiding disastrous experiments, which in the worst case can cost its sovereignty and survival as a nation and people. Focusing on microeconomic issues as the main policy lever (while insulating the country against external shocks and manipulation) is a new approach in theory and practice, replacing or at least complementing the former domination by "culture-free" armchair macroeconomists.

Change the present to restore the past and create the future

> That side the wall, the branches—this side, the broken blossoms,
> Fallen to earth, the playthings of every passing breeze.
> The branches may be bare, but they will put out more flowers—
> The flowers, once adrift, may never regain the trees.
>
> —Ming poem

So, after all has been said, what should China do as a nation? To answer this question, let us first listen to Confucius: "If a man cherishes his old knowledge so as continually to be acquiring new, he may be a teacher of others" (Ying 1995, p. 73, citation 2:11, translated directly from the Chinese). If there is one single bit of advice and a conclusion I would like to communicate to the Chinese government and its hardworking people, it would be this Confucian dictum. A culture with three thousand years of recorded history (and perhaps existing for at least five thousand years), a civilization that, for the first and perhaps last time in human history was close to realizing the dream of an ideal society on Earth, possesses an unimaginable treasure of original and creative ideas. It is a fountain of wisdom that has influenced the minds and deeds of myriad men in the Middle Kingdom and elsewhere. Much of it is so deeply rooted in Chinese mental models and thinking that it does not seem original and valuable anymore. This is the hallmark of all great ideas: the more original the thought, the more obvious and mundane it looks later on. But this does not diminish its greatness in any way. And the comment that ancient Chinese thinking produced a rigid system unable to adapt to new circumstances is wrong. Yes, the Chinese valued stability, in the same way we should cherish it today. But at the same time, imagine all the upheavals in China's history, which were much more dramatic than what is happening today. Our age is far from unique. China's wisdom thus can tell us a lot about how to deal with change.

The past, for China, should not be regarded as a sunk cost; it is an asset that cannot be valued high enough and has not been sufficiently leveraged so far.

Why rely on teachings—for example, from the United States—which, after all are very high-order derivatives and copies of very old wisdom. And the important bits were lost on the way. Do you remember the old children's game in which everybody has to pass a story on by telling it into his friend's ear—the final version is completely different from the original story, and all important elements disappeared. The United States is not famous for its original deep thought, but for the excellent packaging and promotion of the obvious. In contrast to the image of in-novativeness, good thinking there usually develops only when trained brains (or their fruits) are physically imported.

How inefficient would it be for China to have thought and worked so hard, for such a long time, and then brush away everything, declaring it all a failure, and copy from others (who had originally copied from China). This is a clear recipe for always lagging behind. Once something is copied, the copied model will again be one step ahead. The ability to generate a creative capacity always to move faster than others is crucial in a world where speed (if it is associated with cost efficient quality) is a competitive weapon (Schlevogt 1999f; 2000p). The past, for China, should not be re-garded as a sunk cost; it is an asset that cannot be valued high enough and has not been sufficiently leveraged so far. It is like an archive of great recorded classical music that any music company in the world would be desperate to purchase, then free from the dust, and make fortunes. It is like a cellar of great cognac from Napoleonic times that has just been re-discovered. Can you imagine its price? Based on the expected future cash flow resulting from putting it to myriad known or innovative uses, a fi-nancial wizard could immediately translate such physical assets into se-curities that would bring in huge amounts of capital. So far, nobody has recognized that the same valuation and potential for leverage applies for the invisible assets of a whole nation.

Great Walls, once edifices to the genius of man, serving a well thought-through purpose, can turn into mere UNESCO heritage sites if nothing new follows.

At the same time, a society that only looks in the rear mirror as it drives ahead will crash—dramatically. An archeologist or antiquarian cannot provide clear directions respecting things present and future. The "rear mirror" syndrome occurred in China, culminating in a series of humili-ating defeats inflicted by honorless aggressors like the British and the Jap-anese in the nineteenth and twentieth century. A nation should never celebrate itself for having achieved the ideal state, it should always look for improvements (Schlevogt, 1999g). Beauty is in nature and does not depend on a mirror evidencing its magnificence. Perfection will never be reached.

A civilization, even if it is the Middle Kingdom and Land of Dragons, the sole intermediary between heaven and the rest of the earth, has to adapt continuously to changing circumstances or create or shape the en-vironment, and learn constantly from its mistakes and other countries and interact with other countries. Only by following this approach will it in-cessantly progress in absolute and relative terms, avoiding a detrimental international balance of power and knowledge—which is as undesirable as deficits in the balance of trade and balance of payments. Such an "invisible deficit" occurred when China's technology fell back and other nations exploited their absolute and comparative advantages. Great Walls, once edifices to the genius of man, serving a well thought-through purpose, can turn into mere UNESCO heritage sites if nothing new follows. National military defeat in physical war is the equivalent of a devalued currency (as a result of a lost economic war), only costing more lives and causing more material and spiritual damage.

But for China, a stumble may have prevented a fall. After all, it was lucky and did survive. Not all ancient civilizations were that fortunate. See what is left of Egypt, Greece, Carthage, Rome, and the Aztecs—heaps of rubble, and genes and ideas absorbed by their conquerors. And even the original race and ideas are dead, extinct from the universe. These were splendid empires with dreams, passions, and brilliance, full of pioneering spirits and great builders. They were destined to last forever—or so it seemed. But for these civilizations, everything is gone and will never come back. The game is over. The legacy of lost empires is like water splashed on the floor: once spilt, it can never go back into the bucket, even if it creates and nurtures new life elsewhere.

While constant adaptation, learning, and interaction are the secret for survival, the key for a nation's spiritual prosperity is to keep its eternal values, the inner core, stable. Since the traditional values brilliantly answer the elementary needs of the Chinese—as evidenced by the successful track record and permanence of this race—they are garments that never need to be renewed. As with physical human genes, (social) scientists and politicians should not tinker with the soul of a civilization. Its genetic code was programmed in ages gone by with divine insight and subtlety that our age lacks. Once changed, it will unleash unforeseen dynamics. It can never be restored, since we do not possess the knowledge and energy that was needed to design and implement it. Though the core should stay stable, the outside shell should change to make it more suitable to the external environment and to new circumstances. As mentioned, outside forces also can be shaped—adaptation alone is passive.

Web-based Chinese management theory clearly explains much of the success of Chinese economic development in the wake of Deng Xiaoping's reforms, thus confirming the positive impact of stable values that are protected by a fluid cover. Indeed, an analysis of old Chinese thought and new empirical insights reveals that the new Chinese entrepreneurs are on their way to leverage the best of both old and new knowledge. They are corporate archaeologists with a modern Midas touch. They restore old values and modernize the outer shell to make it more effective in the new market environment. Chinese entrepreneurs are the few in this great nation who will save, teach, and cherish it—they represent the hope of a billion people. The basic insight from this study is how relevant past thought is for the present and the future. It creates social capital, flexibility, and cost-efficiency, making the private enterprises quick to adapt and quick to develop. The ancient fountain of wisdom makes them powerful creators of organizations, jobs, wealth, and social cohesion. Their performance is stable, reliable, and solid rather than cyclical, erratic, and based on speculation. And all this miracle is mainly self-initiated and self-financed.

That is why the story which emerges from this book is so inspiring and uplifting. Indeed, China and its entrepreneurs are changing the gloomy present to restore the glorious past creating a future full of promise and opportunity. The reforms have allowed a grassroots-driven revival of the long buried (but not dead) springs of skillful management, deeply rooted in Chinese culture. The old Chinese poem cited at the beginning of this section distinguishes between bare branches and fallen blossoms. Sometimes, things that are beautiful now lack future potential, while presently unappealing things may carry the seeds of greatness. The message from this book is encouraging: the invisible roots that reach far into the origins of life and the visible branches are still there, and will soon bear new fruits, even if this is difficult to imagine based on the present situation. China's brightest buds have been buried under snow, but soon will start to blossom again. The only condition is that central, regional, and local governments continue to protect China from outside danger and keep up internal stability based on law, order, and morality. Otherwise, other external and internal forces will exploit and fill the void, and destroy the nation as a result.

If there is spontaneous and sustained enthusiasm and collective cooperation, the magic will happen, and economic questions will be mere technicalities that will be resolved sooner rather than later.

The way ahead will be stony and progress will be slow—despite all the stories about economic miracles, which are largely destined to inspire hope and maintain morale. Centuries and decades are more appropriate references to gauge China's future development than years and months. Much has been achieved since the start of reforms, but the gap that separates China from the developed world is still huge—and the target is moving. The painful rebuilding of Germany's formerly Soviet occupied zone on a much smaller scale with better starting conditions, and more resources conveys a feeling for the magnitude of the task ahead and a foretaste of the future difficulties. And it is not clear whether the former German Democratic Republic will ever catch up with western Germany. My benchmark for China's progress is whether its myriad villages will attain the political, economic, and social development level of German villages now and in the future instead of being rural deserts. This is a more meaningful comparison than just analyzing some showcase districts or small projects in a few selected cities. Such hardware build-up is easy to achieve. Developing the software and achieving breadth are more challenging pursuits.

A great nation, like a great man, has to endure much darkness of fortune to reach greater power or happiness. If you want a place in the sun for your nation, you have to put up with many cloudy decades first. Perseverance, however, is not a long race; it is many short races, one after another. Despite many quick wins, China will need a long time to catch up and perhaps overtake—and eventually commercially and militarily take over—the West. But with a strong leadership spirit and high energy, the Chinese people and economy and everything else will wake up and rise again.

Confucius was once asked what the most important ingredients of government are. He mentioned sufficiency of food, sufficiency of military equipment, and the confidence of the people in their ruler. He was then asked, if one of these factors would have to be given up, what would be the first one to go. He conceded military equipment. Asked what would be the next factor to be abandoned, he answered, "food," because death is the destiny of man. The only factor he could not give up was faith, for if a people has no faith in its rulers, there is no standing for the state.

Faith in a nation, and the nation itself, is a collective invisible asset that will survive eternally even when individual human beings die, unless it is willfully destroyed by enemies of the nation state. Prussia was turned from a sand box into an empire, Venice from a small city to a great power that dominated the Mediterranean. The leadership spirit makes all the difference, be it that of enlightened and disciplined Prussian kings or the Venetian senate where every word was a fate. Thus, it is not the ability of a state to feed its people, or to protect them or to punish its internal and external enemies, which matters most; it is the confidence of the people that determines its destiny. If there is spontaneous and sustained enthusiasm and collective cooperation, the magic of organized life will happen, and economic questions will be mere technicalities that will be resolved sooner rather than later. John Ruskin highlighted the powerful triad of strong faith, steady hands, and patient souls. They will catalyze the miraculous rebirth of China (and other nations).

A friend is somebody who knows you and still likes you, not somebody who does not know you and nevertheless hates you.

A reminder for all of us "big noses": That's what friends are for

Now let me say something to the Western world, which looks at China's peaceful revolution, in awe and maybe in fear. Old books about the "yellow danger" are read again in dimly lit diplomatic back rooms. Please, forget these immature and irrational ideas and do as the first emperor (Qin Shi-Huang) did with what he unfortunately considered old ballast: burn these books. Think about how to make this great struggle of a great people a success story without equal. The task of other nations is to help China on its way back to glory. They should play the role of a friend. This is our world duty. A friend is somebody who knows you and still likes you, not somebody who does not know you and nevertheless hates you. To deal effectively with China, a leader, first of all, needs a deep understanding of its uniqueness and diversity. All generalizations are wrong. We are also obliged to embrace and accept the differences. Do not blame communism or an "authoritarian regime" for the different weltanschauung—the basic philosophy about the role of the individual in society differs completely from the West. In China, the individual lives to build a great society, not the other way round. The society is the work of the whole race not the playground for one individual. The national and collective interest comes first. Obedience and social cohesion are regarded as more important and more difficult to attain than freedom to do anything without any obligations. Ties of reciprocal responsibility embedded in a community full of peace and harmony are opposed to an opportunistic, ad hoc agglomeration of atomized aggressive individuals waiting for their next move, change, and thrill.

Understanding another culture first requires us to adopt the perspective and thinking of the other culture—a very difficult step for ethnocentric Westerners, who erroneously believe that they are the origin and center of the world, that they invented science and technology, created the most superb art, and generated all human knowledge. Let me illustrate the importance of "(cross) cultural mental mobility." The great German scholar Athanasius Kircher (1601–1680), the "last renaissance man," narrowly failed to decipher the Egyptian hieroglyphs for two reasons. First, he followed the Western concept, imprinted in his mind, that the phonetic symbols (which he correctly identified as such, because he started from the Coptic language) have to correspond to an alphabet. Second, he could not distance himself from the Renaissance mental map of a supposed deeper symbolic meaning of hieroglyphs, with the phonetic value representing only a superficial, commonplace part of the picture. Thus, whereas his original openness that inspired him to ground the research in the other country's culture (Coptic language) helped him to make great initial progress, his ethnocentric frame of mind (Western language and Renaissance symbolism) subsequently kept him from achieving the final breakthrough.

Of course, there will be disappointments in the friendship between East and West. To be sure, the Chinese are far from being angels. As all people, they are at best angels with one wing only. Nevertheless, it might be better to run the risk of being cheated occasionally than to be perpetually suspicious and achieve nothing because of mistrust. Mutual confidence in the honest intentions of each party builds up valuable social capital that will help us all to prosper, both materially and spiritually and to overcome occasional disagreement. Your trust and generosity eventually are likely to be reciprocated.

If mutual understanding, the willingness to adopt the other culture's perspective, and mutual trust do not materialize, I predict a great clash between East and West will begin in the twenty-first century. After increasingly sharp verbal controversy and cold war strategies and tactics, the tensions will find the outlet in direct and indirect regional conflict and, if uncontained, finally culminate in an inter-continental military confrontation at a large scale. Ideas about men and society are simply too different, and are moving ever farther apart. The Chinese cherish the family above all else, whereas many people in the West, especially in the United States, believe that the family is only a temporary mechanism for the satisfaction of economic instead of social and emotional needs. Same-sex marriages horrify the Chinese, who regard them as a sign of the highest stage of moral degradation. When watching these developments, they think that the very foundations of society have never been as shaken before. They believe that humankind will not be able to endure this spectacle for long.

If no understanding is reached through empathetic moderation, this clash of values will lead to an explosion, fuelled by deep-seated Chinese feelings of revenge for a long series of national defeats, humiliation, and shame. Apart from this spiritual energy and impetus the lack of resources to power economic growth and feed more than a billion people will be an additional material push factor motivating a nation struggling for survival to expand to greener pastures. And China (and other Asian nations which are its spiritual allies) probably will be more determined, more cohesive, and thus stronger than the disintegrating Western societies in this titanic struggle.

In China, after the broad currents of feudalism, communism, socialism, and capitalism (materialism), both nationalism and perhaps imperialism will fill the ideological vacuum. They will serve as powerful forces that unite the people against a common enemy who has erroneously relegated the nation state to history books and thus lacks the spirit that could energize its superb military equipment. For example, many Germans after the Second World War tried everything to get rid of their nation and submerge themselves into one faceless and soulless Europe, governed by bureaucrats. The defamation of the military and antiwar propaganda further soften hearts and minds in the West. Sterile propaganda against "rogue states" and "(global) terrorism" will not suffice to stem the tide of a dynamic and disciplined people with huge, motivated armies asserting itself and searching for resources. Because of rapid growth and high invesment into armament, increasingly, China and other Asian countries will also posses the military means to pursue their aspirations. The acquisition of its first aircraft carrier symbolizes China's growing capacity to project its power beyond its borders.

The apparent Westernization of many Chinese is very superficial; the deep and sophisticated cultural roots cannot be changed by primitive forces such as McDonald's and Disneyland. A few "classical leaders" from China or the overseas Chinese community, who have conserved their cultural heritage will be enough to reignite the dormant nationalism that is anchored in every Chinese heart and soul by birth. And China is working hard to grow strong and tall again, in order to face the final confrontation with the West, if necessary. Friendly talk, modesty, and an apparent focus on economic construction should not deceive the West about what is going on in China. The economy of China and other Asia nations serves national goals, especially the provision of funds, healthy people, and hard and soft technology for a military build-up. The country tolerates the sporadic bullying and small insults from the West—including the bombing of its embassy in Belgrade and spying missions on its sovereign territory by the U.S.—for the sake of the greater future mission. As mentioned, the sense of disgrace resulting from two centuries of Western domination is deep. The continuing China bashing and aggressions by the U.S. as part of its hegemonistic schemes (Schlevogt 1999m) makes things worse. The spontaneous feeling of patriotism and pride in their nation, among Chinese both in the motherland and overseas, may be the strongest in any race. Ask Chinese anywhere in the world, and they will tell you that they are proud to be "descendants of the dragon." Fortunately, this feeling has seldom induced aggression by itself nor has it been organized and galvanized for the purpose of military conquests.

To sum up, the strong and shared feeling of Chinese patriotism contrasts sharply with the current attitude of Western peoples. Thus, in any conflict between East and West, the East, because of its stronger faith and unity, will have the better cards. The barbarians are not at the gate anymore. Instead, they have to guard their own fortresses. A spark can ignite the explosive mix of powerful patriotism and deeply felt past humiliation that endures until now. And then it might be the disciplined and tidy Easterners who cut the long pigtails of the wild Westerners, not the other way round.

From East to West to East to West

In the discussion of my study's broader implication, I first focused on China's economic development, policy-making, and cultural revival. Then, I outlined the lessons for the West, which included best case (shared prosperity) and worst case (inter-cultural confrontation) scenarios of future developments. Let me now broaden the perspective again and ask what the findings imply for the world in terms of great historical and philosophical currents. I believe that if China manages to change the present to restore its past glory in a bright future, it once again can become the great teacher of mankind. In terms of historical and philosophical development trends, we see a circular movement of intangibles flowing from East and West, and back again. It is the first time that the circle takes a second turn.

From East to West

In ancient times, China was the fountain of the most influential inventions and innovations in the world: paper, printing, compass, gunpowder, holistic philosophy, bureaucracy, warfare strategy, and medicine . . . you name it. They are basic tools without which the modern world would be unimaginable. And I dare to speculate that not all inventions have been preserved, or documented as originating in China. These original ideas traveled to the West along the Silk Road. When the real or fictitious Marco Polo arrived in China, he stood in amazement before the great achievements of an ancient civilization. Interestingly, the Chinese culture was so strong that it conquered the conqueror. Invaders such as the Mongols (who established the Yuan dynasty) and the Manchus (who founded the Qing dynasty) became very Chinese. They even learned Chinese before they came to China. In view of the Middle Kingdom's intellectual magnetism and radiation, it might have been fashionable to do so—it also was a sign of sophistication for Russians to speak the language of the supposed repository of all culture, France. It is equally intriguing that once the Mongols went back home, they became nomads again. Chinese culture was embedded in the minds of the people, in the patterns of social interactions, and in the make up of institutions and laws in the Chinese motherland—a complex human, intellectual, and social web that apparently was difficult to replicate in Mongolia and elsewhere.

From West to East

But then, after all the Chinese splendor, the flow of ideas reversed. Part of the original problem was that foreigners put China's creations to better, or at least more effective uses. After two oriental invasions, by the Mongols and the Manchus, came Western opium, followed by advanced scientific and less advanced (in the sense of being helpful) social and political ideas and movements: Colonialism was followed by imperialism and communism. Then, for a short time, Stalinism. How much must the pragmatic Chinese have suffered with all these foreign ideological and abstract "-isms," and less abstract poisoning and shame.

From East to West again

Everything moves in circles—as the old Chinese philosophers had already discovered. In recent times, the flow of ideas has again started to move from the East to the West, or at least bidirectionally. China first became original and creative again under Chairman Mao Zedong (1893–1976), a clear turning point in Chinese history. His original vision was great and inspiring, attracting many overseas Chinese who wanted to escape stagnating foreign communities back to the mainland. After at least a century of darkness and passiveness, the Chinese motherland was destined to bloom again. After the Communist revolution, Mao engaged in what might be perceived as the last acts of Chinese "(progressive) conservatism," in the sense of China preserving its own identity, going its own way, and creating something new. The Great Leap Forward—the idea that China could dramatically increase steel production without Western technological support and overtake the West within a few years—and the Great Cultural Revolution—the complete eradication of Western bureaucracy and the bourgeoisie—are the most memorable aspects of this effort. These creative activities started to reverse the flow of ideas back from the East to the West—in this instance, ideas about how *not* to organize society (even though many, especially young, people in the West admired Mao and his alternative model).

This going and coming of ideas on a journey through time and space, physical and virtual, along silk roads and . . . optic cyberways . . . is like a ball game. This time the Chinese are in possession, running for the touchdown . . . but not the final showdown.

What we are witnessing now are new manifestations of Chinese conservatism, even though historians claim that such acts of Chinese (re-)creation died with Mao. We cannot blame them. I am talking about things present and future, not past. Perhaps we should use the term "incremental (or revolutionary) conservatism (or restoration)" which epitomizes my notion of slowly (or radically) changing the present to preserve (or restore) the past. In any case, we see acts of creative revival. As described in this book, we witness the rebirth of a great management model, updated for (post)modern times. Chinese management might become the breakthrough paradigm for the twenty-first century and beyond, well-suited for mastering the great future challenges, such as managing uncertainty and complexity in a turbulent world, achieving quantum leaps in human motivation and the exploitation of human potential, and dealing with increasingly scarce resources, partly by creating new undepletable (invisible) resources that can be multiplied at will with increasing marginal returns instead of the usual decreasing returns.

All these factors will push the production-possibility frontier (the maximum output achieved by different combinations of inputs) outward and increase individual and collective prosperity and happiness in more peaceful and harmonious groups, organizations, and societies. I have discussed in detail what we can learn from the new web-based Chinese management theory, including the inspired leadership, lack of formality, entrepreneurial spirit, and networking based on trust. The Chinese "Renaissance model" might be applied to transform sluggish Western organizations in all walks of life—from companies to charities—and whole societies, injecting Chinese pioneering and entrepreneurial spirit through managerial "familypreneurship" or even "capitalpreneurship."

Which Western set of techniques can show such a long track record of survival and effectiveness? The oldest modern bureaucracy, attributed to the Prussian king Frederick the Great, dates back only to the 18th century and has quickly revealed its limits in dealing with new-age challenges. Chinese management, in contrast, has proven to be a reliable formula for success over uncounted centuries. Even though no patents have been registered to hide it from outsiders, it has not been a very well publicized and obvious model, since its effectiveness results from invisible roots—the eternal Chinese values. I hope this book will change this situation, remove the causal ambiguity, and popularize the art of Chinese management in the whole world—through theory, evidence, and applications.

To sum up, the going and coming of ideas on a journey through time and space, physically and virtually along silk roads and their digital equivalents, optic cyberways (which are also made out of fibers), is like a ball game. This time the Chinese are in possession, running for the touchdown . . . but not the final showdown—yet.

Research limitations and outlook: A call for further studies

Anybody who pretends to have reached perfection or even shows himself satisfied degrades himself and his work. Nobody but God can say, "And behold, it was very good." Research on private enterprises in mainland China is in its infancy. Empirical, survey-based studies on organizational structure, management, context, and effectiveness in China are even younger. It is therefore of paramount importance to expand our knowledge by undertaking more micro-level studies in China's private sector. My work is a pioneering step towards a greater understanding of Chinese organizations. It integrated theory, evidence, and applications, which as I suggested need always go hand in hand, instead of being separated in a functional division of labor among theorists, empiricists, and practitioners. By opening the door, I hope to stimulate future research in this exciting new area.

In view of the inherent imperfection in any human endeavor, I must outline some important general limitations of this research and the concomitant need for future research. More detailed methodological limitations are discussed in appendix A. I propose further research related to the following broad themes that reflect the limitations. I will show how WCM theory can be used as a model for such future studies, especially for generating hypotheses that can be tested with empirical data.

Internal working of WCM

This study represents a first attempt to integrate Chinese management approaches into a new theory and test it with extensive empirical survey data and case studies. It would be interesting to explore deeper levels of

Chinese management and its cultural roots, uncovering more detailed spiritual, emotional, cognitive, and social mechanisms explaining its operation and success. For example, when I discussed the charismatic leadership style of Chinese private entrepreneurs, I mentioned their strongly developed intuition, spontaneous grasp of business situations, unorthodox creativity, and unrivalled ability to spin webs. What are the internal and external processes that facilitate such efficient information absorption, processing, and interpretation? How exactly is social capital and collective energy developed and how do they function? More in-depth qualitative socio-psychological studies, maybe in a laboratory, will be needed to answer this kind of question. I predict that we will make a new discovery. The endproduct-driven, holistic Chinese system thinking that derives its strength from nature, present in the Chinese mind at least since the classic *Book of Changes* appeared, is a very important tool for developing such intuitive and spontaneous grasp and creativity, enhanced by social capital that is generated by Confucian doctrine.

Because of utterly different cultural backgrounds and mental and perhaps also physical genes, thinking and interaction models in China are likely to differ completely from those in the West, and may prove superior to deal with uncertainty and complexity. It certainly helps to think out of (Western) boxes. Westerners could learn from this mental and social approach of the Middle Kingdom, much as they learned from Chinese traditional medicine and Chinese *gongfu* (Kung Fu). When introduced to the West, these oriental approaches were ridiculed, just as the notion of Chinese management might be laughed at in certain "advanced management" circles. WCM is socialized Chinese system thinking, enriched by Confucianism applied to management. Just as we do not yet fully understand the workings of traditional Chinese medicine and Kung Fu, so our knowledge of Chinese management may still be incomplete. It may be possible that the ancient Chinese knew the internal mechanism by which traditional medicine, Kung Fu, and management operated. If we restore the universal and eternal knowledge, and add to it, we could identify and focus on the levers by which Chinese management operates at deeper socio-psychological levels, and thus control the all-powerful collective mind and energy. Then, the charismatic, power-concentrated Chinese leadership style might become the easily malleable acupuncture needle to cure the organizational malaise of the West.

Eventually, we should strive for a synthesis of Western deductive thinking and Eastern inductive mental and social models. In physics, only such an integration brought us to the level of sophistication we have attained today. How about management? In many respects our ability to motivate humans to the fullest extent possible and leverage the complete power of the human brain, as well as to proactively coordinate complex transactions that involve high uncertainty—instead of leaving them to random processes involving invisible hands (of the market and other agents) and hoping that everything will turn out fine—is in a stage that reminds me of the Stone Age. Little do we know about the all-important spiritual, energy-related, (micro-)psychological, social, and systemic forces that move individuals, groups, organizations, nations, international networks, and the world as a whole in a dynamic fashion. But scholars so far have done little work in this decisive area. Even if we cannot measure or explain a phenomenon, it can nevertheless exist and be leveraged. Scientific and technical difficulties are not an excuse for giving up. Where we are looking determines what we will find. We would greatly benefit from a quantum leap in these unchartered waters through a theoretical and empirical synthesis of East and West.

Sources for readoption

In this book I have shown that overseas Chinese management approaches have been readopted in mainland private firms. It would be interesting to analyze in more detail the mechanism by which this distinctive style has been retransmitted to the Chinese motherland. WCM theory is useful to conceptualize the linkage between emphasis on traditional culture and organizational choices and their outcomes. This connection can be tested further through longitudinal surveys of firm-level data, assessing managers' attitudes and correlating them with organizational design, which results in different levels of effectiveness. Longitudinal studies can establish cause and effect relationships by ordering events in time, answering the question of what came first. More qualitative studies will yield additional real-world richness that illuminates these linkages. Based on the case study evidence from China, I make two predictions related to the sources of readoption and the change agents involved. First, there is a conscious desire by many private entrepreneurs to revive traditional Chinese culture. In this case, the knowledge is mainly recycled from older family members and friends who lived in pre–Revolution China, as well as through the study of ancient Chinese books. Second, another hypothesized mechanism is the transfer of management approaches through overseas Chinese investors. They might sit on mainland Chinese boards, and thus formally and informally communicate their distinctive values, which they have inherited from their ancestors. They might also form international webs with mainland Chinese organizations, which facilitate a fluid exchange of ideas and people, whom I regard as "value carriers."

Development of Chinese private enterprises over time

My study was mainly concerned with the present situation of Chinese enterprises. The empirical research adopted a cross-sectional design. It would be interesting to trace back in more detail how private Chinese enterprises developed historically, from the earliest beginnings and especially after 1978. Previous work (Kraus 1991; Young 1995) has covered the early reform area, but new studies need to analyze the subsequent dramatic changes, and link them with earlier periods, distilling key development patterns and trends, as well as potential continuities and discontinuities with pre-Revolution entrepreneurship. In particular, it would be instructive to see how environmental constraints—such as legislation; treatment by the government; supporting infrastructure; and access to investment opportunities, supplies, managerial and technical personnel, and technology—changed over time and how they influenced private entrepreneurs. I predict that such a study would reveal a significant change in the environment, from outright hostility in the past to a much more benevolent situation now. Private enterprises through their webs are likely to be largely insulated against these changes and might even leverage them to their advantage.

It will also be important to follow the future development of private enterprises. Apart from establishing the direction of causality between contextual factors and organizational choices and their outcomes, such long-term observation will show whether the average size of private Chinese enterprises on the mainland will grow or, for cultural reasons, stay small. I predict that private enterprises on average will prefer to remain small, in order to keep all business in the family. However, at present we cannot exclude the possibility that enterprises currently are small only because they are young, and may grow over time instead of proliferating into a large network of small units. However, this scenario seems less likely, based on what we know about the development of overseas Chinese businesses. Even though they had ample time to grow and were constantly exposed to Western business concepts that emphasized the virtues of growth, they remained small.

Finally, as happened overseas, most certainly a handful of large private Chinese conglomerates will emerge on the mainland. It will be instructive to analyze their management model and compare it to that of the smaller companies on the mainland and the overseas conglomerates. Will they usually grow by expanding their core business or will they diversify? Will they coordinate and control their businesses through web-based Chinese management, especially in the form of hub-and-spoke systems? Or will they adopt professional managed designs, such as a multidivisional structure with autonomous units, more integrated networks, or even radical new models? How will they decide between conservation and revolution? And will they expand into foreign markets, and if so, which approaches will they use and with what success? Will there be successful Chinese multinational companies originating from the mainland?

International organizational comparisons

In this book, I have demonstrated that the management model of Chinese private enterprises differs from the model of state enterprises, and thus has been proven to be distinctive domestically. To establish its international distinctiveness, we need to show empirically that web-based Chinese management differs from the management of family businesses in other countries. In particular, the distinctiveness and influence of the Chinese culture construct can finally be demonstrated only in international studies. Cross-sectional comparative research, similar to the Aston studies (Pugh and Hickson, 1976), which used standardized measures of organizational structure that were tested worldwide, would be one option.

In terms of the detailed research design, a cross-national study might compare small Chinese family businesses to small Western family businesses, or compare the few large, private Chinese enterprises to large Western companies. It might compare the mean values for organizational choices (and their outcomes) from my China study to results from other countries and regions, such as Italy's Emilia Romagna, which is famous for its textile subcontractors and their *impannatores* (Brusco 1982; Lazerson 1995). Such a study might also assess statistical differences between countries in the impact of contextual factors on organizational choices (and their relationship with effectiveness), using structural equation models.

In view of the importance of Confucian values (which are unique to Chinese culture) in Chinese family enterprises, I would expect to demonstrate distinctiveness through statistically significant differences (a) in mean levels for structural, managerial, and contextual choices, and (b) in path coefficients from context to organizational design. In turn, the family powered by culturally embedded social capital may also result in greater effectiveness. But again, despite the usefulness of WCM theory for generating hypotheses, only empirical studies will provide the final evidence.

Transferability of the Chinese management model

I have argued that even though the web-based organizational model that is embedded in traditional culture originated in China, it might serve as new management paradigm for Western organizations and societies. It would be interesting to analyze cases of Western organizations that adopted this new model, assessing its impact on various stakeholders, such as employees, managers, and customers. Such studies should also examine the economic and social value it creates, implementation bottlenecks, and approaches for overcoming them. Suitable research designs include field experiments, natural experiments, and action research. Based on WCM theory I predict that organizational effectiveness and efficiency will increase after the company adopted the new model. It will increase trust and flexibility, and will reduce costs. The research should also examine the channels through which the knowledge, skills, and other invisible capital embedded in WCM can be transferred to the West. Those include activity-based learning from Chinese partners through strategic alliances or joint ventures, implanting key Chinese managers into Western companies, and codifying and disseminating "best practice" online or offline (as in this book).

Policy implementation in China and elsewhere

My outline of potential new policies for creating, nurturing, and reforming enterprises in China was preliminary. In particular, more detailed suggestions need to be developed about concrete implementation approaches and change management programs. Plans should outline which concrete action the government should take, specifying what it can do and, in cases when development depends on spontaneous action by organizations, what it *cannot* do. Future studies should also analyze how Western governments can learn from the theory, evidence, and applications of web-based Chinese management to increase the performance of their companies at home and abroad—and their societies at large—and improve relations with China.

Other forms of organization

The study was limited to economic organizations. However, the nature, causes, and outcomes of management in other forms of organization in China, such as the party, army, universities, churches, and charities might differ from the findings of this study. For example, Hinings (1979), referring to the Western context, suggested that there might be political issues in local governments and effects of religious beliefs in church organizations that would not occur in industry. As suggested, the issues outlined in my research agenda are relevant for non-economic organizations: the internal operating mechanism, sources of management styles adopted, development over time, international distinctiveness, transferability of WCM, and concrete policies for the creation, nurturing, and reform of these organizations.

Emergence of a new political and social class

Adopting an anthropological viewpoint, I have argued that Chinese private entrepreneurs potentially will bear the torches of a great Chinese cultural revival, and will play an increasingly important role in society. It will be interesting to adopt a political scientific perspective and analyze whether this new, rising entrepreneurial class in the future will be able to shape the political agenda as well. To test such a proposition, we would need longitudinal data that traces the influence of private entrepreneurs on society through political network analysis. Apart from control over resources, processes, and system design, we could measure power could by the "network centrality" (Ibarra 1993) of the new entrepreneurs within their organizations and society at large. Besides, a sociological analysis will reveal whether this new social class and elite holds different beliefs from the rest of society and might change its tastes and lead its opinions and actions.

If we proceed with this research agenda, we will be able to enhance our understanding of the awakened giant that is soon to become a political, economic, military, and cultural superpower. With this growing importance, it becomes increasingly urgent better to understand organization in China, to identify similarities with the West, and to observe differences that result from diverging cultural backgrounds, ideas, and patterns of social interaction. We will thus improve the quality of advice to managers and politicians in China and abroad, and in general move toward stronger and more successful international cooperation and partnership with this powerful ancient nation that has been born again.

A famous general once said, "Success is how high you bounce when you hit bottom." This will be the final measure for China's great national revival, which will make it a mighty force and only credible power counteracting the global convergence on the Western (American) model. Germany has made it (in material terms), and Japan, too, has shown enormous elasticity in bouncing back after the Second World War. Will China be the next phoenix that rises from the ashes? I sincerely hope so. All my soul, heart, mind, hands, and energy will be with the Chinese people on the long march ahead.

完

End

Summary and conclusions

In this chapter, I discussed the major conclusions and themes of this book. I first showed that we are witnessing a great cultural revival in the Chinese motherland. The management model that had disappeared from the mainland was shown to have returned after Deng Xiao-ping's reforms, together with an emerging renaissance of traditional Chinese values.

Next, I argued that web-based Chinese management is an art, in the sense of doing something well. It combines dexterity, action, and experience. It is even a fine art, because it combines the work of the head, heart, and hand. Shaped by Chinese traditional culture, the Chinese management style is also an artifact. In its savageness, changefulness, naturalism, grotesqueness, "active rigidity" (or active stability), and redundancy, it resembles the inner spirit of Gothic architecture.

Because of internal and external limits to growth combined with ample opportunities at home, I predicted that most private Chinese enterprises will not develop into great international players, but will strengthen their role as formidable niche players in the domestic market(s). Web-based management was shown to drive the development of Chinese private enterprises, which in turn serve as powerful engine of China's progress in many fields. It is a great blueprint for organizations, sectors, economies, and societies, generating great flexibility and dynamism. It absorbs shocks and lessens the likelihood and impact of recessions and depressions. In contrast to conventional macro-economic advice, I suggest that economic policies should mainly focus on the micro level while providing a stable framework at the macro level. The new web-based management model can be used for economic policies targeted at state enterprises and private Chinese and foreign enterprises. It thus improves management in the public sector and promotes the growth of the domestic and foreign-operated private sector through a focus on entrepreneurial leadership, enterprise webs, and invisible capital.

I then broadened the perspective to elaborate on the preconditions for a great national renaissance of China, above all the imperative to revive old Chinese treasures and merge them with new ideas. Next, I discussed some lessons for Western people. To deal effectively with the Chinese and become their permanent friends, they have to learn to adapt their cultural mental maps and try to think "the Chinese way." If mutual understanding does not materialize, a great value clash and confrontation will occur in the new millennium, which the West will probably lose because of its moral weakness. Subsequently, I again broadened my contemplation space to analyze the age-long interchange of ideas from a historical and philosophical standpoint. I suggested that over the centuries we have seen a circular flow of ideas from East to West to East to West. The present national revival and renewal of Chinese ideas, and their global export marks the second turn in this global interchange of intangibles. They constitute the seeds of material manifestations and thus are the source of progress and growth.

Finally, I spelled out the limitations of this study and proposed an agenda for continuing the exciting research on Chinese management and entrepreneurship in mainland China. Researchers need to explore the internal working of WCM, the sources of its readoption, the development of private enterprises over time, international organizational differences, the transferability of WCM, policy implementation, applications to other forms of organization, and the emergence of a new, politically and socially powerful entrepreneurial class. More successor studies to this pioneering research, which combined theory, evidence, and applications, will help us to build the all-important bridge between East and West, making it possible for humankind for the first time in history to walk hand in hand throughout a healthy, prosperous, harmonious, and peaceful millennium, in which individual human potential and the collective genius are leveraged to the fullest extent possible, while distinctive national and cultural traits are cherished and maintained.

Appendices

Appendix A: Detailed Survey Methodology

In this appendix, I will first review the survey design in terms of sample, measures, and procedures and then outline some detailed methodological limitations. For all other details on scale development and validation, exploratory data analysis, and statistical results for each structural equation model, I refer the reader to Schlevogt (1999a).

Sample

Two samples were selected for the survey: one for Beijing (sixty enterprises, 48.4% of total sample), situated in the north, and one for Shanghai (sixty-four enterprises, 51.6%), located in the south. These cities, apart from Hong Kong, were considered to be China's major "growth engines" (Ou, Shi, and Xu 1996, p. 3). About half of the sample (sixty-three enterprises, 50.8%) were state enterprises and half were private enterprises (sixty-one enterprises, 49.2%). The sample was heterogeneous (Gillespie and Mileti 1981, p. 376). It comprised a variety of industries and services. This provided the degree of freedom necessary for testing rival hypotheses, following the approach of the original Aston project (Pugh and Hickson 1976; Pugh et al. 1968; Pugh et al. 1969) and successor studies (see Child 1972a; Mileti and Gillespie 1977; Beyer and Trice 1979). The Aston research achieved a degree of sample diversity that only a few cross-national studies matched (G. Miller 1987, p. 310). Subsequent research confirmed that theories and casual models of organizational structure are applicable to samples of very different organizations (G. Miller, Anderton, and Conaty 1985; G. Miller and Conaty 1982), which suggests that findings from this book may also apply to a wider set of organizations.

Measures

Theoretical rationale for inclusion of variables

Web-based Chinese management theory served as basis for the choice of constructs in this research. The selection captured some important contextual factors, properties, and outcomes of both organizational structure and management practices, which required further research and were considered to be strongly connected to Chinese management.

Operationalization and measurement of variables

So far, no empirical study has adopted my theory and tested all the identified aspects of context, structure, management, and outcome *at the same time*. Therefore, I used an eclectic and creative approach, choosing operational definitions and scales from earlier studies and developing new ones where necessary. Wherever possible, I adopted standard definitions and well-validated scales that had strong theoretical grounding and, through frequent application and replication, were shown to possess desirable psychometric properties. Besides, only by using standardized scales can findings be compared with international data from other studies and knowledge be accumulated. This approach follows common usage in the research literature. As noted by Churchill (1979), when at all possible, the researcher should use existing measurement scales or adapt them for his research purposes. The unnecessary use of new scales makes it difficult to compare and aggregate findings, thereby inhibiting the synthesis of what is known (Segars, 1997 p. 112). It sacrifices intellectual development for the sake of artificial "novelty," which unfortunately is rewarded in many academic quarters.

For the organization structural constructs, the research largely followed the Aston tradition, adopting its operationalizations and measures (Inkson, Pugh, and Hickson 1970; Pugh and Hickson 1976). For management practices and effectiveness, most definitions and scales were chosen from Khandwalla's (1974, 1977) survey of Canadian companies. There were two reasons for this choice. First, Khandwalla and other scholars developed a wealth of theoretical insights on the relationships between these scales and various antecedents. Second, as will be demonstrated below, the psychometric properties of the various scales turned out to be very favorable.

My study used the items for participative leadership, as well as adaptive and planning-driven decision making. The corresponding questionnaire sections and item numbers were reported in the context of the individual models.

Because Khandwalla's original study did not cover strategy, Venkatraman's (1989) scale measuring the strategic orientation of business enterprises was chosen. It is based on an extensive review and synthesis of the theoretical strategy literature and is well validated in a structural equation context. Based on their theoretical importance, the study concentrated on two aspects of strategic orientation, proactiveness and (price-cutting) aggressiveness.

The internal and external contextual scales were chosen from two sources. The scale "CEO need for achievement," is theoretically grounded and empirically validated in psychology research (Steers and Braunstein 1976). It also showed relatively high predictive and nomological validity in a structural equation model that approached the type of model used in this book (D. Miller and Droege 1986). Uncertainty also has been well validated in previous studies, but, despite its theorized importance, failed to show significant effects on the dependent variables in a nomological network (D. Miller and Droege 1986).[1] Khandwalla's (1977) indices of objective absolute and subjectively rated relative performance were used to measure effectiveness. Finally, because of the lack of relevant scales in the literature, two new measures, for (a) emphasis on selected Chinese cultural characteristics, and (b) subcontracting, were developed and tested for this study. The questionnaire also includes several scales and items that were not used for this book, serving the purpose of generating data for subsequent analyses.

An overview of the constructs, operationalizations, and scales used in this research is presented in tables A-1, A-2, and A-3. These tables include detailed information on the procedures used to compute composite scores for the scales. In most cases, the items of a scale that had been shown to be unidimensional and reliable, were summed to arrive at the total scale score. This implies that items loading high on one factor were added. The unweighted additive scoring approach was chosen because it was successfully used by the Aston researchers, and became established as a commonly recognized standard. It makes the factor scores meaningful and easy to interpret, and allows for international comparisons. For the profile comparisons of structural and managerial properties, the scales were standardized to 100%. This means that a company which scored highest on every item of a scale obtained a factor score of 100. Such standardization enables researchers to compare the score means of different scales across different subgroups.

Unweighted addition, however, is a relatively simple method for scoring. It is problematic when the standard deviations of the individual items are not equal across a scale. In this case, items with larger standard deviations have a greater impact on the overall scale. This problem disappears when all variables are first standardized. A more sophisticated alternative approach for deriving factor scores is regression. But even when this method is used, factor scores are not perfectly correlated with the "true" factor, since there is an infinite number of possible factor scores that all possess the same mathematical characteristics (Tabachnick and Fidell 1989, p. 641).

Table A-1 Research scales for contextual variables

Construct	Operationalization	Scales	Type of scale	Items (#)	Scoring procedure	Scale reliability*
Environmental uncertainty	Degree of change and unpredictability of markets and technology (D. Miller and Droege 1986, p. 547)	Miller and Droege's scale (1986, p. 557), based on Khandwalla (1974, 1977) and D. Miller (1983)	7-point Likert	5	Unweighted sum	.74* D. Miller and Droege (1986, p. 560)
Chinese culture	Degree to which family loyalty, respect for seniority, collective orientation, and trust-based relationships are emphasized in the organization	Schlevogt (new scale)	7-point Likert	16	Unweighted sum for selected items	Determined in this study
Government support	Government action that has a positive impact on the organization	Khandwalla (1977) scale	7-point Likert	9	Unweighted sum	Not given
External constraints	Factors in an organization's task environment that limit its access to resources	Khandwalla (1977) scale	7-point Likert	11	Unweighted sum	Not given
Size	Number of full-time employees (Blau and Schoenherr 1971)	Blau (1974)	Open-ended	1	Natural logarithm to base 10 of number of employees	.98‡ (Khandwalla 1977, p. 659)
Technology	Use of mass-production technology (Khandwalla 1974), that is, the large-scale fabrication of standard items.	Khandwalla's mass-production orientation scale (Khandwalla 1977)	7-point Likert	1	Simple item score	N/A (single-item scale)
CEO need for achievement	A person's degree of striving to meet standards of excellence, to accomplish difficult tasks, and to achieve success	Manifest Need Questionnaire (Steers and Braunstein 1976)	7-point Likert	5	Unweighted sum after recoding reversed items	.66*, .72† (Steers and Braunstein 1976, p. 258)

*Cronbach α (recommended to be greater than .70), no α given for single-item scales or if scale was not constructed on the basis of the domain sampling model.
†Test–retest reliability (stability coefficient).
‡Interrater reliability.

Table A-2 Research scales for endogenous structural variables

Construct	Operationalization	Scales	Type of scale	Items (#)	Scoring procedure	Scale reliability
Centralization	Degree to which the authority to make decisions that affect the organization is located at the top of the management hierarchy	Aston centralization scale (Inkson, Pugh, and Hickson 1970; Pugh and Hickson 1976)	5-point scale	11	Unweighted sum	.82* (D. Miller and Droege 1986)
Formalization	Degree to which rules and procedures are *written*	Aston formalization scales (Inkson, Pugh, and Hickson 1970; Pugh and Hickson 1976)	4-point scale / 5-point scale / Binary scale	2 / 1 / 9	Unweighted sum	.65* (D. Miller and Droege 1986)
Specialization	Degree to which an organization's activities are divided into specialist roles	Aston specialization scale (Inkson, Pugh, and Hickson 1970; Pugh and Hickson 1976)	Binary scale	16	Unweighted sum	.80* (D. Miller and Droege 1986)
Control	Planning, coordinating, monitoring, and providing feedback about progress in achieving the stated purpose and objectives of the organization	Khandwalla's (1977) Sophistication of Control and Information Systems (C.I.S.) scale	7-point Likert	10	Unweighted sum	.80*, .64‡ (Khandwalla 1977, p. 662)
Integration	Liaison of organizational activities through structural and processual devices	Miller's structural and process liaison scales (D. Miller 1983)	7-point Likert	6	Unweighted sum for each subscale	.85* Structure (D. Miller and Droege 1986) .74* Process (D. Miller and Droege 1986)

*Cronbach α (recommended to be greater than .70), no α given for single-item scales or if scale was not constructed on the basis of the domain sampling model.
†Test–retest reliability (stability coefficient).
‡Interrater reliability.

Table A-3 Research scales for endogenous managerial variables and organizational outcome variables

Construct	Operationalization	Scales	Type of scale	Items (#)	Scoring procedure	Scale reliability
Strategic orientation	A company's resource deployment pattern used to achieve its stated purpose and objectives	Venkatraman's (1989, pp. 959–960) Strategic Orientation of Business Enterprises (STROBE) scale	7-point Likert	12	Unweighted sum for each of the six subscales	Ranging from .53¶ to .68¶ for the individual dimensions (Venkatraman 1989)
Leadership style	The approach used by a leader to pattern the behavior of a group and elicit followers' voluntary compliance and energy in a broad range of matters	Khandwalla's (1977) scale	7-point Likert	7	Unweighted sum for each of the three subscales	Participation: N/A*, .57‡ (Khandwalla 1977, pp. 660–661) Flexibility: N/A*, .52‡ (Khandwalla 1977, pp. 660–661) Coercion: N/A*, .49‡ (Khandwalla 1977, pp. 660–661)
Decision-making style	The procedure employed by an organization to define its purpose and objectives, design programs of action to realize them, and to allocate resources	Khandwalla's (1977) scale	7-point Likert	3	Simple score on each subscale	N/A*
Communication style	The sending of information (a message) and its receipt, flowing vertically or horizontally (sometimes involving feedback) within an organization	Khandwalla's (1977) scale	7-point Likert	2	Simple score on each subscale	N/A*

Construct	Operationalization	Scales	Type of scale	Items (#)	Scoring procedure	Scale reliability
Subcontracting	The outsourcing of certain activities of the value chain to other organizations in the pursuit of objectives such as focusing on core competencies, increasing flexibility, and reducing costs.	Schlevogt's scale (new)	7-point Likert	11	Unweighted sum	Determined in this study
Organizational effectiveness	Degree to which an organization achieves its stated purpose and objectives	Khandwalla's (1977, p. 662) index of objective performance and index of subjective performance	Objective: open Subjective: 7-point Likert	3 5	Sum of trichotomized scores on three subscales Unweighted sum	Objective: N/A*, 93‡ (Khandwalla 1977 pp. 662–663) Subjective: .84*, .59‡ (Khandwalla 1977, pp. 662–663)

¶Composite measurement reliability, the ratio of trait variance to the sum of trait and error variance (should be greater than .50).

*Cronbach α (recommended to be greater than .70), no α given for single-item scales or if scale was not constructed on the basis of the domain sampling model.

†Test–retest reliability (stability coefficient).

‡Interrater reliability.

Psychometric properties of scales

Scales need to possess desirable psychometric properties, including unidimensionality (Segars 1997, p. 108), reliability (Churchill and Peter 1984, p. 369; Peter 1979, p. 6), and validity (Peter 1981, p. 133). Results from earlier reliability tests of the scales used in this book, including Cronbach Alpha, test–retest reliability, interrater reliability, and composite reliability, are reported in tables A-1 to A-3. The scales showed relatively high degrees of reliability, which formed the basis for their inclusion in this study. The earlier assessment of psychometric properties was not always rigorous and complete. In particular, very few studies provided quantitative evidence on unidimensionality and validity. One of the advantages of structural equation modeling is to measure very accurately all psychometric properties of the scales included in the models. It estimates the parameters related to sets of indicators in the measurement (empirical) model, simultaneously with the estimation of the structural (theoretical) model. The results of this (replicated) validation for my study, as well as an outline of the scale development and testing for the two new scales (emphasis on selected characteristics of Chinese culture and subcontracting) are presented in Schlevogt (1999a).

The multiple-choice questions on CEO sociodemographics and company background are not formally analyzed in this measurement section. They are standardized items that form part of most questionnaires, but, taken alone, do not measure underlying constructs. Additional variables aggregated for the organizational effectiveness model were discussed in chapter 5.

Procedures

This part is organized around four sections. I will first describe the questionnaire design and then outline the data collection approach. After discussing questionnaire administration, I then will elaborate on the design and major findings of the pilot test.

Questionnaire design

The questionnaire consisted of 19 sections totaling 222 questions. They covered the informant's sociodemographic background, contextual factors, organizational structure, management, and effectiveness. Closed questions were used in most cases, including either seven-point Likert scales or multiple-choice questions. In addition, there were several open-ended questions. The detailed statistics are as follows: multiple-item scales: thirty-three; multiple-choice questions: nine; open-ended questions: sixteen. The average response time per questionnaire was an hour and a half.

Data collection method

This study applied an institutional, interorganizational approach for the survey. It combined the key informant method (Phillips 1981; Seidler 1974; Zelditch 1962) with archival records.

Key informants. First used in ethnographic studies (see Osgood 1940; Mead 1953), the key informant method entails selecting a certain number of knowledgeable informants in one or more organizations and asking them to report on aggregate organizational properties that they have observed. It is assumed that the informant's role or status either provides him with comparatively complete and specialized knowledge or that he is in some other respect representative of the unit. The term "informant" is distinguished from "respondent." The latter reports on personal attitudes rather than on aggregate properties (Seidler 1974). Within one study the interviewee on certain occasions may act as informant and on others as respondent.

I conducted face-to-face interviews exclusively in Mandarin Chinese with one informant per company (CEO in 85% of the cases, the rest with the most senior vice president). The interviewee reported on organizational characteristics by responding to the questions of the standardized questionnaire (see appendix D). In some cases the executive brought in staff assistants to answer specific questions in their fields of expertise.

The key informant method was selected because of the following advantages that mattered for this study: aggregation of quantitative data on organizational properties that can be subjected to rigorous statistical testing;[2] generalizability because of large, representative sample of different organizations; high response rate resulting from "one contact solution" for each company; and successful application in China (see J. Tan and Litschert 1994). Some researchers have criticized the key informant method (see Phillips 1981). They question whether the responses of one informant can accurately reflect organizational reality. To eliminate random and systematic measurement error as far as possible, I followed standard practices proposed in the literature (see Mitchell 1994): the use of pretests and concrete and simple questions (Ballweg 1969; Hyman, Levine, and Wright 1967); multiple methods; knowledgeable, "unbiased" informants; standardization of the research situation; personal interviews; and post hoc analysis of data reliability.

Archival records. Archival records included company descriptions, brochures and other promotional material, annual reports, and organizational charts. Whenever available, they were used to verify oral information. Results from the standardized questionnaire and archival records were strongly correlated.

Questionnaire administration

There are three major approaches toward administering questionnaires: interviews in person, by phone, or by mail. Each has strengths and weaknesses that depend on the context. For this study, I decided to use personal interviews. Phone interviews were considered impractical because of the complexity of the questionnaire. The choice between mail and personal interviews was based on the results from the pilot study. Through personal interviews, the interviewer could best control the quality of the interview and explain difficult sections of the questionnaire. In addition, the response rate was significantly higher than for mailed questionnaires. Personal interviews also kept the interest of the interviewee during the interview at high levels. This method elicited a cooperative attitude from the CEO (or the most senior vice president) who on average had to spend an hour and a half of his valuable time to answer the questionnaire.

The field research was conducted in two stages. The first stage (spring 1996) consisted of a field visit to Beijing. In the second stage (spring to summer 1997), a field visit to Shanghai was undertaken. Sampled informants were first contacted in a cover letter asking them to participate in the study. It was printed on high quality paper, which turned out to be very important in China, since it conveys solidity and respect for the recipient. When the CEO did not respond after approximately ten to fourteen days, he was called. In the event of refusal, the company was visited to convince the CEO to participate. The interview was usually conducted in the CEO's office or his meeting room. The interviewee filled in his answers on the questionnaire. The interviewer offered explanations when the informant did not fully understand a question.

Pilot study

The purpose of the pilot study was to discover possible weaknesses, ambiguities, and other problems in the survey research design and to correct them before the full-scale data collection. Following common practice, I did not conduct a pilot test for the qualitative case studies. In terms of detailed objectives, the survey pilot-tested the effectiveness of the research methods, the scales, and the sampling frame (see Moser and Kalton 1971; Sproull 1988). The questionnaire and administrative procedures were pilot-tested with an effective sample size of n = 10. This sample size approximated the 1% level of respondents included in the final sample, recommended in the literature (see Sarantakos 1993, p. 278). The pilot sample consisted of (a) responses from seven personal interviews conducted in Beijing and (b) three responses to mailed questionnaires. The personal interviews included a qualitative discussion on all scales to test face validity and content validity. Interviewees also were asked which sections they considered interesting or difficult. To ensure accurate and valid sampling, the mailed pilot survey randomly selected companies from Ji's (1993) directory that included companies in various parts of China. I evaluated the results of the pilot according to its objectives.

Effectiveness of research methods. Using mailed questionnaires to collect data was shown to be unfeasible in China. Supposedly because of the low efficiency of the postal system and lack of personal interaction, the response rate was extremely low (below 2%). The quality of the returned questionnaires turned out to be unsatisfactory. There were many missing values and "don't know" answers. In contrast, personal interviews elicited a high response rate from CEOs (or their most senior vice president) and complete responses. All seven contacted informants agreed to participate, partly because they thought they could learn from interacting with a Western researcher. In addition, difficult sections of the questionnaire with concepts unfamiliar to the Chinese managers could be clarified. Since none of the informants had ever participated in a survey and answered a pen-and-paper questionnaire, sometimes even the notion and use of a scale had to be explained. The interaction significantly reduced the number of "don't know" answers. Very few informants refused to answer particular questions claiming ignorance. Further, the number of missing values was greatly reduced, because the interviewer could ensure that no question was overlooked. The informants were capable of *distinguishing* the various contextual and organizational questionnaire categories. The questionnaire was considered somewhat lengthy, since it required one to two hours for completion, but the informants willingly cooperated. When there were two informants, such as the CEO and his vice president, their answers corresponded very closely.

In view of these favorable results, personal interviews were chosen for collecting the data. Because of time and budget constraints, the survey had to focus on two geographic locations, Shanghai and Beijing. It could not cover as many locations as mailed questionnaires. I decided that only one key informant per organization would be interviewed for three reasons: the answers from two informants were strongly correlated, other successful studies (including research conducted in China) had used only one informant per company before, and time and budgets were limited. This approach generated high quality data and maximized the number of informants from *different* organizations, at the expense of a broader coverage of multiple informants within one company.[3] Finally, because of the need for a large amount of data to test my theory, I maintained the original length of the questionnaire.

Scale effectiveness. Overall, the scales were easily understood. Some of the more qualitative aspects in the management practice sections had to be explained and were partly reworded after the pilot test, using Chinese technical terms to facilitate understanding. An example is the term "return on net assets," which can be literally translated based on dictionaries. However, many informants did not understand this translation, because the dictionary term did not exist in China. Meanwhile, Chinese accounting law specifies the notion of return on net assets, and the technical term used in this legal application exactly reflected the intended meaning. In other cases, concrete examples, idiomatic expressions, and special formatting (such as underlining words in a sentence) were added to improve understanding. Response categories on the legal status of the company had to be adjusted to accommodate the different ownership modes. In addition, the categories for educational background were expanded to correspond to current educational institutions in China. The new scale for "emphasis on selected Chinese cultural characteristics" showed relatively high face validity. In regards to content validity, respondents indicated some aspects of the domain that, according to their judgment, were not covered, including "trust when dealing with friends." Based on their feedback, I added three items to the final scale. The new "subcontracting" scale was easily understood. It effectively measured the degree to which activities were outsourced. I only added a special function for workers' welfare, which is less common in Western companies.

Effectiveness of sampling frame. The sampling frame proved very reliable in terms of the accuracy of the published data. Names and addresses of the companies were correct. A more detailed analysis related to the representativeness of the sample that was obtained from this frame can be found in appendix C.

Detailed methodological limitations

An ancient Chinese proverb states: "If you think you understand, you do not really understand." The following limitations may affect the validity or generalizability of the results. More detailed limitations on the structural equation analysis are discussed in Schlevogt (1999a).

Further assessment of culture scale

Chinese culture is an abstract concept. Because of its holistic nature, it contains contradictions, ambiguities, and multiple means that are difficult to analyze and understand (Child 1994, p. 285). At the epistemological level, there is some controversy as to whether it can be conceptualized as a uniform construct and measured in any meaningful sense (Tayeb 1994, p. 443). This is especially true if one uses a single scale with relatively few items.

To reflect its variety, culture was conceptualized as a multidimensional construct. The scale was not intended to cover all aspects of Chinese culture. Rather, it attempted to measure a very limited number of characteristics, which were thought to influence organizational properties strongly. Whenever possible, the research literature guided the selection of items. Furthermore, the scale did not measure Chinese culture per se. Otherwise, no difference should be found in a study that analyzes only companies located in China. Instead, it focused on the importance attached to selected cultural values within individual organizations. In addition, the scale represents only a first exploratory attempt. Subsequent studies must replicate the findings reported in this book and further examine the measurement properties of the new scale. Though the reliability coefficient is acceptable for exploratory research, it has to be seen whether it will be higher in replicated studies. The scale's distinctiveness in capturing elements of Chinese culture—its validity—will be proven only when it has been used in cross-cultural studies showing that companies in other countries consistently score low on the dimensions of Chinese culture.

Longitudinal studies

This study adopted a cross-sectional design. Therefore, strictly speaking, no inferences can be made about causal relationships between contextual antecedents and organizational properties and outcomes. Further longitudinal studies analyzing samples of organizations in different time periods are needed to confirm the causal ordering of the variables.

National replication sample

The sample included only companies located in Beijing and Shanghai. In view of China's economic and cultural diversity, inferred differences between the north and the south (and other regions) are tentative. In addition, the sample included only companies located in urban areas. Further studies need to sample companies in the whole of China, including enterprises in different regions and rural areas, such as Township and Village Enterprises (TVEs). In addition, even though the response rate was very high and the inspection of nonresponse cases did not reveal any bias, nonresponse always potentially threatens the representativeness of research findings. A replication study would provide further support for the results.

Appendix B:
Qualitative Research Design

In this appendix I will outline the case study research methodology, covering the choice of companies, validation, and field procedures.

Choice of companies

In addition to the survey, the study reports findings from the in-depth case studies of three Chinese companies and one Western company, as well as several mini case studies. The objective of the cases was to obtain more qualitative data and real-world richness, which supplemented the quantitative findings. The individual Chinese companies were selected because they were judged to be typical examples in terms of ownership mode and geographic location. They also represented extreme points on the private–state spectrum. Because of the different company sizes, it is, however, impossible to draw conclusions that can be *statistically* generalized.

Tiger Corporate Image Design (twenty-five full-time employees, revenues not disclosed, founded in 1992) was chosen to analyze selected aspects of context, structure, and management in a small private family firm based in Beijing.[1] The Cathay Industrial Bank (CIB; 560,000 employees, 580 billion RMB revenues, founded in 1984) served as an example of a state-owned enterprise in Beijing. The third company, Magnolia Education Group (fifty full-time employees, three hundred part-time employees, six million RMB revenues, founded in 1983), was chosen to examine selected characteristics of a medium-size private enterprise in Shanghai. American International Group (AIG) is one of the few Western companies that undoubtedly succeeded in China. It demonstrates the effectiveness of the CHINA framework developed in chapter 7.

The quantity of empirical evidence varied across the four cases. I was an observer at Tiger for one month and collected data from a wide variety of sources. It was not possible to gather such detailed evidence for the other two case studies. I therefore had to focus mainly on interviews with two or three top executives and archival data. Owing to its sensitive government connections, Cathay Industrial Bank was very secretive and tightly controlled. For example, the interviews had to be solicited in writing and be approved at an interdepartmental meeting. Besides, many Shanghainese entrepreneurs are very practical and do not perceive research as particularly useful. The Magnolia Education Group therefore did not agree to a long, observation-based study. For the AIG case study I analyzed newspaper and magazine reports and company reports, and leveraged my personal experience of dealing with this company. The additional mini case studies used newspaper and magazine reports and other public material as input.

Validation

Since the case studies of Chinese companies relied mainly on primary data, I followed the methodological guidelines recommended for empirical case study research (Yin 1994): (a) multiple sources of evidence, (b) a case data book, including table shells, for inspection by other researchers, and (c) a chain of evidence (audit trail) that establishes the high reliability of the data.

Field procedures

In this section I will outline the sources of evidence for the case studies and briefly discuss their strengths and weaknesses.

Interviews

I conducted in-depth interviews with the company's CEO and other top managers, who acted as key informants. The general structure and standardized questions of the survey questionnaire were used as the interview guide and the point of departure for the discussion. I subsequently asked probing questions to collect evidence for each major contextual, structural, and managerial property. The answers were later recorded in the table shells of the individual case records (see M. Miles and Huberman 1984). All CEOs also filled in the standardized questionnaire. The informants were visited in their offices. Since the CEO of CIB held a high political position and correspondingly had a particularly busy schedule, the interview was self-administered. The interviews were not taped, because many interviewees would have felt uncomfortable in the presence of recording devices (Yin 1994, p. 87). Especially in China, many informants worry about the negative consequences that may result from candid answers. Interviews were targeted, focusing directly on the key issues to be examined in the case study, and provided many insights. However, some bias may result from poorly constructed questions, the characteristics of the informant, and inaccuracies because of his poor recall.

Written sources

Newspaper and magazine reports served as sources of written information. Besides, company records, including company descriptions, brochures, and other promotional material, annual reports, and organizational charts were analyzed. Many private firms lacked these written documents, illustrating their low degree of formalization. Public written sources have the advantage of being permanent, unobtrusive, and broad in coverage. Potential disadvantages are selectivity, low retrievability, and reporting bias. Internal archival records, in addition to the advantages and disadvantages of public documents, often include precise and quantitative information. A potential weakness might be limited accessibility because of privacy concerns.

Observation

I directly observed the operations of Tiger to gather behavioral cues on the realities of structure and management, as well as emphasis on family-based traditional values. Direct observation conveys a strong sense of realism and provides information on the context of events and actions. Both aspects were very important, particularly to elucidate the "soft" aspects of management and culture. However, observation is time-consuming; potentially selective, costly, and obtrusive; and might influence the cause of events.

Artifacts

Physical artifacts were examined at Tiger. They included corporate identity designs displayed in a small exhibition organized by the CEO. This exhibition enabled me to assess the innovativeness and quality of the company's products. An advantage of this method is that physical artifacts reveal cultural, technical, and operational features of an organizations, which may not become apparent from interviews and other methods. However, they constitute only a selection and may not be easily available.

Appendix C: Sample Characteristics

Particularly in cross-cultural research, it is important to present detailed descriptive statistics for the sample (Brislin, Lonner, and Thorndike 1973, p. 22). I will discuss all sample characteristics that could potentially influence the results of the survey or their interpretation: response rate, informant characteristics, and company characteristics.

Response rate

A total of 124 enterprises (of 157 contacted) agreed to participate in the survey. With thirty-three nonrespondents, the response rate for the whole sample was 79%, which compares very favorably against the extremely low response from the mailed pilot test. This result underlines the effectiveness of personal interviews, at least in China. As in the pilot, test, higher response rates were obtained by systematically following up on nonresponses, first by calling the prospective interviewee and then, in case of continued nonresponse, by visiting the company. The informants readily participated in the survey for similar reasons as in the pilot test. Many CEOs were curious about the research because they had never participated in such a survey. Further, they hoped to learn from an Oxford scholar. Some respondents asked for a blank copy of the questionnaire for use as a diagnostic tool in their company. For example, the CEO of a hotel in Beijing pledged that he would measure the company's progress in increasing management sophistication on a monthly basis, using my questionnaire. Finally, many CEOs hoped to establish a new important contact with the Western world. The research thus profited from its pioneering nature. Especially in view of the extensive nature of the questionnaire, response rates in the West certainly would have been significantly lower.

To assess potential nonresponse bias, I analyzed whether sampled companies that refused to participate in the survey differed from the participating companies. I examined potential differences for five variables: reason for refusal, company size, geographic location, ownership mode, and industry category. The reasons for not participating did not suggest any particular bias. Some CEOs simply were not interested in spending time on the research. This is similar to the reason why companies in the West do not participate in surveys. The mean size (number of employees) of nonrespondent and respondent private and state enterprises are reported in table C-1. The mean size of nonrespondent private enterprises ($\bar{x}=95$, $\Delta\bar{x}=36$, $p>.05$, $df=77$) and state enterprises ($\bar{x}=7,279$, $\Delta\bar{x}=5,517$, $p>.05$, $df=76$) did not differ significantly from the mean size of participating private and state enterprises, respectively.[1]

There were nineteen nonrespondent companies in Shanghai and fourteen in Beijing. Because those numbers did not differ significantly, there was no bias in terms of geographic location. The slightly higher nonresponse rate in Shanghai might reflect the stronger commercial orientation of Shanghainese companies. Some do not perceive research as valuable. There were eighteen nonrespondent private enterprises and fifteen nonrespondent state enterprises. Once again, the two subgroups did not differ significantly. I therefore concluded that there was no nonresponse bias in terms of ownership mode. Finally, an industry comparison of all nonrespondent with respondent companies showed that the groups were relatively similar (see figure C-1), with the only slight difference that there were somewhat more service companies in the nonrespondent group. However, an analysis of the individual businesses within the broad industry categories did not reveal any systematic response bias. For each nonrespondent company, there was at least one company in the same business that agreed to participate. Thus, no business type was excluded for systematic reasons. Although no sys-

Table C-1 Comparison of respondent and nonrespondent company size (number of employees)

Enterprise	Respondents			Nonrespondents			Mean comparison		
	$\bar{x}$	s	N	$\bar{x}$	s	N	$\Delta\bar{x}$	t	df
Private	59	96	61	95	66	18	36*	1.80	77
State	12,796	76,054	63	7,279	22,909	15	5,517*	.48	76

*Levene's test significant, therefore inequal variance t-test used.
$\bar{x}$ = mean company size (number of employees).
$\Delta\bar{x}$ = mean difference.
s = standard deviation.
df = degrees of freedom.
N = sample size.
All employee numbers are rounded (no decimal points).

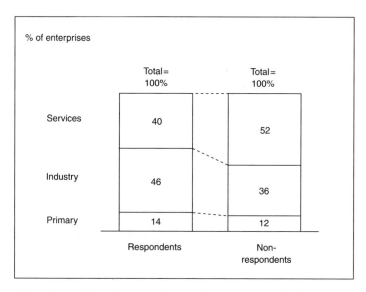

% of enterprises

	Respondents Total= 100%	Non-respondents Total= 100%
Services	40	52
Industry	46	36
Primary	14	12

Figure C-1 Comparison of respondent and nonrespondent industries

tematic differences between sample members and nonrespondents could be detected with respect to the five variables tested, it can never, with absolute certainty, be stated that there are no internal differences of any importance.

Informant characteristics

Table C-2 shows the average age, time with the company, and tenure of current position for all interviewees.

Figure C-2 displays the age of informants. It ranged from 27 to 67 years, with an average of 45 years, and standard deviation of 8 years (122 valid cases).

The majority of informants were CEOs (85%). The remainder were the most senior vice presidents in the company. In terms of international experience, seventy-nine respondents (64%) had been to the West. Inform-

Table C-2 Work experience of informants

Characteristic	x̄	s	Valid cases
Age (years)	45	8	122
Time with company (months)	124	131	123
Time in current position (months)	54	44	123

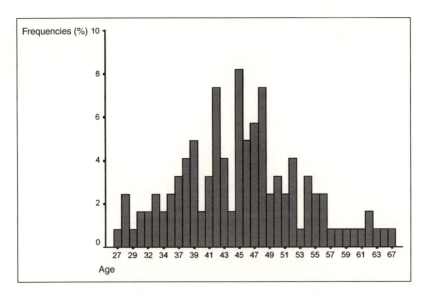

Figure C-2   Frequency distribution of respondent age (n=122)

ants were predominantly male (87%), which accurately reflects the reality of corporate business in China. Most interviewees had earned a degree either from a professional school or a bachelor's degree from a university (see figure C-3).

Company characteristics

Descriptive statistics relating to company size (measured in sales and employees) are reported in table C-3. The frequency distribution of sales is shown in table C-4. Private enterprises are on average significantly smaller than state enterprises.

Table C-3 Size of companies

	Sales	('000 RMB)		Employees		
	Total sample	Private	State	Total sample	Private	State
Mean	168,000	22,429	311,000	5,637	101	10,998
Median	15,000	5,750	60,000	100	25	600
Standard deviation	559,000	47,721	762,000	50,332	197	70,458
Minimum	50	50	200	5	5	6
Maximum	5,000,050	282,000	5,000,050	560,000*	1,000	560,000
Total valid	117	58	59	124	61	63

*Cathay Industrial Bank (name changed for confidentiality reasons).

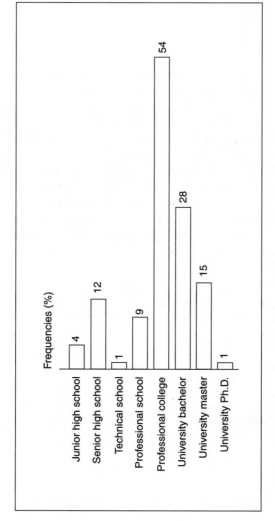

Figure C-3 Frequency distribution of informant education (n=124)

Table C-4 Frequency distribution of sales

Sales (million RMB)	Frequency	Valid %
0–5	41	35.0
5–15	19	16.3
15–50	18	15.4
50–100	15	12.8
>100	24	20.5
Total valid	117	

Company age varied from one year to a century, with a mean value of twenty-one years and standard deviation of twenty-six years (121 valid cases). A wide variety of industries and services was represented in the sample (see table C-5). They included timber, cotton mills, chemicals, pharmaceuticals, industrial equipment, handicrafts, food and beverages, home appliances, electronics, construction, real estate, trading, financial services, and publishing. About 46% of the companies belonged to the secondary (industry) sector. No single business segment (within broad industry groups) accounted for more than 5% of the total sample. The frequency distribution of the ownership structure scale (see company questionnaire, appendix D, section 2.7) is presented in table C-6. In the state sector, the great majority of companies were state-owned enterprises

Table C-5 Types of industry/service

Type of industry/service	Frequency	Valid percent
Basic materials & chemicals	17	13.7
Manufacturing and assembly	30	24.2
Consumer goods	27	21.8
Diversified financial services	11	8.9
Media and entertainment	14	11.3
Miscellaneous services	25	20.2
Total	124	

Table C-6 Ownership structure of sampled companies

Ownership category	Frequency	Valid percent
State-owned	54	43.5
Collective	9	7.3
Joint-venture	14	11.3
Wholly Chinese owned	47	37.9
Total	124	100.0

(43.5% of total sample). In the private sector, most companies were fully Chinese owned (37.9% of the total sample). The joint-venture partners were all private enterprises.

To assess the representativeness of the sample further, I needed to get a rough idea of the correspondence between sampled companies and the underlying population. I therefore compared the proportion of industrial sectors represented in the sample to the national average (% of GDP). The sample roughly mirrored the underlying population (see figure C-4), with the only minor exception that the service sector was slightly overweighed. This might be because a sample that contains data for two cities was compared to the *national* population. We would expect the industry structure for some of the most advanced cities to differ somewhat from the national average, featuring a higher proportion of more advanced service sector companies. Unfortunately, when the study was undertaken, there were no data relating to the city's industry composition. Such information might have clarified the issue. More generally, the similar number of respondents in industry and services has strong benefits. It avoids the oversampling of manufacturers in most earlier Aston studies. Even though the sample seems to adequately represent the two locations, it cannot be claimed that it exactly mirrors the complete company population of the whole of China, because budget and time constraints limited the study to selected urban areas.

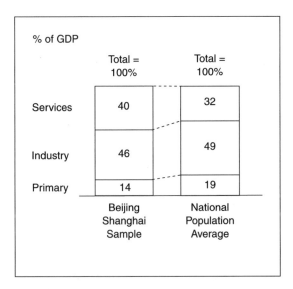

Figure C-4 Comparison of sample and population industry structure. Source: Schlevogt China study Datastream.

Appendix D. Retranslated Company Questionnaire in English

Company questionnaire instructions

1. This questionnaire has to be filled out personally by the company's CEO (factory director) or, if he is not available, by the company's vice president (deputy factory director).
2. "The firm" means the entity of which you are the senior executive, whether it be a division, a subsidiary, or an independent corporation. Answers to all questions, unless otherwise stated, refer to this entity's operations, policies, and environment.
3. Most of the questions are rating scales. Please circle the number in each scale that seems closest to describing the reality of your company as you perceive it. Feel free to make any additional explanatory or qualifying comments under the relevant scale. For all scale items, there are *two extreme points*: 1 represents the statement on the left and 7 the statement on the right; numbers between 1 and 7 represent degrees of the extremes. Please tick only one answer. Do not write on or mark shaded areas.

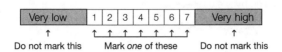

4. Please answer *all* questions; incomplete questionnaires create severe problems in subsequent statistical and data analysis. After completing the questionnaire, please check to see that no questions are left unanswered.
5. Service-oriented firms (such as banks), please note: In the questionnaire, (a) "sales" = "revenues"; (b) "product" = "service"; (c) "manufacturing" or "production"= *principal* operations of firm (e.g., banking operations). Write "N.A." where an item appears to be clearly irrelevant to your type of business.
6. Please do not use a pencil to fill in this questionnaire.

Thank you very much for your cooperation.

Kai-Alexander Schlevogt (Shi Kai Ya)
University of Oxford, School of Management Studies

1. CEO personal information

1. Age: _____

2. Sex:
   (a) Male   (b) Female

3. Education:
   (a) Junior high school   (d) Professional school   (g) University master
   (b) Senior high school   (e) Professional college   (h) University Ph.D.
   (c) Technical school   (f) University bachelor

3A. If higher education, which subject did you study? _____

4. Have you ever been to at least one country of the Western developed world (US, Canada, Western Europe, Japan, Australia)?
   (a) Yes   (b) No

4A. If you have been abroad, what was the main objective of the visit?
   (a) Study   (d) Travel
   (b) Work   (e) Other _____
   (c) Business study tour

4B. If you studied abroad, in which country/ies did you study? _____

5. Position:
   (a) CEO   (b) Others _____

5A. If you are not CEO, what are your responsibilities? _____

6. How long have you been working for the company?   _____ Years   _____ Months

7. How long have you held your current position?   _____ Years   _____ Months

2. Company information

1. To which category does your company belong?
   (a) Independent corporation   (b) Subsidiary   (c) Division

2. Nature of your company's business: _____

3. Approximate annual revenues (RMB): _____

4. Approximate number of employees: ____

5. How many years ago was the company founded? ____

6. Legal form of your company:
   (a) Unlimited company   (c) Shareholders' company
   (b) Limited company   (d) Joint venture

7. Ownership structure of your company:
   (a) State   (c) Foreign (solely owned, joint venture, alliance)
   (b) Collective   (d) Private

8. Share structure (total 100%):
   (a) State: ____% of shares   (d) Family members: ____% of shares
   (b) Collective: ____% of shares   (e) Other Chinese private: ____% of shares
   (c) Foreign: ____% of shares

3. Goals

1. Performance aspirations: How important are the following goals to your firm's top management in making strategic decisions or commitments of a long-term nature (i.e., more than 5 years)?

	Little importance ↓					Extreme importance ↓

(a) Earning a high, above-average profit

1	2	3	4	5	6	7

(b) Achieving a high, above-average rate of growth in sales or revenues

1	2	3	4	5	6	7

(c) Retaining or securing high, above-average liquidity and financial strength

1	2	3	4	5	6	7

(d) Maintaining or securing high, above-average employee morale, job satisfaction, and commitment to firm's objectives

1	2	3	4	5	6	7

(e) Achieving or maintaining an excellent public image

1	2	3	4	5	6	7

2. Orientation to diversification and vertical integration: what is the operating top management *philosophy*?

   (a) Concentration on a single group of related products or a single industry; great emphasis on defining one's industry and sticking to it

1	2	3	4	5	6	7

   Strong emphasis on diversification of products or services, even if it means venturing into unrelated industries

   (b) Strong avoidance of vertical integration

1	2	3	4	5	6	7

   Strong tendency to integrate vertically, such as by acquiring raw material sources and processing facilities, and/or by acquiring wholesaling and even retailing channels

3. Orientation to diversification and vertical integration: What is the *existing* structure of the company?

(a) Concentration on a single group of related products or a single industry; great emphasis on defining one's industry and sticking to it

1	2	3	4	5	6	7

Strong emphasis on diversification of products or services, even if it means venturing into unrelated industries

(b) Strong avoidance of vertical integration

1	2	3	4	5	6	7

Strong tendency to integrate vertically, such as by acquiring raw material sources and processing facilities, and/or by acquiring wholesaling and even retailing channels

4. How much attention does top management pay to the following characteristics of your main industry? In other words, considering their impact on long-term profitability or growth, how much importance does your top management attach to these aspects?

	Little importance ↓					Extreme importance ↓	
(a) Competition in delivery and after-sales services in your industry	1	2	3	4	5	6	7
(b) Innovation of new or better operating processes	1	2	3	4	5	6	7
(c) Price competition in the industry	1	2	3	4	5	6	7
(d) Rate at which products or services are getting obsolete	1	2	3	4	5	6	7
(e) Competition for technical manpower	1	2	3	4	5	6	7
(f) Competition in promotion, advertising, selling, distribution, etc.	1	2	3	4	5	6	7
(g) Competition for purchases of inputs (e.g., raw materials), parts, equipment	1	2	3	4	5	6	7
(h) Competition in *quality* and variety of products and services	1	2	3	4	5	6	7

4. Strategy

1. How much importance does top management attach to the following aspects of strategy?

	Little importance ↓					Extreme importance ↓	
(a) Sacrificing profitability to gain market share	1	2	3	4	5	6	7
(b) Cutting prices to increase market share	1	2	3	4	5	6	7
(c) When confronted with a major decision, I usually try to develop thorough analysis	1	2	3	4	5	6	7
(d) Information systems provide support for decision making (the information system incorporates operative data of the company, such as costs, products, etc.)	1	2	3	4	5	6	7

(e) Significant modifications to manufacturing technology

1	2	3	4	5	6	7

(f) Use of production management techniques

1	2	3	4	5	6	7

(g) Our criteria for resource allocation generally reflect short-term considerations

1	2	3	4	5	6	7

(h) Forecasting key indicators of performance

1	2	3	4	5	6	7

(i) Constantly seeking new opportunities related to the present operations

1	2	3	4	5	6	7

(j) Usually the first to introduce new brands or products in the market

1	2	3	4	5	6	7

(k) Our operations can be generally described as high-risk

1	2	3	4	5	6	7

(l) A tendency to support projects where the expected returns are certain

1	2	3	4	5	6	7

5. Leadership style

1. *Participation*: To what extent is decision making at top levels in your firm characterized by participative, group, or democratic decision making, in relation to the following classes of decisions?
   (a) Product- or service-related decisions concerning level of operations, marketing strategy, research and development of new products or services, etc.:

No participation; the responsible top executives make the decisions, using existing information

1	2	3	4	5	6	7

Decisions made by top management groups or committees after full discussion and attempt to reach consensus—failing which, decisions are taken by majority vote

   (b) Capital budgeting decisions (selection and financing of long-term investments):

No participation; the responsible top executives make the decisions, using existing information

1	2	3	4	5	6	7

Decisions made by top management groups or committees after full discussion and attempt to reach consensus—failing which, decisions are taken by majority vote

   (c) Long-term strategy of growth, diversification, etc. and decisions related to changes in the firm's operating philosophy:

No participation; the responsible top executives make the decisions, using existing information

1	2	3	4	5	6	7

Decisions made by top management groups or committees after full discussion and attempt to reach consensus—failing which, decisions are taken by majority vote

2. *Flexibility*: An operating top management philosophy of:
   (a) A strong emphasis on holding fast to tried-management principles despite any changes in business conditions

1	2	3	4	5	6	7

A strong emphasis on adapting freely to changing circumstances without too much concern for past practice

(b) Tight control of most operations by means of sophisticated control and information systems

| 1 | 2 | 3 | 4 | 5 | 6 | 7 |

Loose, informal control; heavy dependence on informal relationships and norms of cooperation for getting work done

3. *Coercion:*

(a) To what extent within your firm do you observe senior managers using force as a mode of resolving their disagreements over personal matters and corporate issues ("Might overcomes right"; "If you cannot make a man think as you do, make him do as you think")?

Seldom used

| 1 | 2 | 3 | 4 | 5 | 6 | 7 |

Used very often

(b) In attempting to institute organizational changes, overcome the resistance of personnel to these changes, and get their required commitment, management issues orders and implicitly or explicitly warns personnel of serious consequences of resisting management orders.

Seldom used

| 1 | 2 | 3 | 4 | 5 | 6 | 7 |

Used very often

6. Decision-making style

Researchers have indicated that decision making in organizations takes place in three distinct (but not necessarily mutually exclusive) modes or styles. Please indicate how closely each of the following modes resembles the way decisions get made at the top levels of your firm.

1. Mode A: Adaptive. Characterized by a cautious, pragmatic, one small step at a time adjustment to problems. Decisions are generally compromises between the conflicting demands of owners, unions, government, managers, customers, etc. They are made locally more often than centrally, and the primary concern is with stability and steady growth.

Little resemblance to style of top-level decision making in firm

| 1 | 2 | 3 | 4 | 5 | 6 | 7 |

Very great resemblance to style of top-level decision making in firm

2. Mode B: Entrepreneurial. Characterized by active search for big new opportunities; large, bold decisions despite the uncertainty of their outcomes; a charismatic decision maker at the top, wielding great power; rapid growth as the dominant organizational goal.

Little resemblance to style of top-level decision making in firm

| 1 | 2 | 3 | 4 | 5 | 6 | 7 |

Very great resemblance to style of top-level decision making in firm

3. Mode C: Planning. Characterized by systematic search for opportunities, as well as anticipation of problems; a systematic consideration of costs and benefits of alternatives; and a conscious attempt to integrate programs of action to achieve specified goals efficiently. The accent is on profit maximization, long-term planning, very careful screening of investments to minimize risks, and the extensive use of expertise and solid research before making decisions.

Little resemblance to style of top-level decision making in firm

| 1 | 2 | 3 | 4 | 5 | 6 | 7 |

Very great resemblance to style of top-level decision making in firm

7. Communication

1) An operating top management philosophy of:

Highly structured *vertical* channels of communication and highly restricted access to important financial and operating information

1	2	3	4	5	6	7

Open channels of communication and important financial and operating information flowing quite freely throughout the organization

2) How often does your company use the following meetings?

Seldom used →   Used very often ↓

Departmental meetings that are set up to allow members of the same department to engage in joint decision making

1	2	3	4	5	6	7

8. Culture/trust

8.1. *Chinese values*

1. How important are the following factors in daily business transactions?

Little importance ↓   Extreme importance ↓

(a) Keeping one's face

1	2	3	4	5	6	7

(b) Having respect for seniority

1	2	3	4	5	6	7

(c) Loyalty to one's family

1	2	3	4	5	6	7

(d) Loyalty to one's company

1	2	3	4	5	6	7

(e) Personal relations (*guanxi*)

1	2	3	4	5	6	7

(f) Using strategies from classical Chinese warfare literature to succeed

1	2	3	4	5	6	7

(g) Using strategies from Western management textbooks to succeed

1	2	3	4	5	6	7

(h) Solving problems in teams, not alone

1	2	3	4	5	6	7

(i) Using common sense and intuition, instead of complicated and theoretical reasoning, to solve problems

1	2	3	4	5	6	7

(j) Looking for integrative solutions to problems, not partial ones

1	2	3	4	5	6	7

(k) Trust in the people with whom you are doing business

1	2	3	4	5	6	7

(l) Collective orientation (i.e., belonging to a group, such as family, company, organization)

1	2	3	4	5	6	7

(m) Taking risks

1	2	3	4	5	6	7

2. How far do you agree with the following statements?

Completely disagree ↓   Completely agree ↓

(a) "I trust members of my family more than outsiders, therefore I always try to keep business within my family."

1	2	3	4	5	6	7

(b) "When dealing with outsiders, whenever possible I prefer to deal with foreigners, instead of with my fellow country-men."

1	2	3	4	5	6	7

(c) "I value the substance of the cooperation and do not dis-tinguish between foreigners and fellow countrymen; the important thing is that the person I am dealing with is my friend and can be trusted."

1	2	3	4	5	6	7

8.2. Corporate culture

Consider the organization you work for as a whole. What set of values, what beliefs, what forms of behavior could be said to be typical of it? Please indicate the degree to which the following statements represent values held by the organization. *Please do not state your own values and preferences.*

1. A good boss . . .

Does not represent values held in our organization at all ↓   Exactly represents values held in our organization ↓

(a) . . . is strong, decisive, and firm but fair. He is protective, generous, and indulgent to loyal subordinates.

1	2	3	4	5	6	7

(b) . . . is impersonal and correct, avoiding the exercise of au-thority for his own advantage. He demands from subordi-nates only that which is required by the formal system.

1	2	3	4	5	6	7

(c) . . . is egalitarian and can be influenced in matters con-cerning the task. He uses his authority to obtain the re-sources needed to get on with the job.

1	2	3	4	5	6	7

(d) . . . is concerned about and respectful of the personal needs and values of others. He provides satisfying and growth-stimulating work opportunities for subordinates.

1	2	3	4	5	6	7

2. A good subordinate . . .
(a) . . . is hardworking, loyal to the interests of his superior, resourceful, and trustworthy.

1	2	3	4	5	6	7

(b) . . . is responsible and reliable, meeting the duties and re-sponsibilities of the job and avoiding actions that surprise or embarrass his superior.

1	2	3	4	5	6	7

(c) . . . is self-motivated to contribute his best to the task and is open to ideas and suggestions. Is willing to give the lead to others when they show greater expertise or ability.

1	2	3	4	5	6	7

(d) . . . is vitally interested in the development of his own po-tential and is open to learning and receiving help. Also re-spects the needs and values of others, and is willing to give help and contribute to their development.

1	2	3	4	5	6	7

3. The organization treats the individual . . .
(a) . . . as a trusted agent whose time and energy are at the disposal of those who run the organization.

1	2	3	4	5	6	7

(b) . . . on the basis that his time and energy are available through a contract that defines the rights and responsibili-ties of both sides.

1	2	3	4	5	6	7

(c) . . . as a coworker who has committed his skills and abilities to the common cause.

| 1 | 2 | 3 | 4 | 5 | 6 | 7 |

(d) . . . as an interesting and talented person in his own right.

| 1 | 2 | 3 | 4 | 5 | 6 | 7 |

4. People are controlled and influenced by . . .
   (a) . . . the personal exercise of rewards, punishment, or charisma.

| 1 | 2 | 3 | 4 | 5 | 6 | 7 |

   (b) . . . impersonal exercise of economic and political power to enforce procedures and standards of work performance.

| 1 | 2 | 3 | 4 | 5 | 6 | 7 |

   (c) . . . communication and discussion of task requirements motivating personal commitment to goal achievement, which leads to appropriate action.

| 1 | 2 | 3 | 4 | 5 | 6 | 7 |

   (d) . . . intrinsic interest in and enjoyment of the activities to be done, and/or concern and caring for the needs of the other people involved.

| 1 | 2 | 3 | 4 | 5 | 6 | 7 |

5. It is legitimate for one person to control another's activities . . .
   (a) . . . if he has more power and influence in the organization.

| 1 | 2 | 3 | 4 | 5 | 6 | 7 |

   (b) . . . if his role prescribes that he is responsible for directing the other.

| 1 | 2 | 3 | 4 | 5 | 6 | 7 |

   (c) . . . if he has more knowledge relevant to the task at hand.

| 1 | 2 | 3 | 4 | 5 | 6 | 7 |

   (d) . . . if he is accepted by those he controls.

| 1 | 2 | 3 | 4 | 5 | 6 | 7 |

6. The basis for task assignment is . . .
   (a) . . . the personal needs and judgment of those who run the place.

| 1 | 2 | 3 | 4 | 5 | 6 | 7 |

   (b) . . . the formal divisions of functions and responsibility in the system.

| 1 | 2 | 3 | 4 | 5 | 6 | 7 |

   (c) . . . the resource and expertise requirements of the job to be done.

| 1 | 2 | 3 | 4 | 5 | 6 | 7 |

   (d) . . . the personal wishes and needs for learning and growth of organization members.

| 1 | 2 | 3 | 4 | 5 | 6 | 7 |

9. Conflict

Three areas of a firm often have conflicts with one another. One is marketing; another is operations; and the third is R&D and design. Please rate the extent of conflict between pairs of these in your firm. If any item is irrelevant to your firm, please write "N.A." For manufacturing firms, operations cover production-related activities.

	No conflicts				Strong disagreement between personnel of two areas		
	↓						↓

(a) Marketing and operations | 1 | 2 | 3 | 4 | 5 | 6 | 7 |

(b) R&D/design and marketing | 1 | 2 | 3 | 4 | 5 | 6 | 7 |

(c) Operations and R&D/design | 1 | 2 | 3 | 4 | 5 | 6 | 7 |

10. CEO's personality

Below are several statements that describe various things people do or try to do on their jobs. I would like to know which of these statements you feel most accurately describe *your own behavior* when you are at work. Please circle the number above the word(s) that best describe your own actions. There are no right or wrong answers. Please answer all questions frankly.

1. I do my best work when my job assignments are fairly difficult.

| 1 Always | 2 Almost always | 3 Usually | 4 Sometimes | 5 Seldom | 6 Almost never | 7 Never |

2. I try very hard to improve on my past performance at work.

| 1 Always | 2 Almost always | 3 Usually | 4 Sometimes | 5 Seldom | 6 Almost never | 7 Never |

3. I take moderate risks and stick my neck out to get ahead at work.

| 1 Always | 2 Almost always | 3 Usually | 4 Sometimes | 5 Seldom | 6 Almost never | 7 Never |

4. I try to avoid any added responsibility on my job.

| 1 Always | 2 Almost always | 3 Usually | 4 Sometimes | 5 Seldom | 6 Almost never | 7 Never |

5. I try to perform better than my coworkers.

| 1 Always | 2 Almost always | 3 Usually | 4 Sometimes | 5 Seldom | 6 Almost never | 7 Never |

11. Organizational effectiveness

Compared to your industry's average or, if yours is a very diversified firm, in relation to comparable firms, how do you compare on each of the following?

1. Long-run level of profitability

Very low | 1 | 2 | 3 | 4 | 5 | 6 | 7 | Very high

2. Annual growth rate of sales or revenues

Very low | 1 | 2 | 3 | 4 | 5 | 6 | 7 | Very high

3. Employee morale, job satisfaction, and commitment to firm's objectives

Very low | 1 | 2 | 3 | 4 | 5 | 6 | 7 | Very high

4. Financial strength (liquidity and ability to raise financial resources)

Very low | 1 | 2 | 3 | 4 | 5 | 6 | 7 | Very high

5. Public image and goodwill

Very low | 1 | 2 | 3 | 4 | 5 | 6 | 7 | Very high

6. Stability of profitability:
   (a) What was the lowest (before tax) rate of return on net worth during the past 5 years?
   _____% (if the lowest rate was a loss, please place a minus sign before the percent).

   (Method of calculation: Rate of return on net worth $= \dfrac{\text{Annual pretax profit}}{\text{Net worth*}} \times 100$)

   *Net worth = shareholders' funds, or total assets minus total liabilities

   (b) What was the highest (before tax) rate of return on net worth during this period?
   _____% (if the lowest rate was a loss, please place a minus sign before the percent).

7. Growth: What was the average rate of growth of sales or revenues during the past 5 years? _____%
   (Method of calculation: Add sales growth rates for each year from 1990 to 1995, then divide total by 5)

12. Specialization

A function is specialized when at least one person performs that function and *does not perform any other function*. No account is taken of either (a) the specialist's status or (b) whether an organization has many specialists or only one. For each of the following activities for which there is a specialist, please mark "1", otherwise mark "0".

	No ↓	Existing ↓
(a) Develop, legitimize, and symbolize the organization's charter (e.g., public relations, advertising, etc.)	0	1
(b) Dispose of, distribute, and service the output (e.g., sales and service, customer complaints, etc.)	0	1
(c) Transport outputs and resources from place to place	0	1
(d) Acquire and allocate human resources (e.g., hiring, etc.)	0	1
(e) Develop and transform human resources (e.g., education and training)	0	1
(f) Maintain human resources and promote their identification with the organization (e.g., welfare, healthcare, safety, corporate magazine, sports and social activities, etc.)	0	1
(g) Obtain and control materials and equipment (e.g., purchasing, material control, storage, stock control, etc.)	0	1
(h) Erect and maintain buildings and equipment (maintenance, works engineer, etc.)	0	1
(i) Record and control financial resources (e.g., accounts, costs, wages, etc.)	0	1
(j) Control the work flow (e.g., planning, implementation, etc.)	0	1
(k) Control the quality of materials, equipment, and outputs (e.g., inspection, testing, etc.)	0	1

(l) Devise and assess ways of producing the output (e.g., work study, operational research, pricing, methods study, etc.)

0	1

(m) Devise new outputs, equipment, and processes

0	1

(n) Develop and operate administrative procedures (e.g., registry, filing, statistics, organization and methods, etc.)

0	1

(o) Deal with legal and insurance requirements (e.g., legal matters, registration, insurance, licensing, etc.)

0	1

(p) Acquire information on the operational field (market research)

0	1

13. Formalization

The degree of formalization of role definition in the organization is given by (a) the number of specific role-defining documents that exist in the organization and (b) in some cases, the extent of their distribution or application.

(a) Information booklets given to

| 0 | None | 1 | Few employees | 2 | Many employees | 3 | All employees |

(b) Number of information booklets

| 0 | None | 1 | One | 2 | Two | 3 | Three | 4 | Four or more |

(c) Organization chart given to

| 0 | None | 1 | CEO only | 2 | CEO plus one other executive | 3 | CEO plus all/most department heads |

	None ↓	Existing ↓
(d) Written operating instructions	0	1
(e) Written terms of reference or job descriptions for direct workers	0	1
(f) Written terms of reference or job descriptions for line supervisors	0	1
(g) Written terms of reference or job descriptions for staff (staff assists top management in strategy and administration)	0	1
(h) Written terms of reference or job descriptions for CEO	0	1
(i) Manual of work procedures	0	1
(j) Written organizational policies	0	1
(k) Work flow schedule or production program	0	1
(l) Written research program or reports	0	1

14. Centralization

Which hierarchical level in your firm has the authority to make the following decisions? (0 = above the chief executive—this would be the board of directors or owner; 1 = chief executive; 2 = divisional or functional manager, such as production or sales manager; 3 = subdepartment head; 4 = first-level supervisor; 5 = operatives at the shop level). Please circle the appropriate number.

Decisions concerning:

	Above CEO ↓				Operatives ↓	
(a) The number of workers required	0	1	2	3	4	5
(b) Whether to employ a worker	0	1	2	3	4	5
(c) Internal labor disputes	0	1	2	3	4	5
(d) Overtime to be worked at shop level	0	1	2	3	4	5
(e) Delivery dates and priority of orders	0	1	2	3	4	5
(f) Production plans to be worked on	0	1	2	3	4	5
(g) Dismissal of a worker	0	1	2	3	4	5
(h) Methods of personnel selection (e.g., hiring criteria)	0	1	2	3	4	5
(i) Method of work to be used (e.g., choice of Total Quality Management as management method)	0	1	2	3	4	5
(j) Machinery or equipment to be used	0	1	2	3	4	5
(k) Allocation of work among available workers	0	1	2	3	4	5

15. Technology

To what extent are each of the following technologies used in your firm?

1. "Custom" technology (production or fabrication of a *single unit* or a *few units* of products or services to customer specifications or needs; e.g., missile prototypes, patient care in exclusive private clinics).

Not used at all or minimally used | 1 | 2 | 3 | 4 | 5 | 6 | 7 | Very extensively used: over 70% of value added by operations attributable to this

2. "Small batch, job shop" technology (creation of small batches of similar units, such as fashionable dresses, tools and dies).

Not used at all or minimally used | 1 | 2 | 3 | 4 | 5 | 6 | 7 | Very extensively used: over 70% of value added by operations attributable to this

3. "Large batch" technology (e.g., used in manufacturing drugs and chemicals, parts, yarn; in university, used for instructing large groups of students in required courses).

Not used at all or minimally used | 1 | 2 | 3 | 4 | 5 | 6 | 7 | Very extensively used: over 70% of value added by operations attributable to this

4. "Mass production" technology (e.g., used in production of cars and standard textiles).

Not used at all or minimally used | 1 | 2 | 3 | 4 | 5 | 6 | 7 | Very extensively used: over 70% of value added by operations attributable to this

5. "Continuous process" technology (e.g., used in oil refining and other *automated* industries, in which the output is highly standardized and mechanized, and is produced continuously rather than in batches or shifts).

Not used at all or minimally used | 1 | 2 | 3 | 4 | 5 | 6 | 7 | Very extensively used: over 70% of value added by operations attributable to this

6. "Service technology" used by firms to serve their widely distributed clientele through *branches*, dealers, etc. (e.g., banks, insurance companies, telephone companies, after-sales service in consumer goods industries).

Not used at all or minimally used | 1 | 2 | 3 | 4 | 5 | 6 | 7 | Very extensively used: over 70% of value added by operations attributable to this

7. *Automaticity* mode and automaticity range:
   a) Mode: What is the *bulk* of equipment used by the organization for its work flow?

0	1	2	3	4	5
Hand tools and manual machines	Powered machines and tools	Single-cycle automatics and self-feeding machines	Automatic: repeats cycle	Self-measuring and adjusting: feedback	Computer control: automatic cognition

   b) Range: Please mark the *highest* scoring piece of equipment, in terms of automaticity, that the organization uses.

0	1	2	3	4	5
Hand tools and manual machines	Powered machines and tools	Single-cycle automatics and self-feeding machines	Automatic: repeats cycle	Self-measuring and adjusting: feedback	Computer control: automatic cognition

16. Control

Please rate the extent to which the following control devices are used to gather information about the performance of your firm:

Used rarely or for small part of operation ↓   Used frequently or throughout the firm ↓

(a) A comprehensive management control and information system (the two systems both contain data on costs, products, etc.) | 1 | 2 | 3 | 4 | 5 | 6 | 7 |

(b) Use of cost centers (i.e., aggregating and allocating cost-generating units, such as departments or factory shops) for cost control | 1 | 2 | 3 | 4 | 5 | 6 | 7 |

(c) Use of profit centers (i.e., aggregating and allocating profit-generating units, such as departments or factory shops) for cost control | 1 | 2 | 3 | 4 | 5 | 6 | 7 |

(d) Quality control of operations by using sampling and other techniques | 1 | 2 | 3 | 4 | 5 | 6 | 7 |

(e) Cost control by fixing standard costs and analyzing variations

1	2	3	4	5	6	7

(f) Formal appraisal of personnel

1	2	3	4	5	6	7

(g) Internal auditing

1	2	3	4	5	6	7

(h) Break-even analysis in making investment or pricing decisions

1	2	3	4	5	6	7

(i) Computation of present values, or internal rates of return for evaluating investments

1	2	3	4	5	6	7

(j) Control of inventories, cash, etc. and scheduling of operations by means of mathematical techniques (simulation, linear programming, etc.)

1	2	3	4	5	6	7

17. Integration/coordination

17.1. Structural liaison devices

In assuring the compatibility of decisions in one areas (e.g., marketing) with those in other areas (e.g., production), to what extent are the following integrative mechanisms used?

Used rarely   Used very frequently
↓   ↓

(a) Interdepartmental committees, set up to allow departments to engage in joint decision making

1	2	3	4	5	6	7

(b) Task forces, which are temporary bodies set up to facilitate interdepartmental collaboration on a specific project

1	2	3	4	5	6	7

(c) Liaison personnel whose specific job it is to coordinate the efforts of several departments for purposes of a specific project

1	2	3	4	5	6	7

Rare use of committees or infrequent informal collaboration   Frequent use of committees and/or informal interdepartmental collaboration
↓   ↓

(d) Product or service decisions concerning production, marketing, and R&D

1	2	3	4	5	6	7

(e) Capital budgeting decisions—the selection and financing of long-term investments

1	2	3	4	5	6	7

(f) Long-term strategies (of growth, diversification, etc.) and decisions related to changes in the firm's operating philosophy

1	2	3	4	5	6	7

17.2. Process liaison devices

In assuring the compatibility of decisions between departments (e.g., marketing and production), to what extent are the following integrative mechanisms used?

Used rarely   Used very frequently
↓   ↓

(a) Planning—so that decisions are coordinated via some master plan

1	2	3	4	5	6	7

(b) Bargaining among the heads of departments

1	2	3	4	5	6	7

(c) Each department makes decisions more or less on its own, without regard to other departments

1	2	3	4	5	6	7

There is a great deal of departmental interaction on most decisions

(d) Often there is a lack of complementarity between the decisions of different departments

1	2	3	4	5	6	7

Decisions of the different departments are mutually reinforcing

18. Shape of hierarchy

1. Number of sites: What is the number of operating sites (e.g., plants and branches) of your firm? _____
2. What is the proportion of managerial personnel to total personnel? _____%
3. How many vertical levels are there in the organization? Count the number of levels in the longest line between direct worker and the chief executive (include both levels) in the production or service function. _____
4. To what extent are you contracting out the following functions to *other companies*?

Performed entirely by *company itself* ↓   Completely contracted out ↓

(a) Production (e.g., components, etc.)

1	2	3	4	5	6	7

(b) Assembly

1	2	3	4	5	6	7

(c) Logistics/transport

1	2	3	4	5	6	7

(d) R&D

1	2	3	4	5	6	7

(e) Marketing/sales

1	2	3	4	5	6	7

(f) Worker welfare

1	2	3	4	5	6	7

(g) Human resource management

1	2	3	4	5	6	7

(h) Security

1	2	3	4	5	6	7

(i) Accounting/finance

1	2	3	4	5	6	7

(j) Information processing

1	2	3	4	5	6	7

(k) Administration

1	2	3	4	5	6	7

19. Environment

1. Please answer the following questions concerning the degree and speed of change in the industry that accounts for the largest percentage (%) of your sales (in other words, your *principal industry*). Unless otherwise stated, please circle the number in each scale that best approximates the actual conditions.

(a) Our firms rarely must change marketing practices to keep up with the market and competitors

1	2	3	4	5	6	7

Our firm must change marketing practices frequently (e.g., semiannually)

(b) The rate at which products/services are getting obsolete is very slow (e.g., basic metals like copper)

| 1 | 2 | 3 | 4 | 5 | 6 | 7 |

The rate of obsolescence is very high (e.g., fashion goods)

(c) Actions of competitors are quite easy to predict (as in some primary industries)

| 1 | 2 | 3 | 4 | 5 | 6 | 7 |

Actions of competitors are almost unpredictable (e.g., high-fashion goods)

(d) Demand and consumer tastes are fairly easy to forecast (e.g., milk companies)

| 1 | 2 | 3 | 4 | 5 | 6 | 7 |

Demand and consumer tastes are almost unpredictable (e.g., high-fashion goods)

(e) The production/service technology is not subject to very much change and is well established (e.g., steel production)

| 1 | 2 | 3 | 4 | 5 | 6 | 7 |

The modes of production/service change often in a major way (e.g., advanced electronic components)

2. What are the main constraints or bottlenecks affecting the growth of your firm? Please rate the extent to which each of the following slows your sales growth.

Not important as constraint ↓   Very great constraint on growth ↓

(a) Insufficient capital (e.g., inadequate retention of earnings, high interest rates)

| 1 | 2 | 3 | 4 | 5 | 6 | 7 |

(b) Shortage of managerial talent (e.g., to manage new ventures or to expand ventures)

| 1 | 2 | 3 | 4 | 5 | 6 | 7 |

(c) Lack of investment or growth opportunities (e.g., due to stagnant markets)

| 1 | 2 | 3 | 4 | 5 | 6 | 7 |

(d) Lack of cooperation of white-collar employees (e.g., interdepartmental squabbles, low motivation to work)

| 1 | 2 | 3 | 4 | 5 | 6 | 7 |

(e) Shortage of technical manpower (e.g., scientists, engineers, accountants, statisticians, etc.)

| 1 | 2 | 3 | 4 | 5 | 6 | 7 |

(f) Government regulations (e.g., price control, control over expansion or diversification)

| 1 | 2 | 3 | 4 | 5 | 6 | 7 |

(g) Managers' resistance to changes needed for company growth (e.g., too many tradition-bound and conservative managers)

| 1 | 2 | 3 | 4 | 5 | 6 | 7 |

(h) High inflation rate

| 1 | 2 | 3 | 4 | 5 | 6 | 7 |

(i) Labor troubles (e.g., strikes, slowdowns)

| 1 | 2 | 3 | 4 | 5 | 6 | 7 |

(j) Insufficient infrastructure (e.g., transport, electricity)

| 1 | 2 | 3 | 4 | 5 | 6 | 7 |

(k) Political instability

| 1 | 2 | 3 | 4 | 5 | 6 | 7 |

3. What effect did government legislation, regulations, or action in the following areas, have on your firm? If any item is irrelevant or had no effect, please circle 4. "Government" covers local, provincial, national, and, where relevant, supranational governments.

Very negative effect ↓   Very positive effect ↓

(a) Labor legislation covering working conditions

| 1 | 2 | 3 | 4 | 5 | 6 | 7 |

(b) Antitrust or antimonopoly regulations

1	2	3	4	5	6	7

(c) Regulations protecting the environment from industrial wastes

1	2	3	4	5	6	7

(d) Tariffs on imports/exports

1	2	3	4	5	6	7

(e) Tax relief or subsidies

1	2	3	4	5	6	7

(f) Export aid (e.g., the government provides export incentives)

1	2	3	4	5	6	7

(g) Incentives for operations in designated areas

1	2	3	4	5	6	7

(h) Special regulatory bodies or legislation for industry

1	2	3	4	5	6	7

(i) Advertising and promotion regulation

1	2	3	4	5	6	7

Appendix E. Pearson Correlation Matrices for Research Models

Table E-1 Pearson correlation matrix for organizational structure model

Variable	Mean	S.D.	1	2	3	4	5	6	7	8	9	10	11	12	13	14	15	16	17	18	19	20
1. LG10SIZE	2.15	.96	1.00																			
2. MSTECH	3.01	2.38	.47	1.00																		
3. UNCERT_1	13.38	4.15	-.14	.01	1.00																	
4. UNCERT_2	7.89	3.23	-.24	-.09	.73	1.00																
5. NACH_1	17.12	2.40	.01	-.04	.25	.29	1.00															
6. NACH_2	9.89	1.99	.04	.11	.33	.32	.48	1.00														
7. CONSTR_1	13.94	5.55	.03	.22	-.04	-.08	-.21	-.05	1.00													
8. CONSTR_2	15.15	5.63	.11	.30	-.08	-.09	-.13	.03	.70	1.00												
9. CONSTR_3	11.05	4.45	.11	.18	-.05	-.16	-.18	-.09	.63	.64	1.00											
10. RESPECT	10.93	3.16	-.06	.08	.17	.18	.00	.05	.11	.04	.01	1.00										
11. COLLECT	5.77	1.34	.03	.09	.06	.01	.20	.10	.01	.10	.05	.25	1.00									
12. GUANXI	5.87	1.20	.05	.10	.32	.11	.14	.23	.08	.00	.15	.21	.17	1.00								
13. FORMAL	11.51	5.22	.46	.38	-.09	-.12	.07	-.02	.09	.19	.14	.00	.12	.04	1.00							
14. CONTROL	44.53	11.77	.25	.39	.18	.10	.18	.14	.02	.17	.10	.24	.31	.14	.53	1.00						
15. SPEC	11.13	4.48	.46	.31	.29	.22	.29	.18	.03	.08	.06	.17	.18	.11	.46	.47	1.00					
16. CENT_1	12.76	2.94	-.19	-.11	.04	.05	.08	.22	-.14	-.14	-.11	.02	-.01	.17	-.12	-.06	-.32	1.00				
17. CENT_2	11.44	3.40	-.21	-.19	.06	.01	.01	.22	-.11	-.08	-.09	.05	-.10	.10	-.13	-.10	-.35	.69	1.00			
18. CENT_3	8.53	2.23	-.25	-.18	.07	.07	.11	.33	-.18	-.13	-.05	.00	-.01	.13	-.07	-.05	-.27	.69	.72	1.00		
19. LIASTRUC	21.73	10.33	.49	.42	-.10	-.21	-.14	-.13	.18	.21	.21	.04	.11	.10	.63	.52	.37	-.26	-.31	-.22	1.00	
20. LIASDMG	17.48	5.38	.18	.38	.11	-.05	.00	.11	-.07	-.08	.03	.14	.09	.22	.40	.47	.23	.01	.00	.00	.45	1.00

Notes: For a sample size of 124, a correlation of $\pm$ .18 is significant at the 5% level (both tails); $\pm$ .24 is significant at the 1% level.

A covariance matrix was used as input for the model.

Table E-2 Pearson correlation matrix for managerial practice model

Variable	Mean	S.D.	1	2	3	4	5	6	7	8	9	10	11	12	13	14	15	16	17	18	19	20	21
1. LG10SIZE	2.15	.96	1.00																				
2. UNCERT_1	13.38	4.15	-.14	1.00																			
3. UNCERT_2	7.89	3.23	-.24	.73	1.00																		
4. NACH_1	17.12	2.40	.01	.25	.29	1.00																	
5. NACH_2	9.89	1.99	.04	.33	.32	.48	1.00																
6. CONSTR_1	13.94	5.55	.03	-.04	-.08	-.21	-.05	1.00															
7. CONSTR_2	15.15	5.63	.11	-.08	-.09	-.13	.03	.70	1.00														
8. CONSTR_3	11.05	4.45	.11	-.05	-.16	-.18	-.09	.63	.64	1.00													
9. RESPECT	10.93	3.16	-.06	.17	.18	.00	.05	.11	.04	.01	1.00												
10. COLLECT	5.77	1.34	.03	.06	.01	.20	.10	.01	.10	.05	.25	1.00											
11. GUANXI	5.87	1.20	.05	.32	.11	.14	.23	.08	.00	.15	.21	.17	1.00										
12. OPPORT	6.20	1.01	-.07	.15	.20	.12	.13	.06	-.02	-.07	-.01	.21	.12	1.00									
13. NEWPROD	4.90	2.02	.13	.06	.21	.05	-.12	.03	.20	.10	.08	.16	-.06	.24	1.00								
14. PHODPART	4.31	2.00	.30	.02	-.09	-.03	-.02	.21	.22	.15	-.04	.06	.15	.00	.19	1.00							
15. FINPART	4.19	2.20	.32	.02	-.07	-.09	-.08	.22	.31	.23	.03	.03	.10	-.07	.20	.73	1.00						
16. STRAPART	4.38	2.19	.37	-.08	-.07	-.06	-.05	.23	.27	.19	.01	.05	-.04	.08	.18	.69	.81	1.00					
17. ADAPT	4.36	1.96	.05	.01	-.06	-.12	-.22	.12	.17	.16	.13	.04	.02	.09	.19	.14	.15	.13	1.00				
18. HORCOM	4.39	1.92	.37	-.18	-.14	.04	.09	.17	.25	.16	-.14	.16	-.03	.10	.21	.41	.38	.42	.22	1.00			
19. SUBCON_1	9.27	4.43	-.31	.19	.29	-.10	-.05	.06	-.04	-.01	.10	-.06	-.09	.11	-.10	-.16	-.05	-.11	.04	-.14	1.00		
20. SUBCON_2	8.37	4.67	-.25	.14	.19	-.04	.06	.04	.07	.01	.02	-.01	-.21	.00	.04	.01	.12	.03	-.01	.10	.69	1.00	
21. SUBCON_3	7.25	3.85	-.16	-.01	.07	-.02	-.02	.15	.23	.18	-.02	.01	-.22	-.09	.10	-.02	.06	-.04	.04	.06	.49	.63	1.00

Notes: For a sample size of 124, a correlation of $\pm$ .18 is significant at the 5% level (both tails); $\pm$ .24 is significant at the 1% level.
A covariance matrix was used as input for the model.

Table E-3 Pearson correlation matrix for effectiveness model

Variable	Mean	S.D.	1	2	3	4	5	6	7	8	9	10	11	12	13	14	15	16	17	18	19	20	21	22	23	24	25	26	27	28	29	30
1. LG10SIZE	2.15	.96	1.00																													
2. LG10SALE	7.25	1.03	.74	1.00																												
3. CONSTR_1	13.94	5.55	.03	-.08	1.00																											
4. CONSTR_2	15.15	5.63	.11	.06	.70	1.00																										
5. CONSTR_3	11.05	4.45	.11	-.02	.63	.64	1.00																									
6. REGULAT	38.70	9.00	.05	.09	-.15	-.06	-.16	1.00																								
7. FIRM_AGE	20.97	25.36	.49	.37	.11	.10	.09	.12	1.00																							
8. PRIVATE	1.49	.50	-.60	-.42	-.11	-.14	-.13	.03	-.63	1.00																						
9. INDIVID	3.65	2.47	-.61	-.46	-.02	-.08	-.07	-.08	-.82	.88	1.00																					
10. OPPORT	6.20	1.01	-.07	.02	.06	-.02	-.07	.13	.00	.03	.04	1.00																				
11. NEWPROD	4.90	2.02	.13	.14	.03	.20	.10	.06	.14	-.14	-.13	.24	1.00																			
12. CUTPRICE	4.09	1.82	-.06	.01	.13	.19	.13	-.08	-.02	.13	.19	-.14	.09	1.00																		
13. SACPROFI	3.85	1.66	-.06	.00	.13	.15	.21	-.16	-.09	.01	.07	-.16	-.01	.56	1.00																	
14. PRODPART	4.31	2.00	.30	.19	.21	.22	.15	-.06	-.24	-.21	-.24	.00	.19	.00	-.03	1.00																
15. FINPART	4.19	2.20	.32	.19	.22	.31	.23	-.02	.31	-.31	-.32	-.07	.20	-.05	.02	.73	1.00															
16. STRAPART	4.38	2.19	.37	.22	.23	.27	.19	-.04	.30	-.32	-.30	-.08	.18	-.03	.01	.69	.81	1.00														
17. PLANNING	4.85	1.88	.07	.10	.14	.24	.17	.10	.04	-.14	-.16	.20	.38	-.09	-.13	.11	.08	.07	1.00													
18. SUBCON_1	9.27	4.43	-.31	-.12	.06	-.04	-.01	.05	-.15	.14	.21	.11	-.10	.01	.08	-.16	-.05	-.11	-.07	1.00												
19. SUBCON_2	8.37	4.67	-.25	-.12	.04	.07	.01	.04	.01	-.05	-.02	.00	.04	-.08	.05	.01	.12	.03	-.01	.69	1.00											
20. SUBCON_3	7.25	3.85	-.16	-.10	.15	.23	.18	-.11	.09	.07	-.09	.10	.07	-.02	.06	-.04	.20	.09	-.07	.49	.63	1.00										
21. ABROAD	1.64	.48	.51	.49	-.08	-.03	-.03	.15	.37	-.53	-.61	.00	.21	-.10	-.08	.10	.16	.20	.09	-.20	-.08	-.10	1.00									
22. EDUCAT	4.98	1.51	.17	.20	-.18	.00	.03	.09	.08	-.25	-.28	-.04	.11	-.11	.00	.24	.38	.32	.08	.07	.10	-.01	.05	1.00								
23. FIRMTIME	124.29	130.10	.54	.41	.08	.11	.09	.06	.58	-.54	-.49	-.07	.11	.00	.04	.07	.15	.18	.05	-.03	.03	-.03	.34	.12	1.00							
24. CEO_AGE	45.05	8.35	.45	.39	.13	.16	.12	.14	.45	-.50	-.46	.01	.14	-.09	-.11	.24	.38	.32	.08	.07	.10	-.01	.36	-.04	.53	1.00						
25. STRUCTUR	3.23	1.30	.07	.07	.03	.00	.03	-.04	.02	-.12	-.08	.00	-.07	.03	.18	.02	.07	.12	-.03	-.04	-.04	-.01	.08	.00	-.01	.03	1.00					
26. PROFIT	4.44	1.43	.18	-.06	.02	-.03	.24	.18	-.03	-.12	.19	.23	-.04	.04	.14	.09	.07	.37	.05	.13	.19	.17	.11	.04	.13	.23	1.00					
27. REVENUES	4.61	1.45	.19	.27	-.05	.00	-.04	.19	.22	-.06	-.16	.17	.22	-.06	-.03	.15	.09	.14	.32	-.03	.02	.14	.20	.10	.07	.06	.12	.75	1.00			
28. MORALE	4.76	1.36	.09	.14	-.05	.00	-.07	.10	.15	-.09	-.16	.22	.18	-.19	-.04	.16	.16	.08	.22	.05	.09	.08	.09	.03	.01	.03	.02	.48	.52	1.00		
29. LIQUID	4.33	1.46	.13	.15	-.11	-.01	-.16	.15	.08	-.04	-.08	.12	.02	-.16	-.08	.14	.17	.08	.11	.08	.19	.07	.11	.01	.07	.14	.07	.46	.42	.42	1.00	
30. IMAGE	5.55	1.16	.34	.29	-.17	.06	-.13	.20	.29	-.34	-.40	.23	.22	-.02	-.09	.18	.18	.25	.27	-.11	.09	.02	.27	.10	.25	.25	-.06	.42	.46	.42	.39	1.00

Notes: For a sample size of 124, a correlation of $\pm$ .18 is significant at the 5% level (both tails); $\pm$ .24 is significant at the 1% level.
A covariance matrix was used as input for the model.

Glossary

Aston formalization   The extent to which rules, procedures, instructions, and communications are written.

Bureaucracy   A multidimensional construct for the conceptualization of organizational structure, including an organization's degree of (a) Aston formalization, (b) Aston specialization, (c) control, and (d) integration.

Centralization   The degree to which the authority to make decisions that affect the organization is located at the top of the management hierarchy.

CEO need for achievement   A CEO's degree of striving to meet standards of excellence, to accomplish difficult tasks, and to achieve success. This need for achievement represents a way of life or a basic attitude toward it, rather than a simple drive.

CEO tenure   The number of years a CEO has been working for the organization.

Chinese culture   Degree to which family loyalty, respect for seniority, collective orientation, and trust-based relationships are emphasized in the organization.

Chinese management   *see* Web-based Chinese management.

Communication style   The sending of information (a message) and its receipt (sometimes involving feedback), flowing vertically or horizontally within an organization.

Company age   The number of years a company exists.

Complexity   *see* Organizational complexity.

Constraints   Factors in an organization's task environment that limit its access to resources.

Control   *see* Management control.

Coordination   The design of integrative systems to move the different activities in the value chain together toward a common goal (*see* Liaison).

Corporate culture   A set of shared beliefs and values, precedents, expectations, stories, routines, and procedures in a firm that help define its way of doing things, and serve as a behavioral guide for those within the firm.

Corporate strategy   The determination of the basic purpose and long-term objectives of the enterprise, as well as the adoption of courses of action and the allocation of resources for carrying out these goals.

Decision-making style (or process)   The procedure employed by an organization to define its purpose and objectives, to design programs of action, and to allocate resources to realize them. It involves the thinking associated with a sequence of choices as well as the choices themselves.

Environmental uncertainty   The degree of change and unpredictability of demand, customer tastes, competitive behavior, technology, product obsolescence, and supply.

Fit   A match between contextual and organizational factors that leads to an increase in performance.

Formalization   *see* Structuring of activities.

Functional specialization   The distribution of official duties among a number of positions. It is measured by the number of discrete, identifiable functions performed by at least one full-time specialist, who performs that function and no other.

Government support   Government action that has a positive impact on the organization.

Horizontal span of control   *see* Lateral span of control.

Hierarchy   (1) An arrangement of authority in which each person has only one boss and the organization has a single top officer. (2) A system of ranking employees.

Horizontal communication   The lateral flow of information across departments.

Horizontal integration   Expansion of a firm by acquisition of or merger with competitors, or into a related activity that does not involve vertical integration.

Integration   *see* Liaison.

Interdepartmental (standing) committees   Relatively *stable* (interdepartmental) bodies set up to allow departments to engage in regular joint decision making.

Lateral (horizontal) span of control   The number of subordinates that report to one executive, or the ratio of subordinates to first-line supervisor.

Leadership   The ability, based on the personal qualities and behavior of the leader, to pattern the behavior of a group and thus to elicit the followers' voluntary compliance and energy in a broad range of matters.

Leadership style   The approach used by a leader to pattern the behavior of a group and to elicit the followers' voluntary compliance and energy in a broad range of matters.

Liaison   The integration of organizational activities through Structural integrative devices and Processual integrative devices.

Liaison personnel   Managers who coordinate the efforts of several departments (or other organizational units) for a specific project.

Management control   Planning, coordinating, monitoring, and providing feedback about progress in achieving the purpose and objectives of the organization.

Management model (or style)   The contextual, structural, and managerial choices of a company.

Mass production   The large-scale fabrication of standard items.

National culture   Set of values and beliefs held by the members of a nation.

Organization   Collectivity oriented to the pursuit of specific purposes and objectives, and exhibiting formalized social structures.

Organizational complexity   A multidimensional construct comprising (a) vertical span of control, (b) lateral span of control, and (c) spatial dispersion (i.e., number of operating sites).

Organizational effectiveness   The degree to which an organization achieves its stated purpose and objectives.

Organizational efficiency   The productivity with which inputs are transformed into outputs.

Organizational performance   see Organizational effectiveness.

Organizational structure   The distribution of people among social positions.

Ownership structure   The distribution of shares of an organization.

Processual integrative devices   Processes such as planning and bargaining that promote interaction between departments (or other organizational units) and ensure the compatibility and synergy of decisions.

Role specialization   The degree to which specialist roles exist within functional areas. It is measured by the specificity and narrowness of the tasks assigned to any particular role performed by an individual.

Size   The number of full-time employees of an organization.

Specialization   The degree to which an organization's activities are divided into specialist roles; total degree of Functional specialization and Role specialization.

Standardization   The extent to which there are rules or definitions that purport to cover all circumstances and that apply invariably.

Strategic orientation   A company's resource deployment pattern used to achieve its stated purpose and objectives.

Structural integrative devices   Structures such as Interdepartmental committees, Task forces, and Liaison personnel that promote interaction between departments (or other organizational units) and ensure the compatibility and synergy of decisions

Structuring of activities   The degree to which the desired behavior of employees is overtly defined.

Subcontracting   The outsourcing of certain activities of the value chain to other organizations, in the pursuit of objectives such as focusing on core competencies, increasing flexibility, and reducing costs.

Task environment   The collectivity of external individuals, groups, and organizations that are linked to a focal organization and influence it. That part of the total environment of management which is potentially relevant to the setting and attainment of the focal organization's purpose and objectives.

Task force   Temporary body set up to facilitate the collaboration between departments (or other organizational units) on a specific project.

Technology   The means or processes used to transform inputs into outputs.

Vertical communication   The flow of information up or down the hierarchy in an organization.

Vertical integration   Uniting two or more stages in the value chain under common ownership and management.

Vertical span of control   Number of job positions between the chief executive and the employees working directly on the output (including both levels).

Web-based Chinese management (WCM)   A particular way of establishing purpose and objectives and leading resources toward their achievement, practiced by private Chinese firms in mainland China and overseas. It is characterized by (a) a high degree of centralization, (b) a low degree of bureaucracy, (c) strong entrepreneurship, (d) extensive enterprise networks, (e) emphasis on traditional Chinese family-based cultural values, and (f) choice of small organizational size.

Notes

1. Recent excavations have uncovered a piece of jade that probably dates back more than five thousand years and is a sign of an early civilization in China. It might have been used in ritual ceremonies. Zhang Jingguo, the senior archaelogist who led the project in Lingjiatan, a village in Hanshan County, in eastern China's Anhui Province, stated: "I can find no word to describe how far the ancient Chinese went in their search for beauty and perfection" (Xing 1999, p. 9).

2. "Management model" is synonymous with "organizational design," which denotes macrolevel organizational properties. Daft and Lewin (1990, p. 3), for example, mentioned the following aspects in their definition of organizational design: the organization's formal architecture, culture, decision-making norms, ethics, structure of employment relationships, and strategy. The distinctive elements included in this study will be discussed in chapter 2.

3. The word "mandarin" was originally given to the native officials in Macao by the Portuguese and is of Portuguese origin (*mandar* means "to command").

4. Mainstream economists would confidently state that all these "soft" issues had nothing to do with the decline. They would argue that economic factors caused the collapse. Although there were some structural problems, the obvious splendor of the late Song dynasty make it difficult to defend such a view point.

5. Contingency theory states that there is no "one best way" of structuring activities. Structural choices have to fit different contingencies in the internal and external environments. For example, a large organization, ceteris paribus, needs more formal bureaucratic controls than a small firm in order to succeed.

6. Liu Shaoqui, China's nominal head of state (*guojia zhuxi*), was removed during the Cultural Revolution.

7. Official statistics in China tend to overstate FDI, since they include foreign debt that is disguised as foreign investment and money from "round-tripping." This denotes the practice of mainland Chinese companies investing in China from a newly established base in Hong Kong to secure privileges granted only to foreign-funded enterprises.

8. The Chinese call themselves "descendants of the dragons" (*long de chuangren*).

9. Since "strategic choice" is difficult to model, and may be to some extent random, I assume that part of the unexplained variation in structure and management results from strategic choice. I will formally model the influence of the CEO's personality, his motivation, and objectives as need for achievement.

10. The few cases (11.3% of total sample) that officially were registered as joint ventures (see company questionnaire, appendix D, section 2.7, item c) were completely controlled by Chinese owners and managers. The "foreign" share usually was made up by passive investments from overseas Chinese or the capital of the Chinese owners that "round-tripped" from Hong Kong to secure the privileged treatment that joint ventures obtain on the mainland.

11. Although no systematic differences between respondents and nonrespondents could be detected with respect to company size, location, ownership mode, industry, and reason for refusal, it can never be stated with absolute certainty that there were no differences of any importance.

12. Following common usage (see Gupta 1988; Lewin and Stephens 1994, p. 208), I use the term CEO throughout the book. It includes general managers who might have other official job titles (e.g., plant manager).

13. A latent construct is an unobserved phenomenon (such as intelligence), whose existence can be deduced from certain indicators (such as verbal ability).

CHAPTER 2

1. Strictly speaking, cross-sectional studies like this do not allow for definite conclusions on causality. Subsequent longitudinal studies will be necessary to confirm the hypothesized causal relationships. In addition, social science models involve voluntaristic human beings (Burrell and Morgan 1979, p. 6) whose behavior is never completely *determined* by influencing factors that operate in a stable, mechanistic, and predictable manner.

2. Deng Xiaoping, commenting on the nature of socialism, once said that it does not matter "whether the cat is black or white; as long as it can catch mice, it's a good cat."

3. Social capital here is defined as a "set of resources rooted in relationships" (Nahapiet and Ghoshal 1998, p. 243). They are valuable for conducting social affairs.

4. Boisot and Child (1996) called this phenomenon "network capitalism."

5. Besides Hong Kong, Taiwan, and Singapore, I include Eastern countries that have Chinese ethnic enclaves, such as Malaysia, Thailand, Indonesia, and the Philippines, and Western countries with Chinese communities, such as the United States, as areas with free Chinese capitalism.

6. The failure to move from family management to professional management contrasts sharply with the development of American companies, which also often started as family firms, but then moved to professional management (Chandler 1984).

7. The defensive behavior of state enterprises is not attributable to government constraints. Actually, the government would prefer state enterprises *not* to lay off people.

8. In other countries, many firms in the private sector were also small

and owned by families at the beginning but eventually grew. In contrast, because of the importance of traditional cultural values (as seen in overseas Chinese businesses), most small firms in China are less likely to grow considerably in subsequent periods. Instead, they prefer to "proliferate." In Hong Kong, the size of private firms actually *decreased* at times (Hickson and Pugh 1995, p. 170). There is no comparable long-term data for the P.R.C., since private firms have re-emerged comparatively recently and have been neglected by researchers. Instead of analyzing time series, this book adopts a cross-sectional research design. A subsequent longitudinal study needs to provide the final proof for my prediction that the average size of private enterprises in mainland China will not grow dramatically, and that the private sector as a whole nevertheless will increase significantly owing to the proliferating dynamic networks.

CHAPTER 3

1. In the graphs, the value ranges of the scales have been limited to the actual scores, such as a minimum of 40 and a maximum of 80 for figure 3-1 and other ranges for subsequent graphs. This highlights the differences and avoids unnecessary empty space.

2. "Structuring of activities" is the degree to which the intended behavior of employees is overtly defined (Pugh et al. 1968, pp. 85–86).

3. A latent construct is an unobserved phenomenon (such as intelligence), whose existence can be deduced from certain indicators (such as verbal ability).

4. Because of the skewed distribution of size, which is common in most orgnizational research (see McMillan et al. 1973), I used log10 of size as input for the mean difference tests and the subsequent structural equation analysis.

5. Company names have been changed for confidentiality reasons.

6. Confucius is called Kong Zi in Chinese. Mr. Kong thus has the same surname (Kong) as Confucius.

CHAPTER 4

1. The term "formalization" is used here to follow the terminology of previous researchers (Hall 1991, p. 65; Van de Ven 1976). This generic concept combines role formalization together with other dimensions, specialization, and standardization.

2. A relationship is *spurious* when two variables seem to be related only because both are caused by one or more extraneous third variables. The effect of these third variables is similiar to a force that pulls two buckets of water on two separate strings upwards. The movement of one bucket is not caused by the other one. For example, the number of fire engines and average fire damage may be strongly positively related, suggesting that fire engines cause the damage. But if the size of the fire is held constant (called partialled out) by analyzing only fires of a fixed size (such as the subgroup of medium size fires), the original relation may disappear. In an *intervening* relationship, two variables are correlated, because the first variable causes another extraneous (intervening) variable that affects the second variable. For example, company size may be positively correlated with conflicts only because large companies tend to be more diverse, which increases the likelihood of conflict. Apart from producing the appearance of correlation, third

variables may suppress or distort true relationships between two other variables. These accidental relationships arise only when a model does not include a potent confounding variable. To detect true relationships, the researcher may use partial correlation analysis for simple cases involving only two variables and multivariate regression or SEM for a larger number of variables.

3. For comparisons between baseline models and *nested* models, the chi-square difference statistic ($\Delta\chi^2$) with degrees of freedom (*df*) equal to the difference in *df* between the two models, tests the null hypothesis of no significant difference in fit between the two models. Significant chi-square difference statistics ($p<.05$) imply rejection of the more constrained model and demonstrate that a path is statistically significant.

4. In the absence of longitudinal data, we can never prove causality. The influence may flow in the opposite direction. For example, larger companies may value culture less. However, because of the strong theoretical basis, I favor the explanation that culture influences contextual and organizational properties.

CHAPTER 5

1. All findings apply to the total sample of private and state enterprises. The model holds all other factors constant, including private family-based ownership.

2. Different strategies (and other factors) may affect the individual *dimensions* of performance differently (Galbraith and Schendel 1983; Hambrick 1983). For example, price cutting may increase revenues, but undermine profitability, liquidity, morale, and image. Subsequent studies should refine the insights from this book by analyzing differential performance effects.

3. The two samples, strictly speaking, are representative only of the two cities. Extensions to comparisons between the north and south are only tentative.

4. I ignore statistically significant differences when coefficients are insignificant in *both* subgroups, which applies to proactive strategy. But I comment on factors when at least one coefficient is statistically significant. The discussion of statistically insignificant coefficients is tentative and exploratory.

5. If equity were higher (as in many sectors outside the finance industry), economic value would be even lower. The same returns would be spread over a larger equity base and the resulting lower return on equity ratio would be reduced by higher costs of capital.

CHAPTER 6

1. The market works so well for commodity markets because they closely match the radical assumptions of perfect competition, such as an unlimited number of buyers and sellers, no barriers to entry, and perfect information. Most other areas in the economy do not even approximate these requirements. In my view, the essence of strategy is to *avoid* competition by creating monopoly advantages that make the market inefficient and thus create economic rents. With strong brands, control over distribution, and other barriers to entry, the lessons derived from market economics do not apply at all. Since in these cases, the market is not an efficient mechanism for allocating

resources, strategic leadership by the state will be required. Ideological dogmatists, who praise the market as the best economic model available, often try to disguise this situational ineffectiveness of the market.

2. Lao Zi is the legendary founder of Taoism and the traditional author of its most sacred scripture, *Yi Jing* (*The Book of Changes*).

3. To use modern terminology, tacit, activity-based embodied knowledge and thinking-based embrained knowledge was transformed into explicit embedded knowledge contained in rules, procedures, and technologies.

4. This study did not examine the management of private rural enterprises, such as township and village enterprises (TVEs), which may differ from this model.

5. Quoted in Gilder (1992, p. 145).

6. The main task of expert consultants is to invent completely new, customized products and services for a client company, which later manufactures and commercializes these inventions (Robertson and Swan 1998).

CHAPTER 7

1. In all empirical studies that use interviews, there are potentially other sources of respondent bias that, however, can be controlled to some degree. Strategies for reducing such bias used in this study include: standardized questionnaires, the promise of confidentiality and anonymity, simple questions asking for information that can be objectively verified, and the triangulation of responses with other evidence.

2. Best practice should be understood as an evolving portfolio of effective management approaches. If it is perceived as the final word on how to do business, it generates closure around the knowledge base and can become a major obstacle to innovation (Scarbrough 1995).

3. The key success factors for Western companies might be discussed at an even more detailed level. One example would be concrete strategies for entering or operating in China. Such issues might include the selection of the right joint-venture partner and the management of strategic alliances. Here, I am concerned primarily with general strategic principles that will guide and inform these kinds of decisions. A subsequent work might deal with these detailed operational questions.

4. Large companies, *because of their size*, can not dispense with sophisticated control and coordination devices, especially when they lack strong values. These devices are functional—contrary to what many management revolutionaries are claiming. The deep problem thus is not the control and coordination system, but the large company size that requires these stifling organizational arrangements. Apart from decreasing size, the *type* of control can be changed.

5. Proactive strategy, despite its large coefficient, was not statistically significant.

CHAPTER 8

1. This and the following citations were found in Ruskin (1985).

2. Even though the style is called Gothic, it was not invented by the Goths. The term originally described the "savageness" of buildings belonging to this architectural style. They reminded people of Gothic wildness, contrasting with the more regular shapes of other schools.

3. OEM is the process whereby a company manufactures products for another business that designs and markets them. The OEM manufacturer often leverages their customer's strengths which add high value, such as a strong R&D capacity, an established brand name, and a powerful distribution network. They are engaged by many Western companies to benefit from the comparatively low labor costs in Asia and other developing countries.

4. For later generations who read this book, I should explain that Christo is an "artist" who specializes in wrapping up large objects, such as the Reichstag in Berlin. His name will probably not survive long.

APPENDIX A

1. Miller and Droege's (1986) uncertainty scale synthesizes scales used in earlier studies (Khandwalla 1974, 1977; D. Miller 1983).

2. Because knowledgeable and articulate informants do calculations and summaries for the researcher, they are considered to be representative of all members of the organization but, in terms of sampling, do not have to represent all members (Seidler 1974).

3. Seidler (1974) recommended two to five informants, but suggested that fewer informants are needed when informants are known to be objective and questions do not produce bias. Simonin (1997) is an example of a successful study that focused on one informant (p. 1169). In the People's Republic of China, Tan and Litschert (1994, p. 8) found that the responses from two executives had high interrater reliability (between .7 and .9).

APPENDIX B

1. I changed the names of all companies and individuals, since I promised anonymity and confidentiality. The private enterprises in particular worried about the disclosure of commercially sensitive information. Because of bad experiences in the past, they attempt to guard against unexpected repercussions from state officials. Those may misuse the information, for example, by extorting fees on the basis of high reported profits.

APPENDIX C

1. The convention is followed that $\bar{x}$ and s denote sample *statistics*, whereas μ and σ denote population *parameters*.

Bibliography

Adler, Nancy J., Nigel Campbell, and Andre Laurent. 1989. "In Search of Appropriate Methodology: From Outside the People's Republic of China Looking In." *Journal of International Business Studies* 20:61–74.

Alston, Jon P. 1989. "Wa, Guanxi, and Inhwa: Managerial Principles in Japan, China and Korea." *Business Horizons* 32:26–31.

Ambler, T. 1994. "Marketing's Third Paradigm: Guanxi." *Business Strategy Review* 5:69–80.

Ansoff, Igor, et al. 1970. "Does Planning Pay? The Effect of Planning on Success of Acquisitions in American Firms." *Long-Range Planning* (December).

Arbuckle, J. L. 1989. "AMOS: Analysis of Moment Structures." *American Statistician* 43:66–67.

Arbuckle, James L. 1997. *AMOS User's Guide Version 3.6*. Chicago: SmallWaters.

Argyris, Chris. 1957. *Personality and Organization*. New York: Harper Row.

Baird, I. S., M. A. Lyles, and R. Wharton. 1990. "Attitudinal Differences Between American and Chinese Managers Regarding Joint Venture Management." *Management International Review* Spec. Iss. 30:53–68.

Baker, Hugh. 1979. *Chinese Family and Kinship*. New York: Columbia University Press.

Ballweg, John A. 1969. "Husband–Wife Response Similarities on Evaluative and Non-evaluative Survey Questions." *Public Opinion Quarterly* 33:249–254.

Barton, C. A. 1983. "Trust and Credit: Some Observations Regarding Business Strategies of Overseas Chinese Traders in Vietnam." In *The Chinese in Southeast Asia*, Vol. 1, *Ethnicity and Economic Activity*, edited by L. Y. L. Lim and L. A. P. Gosling, pp. 46–64. Singapore: Maruzen Asia.

Berger, Peter. 1994. "Our Economic Culture." In *The Cultural Context of Economics and Politics*, edited by T. William Boxx and Gary M. Quinlivan. Lanham, Md.: University Press of America.

Beyer, Janice M., and Harrison Trice. 1979. "A Reexamination of the Relations Between Size and Various Components of Organizational Complexity." *Administrative Science Quarterly* 24:48–64.

Birch, Cyril. 1968. *Stories from a Ming Collection: The Art of the Chinese Story-Teller*. New York: Grove Press.

Blackler, F. 1995. "Knowledge, Knowledge Work and Organizations: An Overview and Interpretation." *Organization Studies* 16:1021–1046.

Blau, Peter M. 1974. *On the Nature of Organizations*. New York: John Wiley.

Blau, Peter M., and Richard A. Schoenherr. 1971. *The Structure of Organizations*. New York: Basic Books.

Boisot, Max, and John Child. 1996. "From Fiefs to Clans and Network Capitalism: Explaining China's Emerging Economic Order." *Administrative Science Quarterly* 41:600–628.

Boisot, Max, and Xing Guo Liang. 1992. "The Nature of Managerial Work in the Chinese Enterprise Reforms. A Study of Six Directors." *Organization Studies* 13:161–184.

Bond, Michael H., and P. W. H. Lee. 1981. "Face Saving in Chinese Culture: A Discussion and Experimental Study of Hong Kong Students." In *Social Life and Development in Hong Kong,* edited by Rance P. L. Lee and A. Y. C. King, pp. 289–304. Hong Kong: Chinese University Press.

Brislin, Richard W., Walter J. Lonner, and Robert M. Thorndike. 1973. *Cross-Cultural Research Methods*. New York: John Wiley & Sons.

Brown, Donna. 1989. "Race for the Corporate Throne." *Management Review* 78:26–27.

Brusco, S. 1982. "The Emilian Model: Productive Decentralization and Social Integration." *Cambridge Journal of Economics* 6:167–184.

Burrell, Gibson and Gareth Morgan. 1979. Sociological Paradigms and Organizational Analysis: Elements of the Sociology of Corporate Life. Aldershot, Hants, England: Ashgate Publishing.

Cai, Peng Hong. 1997. "Chinese Family Enterprises." *Wenhui Bao*, October 15. (Overseas Observation section; in Chinese).

Carmines, E. G., and J. P. Mclver. 1981. "Analyzing Models with Unobserved Variables." In *Social Measurement: Current Issues*, edited by G. W. Bohrnstedt and E. F. Borgatta. Beverly Hills, Calif.: Sage.

Chan, Adrian. 1996. "Confucianism and Development in East Asia." *Journal of Contemporary Asia* 26:28–45.

Chan, Wellington K. K. 1977. *Merchants, Mandarins, and Modern Enterprise in Late Ch'ing China*. Cambridge: East Asian Research Center.

Chan, Wellington K. K. 1982. "The Organizational Structure of the Traditional Chinese Firm and Its Modern Reform." *Business History Review* 56: 218–235.

Chandler, Alfred D. 1962. *Strategy and Structure: Chapters in the History of the American Industrial Enterprise*. Cambridge, Mass.: MIT Press.

Chandler, Alfred D. 1984. "The Emergence of Managerial Capitalism." *Business History Review* 58:473–503.

Chen, M., ed. 1995. *Asian Management Systems*. London: Routledge.

Chia, Robert, and Ian W. King. 1998. "The Organizational Structuring of Novelty." *Organization* 5:461–478.

Child, John 1972a. Organization structure and strategies of control: a replication of the Aston study. *Administrative Science Quarterly, 17*(2), 163–177.

Child, John. 1972b. "Organizational Structure, Environment and Performance: The Role of Strategic Choice." *Sociology* 6:1–22.

Child, John. 1994. *Management in China During the Age of Reform*. Cambridge: Cambridge University Press.

Child, John, and Yuan Lu. 1990. "Industrial Decision-making Under China's Reform 1985–1988." *Organization Studies* 11:321–351.

China Statistical Press. 1997. *China Foreign Economic Statistical Yearbook*. Beijing: China Statistical Press.

Chu, G. C., and Y. Ju. 1993. *The Great Wall in Ruins: Communication and Cultural Change in China.* Albany: State University of New York Press.

Churchill, Gilbert A., Jr. 1979. "A Paradigm for Developing Better Measures of Marketing Constructs." *Journal of Marketing Research* 16:64–73.

Churchill, Gilbert A., Jr., and J. Paul Peter. 1984. "Research Design Effects on the Reliability of Rating Scales: A Meta-analysis." *Journal of Marketing Research* 21:360–375.

Clad, J. 1989. *Behind the Myth: Business, Politics and Power in Southeast Asia.* London: Unwin Hyman.

Clark, R. 1979. *The Japanese Company.* New Haven, Conn.: Yale University Press.

Clayre, Alasdair. 1984. *The Heart of the Dragon.* London: Collins.

Cohen, Daniel. 1990. "The Fall of the House of Wang." *Business Week* 135: 22–31.

Connell, James P. 1987. "Structural Equation Modeling and the Study of Child Development: A Question of Goodness of Fit." *Child Development* 58: 167–175.

Cook, E. T., and Alexander Wedderburn, eds. 1903–1912. *The Library Edition of the Works of John Ruskin.* London: George Allen.

Daft, R. L., and A. Y. Lewin. 1990. "Can Organization Studies Begin to Break Out of the Normal Science Straitjacket? An Editorial Essay." *Organization Science* 1:1–19.

Dalton, Gregory R. 1990. "Training China's Business Elite." *China Business Review* 17:46–48.

Davies, H. 1995. "Interpreting Guanxi: The Role of Personal Connections in a High Context Transitional Economy." In *China Business: Context & Issues,* edited by H. Davies, pp. 155–169. Hong Kong: Longman Asia.

Davis, Anne S. 1997. "Handling Uncertainty: Do Managers in the People's Republic of China, the US, and the UK Differ?" *Academy of Management Executive* 11:121–122.

Economist, 1999. "Infatuations End." *The Economist.* 9/25/99.

Economist. 1998. "Overdosed—Pharmaceuticals in China." *The Economist,* 11/17/98, pp. 71–72.

European Foundation for Management Development (ECAM). 1986. *Chinese Culture and Management.* Brussels: ECAM.

Fama, E. F., and M. C. Jensen. 1983. "Separation of Ownership and Control." *Journal of Law and Economics* 26: 301–326.

Far Eastern Economic Review. 1997. "Review 200: Asia's Leading Companies." *Far Eastern Economic Review* 43–98.

Feuerwerker, Albert. 1958. *China's Early Industrialization: Sheng Hsuan-huai and Mandarin Enterprise.* Cambridge, Mass.: Harvard University Press.

Feuerwerker, Albert. 1969. *The Chinese Economy ca. 1870–1911.* Ann Arbor: University of Michigan Press.

Fitzgerald, C. P. 1986. *China: A Short Cultural History.* Bungay, U.K.: Richard Clay.

Forney, Matt. 1996. "Trials by Fire." *Far Eastern Economic Review* 62–69.

Freedman, Maurice. 1971. *Chinese Lineage and Society: Fukien and Kwangtung.* London: Athlone Press.

Freedman, Maurice. 1979. *The Study of Chinese Society.* Stanford, Calif.: Stanford University Press.

Fukuda, John. 1989. "China's Management: Tradition and Reform." *Management Decision* 27: 45–49.

Fukuyama, Francis. 1995. *Trust: The Social Virtues and the Creation of Prosperity.* Harmondsworth, U.K.: Hamish Hamilton/Penguin.

Galbraith, C., and D. Schendel. 1983. "An Empirical Analysis of Strategy Types." *Strategic Management Journal* 4:153–173.

Gao, Shangquan, and Fulin Chi (eds.) 1996. *The Development of China's Nongovernmentally and Privately Operated Economy*. Beijing: Foreign Languages Press.

Gernet, Jacques. 1962. *Daily Life in China on the Eve of the Mongol Invasion 1250–1276*. Stanford, Calif.: Stanford University Press.

Gilder, George. 1992. *Recapturing the Spirit of Enterprise*. San Francisco: ICS Press.

Gillespie, David F., and S. Mileti. 1981. "Heterogeneous Samples in Organizational Research." *Sociological Methods & Research* 9:375–388.

Goffman, E. 1961. *Asylums*. London: Penguin.

Goodman, P. S., R. S. Atkin, and F. D. Schoorman, eds. 1983. *On the Demise of Organizational Effectiveness Studies*. New York: Academic Press.

Greenhalgh, Susan. 1990. "Land Reform and Family Entrepreneurialism in East Asia." In *Rural Development and Population: Institutions and Policies*, edited by G. McNicoll and Mead Cain. New York: Oxford University Press.

Gupta, A. K. 1988. "Contingency Perspectives in Strategic Leadership." In *The Executive Effect: Concepts and Methods for Studying Top Managers*, edited by D. C. Hambrick, pp. 141–178. Greenwich, Conn.: JAI Press.

Hall, R. H., and Weiman Xu. 1990. "Research Note: Run Silent, Run Deep—Cultural Influences on Organizations in the Far East." *Organization Studies* 11:569–576.

Hall, Richard H. 1991. *Organizations: Structures, Processes, and Outcomes*. Englewood Cliffs, N.J.: Prentice-Hall.

Hambrick, D. C. 1983. "Some Tests of the Effectiveness and Functional Attributes of Miles and Snow's Strategic Types." *Academy of Management Journal* 26:5–26.

Hamilton, Gary L., and Nicole Biggart Woolsey. 1988. "Market, Culture, and Authority: A Comparative Analysis of Management and Organization in the Far East." *American Journal of Sociology* 94:S52–S94.

Harding, James. 1998a. "Europe 'Overestimated' China's Market." *Financial Times*, 2/16/98. p. 2.

Harding, James. 1998b. "Plumbed in to Success." *Financial Times*, 3/20/98. p. 14.

Hareven, Tamara. 1987. "Reflections on Family Research in the People's Republic of China." *Social Research* 54:663–689.

Harrel, Stevan. 1985. "Why Do the Chinese Work So Hard? Reflections on an Entrepreneurial Ethic." *Modern China* 11:203–226.

Harrison, Graeme. 1994. "Culture and Management." *Australian Accountant* 64:14–22.

Helburn, I. B., and J. C. Shearer. 1984. "Human Resources and Industrial Relations in China: A Time of Ferment." *Industrial and Labour Relations Review* 38:3–15.

Heller, Robert. 1991. "How the Chinese Manage to Keep It All in the Family." *Management Today* (November):31–34.

Herold, David, Stanley Thune, and Robert House. 1972. "Long Range Planning and Organizational Performance." *Academy of Management Journal* 15:91–104.

Hicks, George L., and S. Gordon Redding, eds. 1982. *Culture and Corporate Performance in the Philippines: The Chinese Puzzle*. Manila: Philippines Institute for Development Studies.

Hickson, David J., and Derek S. Pugh. 1995. *Management Worldwide: The Impact of Societal Culture on Organizations Around the Globe*. London: Penguin Books.

Hinings, C. R. 1979. "Continuities in the Study of Organizations: Churches and Local Government." In *Organizations Alike and Unlike*, edited by C. J. Lammers and D. J. Hickson. London: Routledge.

Ho, David Yau-fai. 1976. "On the Concept of Face." *American Journal of Sociology* 81:867–884.

Hofstede, Geert. 1980. *Culture's Consequences: International Differences in Work-related Values*. Beverly Hills, Calif.: Sage.

Hofstede, Geert, and Michael Harris Bond. 1988. "The Confucius Connection: From Cultural Roots to Economic Growth." *Organizational Dynamics* 16: 4–21.

Hsu, Francis. 1967. *Under the Ancestor's Shadow: Kinship, Personality, and Social Mobility in Village China*. Garden City, N.Y.: Anchor Books.

Hu, Hsien-chin. 1944. "The Chinese Concepts of Face." *American Anthropologist* 46:45–64.

Huber, G. P. 1991. "Organizational Learning: The Contributing Processes and the Literature." *Organization Science* 2:88–115.

Hunt, R. G., and G. Yang. 1990. "Decision Making and Power Relations in the Chinese Enterprise: Managers and Party Secretaries." In *Advances in Chinese Industrial Studies: Reform Policy and the Chinese Enterprise*, edited by J. Child and M. Lockett, pp. 227–245. Greenwich, Conn.: JAI Press.

Hwang, K. K. 1987. "Face and Favor: The Chinese Power Game." *American Journal of Sociology* 92:944–974.

Hyman, Herbert H., Gene N. Levine, and Charles R. Wright. 1967. "Studying Expert Informants by Survey Methods: A Cross-national Inquiry." *Public Opinion Quarterly* 31:9–26.

Ibarra, H. 1993. "Network Centrality, Power, and Innovation Involvement: Determinants of Technical and Administrative Roles." *Academy of Management Journal* 36:471–501.

Inkson, J. H. K., Derek S. Pugh, and David J. Hickson. 1970. "Organizational Context and Structure: An Abbreviated Replication." *Administrative Science Quarterly* 15:318–329.

Jackson, Sukhan. 1992. *Chinese Enterprise Management Reforms in Economic Perspective*. Berlin and New York: De Gruyter.

Jacobs, J. B. 1979. "A Preliminary Model of Particularistic Ties in Chinese Political Alliances: Kan-ch'ing and Kuan-hsi in a Rural Taiwanese Township." *China Quarterly* 78:237–273.

Jenner, W. J. F. 1992. *The Tyranny of History*. London: Allen Lane/Penguin.

Jensen, Michael C., and William H. Meckling. 1976. "Theory of the Firm: Managerial Behavior, Agency Costs and Ownership Structure." *Journal of Financial Economics* 3:305–360.

Ji, Kang. 1993. *Directory of Enterprises and Institutions*. Beijing: Kai Ming Publishing House.

Johnson, Mike. 1996. "China: The Last True Business Frontier." *Management Review* 85:39–43.

Judge, William Q., Jr. 1994. "Correlates of Organizational Effectiveness: A Multilevel Analysis of a Multidimensional Outcome." *Journal of Business Ethics* 13:1–10.

Kao, John. 1993. "The Worldwide Web of Chinese Business." *Harvard Business Review* 71:24–34.

Kelley, R. 1990. *The Gold-Collar Worker: Harnessing the Brainpower of the New Work Force.* Reading Mass.: Addison-Wesley.

Kenney, Charles C. 1992. "Fall of the House of Wang." *Computerworld* 26:67–69.

Khandwalla, Pradip N. 1974. "Mass Output Orientation of Operations Technology and Organizational Structure." *Administrative Science Quarterly* 19:74–97.

Khandwalla, Pradip N. 1977. *The Design of Organizations.* New York: Harcourt Brace Jovanovich.

Kogut, B., and U. Zander. 1992. "Knowledge of the Firm, Combinative Capabilities, and the Replication of Technology." *Organization Science* 3:383–397.

Komroff, Manuel, ed. 1926. *The Travels of Marco Polo (The Venetian).* New York: Garden City Publishing.

Kraus, Willy. 1991. *Private Business in China: Revival Between Ideology and Pragmatism.* Honolulu: University of Hawaii Press.

Krone, Kathleen, Mary Garrett, and Ling Chen. 1992. "Managerial Communication Practices in Chinese Factories: A Preliminary Investigation." *Journal of Business Communication.* 29:229–252.

Kuhn, Thomas S. 1970. *The Structure of Scientific Revolutions.* Chicago: University of Chicago Press.

Laaksonen, O. 1988. *Management in China During and After Mao in Enterprises, Government, and Party.* Berlin and New York: Walter de Gruyter.

Lambert, P. 1982. "Selecting Japanese Management Practices for Import." *Personnel Management* 14:38–41.

Lazerson, M. 1995. "A New Phoenix? Modern Putting-out in the Modena Knitwear Industry." *Administrative Science Quarterly* 40:34–59.

Lee, Jean. 1996. "Culture and Management: A Study of Small Chinese Family Business in Singapore." *Journal of Small Business Management* 34:63–67.

Lee, Shu-Ching. 1953. "China's Traditional Family, Its Characteristics and Disintegration." *American Sociological Review* 18:272–280.

Leung, Frankie Fook-Lun. 1995. "Overseas Chinese Management: Myths and Realities." *East Asian Executive Reports* 17:6–13.

Levy, Marion J. 1949a. *The Family Revolution in Modern China.* Cambridge; Mass.: Harvard University Press.

Levy, Marion J. 1949b. *The Rise of the Modern Chinese Business Class.* New York: Institute of Pacific Relations.

Lewin, Arie Y., and Carroll U. Stephens. 1994. "CEO Attitudes as Determinants of Organization Design: An Integrated Model." *Organization Studies* 15:183–212.

Likert, R. 1961. *New Patterns of Management.* New York: McGraw-Hill.

Lin, Yu-tang. 1977. *My Country and My People.* Hong Kong: Heinemann.

Lindblom, Charles. 1959. "The Science of 'Muddling Through.' " *Public Administration Review* 19:79–88.

Lintner, John. 1965. "The Valuation of Risk Assets and the Selection of Risky Investments in Stock Portfolios and Capital Budgets." *Review of Economics and Statistics* 47:13–37.

Littlefield, David. 1996. "A Chinese Puzzle for Employers." *People Management* 2:8.

Lockett, Martin. 1988. "Culture and the Problem of Chinese Management." *Organization Studies* 9:475–496.

Lui, Alice Y. L. 1996. "Trends in International Business Thought and Literature: Parallels Between the East and the West. The Teachings of Ancient Chinese Philosophers and the Echoes from Western Management Theorists." *International Executive* 38:389–401.

Mackie, J. A. C. 1992. "Overseas Chinese Entrepreneurship." *Asian–Pacific Economic Literature* 6:41–64.

Mayo, Elton. 1933. *The Human Problems of an Industrial Civilization.* New York: Macmillan.

McClelland, David C. 1961. *The Achieving Society.* Princeton, N.J.: Van Nostrand.

McClelland, David C., J. Atkinson, R. Clark, and E. Lowell. 1953. *The Achievement Motive.* New York: Appleton Century Crofts.

McGregor, D. V. 1960. *The Human Side of Enterprise.* New York: Harper & Row.

McMillan, C. J., D. J. Hickson, C. R. Hinings, and R. E. Schneck. 1973. "The Structure of Work Organization Across Societies." In *Organization and Nation: The Aston Program IV,* edited by David J. Hickson and Charles J. McMillan, pp. 37–47. Farnborough, U.K.: Gower.

Mead, Margaret. 1953. "The Study of Culture at a Distance." In *The Study of Culture at a Distance,* edited by Margaret Mead and Rhoda Metraux, pp. 3–53. Chicago: University of Chicago Press.

Mecham, Michael. 1995. "Boeing Extends Training Help to China's Airlines." *Aviation Weeks & Space Technology* 143:51–52.

Meyer, John W., W. Richard Scott, and Terence E. Deal, eds. 1983. *Institutional and Technical Sources of Organizational Structure: Explaining the Structure of Educational Organizations.* Beverly Hills, Calif.: Sage.

Miles, M. B., and A. M. Huberman. 1984. *Qualitative Data Analysis: A Sourcebook for New Methods.* Beverly Hills, Calif.: Sage.

Miles, R. E., and C. C. Snow. 1978. *Organizational Strategy, Structure and Process.* New York: McGraw-Hill.

Mileti, Dennis S., and David G. Gillespie. 1977. "Size and Structure in Complex Organizations." *Social Forces* 56:208–217.

Milgrom, Paul, and John Roberts. 1992. *Economics, Organization and Management.* Englewood Cliffs, N.J.: Prentice-Hall International.

Miller, Danny. 1983. "The Correlates of Entrepreneurship in Three Types of Firms." *Management Science* 29:770–791.

Miller, Danny, and Cornelia Droege. 1986. "Psychological and Traditional Determinants of Structure." *Management Science* 31:539–560.

Miller, George A. 1987. "Meta-analysis and the Culture-free Hypothesis." *Organization Studies* 8:309–326.

Miller, George A., Douglas L. Anderton, and Joseph Conaty. 1985. "Assessing the Samples of Prior Organization Research." *Journal of Management* 22: 369–383.

Miller, George A., and Joseph Conaty. 1982. "Comparative Organizational Analysis: Sampling and Measurement." *Social Science Research* 11:141–152.

Mitchell, Vincent Wayne. 1994. "Using Industrial Key Informants: Some Guidelines." *Journal of the Market Research Society* 36:139–144.

Montagu-Pollock, Matthew. 1991. "All the Right Connections." *Asian Business* 27:20–24.

Morgan, Gareth. 1986. *Images of Organization.* London: Sage.

Moser, C. A., and G. Kalton. 1971. *Survey Methods in Social Investigation.* London: Heinemann.

Mun, K. C. 1990. "Stakeholder in the Chinese Enterprises: An Examination of Li Yingling's Ownership Reform Model." In *Advances in Chinese Industrial Studies: Reform Policy and the Chinese Enterprise*, edited by J. Child and M. Lockett, pp. 109–124. Greenwich, Conn.: JAI Press.

Myers, Ramon H., ed. 1986. *The Economic Development of the Republic of China on Taiwan, 1965–1981*. San Francisco: Institute for Contemporary Studies.

Nahapiet, Janine, and Sumantra Ghoshal. 1998. "Social Capital, Intellectual Capital, and the Organizational Advantage." *Academy of Management Review* 23:242–266.

National Bureau of Statistics. 2000. *Statistical Communique of the People's Republic of China on the 1999 National Economic and Social Development*. Beijing: National Bureau of Statistics, People's Republic of China.

National Bureau of Statistics 1999. *China Statistical Yearbook*. Beijing: National Bureau of Statistics, People's Republic of China.

Nonaka, I., and H. Takeuchi. 1995. *The Knowledge Creating Company*. London: Oxford University Press.

Osgood, C. (1940). Informants. In *Ingalik Material Culture*, edited by C. Osgood, pp. 50–55. New Haven, Conn.: Yale University Publications in Anthropology #22.

Ou, Ren, Yong Shi, and Xin Xu. 1996. *Business in the South and North: The Different Regional Styles and Business Cultures of Chinese Businessmen*. Hainan: International News Press.

Pascale, R. T., and A. G. Athos. 1981. *The Art of Japanese Management*. New York: Werner.

Peter, J. Paul. 1979. "Reliability: A Review of Psychometric Basics and Recent Marketing Research Practices." *Journal of Marketing Research* 16:6–17.

Peter, J. Paul. 1981. "Construct Validity: A Review of Basic Issues and Marketing Practices." *Journal of Marketing Research* 18:133–145.

Peters, Thomas B., and Robert H. Waterman. 1982. *In Search of Excellence: Lessons from America's Best-Run Companies*. New York: Harper & Row.

Phillips, Lynn W. 1981. "Assessing Measurement Error in Key Informant Reports: A Methodological Note on Organizational Analysis in Marketing." *Journal of Marketing Research* 18:395–415.

Polanyi, M. 1962. *Personal Knowledge: Towards a Post-critical Philosophy*. London: Routledge and Kegan Paul.

Polanyi, M. 1967. *The Tacit Dimension*. London: Routledge and Kegan Paul.

Pucik, Vladimir, and Nina Hatvany. 1983. "Management Practices in Japan and Their Impact on Business Strategy." In *The Strategy Process: Concepts, Context, Cases*, edited by Henry Mintzberg and James Brian Quinn, pp. 358–368. Englewood Cliffs, N.J.: Prentice-Hall.

Pugh, D. S., and D. J. Hickson. 1976. *Organization Structure in Context: The Aston Programme I*. Farnborough, U.K.: Saxon House.

Pugh, D. S., D. J. Hickson, C. R. Hinings, and C. Turner. 1968. "Dimensions of Organization Structure." *Administrative Science Quarterly* 13:65–105.

Pugh, D. S., D. J. Hickson, C. R. Hinings, and C. Turner. 1969. "The Context of Organization Structures." *Administrative Science Quarterly* 14:91–114.

Pye, Lucian W. 1992. *Chinese Commercial Negotiating Style*. New York: Quorum Books.

Pye, Lucian W. 1985. *Asian Power and Politics: The Cultural Dimensions of Authority*. Cambridge, Mass.: Harvard University Press.

Quinn, Robert E., and John Rohrbaugh. 1983. "A Spatial Model of Effectiveness Criteria: Towards a Competing Values Approach to Organizational Analysis." *Management Science* 29:363–377.

Redding, S. Gordon. 1980. "Cognition as an Aspect of Culture and Its Relation to Management Processes: An Exploratory View of the Chinese Case." *Journal of Management Studies* 17:127–148.

Redding, S. Gordon. 1990. *The Spirit of Chinese Capitalism*. Berlin: De Gruyter.

Redding, S. Gordon, and Michael Ng. 1982. "The Role of 'Face' in the Organizational Perceptions of Chinese Managers." *Organization Studies* 3:201–219.

Redding, S. Gordon, and Y. Y. Wong, eds. 1986. *The Psychology of Chinese Organizational Behavior*. Hong Kong: Oxford University Press.

Reich, R. 1991. *The Work of Nations: Preparing Ourselves for 21st Century Capitalism*. London: Simon and Schuster.

Robertson, Maxine, and Jacky Swan. 1998. "Modes of Organizing in an Expert Consultancy: A Case Study of Knowledge, Power and Egos." *Organization* 5:543–564.

Roehrig, M. F. 1994. *Foreign Joint Ventures in Contemporary China*. New York: St. Martin's.

Ruskin, John. 1985. *Unto This Last and Other Writings*. London: Penguin Classics.

Salaff, Janet. 1981. *Working Daughters of Hong Kong*. Cambridge: Cambridge University Press.

Sarantakos, Sotirios. 1993. *Social Research*. Houndsmill, U.K.: Macmillan.

Scarbrough, H. 1995. "Blackboxes, Hostages and Prisoners." *Organizational Studies* 16:991–1020.

Schendel, D., and G. R. Patton. 1978. "A Simultaneous Equation Model of Corporate Strategy." *Management Science* 24: 1611–1621.

Schermerhorn, John R., Jr. 1987. "Organizational Features of Chinese Industrial Enterprise: Paradoxes of Stability in Times of Change." *Academy of Management Executive* 1:343–347.

Schlevogt, K.-A. 1998. *Power and Control in Chinese Private Enterprises: Organizational Design in the Taiwanese Media Industry*. Parkland, Fla.: Dissertation Publisher.

Schlevogt, K.-A. 1999a. *Inside Chinese Organizations: An Empirical Study of Business Practices in China*. Parkland, Fla.: Dissertation Publisher.

Schlevogt, K.-A. 1999b. "Web-based Chinese Management (WCM): Toward a New Management Paradigm for the Next Millennium?" *Thunderbird International Business Review* (formerly *The International Executive*), 41 (6), 655-692.

Schlevogt, K.-A. 1999c. "Fortune Blesses Only Successful Development." *China Daily*, September 29, p. 4.

Schlevogt, K.-A. 1999d. "How to Become a Master Corporate Designer" (in Chinese). *China Business Times*, Enterprise Weekly section, 11/22/99, p. 7.

Schlevogt, K.-A. 1999e. "Internet has Hidden Flaws." *China Daily*, 9/21/99, p. 4.

Schlevogt, K.-A. 1999f. "Obstacles Remain in China's Way." *China Daily*, 10/21/99, p. 4.

Schlevogt, K.-A. 1999g. "Time to Celebrate Successes." *China Daily*, 10/5/99, p. 4.

Schlevogt, K.-A. 1999h. "The Art of Chinese Management: Towards a New

Management Paradigm for the 21st Century." In *Proceedings of the Sixth Annual International Conference on Advances in Management* (Vol. 6, pp. 65–66) edited by P. Minors, Bowling Green, Ky.: Center for Advanced Studies in Management.

Schlevogt, K.-A. 1999i. "China Runs on Two-track Path." *China Daily,* 10/20/99, p. 4.

Schlevogt, K.-A. 1999j. "Deflation Necessitates Micro-adjustments in China." *China Daily,* 10/8/99, p. 4.

Schlevogt, K.-A. 1999k. "Medium-term Development: At the Same Time Extremely Fast and Extremely Slow" (in German). *China-Contact.* Issue 12 (December): 6–8.

Schlevogt, K.-A. 1999l. "US Follows Double-standard Principle." *China Daily,* 10/30/99, p. 4.

Schlevogt, K.-A. 1999m. "World Policeman Endangers Peace." *China Daily,* 10/29/99, p. 4.

Schlevogt, K.-A. 1999n. "Policy Needed to Make Web a Power for Life." *China Daily,* 9/22/99, p. 4.

Schlevogt, K.-A., & Donaldson, L. 1999. "Measuring the Concept of Contingency Fit in Organizational Research: Theoretical Advances and New Empirical Evidence from China." In *Proceedings of the 59th Annual Meeting of the Academy of Management,* edited by S. J. Havlovic, August 6–11 (pp. 42–43). Chicago, Ill.: Academy of Management.

Schlevogt, K.-A. 2000a. "Doing Business in China, Part I: The Business Environment in China—Getting to Know the Next Century's Superpower." *Thunderbird International Business Review* (formerly *The International Executive), 42*(1): 85–111.

Schlevogt, K.-A. 2000b. "Doing Business in China, Part II: Investing and Managing in China—How to Dance with the Dragon." *Thunderbird International Business Review* (formerly *The International Executive), 42*(2): 201–226.

Schlevogt, K.-A. 2000c. "Doing Business in the Russian Federation: Time for Anti-cyclical Investments." *Thunderbird International Business Review* (formerly *The International Executive), 42*(6): 707–734.

Schlevogt, K.-A. 2000d. "Fractured State: Do the Disparities of Wealth Threaten the Stability of China? Interview with Kai-Alexander Schlevogt, Permanent Foreign Professor at Peking University." *BBC World Service,* December 11. Interviewer: Christopher Gunnes.

Schlevogt, K.-A. 2000e. "Interview: Call for the Emigrants—Experts Should be Invited Back, Universities Should be Floated at the Stock Exchange" (in German). *DieWoche,* 5/26/00, p. 29.

Schlevogt, K.-A. 2000f. "The Branding Revolution in China: Chinese Entrepreneurs are Waking Up to the Value of Brands." *China Business Review, 27*(3): 52–57.

Schlevogt, K.-A. 2000g. "Call for a Knowledge Crusade: On the Mistake to Bring Intellectual Guest Workers as Stopgap to Germany" (in German). *Wirtschaftswoche* (*German Business Weekly*). (14): 30.

Schlevogt, K.-A. 2000h. "Let's Get Ideas, Not Heads for the Country: The Knowledge Age and the Green Card—A Reflection" (in German). *Frankfurter Rundschau,* 4/20/00, p. 6.

Schlevogt, K.-A. 2000i. "China's Western Campaign." *Far Eastern Economic Review, 163* (33): 29.

Schlevogt, K.-A. 2000j. "Preparing for Powerful Change: How to Develop a

World-class Leadership Platform and Agenda." (in Chinese) *China Marketing*, 4 (April): 20–22.

Schlevogt, K.-A. 2000k. "Energizing the Organization for Your Change Mission: Getting your Troops Ready for the Battle" (in Chinese). *China Marketing*, 5 (May): 22–25.

Schlevogt, K.-A. 2000l. "Executing Your Change Agenda to Achieve Strong Impact and Continuous Improvements: The Journey is the Reward." *China Marketing* 7 (July): 14–17.

Schlevogt, K.-A. 2000m. "From America—Without Love." *European Business Forum,* 1(1), 58–60.

Schlevogt, K.-A. 2000n. "The Nascent Chinese Consulting Market: Opportunities and Obstacles." *C2M: Consulting to Management* (formerly *Journal of Management Consulting),* 11 (2): 28–34.

Schlevogt, K.-A. 2000o. "The Nascent Chinese Consulting Market: Best-practice Approaches." *C2M: Consulting to Management* (formerly *Journal of Management Consulting).* 11(3): 15–22

Schlevogt, K.-A. 2000p. "Snail Track Instead of 'Leapfrogging': The Other Side of Development" (in German). *China-Contact* 5 (May): 26–28.

Schlevogt, K.-A. 2000q. "Strategies, Structures and Processes for Managing Uncertainty and Complexity: Worldwide Learning From the Chinese Organizational Model of Private Enterprises," edited by M. A. Rahim, R. T. Golembiewski, & K. D. MacKenzie (Eds.), in *Current Topics in Management* Vol. 5, pp. 305–328. Stamford, Connecticut: JAI Press.

Schlevogt, K.-A. 2000r. "The Honor of the Debtors" (in German). *Die Welt,* 9/23/00, p. 11.

Schlevogt, K.-A. 2000s. "Today's Asia for Tomorrow's Europe—It's Time for National Visions in a New 'Age of Empire.' " *European Business Forum,* 1(2): 76–78.

Schlevogt, K.-A. 2000t. "Developing International Management Education in Emerging Markets for the 21st Century: Challenges and Solution Blueprints for Chinese Universities and their Global Educational Web-partners." Conference paper. *Second Asia Academy of Management Conference, Conference theme: Managing in Asia—Challenges and Opportunities in the New Millennium.* December 15–17. Singapore. Extended abstract included in Best Papers Proceedings.

Schlevogt, K.-A. 2000u. "Key Success Factors in the Land of Dragons: The CHINA Framework for High Organizational Effectiveness." In *Best Paper Proceedings of the Second Asia Academy of Management Conference, Conference theme: Managing in Asia—Challenges and Opportunities in the New Millennium. December 15–17,* edited by N. Pangarkar, pp. 1–10. Singapore: Asia Academy of Management.

Schlevogt, K.-A. 2001a. "The Great Leap Nowhere: China's Western Campaign is Fraught with Difficulty." *Asian Business.* 2001. 37. (1) (January): 40–42.

Schlevogt, K.-A. 2001b. "Leaders Should Manage Crises." *China Daily,* 3/8/01, p. 4.

Schlevogt, K.-A. 2001c. "The Building of a Powerful Nation: Ten Theses Regarding China's Medium-term Development" (in Chinese). In *Dialogue with 21st Century's China.* Volume: Development, pp. 376–389. Beijing: Central Document Publisher.

Schlevogt, K.-A. 2001d. " 'Stakeholder Value' Instead of Value Destruction: How to Create Real Fortunes" (in Chinese). In *Dialogue with 21st*

Century's China. Volume: Reform, pp. 202–207. Beijing: Central Document Publisher.

Schlevogt, K.-A. 2001e. "Managing Radical Change." *Academy of Management Executive*. Vol. 15. Issue 2 (May): 134–135.

Schlevogt, K.-A. 2001f. "The Distinctive Structure of Chinese Private Enterprises: A Comparison Between the State and Private Sector." *Asia Pacific Business Review 7*(3): 1–33.

Schlevogt, K.-A. 2001g. "Doing Business in India: Planting an Emerging Market Growth Option" in the Subcontinent of Paradoxes." Working Paper.

Schlevogt, K.-A. 2001h. "Invisible Virtues Foster Dynamism." *China Daily*, April 16, p. 4.

Schlevogt, K.-A. 2001i. "How Dragons Can Mutate into Paper Tigers." *European Business Forum* (6): 71–72.

Schlevogt, K.-A. 2001j. "Training China to Become World-class." *China Daily*, 5/12/01, p. 4.

Schlevogt, K.-A. 2001k. "China to Offer Great Games." *China Daily*, 7/16/01, p. 4.

Schlevogt, K.-A. 2001l. "Cultivating Loyalty." *China Economic Review 11*(7): 1, 18–19.

Schlevogt, K.-A. 2001m. "Bonding Loyalty." *China Economic Review 11*(8): 16–18.

Schollhammer, H. 1982. "Internal Corporate Entrepreneurship." In *Encyclopedia of Entrepreneurship*, edited by C. A. Kent, D. L. Sexton, and K. H. Vesper, pp. 209–223. Englewood Cliffs, N.J.: Prentice-Hall.

Segars, A. H. 1997. "Assessing the Unidimensionality of Measurement: A Paradigm and Illustration Within the Context of Information Systems Research." *Omega* 25:107–121.

Seidler, John. 1974. "On Using Informants: A Technique for Collecting Quantitative Data and Controlling Measurement Error in Organizational Analysis." *American Sociological Review* 39:816–831.

Sharpe, William F. 1964. "Capital Asset Prices: A Theory of Market Equilibrium Under Conditions of Risk." *Journal of Finance* 19:425–442.

Shenkar, Oded 1984. "Is Bureaucracy Inevitable? The Chinese Experience." *Organization Studies* 5:289–308.

Shenkar, Oded 1989. "The Chinese Case and the Radical School in Organization Studies." *Organization Studies* 10:117–122.

Shenkar, Oded. 1994. "The People's Republic of China: Raising the Bamboo Screen Through International Management Research." *International Studies of Management and Organization* 24:9–34.

Shenkar, Oded, and Mary Ann von Glinow. 1994. "Paradoxes of Organizational Theory and Research: Using the Case of China to Illustrate National Contingency." *Management Science* 40:56–71.

Silin, Robert. 1976. *Leadership and Values: The Organization of Large-Scale Taiwanese Enterprises*. Cambridge, Mass.: Harvard University Press.

Simonin, Bernard L. 1997. "The Importance of Collaborative Know-how: An Empirical Test of the Learning Organization." *Academy of Management Journal* 40:1150–1174.

Smart, Josephine, and Alan Smart. 1993. "Obligation and Control: Employment of Kin in Capitalist Labor Management in China." *Critique of Anthropology* 13:7–31.

Smith, Craig S. 1996. "AIG Reshapes China's Insurance Industry: Firm's Success May Lead to Curbs on Foreign Insurers." *Wall Street Journal*, 2/9/96.

Smith, K. G., and C. M. Grimm. 1987. "Environmental Variation, Strategic Change and Firm Performance: A Study of Railroad Deregulation." *Strategic Management Journal* 8:363–376.

Smith, Peter B., Mark F. Peterson, and Zhong Ming Wang. 1996. "The Manager as Mediator of Alternative Meanings: A Pilot Study from China, the USA and U.K." *Journal of International Business Studies* 27:115–137.

Solt, Michael E. 1995. "Perceptions About Managerial Advancement in the People's Republic of China." *International Executive* 37:415–435.

Sproull, N. L. 1988. *Handbook of Research Methods: A Guide for Practitioners and Students in the Social Sciences.* London: Scarecrow Press.

Steers, Richard M., and Daniel N. Braunstein. 1976. "A Behaviorally-Based Measure of Manifest Needs in Work Settings." *Journal of Vocational Behavior* 9:251–266.

Stichcombe, Arthur L. 1965. "Social Structure and Organizations." In *Handbook of Organizations*, edited by James G. March, pp. 142–193. Chicago: Rand McNally.

Strange, Roger, Syed Kamall, and Hui Tan, eds. 1998. *Operating as a Foreign Company in China: Introduction and Overview.* London: Frank Cass.

Sung, Yun-wing, and Thomas M. H. Chan. 1987. "China's Economic Reform I: The Debates in China." *Asian-Pacific Economic Literature* 1:1–25.

Sunzi. (1999/ca. 500 BC). *The Art of War.* Beijing: Foreign Languages Press.

Tabachnick, Barbara G., and Linda S. Fidell. 1989. *Using Multivariate Statistics.* New York: HarperCollins.

Tam, Simon, ed. 1990. *Centrifugal Versus Centripetal Growth Processes: Contrasting Ideal Types for Conceptualizing the Developmental Patterns of Chinese and Japanese Firms.* Berlin: De Gruyter.

Tan, J. Justin, and Robert J. Litschert. 1994. "Environment–Strategy Relationship and Its Performance Implications: An Empirical Study of the Chinese Electronics Industry." *Strategic Management Journal* 15:1–20.

Tayeb, Monir. 1994. "Organizations and National Culture: Methodology Considered." *Organization Studies* 15:429–446.

Taylor, Frederick W. 1911. *The Principles of Scientific Management.* New York: Harper Bros.

Thompson, James D. 1967. *Organizations in Action: Social Science Bases of Administrative Theory.* New York: McGraw-Hill.

Thune, Stanley, and Robert House. 1970. "Where Long Range Planning Pays Off." *Business Horizons* 13: 81–87.

Tien, H. Yuan, and Che-fu Lee. 1988. "New Demographs and Old Designs: The Chinese Family amid Induced Population Transition." *Social Forces* 69:605–628.

Tsang, Eric W. K. 1998. "Can Guanxi Be a Source of Sustained Competitive Advantage for Doing Business in China?" *Academy of Management Executive* 12:64–73.

Turpin, Dominique V. 1998. "Challenge of the Overseas Chinese." *Financial Times, Mastering Global Business Series*, part 2. 2/6/98, p. 8.

Van de Ven, Andrew. 1976. "A Framework for Organizational Assessment." *Academy of Management Review* 1:64–78.

Venkatraman, N. 1989. "Strategic Orientation of Business Enterprises: The Construct, Dimensionality, and Measurement." *Management Science* 35: 942–962.

Verbrugge, J., and S. Goldstein. 1978. "High Performers Versus Low Performers: What Makes the Difference." *Savings and Loan News* November: 64–69.

Vogel, E. 1989. *One Step Ahead in China: Guangdong Under Reform.* Cambridge, Mass.: Harvard University Press.

Walder, Andrew. 1986. *Communist Neo-traditionalism: Work and Authority in Chinese Industry.* Berkeley: University of California Press.

Waley, Arthur. 1939. *Three Ways of Thought in Ancient China.* Stanford, Calif.: Stanford University Press.

Wall, James A., Jr. 1990. "Managers in the People's Republic of China." *Academy of Management Executive* 4:19–32.

Watson, James L. 1975a. "Agnates and Outsiders: Adoption in a Chinese Lineage." *Man* 10:293–306.

Watson, James L. 1975b. *Emigration and the Chinese Lineage.* Berkeley: University of California Press.

Weber, Max. 1930. *The Protestant Ethic and the Spirit of Capitalism.* London: Allen and Unwin. (First published in 1904–1905).

Weber, Max. 1947. *The Theory of Social and Economic Organization.* New York: Free Press. (First published in 1924).

Weber, Max. 1951. *The Religion of China.* Glencoe, Ill.: Free Press. (First published in 1916).

Weidenbaum, Murray. 1996. "The Chinese Family Business Enterprise." *California Management Review* 38:141–156.

Weidenbaum, Murray, and Samuel Hughes. 1996. *The Bamboo Network: How Expatriate Chinese Entrepreneurs Are Creating a New Superpower in Asia.* New York: Free Press.

Weihrich, Heinz. 1990. "Management Practices in the United States, Japan, and the People's Republic of China." *Industrial Management* 32:3–7.

Whitley, Richard D. 1990. "Eastern Asian Enterprise Structures and the Comparative Analysis of Forms of Business Organization." *Organization Studies* 11:47–74.

Whitley, Richard D. 1991. "The Social Construction of Business Systems in East Asia." *Organization Studies* 12:1–28.

Whitley, Richard D. 1994. "Dominant Forms of Economic Organization in Market Economies." *Organization Studies* 15:153–182.

Whyte, Martin King. 1995. "The Social Roots of China's Economic Development." *China Quarterly* 144:999–1019.

Wilhelm, R. 1930. *Chinesische Wirtschaftspsychologie.* Leipzig: Deutsche Wissenschaftliche/Buchhandlung.

Williamson, Oliver E. 1970. *Corporate Control and Business Behavior: An Inquiry into the Effects of Organization Form on Enterprise Behavior.* Englewood Cliffs, N.J.: Prentice-Hall.

Williamson, Peter. 1997. *New Competitive Strategies in Asia: How Should Western Companies Respond?* Hong Kong: Financial Times.

Wilson, R. W. 1970. *Learning to Be Chinese: The Political Socialization of Children in Taiwan.* Cambridge, Mass.: MIT Press.

Wolf, Margery. 1968. *The House of Lim: A Study of a Chinese Farm Family.* Englewood Cliffs, N.J.: Prentice-Hall.

Wong, Gilbert Y. Y., and Philip H. Birnbaum-More. 1994. "Culture, Context and Structure: A Test on Hong Kong Banks." *Organization Studies* 15: 99–123.

Wong, Siu-lun, ed. 1988. *The Applicability of Asian Family Values to Other Sociocultural Settings.* New Brunswick, N.J.: Transaction Books.

World Executive's Digest. 1996. "Creating Asia's Leaders." *World Executive's Digest* December, pp. 17–22.

Wu, Yanrui. 1993. "Productive Efficiency in Chinese Industry." *Asian-Pacific Economic Literature* 7:58–66.

Wu, Yuan li, and Chun-hsi Wu. 1980. *Economic Development in Southeast Asia: The Chinese Dimension*. Stanford, Calif.: Hoover Institution Press.

Xing, Fan. 1995. "The Chinese Cultural System: Implications for Cross-cultural Management." *SAM Advanced Management Journal* 60:14–20.

Xing, Li. 1999. "Jade Offers Clues to Earliest Civilization." *China Daily*, 3/30/99, p. 9.

Xu, Chonghua. 1992. "Structure and Operation of Electronic Mass Media in China." *International Journal of Technology Management* 7:537–546.

Yan, Rick. 1998. "Short-term Results: The Litmus Test for Success in China." *Harvard Business Review* 76:61–75.

Yang, C. K. 1961. *Religion in Chinese Society: A Study of Contemporary Social Functions of Religion and Some of Their Historical Factors*. Berkeley: University of California Press.

Yeung, I. Y. M., and R. L. Tung. 1996. "Achieving Business Success in Confucian Societies: The Importance of Guanxi (Connections)." *Organizational Dynamics* 25 (Autumn): 54–65.

Yin, Robert K. 1994. *Case Study Research: Design and Methods*. Thousand Oaks, Calif.: Sage.

Ying, Qin, ed. 1995. *The Four Books*. Changsha: Hunan Publisher.

Yoshihara, Kunio. 1988. *The Rise of Ersatz Capitalism in South-East Asia*. Singapore: Oxford University Press.

Young, Susan. 1995. *Private Business and Economic Reform in China*. Armonk, N.Y.: M. E. Sharpe.

Yuan, Zhang. 1999. "Shaoxing Steeped in History." *China Daily*, 3/27/99, p. 5.

Zelditch, Morris, Jr. 1962. "Some Methodological Problems of Field Studies." *American Journal of Sociology* 67:266–276.

Index

revival in making, 253
understanding another, 295
Customers, location, 14

DaimlerChrysler, harassment, 15
Data collection, 25
Decision making
  Magnolia case study, 98
  optimizing through planning, 217–221
  private vs. state, 77
  private vs. state enterprises, 57
Development
  forecasting, 218–219
  macroeconomy, 279–280
  private economy, 278–279
  Western arrogance, 183
Dexterity, management, 257–258
Diaspora, uniting Chinese, 256–257
Dictatorial style, case studies, 84–85
Dictatorship, Tiger case study, 92–94
Dictatorship by owner-manager, 35–36
Differences, regional, 242–245
Differentiation, strategies, 216–217
Director responsibility system, 11
Distinctive management model, 13
Distinctiveness
  Chinese management, 53–59, 261
  cultural emphasis, 58
  enterprise networks, 57–58
  entrepreneurship, 56–57
  low bureaucracy, 55–56
  North China, 150–151
  small company size, 59
  South China, 151
  strong centralization, 55
  term, 53–54
  web-based Chinese management, 166–167

East and West
  east to west, 299, 300–301
  friendship disappointments, 297
  mutual understanding, 297
  west to east, 298
Economic development/policy making
  entrepreneurial leadership, 288–289

failure of macroeconomic cures, 283–286
growth/reform at micro level, 286–288
malaise of state enterprises, 280–283
social capital, 290–291
strong enterprise webs, 289–290
Economic importance, China, 3
Economic system, 10
Economy, development, 278–280
Education, tacit knowledge, 259–260
Effectiveness
  Chinese management, 52–53
  hypotheses of Chinese management, 60
  See also Organizational effectiveness
Effectiveness studies, management, 48
Empirical evidence, 48
Empirical findings, book, 27
Employment, nonstate-owned sector, 13
Emulation
  private family ownership, 190–198
  web-based Chinese management, 181–190
Enlightened Western approach, 227
Enterprise networks
  American International Group, 240
  building, 227–229
  case studies, 84, 106–107
  flexibility, 171
  private Chinese management, 167
  private vs. state enterprises, 57–58
  Tiger case study, 91f
  See also Networks
Enterprise webs
  creating strong, 289–290
  summary, 111
  web-based Chinese management, 37–38
  Western businessmen, 228
Entrepreneurial revolution, 3–4
Entrepreneurial style
  case studies, 84
  instilling leadership, 286–287

uniting Chinese diaspora, 256–
257
vs. overseas Chinese, 48, 254–257
Management
basic research model, 23
coordination and control, 7
mainland vs. overseas Chinese,
256–257
Si Mu Wu tetrapod story, 7
term, 54
Tiger case study, 94
Management expertise
effectiveness model, 146
measurement model, 138
north, 243
Management model, term, 54
Management practices
basic unconstrained model, 126
cultural impact, 129–130
decision tree for testing, 127*f*
direct impact of culture, 130, 132–
133
empirical model, 125–126
fit indices for stacked model, 129*t*
indirect impact of culture, 133
individual comparisons, 130
influencing factors, 125–133
nested for stacked model, 128*t*
nested model tests, 130, 132–133
private and state enterprises, 129
specification of model, 125–126
standardized path coefficients,
131*t*
structural model, 125
Western companies, 21–22
Management style, 144–145
Managerial profiles,
entrepreneurship, 74–78
Managers, CHINA framework, 208–
209
Mandarin, term, 8
Market economy, China's transition,
22
Masterclass, Western, 227–228
Mean difference tests
company size, 83*t*
emphasis on culture, 79*t*
management, 75*t*
structure, 66*t*
Measurement model, 52, 116, 118,
137–140

Mencius, 8–9
Microeconomic factors, 282–283
Ming dynasty, Zhu Yuan Zhang, 9
Mission, research gap, 5–6
Models
basic research, 23–24
capital asset pricing, 18
empirical for management, 125–
126
family-based enterprises, 44*f*
general research, 23*f*
management practices, 125–126
measurement, 116, 118, 137–140
organizational, 186
Stalinist, 186
structural, management, 125
structural, 115–116, 136–137
structural equation modeling, 114–
115
web-based Chinese management,
4
See also Organizational
effectiveness; Organizational
structure; Web-based Chinese
management (WCM)
Modernism, 13th-century China, 9
Mongols, 10
Motivation, 195*f*, 196
Multiculturalism, 184–185
Multinational companies, 14

Nanyang, 32
Natural experiment, 10
Naturalism, management, 269–270
Natural organizational experiment,
19
Nature, Chinese management, 51
The Nature of Gothic, 264–265
Nepotism, family-based enterprises,
47
Networks
building, 221–230
cost efficiency, 171–175
guanxi with government, 221–227
Magnolia case study, 98–99
private vs. state, 57–58, 78
south, 244–245
Tiger case study, 86–90, 91*f*
See also Enterprise networks
Ningjuli, 40
Nonstate-owned enterprises, 11–13